Billy Boy

THE STORY OF A LANCASHIRE WEAVER'S SON

William Woodruff

Ryburn Publishing

First published in 1993
Ryburn Publishing Limited
Krumlin Halifax

ISBN 1 85331 047 6

Composed by Ryburn Publishing Services
Printed and bound in Bodmin, Cornwall
by Hartnolls Limited for
Ryburn Book Production
Halifax England

Billy Boy

THE STORY OF A LANCASHIRE WEAVER'S SON

William Woodruff was born in 1916 into a family of Lancashire cotton workers. Leaving school at 13, he became a delivery boy in a grocer's shop. In 1933, with bleak prospects in the north of England, he decided to try his luck in London. In 1936, with the aid of a London County Council Scholarship, he went to Oxford University. Throughout the Second World War he fought in North Africa and the Mediterranean region. In 1946 Woodruff renewed his academic career. In 1952 he went as a Fulbright scholar to Harvard University. Subsequently he held professorships at the Universities of Illinois, Melbourne (Australia), and Gainesville, Florida. Along the way he obtained degrees from Oxford, London, Nottingham, and Melbourne (honorary) and was guest professor at a number of universities, including Waseda University, Tokyo, the Free University, Berlin, the Institute for Advanced Study, Princeton, and St Antony's College, Oxford. He is the author of many books in economics and history. The most recent is *A Concise History of the Modern World* (Macmillan, 1991). He is also the author of a widely published and translated autobiographical novel *Vessel of Sadness*, based on his World War II experiences with the British infantry, and of an allegory, *Paradise Galore*. Woodruff has seven children. He lives in Gainesville, Florida.

Dedication

To the memory of grandmother Bridget
who always called me Billy Boy

Contents

Principal Characters*

Family:

Billy Woodruff: youngest child of
William Woodruff (*Will*), weaver, and
Margaret Kenyon Woodruff (*Maggie*), cardroom hand.
    Other Woodruff children are *Jenny, Brenda* and *Dan.*
Arne Woodruff: Billy's paternal great-grandfather
Bridget Gorman Kenyon: Billy's maternal grandmother.
    Edward, Eric, Alice, and *Maggie* are her children.
Thomas Kenyon: Billy's maternal grandfather.
Selma Nilson Woodruff: Billy's paternal grandmother.
William Woodruff: Billy's paternal grandfather.
Mat and *Hessie Nilson:* textile workers at Fall River, Massachusetts.
Henry Nilson: shipping agent at Liverpool.

Others (*alphabetically*):

Christine Bailey marries Dan Woodruff.
Elsie Briggs: spinner.
Arthur Dimbleby: foreman at Darwen Brick Works.
Harry Entwistle: boilerman at Dougdale's Mill.
Willie Gill: Grand Knight of St. Columbus. *Rosie* is his daughter.
Dr. Grieves: physician.
Charles Grimshaw: grocer; *Mrs. Grimshaw;*
    Mildred and *Nancy* are their daughters;
    Cyril and *Arthur* are his shop assistants.
Simon Gripper: purveyor of holy pictures.
Betsy and *Grace Kenyon:* Billy's aunts in Bamber Bridge.
Mr. and Mrs. Lambert: neighbours in Griffin Street.
George and *Madge Latham:* newsagents.
Miss Little: teacher at St. Peter's.
Sister Loyola and *Sister Lucy:* nuns at St. Peter's.
Mr. Manners: teacher at St. Philip's.
Mr. and Mrs. Morgan, and their daughter *Annie:* neighbours
    in Griffin Street.
Patrick Murphy: overseer at Hornby's Mill.
Terence Peek: Billy's neighbour in Livingston Road.
    Agnes is his wife; *Millicent, Roger* and *John* are his children.
Peter Shad: a Communist activist.
Adam and *Emily Sims:* emigrants to America.
Harold Watkins: weaver and Billy's close friend.
Gordon Weall marries Jenny Woodruff.
Betty Weatherby: daughter of a cotton manufacturer.

*several names have been changed.

Family Tree

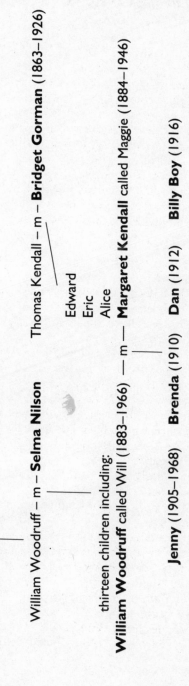

George Woodruff († 1856)

Arne Woodruff (1849–†?) – m – Eva Anders

William Woodruff – m – **Selma Nilson**

Thomas Kendall – m – **Bridget Gorman** (1863–1926)

thirteen children including:
William Woodruff called Will (1883–1966) — m — **Margaret Kendall** called Maggie (1884–1946)

Edward
Eric
Alice

Jenny (1905–1968) **Brenda** (1910) **Dan** (1912) **Billy Boy** (1916)

7

1 Prologue

They said I should not go. They said it was madness for an old man to cross the Atlantic to seek out his birthplace.

"You'll find nothing but ghosts there. Why don't you go and see the Grand Canyon?"

Others thought that anybody over seventy had every right to do as he pleased.

"Time's a-wasting," they said, noting my faulty gait.

So I went.

And when I reached the north of England and came to Blackburn, the town of my birth, and asked the taxi driver to take me to Griffin Street, he eyed my white hair cautiously.

"Are you sure you want to go there?"

"Oh yes," I answered, "I was born there. I've come a long way to see it."

"You're the boss," he said, taking my bags and holding the door so that I could climb in. A cold north wind – the wind I'd known as a boy and had long since forgotten – tugged at my coat. I began to regret having arrived in thin Florida clothing.

As we moved off I caught sight of several high-rise apartment buildings I'd never seen before; they were harsh to the eye.

"Council flats," the driver said.

But then came landmarks I'd known as a child. The reddish-brown cathedral still dominated the centre of town. When my great-grandfather Arne Woodruff fled from Westmorland to Blackburn more than a hundred years ago, there were cows grazing around the church. I wondered if the image of Christ crucified was still inside; the Christ with the big hands: worker's hands.

We passed Queen Victoria's statue on the Parade – it was as ugly as ever, still covered with bird dirt. The statue of Robert Peel, the famous nineteenth-century statesman and cotton manufacturer, stood, equally dirty, at the other side of the cathedral. Both statues had started out a golden bronze but were now green with age.

As we crossed King William Street, I stared at the clock tower above the Market Hall. A touch of Italy in the north of England. My father, recently arrived from America in 1914, had paraded under that clock before going to war.

The King's Arms pub appeared on our left. It looked much older, but was otherwise unchanged. It still had the same great marble pillars at the entrance that looked like potted meat. As a small child, I'd pressed my back against that "potted meat" while the first automobile in my life drove by. Mother had warned me that a motor-car was in town, and that I should watch out for it carefully. "Look out!" the crowd had shouted, "It's coming!" As I turned and looked in the direction they were pointing,

I saw a large black beetle with a shiny nose crawling across the cobble-stones toward me. Its deep cough and trail of smoke added to my fears. I couldn't have been more scared or more amazed had an extinct reptile walked by.

But what was this nagging feeling I was experiencing? The more I stared through the car window, the more convinced I became that this was not the town of my birth. Had I come to the wrong place?

Of course not. The grey-roofed factories with their fortress-like walls were still there. So was Hornby's Mill; it seemed so small. Its windows were dirty and broken. As we turned a corner I could see endless rows of weavers' cottages running across the town into the surrounding hills. The wet roofs glistened in the evening light; they seemed to be sagging. Using the local, almost inexhaustible supplies of stone, slate, and clay, the cottages had been thrown together in the second half of the nineteenth century when the Lancashire cotton textile industry was booming. Whoever had built them had insisted on uniformity, if not downright ugliness. People lived and died in almost identical cottages that were little more than ramshackle barracks.

Except that they looked dirtier and older, most of the public buildings we passed – the gas works, the chapels and the churches – were as I had left them many years before.

I asked the driver to go past the two church schools where seventy years ago I had been a pupil. All that was left of St. Philip's, was a gaunt, lonely church tower. It stood there forlorn, an island of stone.

"School fell down, church wasn't needed," the driver said.

My parents had walked through the cobbled streets to be married at St. Philip's in September 1904, "according to the rights and ceremonies of the Established Church." I had approached this same tower as a small, rather frightened schoolboy of four in 1920.

My other school, St. Peter's, was still standing, though propped up at the sides with metal supports. Its grimy walls had the same forbidding appearance that they had had when I looked upon them as a child.

We crossed the Blakewater river still running black.

In the far distance, from a high point, I caught a glimpse of the slag heaps on which as a boy I had fought with gangs of other children; they stood pyramid-like against the sky as they had always done.

Yet the nagging feeling remained. The Blackburn of my childhood had had a forest of red brick chimneys belching great twisting coils of smoke. Where were they? The few tall chimneys I could see were cold and smokeless. I looked at my watch. It was 5:30 p.m. The light was fading. Seventy years ago, at this hour, Blackburn's streets would have been filled with the clip-clap sound of clogs as thousands of factory workers, the women in grey shawls, the men wearing dark caps, hastened home from work. Now there were few people on the streets; they were better dressed – no shawls, few caps, no clogs – but there was no haste in their step.

10

At 5:30 in the evening, the Blackburn into which I was born had been noisy, urgent, crowded, vibrant, alive.

The Blackburn I saw through the taxi window was becalmed – like a demasted ship after a storm.

"Slum clearance," the driver mused, picking his teeth, as we stood in what had been Griffin Street and surveyed a windswept, rubble-strewn wasteland covering many acres. "Had to do it," he said, " 'Pakies'[†] were moving in."

I stared at a pile of broken glass and rusty wire where my cottage had been.

"It's a pity you came all the way from America to find everything gone," he said glumly.

"Oh, no," I answered. "On the contrary, ... everything is here."

II Griffin Street

The fierce rattling of my bedroom window-pane first roused me from the long sleep of birth. Mr. Smalley, whom we always called t' knocker-up man, came with his wire-tipped pole in the dark six mornings a week to shake our window until father stirred and shouted loud enough to be heard in the street below, "We're up!" Whereupon Mr. Smalley went next door and rattled the bedroom window of our neighbour, Mr. Morgan, the coal hauler. I often lay in bed listening to Mr. Smalley coming down the street. With his coming, Griffin Street began to stir. Daylight followed.

The first sights I recall were of the bedroom which my brother Dan and I shared with our parents. I remember the small-paned window and the flaking paint, the whitewashed walls and the two metal beds with straw mattresses which rested on thin metal slats. Sometimes the slats would sag, leaving a pocket into which one sunk one's hip. I think the straw mattresses must have encouraged bugs, for I recall mother sitting on the side of the bed running her fingers down the seams of blankets and sheets. I didn't find anything strange about her crushing the bugs between her thumb nails, though it did get bloody at times.[†] It was a never-ending battle; there were always more bugs coming through the walls. Yet neither sagging slats nor bugs denied me the exquisite sleep of childhood.

The pegmat which lay at my bedside, and which protected my feet from the freezing floor in winter, is so engraved on my mind that I could draw its shape and colours without hesitation. In our house there was always one at the side of every bed as well as before the two fireplaces downstairs. They were made from strips an inch or two wide and several inches long of discarded clothing. They could be of all colours dependent on the colour of the garments used. The women made them at night, working the materials across their knees. The cuttings were pulled through a stiff piece of fabric with a rughook that had a round wooden handle. Sometimes several women worked together, chattering and laughing into the night. Pegmats were not only solid and warm; they meant that no garment, however old, was wasted. The pegmats in the house were kept clean by beating them against the outside wall.

There was not much else in the room: a lace curtain, a tiny black iron fireplace, and an empty orange crate scavenged from the fruit market in town, which served as a bedside table. The crate's two compartments were brightly painted and decorated with a linen cloth at the front. There were also two pisspots – I did not know the word chamber-pot until I had left school – an open-flame gas light, the flame blue at the bottom, white at the top, and a cracked wooden door with a latch. Clothing, what little we had, hung on hangers or rails on the plastered walls, which were sometimes damp. To protect the garments from the damp, sheets of brown paper separated them from the plaster.

My brother and I slept so close to our parents that we could touch them. It gave us a sense of belonging. No one noticed the lack of privacy, or the crowded conditions; it was natural for us to be so close; it made us feel safe and secure. Privacy I learnt about and came to value much later. I knew about the procreation process long before I understood it. It seemed as natural as somebody using the pisspot. It didn't disturb me, or confuse me, or revolt me. Like father's deep snoring, I ignored it. Living in such a confined place as a weaver's cottage meant everybody shared everybody else's joys and sorrows.

Not long after t' knocker-up had finished rattling our window-pane, a stream of wood-shodden workers began to hurry past my window on its way to the mills: in the Blackburn of seventy years ago, more than 200 factory and workshop chimneys were belching smoke by 5:00 a.m. Muffled voices and morning greetings flew up from the crowded street to where I lay. As the grey light grew in the sky, and the night's bright stars paled, the stream of passers-by became a river, and then a flood. The clip-clap sound of the clogs† passing over the cobbles drowned out all other noises. In winter, deadened clogs meant a heavy snow; clogs that rang meant a heavy frost.

Once the flow of workers passing my window had subsided, except for the rattle of a cart in the distance, all was still again: still enough, that is, until I heard the last running footsteps dash by – someone trying to reach the mill before the whistle sounded and the tall iron gates were shut. Latecomers never failed to excite me. Sometimes, with nothing on but my grey flannel shirt, I'd jump out of bed and, with my face pressed against the cold glass, watch the last workers rush by. "Hurry," I shouted, "you'll make it!" Back in bed, I had visions of the runners squeezing through the heavy factory gates as they clanged to. Those shut out of the mills usually came traipsing back beneath my window. I could tell from the ring of their clog-irons that they had failed. Time was a much harder master then.

By mid-morning the stream of clogs passing our house had been replaced by an equally crowded stream of horse-drawn carts, clippety-clopping their way to the railway station with mountains of grey cloth. Some of the cloth, which we called "duties" – after the Indian word dhotis – was on its way to be bleached, dyed, and printed in Manchester twenty-five miles to the south; the bulk of it would then go to the port of Liverpool, thirty-five miles to the south-west, on its way to India, wherever that was. India must have been very important to Blackburn because I seemed to hear more about India as a child than I did about England.

The long columns of horse-drawn carts passed within an arm's reach of our front door. I watched the wind tugging at the tarpaulins that covered the cloth. With marked regularity, the tarpaulin buckles smacked against the sides of the carts. The journey to the station was a race in which the whip was not spared. I wondered if the horses which did not move fast enough were shut out of the station as the workers were shut out of the factories.

I also heard the coming and going of our neighbour, Mr. Morgan, the coal hauler, who left his house later than the mill workers. Mr. Lambert on the other side of our house sometimes used to walk to his job at the gas works with Mr. Morgan. About this time the lamplighter passed down the street with his long pole with a hook on the end of it, and the bright street lamps were extinguished.

As the day wore on, I heard the call of the rag-and-bone man who cried his wares from a donkey cart in the street. In exchange for a handful of rags, a bare bone or two, some old medicine or pickled-onion bottles, or old newspapers, or any old piece of metal, he gave mother a donkey stone – a piece of hard chalk – to colour the kitchen hearthstone and sometimes the front doorstep on the street. Everybody knew that the rag-and-bone man was not as poor as he looked. I also heard the scissors-grinder. For a penny or two, he sharpened scissors and knives with a foot-driven grinding wheel amid a shower of sparks. There were other peddlers, such as the thread, needles, and ribbon seller, who cried their wares. My favourite was the tinker who shouted his skills at mending pots and pans. Because it was one of the main highways to the mills, there was no lingering in my street for man or beast until darkness came.

At the end of the working day, shortly after 5:00 p.m., as the last empty carts often drawn by exhausted froth-covered horses returned to the mills, the tide of workers, the women walking arm in arm, surged past our cottage door again homeward bound. Their step was not as brisk as it had been at the beginning of the day. After that, apart from the plaintive

13

shriek of a train in the distance, or the haunting sound of a lonely concertina being played by a passerby, silence reigned. To keep up steam the thump of the mill engines went on all night, but that didn't bother anybody. The workers never noticed noises that brought them bread.

In time I became familiar with the other parts of my home. Every detail of it has remained etched in my mind. The cottage consisted of four white-washed rooms, two up and two down. It took six paces to go from one end of the house to the other. The rooms were about seven feet high, and eight or nine feet square. The outside of the cottage was brick, the inside plaster. The downstairs floors were made of large flagstones, cut from local quarries and covered with a scattering of clean sand which was swept up and renewed weekly; the ceilings were the wooden floor boards of the upper rooms; the roof was grey slate. There was a tiny yard at the rear, where the rain sat between the cobbles, which led into an alley and backed on to an identical dwelling.

Because of the small, wooden staircase, the back bedroom, where my two sisters slept, was slightly smaller than the front bedroom. There was only space for one bed and a large wooden trunk filled with linen and bedding. My sisters' clothing also hung on the walls. In 1916, when I was born, Jenny was eleven; Brenda was six. There was the same kind of fireplace, orange crate, pisspot, pegmat, gas lamp, thin wooden door, and a window looking directly into a similar window across the alleyway.

The kitchen, which was beneath the back bedroom, was the centre of family activities. It was both a place of relaxation and work. An unending process of washing, ironing, baking, and cooking took place there. The room contained a small, plain deal bench which served as table, two rush-bottomed stand chairs – small children always stood for meals – two foot-stools, two rocking chairs, a peg hearth-rug, a cupboard for groceries, hooks for pots and pans, the bread-mug, a large clay bowl with a clay lid in which we kept bread, margarine, and other food, and another large clay bowl in which the bread was made. There was yet another large earthenware dish which could be used for any purpose. As the kitchen was three paces one way and two-and-a-half paces the other, there was not a lot of room to move around. In that confined space one had to learn to sit still. That, I suppose, is why young children didn't sit at table. There simply wasn't room for more chairs. Later on I seem to remember sitting on a bench. But until I was about ten, like my siblings, I stood for meals.

The coal-burning open fire range had an oven at one side, and an oblong tank for heating water at the other. The water was rusty, but it could be used for all kinds of cleaning jobs. Directly in front of the fire was a top-bar on which the kettle might stand. Farther back was a chain on which to hang the kettle over the fire. Steel fire irons stood on the hearth which had a metal surround. The whole range was kept clean with black-lead and ammonia. The hearth was kept white or yellow with a

14

donkey stone. Ashes from the fire, which fell into a stone-lined hole in the floor, were shovelled into a bucket and thrown into the midden in the backyard. Coal for the fire was dumped in the kitchen under the stairs, a sack at a time. It kept dry there. It was brought by our neighbour, Mr. Morgan, who staggered through the front room into the kitchen with a hundred pound sack on his back.

The cloud of dust that flew up when Mr. Morgan poured the coal on the ground – though on our behalf he was ever careful – took time to settle. The worst thing that could happen was for Mr. Morgan to arrive while the family was eating. With a sack of coal being shaken out almost against the dining table, it was impossible not to eat coal dust.

When done, Mr. Morgan would quietly fold his sack, adjust his leather hood which protected his ears as well as his head, reposition the studded leather guard which prevented the coal from digging into his back, pick up his shilling and leave. I never knew Mr. Morgan to stand in our kitchen talking – perhaps because he was so dirty.

Above the fireplace was a gas light, which was capped with a one-penny asbestos mantle – about the size and shape of a white clay pipe bowl. Beneath the gas light was a shelf on which sat two red and white earthenware dogs.

Under the window there was a stone sink and a slopstone, sometimes called a draining board. Above the sink was the only tap in the house. Between the sink and the fireplace, in the corner of the room, was a deep, large metal basin called a setpot or copper. It had a small fireplace beneath it, heated with orange-box wood, and a chimney connected to the main fire range. A single metal gas ring stood next to the setpot for cooking. Like the gas light, the gas ring was serviced by a penny meter under the stairs. If the gas gave out and we didn't have a penny, we used a candle; if we didn't have a candle we sat by the fire or went to bed. Clean water, water free of rust, was boiled in the setpot. All clothes washing was done there. Washing was soaked, boiled, rotated with a wooden dolly, rinsed, and starched in this small corner. The steaming wet washing was run through a wringer which stood in the yard and, weather permitting, hung out to dry. On rainy days it was hung indoors on a clothes rack, which could be lowered and raised, fixed to the already low ceiling in front of the range. Damp clothing usually hung above our heads for half the week. Finally, there were two doors, one leading to the cobbled yard and the alleyway beyond, the other to the front room.

The front room downstairs, the 'best room', was the same size as the front room upstairs, about nine feet by nine feet. When you opened the front door and stepped down one step you stood in the street. In winter a heavy curtain was put up behind the front door to stop drafts. Some people called this room the parlour, but that was putting on airs. It had the same window, the same lace curtains, the same pegrug, the same gas light, the same fireplace as the front bedroom upstairs. It also had two rocking chairs, some stools, and another large chest for clothing and belongings. The fire-irons and metal surround in the best room, as custom decreed, were made of brass, not steel as in the kitchen. On the Singer sewing machine in front of the window stood an aspidistra which was periodically washed with soap and water and put out for air. Mother's cut-glass punch bowl stood on a small table against the wall. The sewing machine and the punch bowl were the prized possessions that mother had brought back from America. My parents had migrated to America with my sister Jenny in 1906. On the shelf above the fireplace were several framed pictures of relatives. There also was a coloured picture of Blackpool tower and the earlier big wheel. The front room was used for special entertaining, for holidays such as Christmas, and if coal was available, at weekends. Except on the hottest days of summer it was always too cold to sit in the front room without a fire. None of the rooms had a chest of drawers or a clock. Time in the house was kept by a steel watch which hung on a hook by the kitchen fire.

For me, the cobbled yard at the back of the house was another world. It could be traversed with a hop, skip, and a jump. In the yard, underneath the kitchen window, was a tap over a drain where the pisspots stood after being rinsed. In frosty weather the tap froze and the pots had to be washed inside. In one corner of the yard was a tiny roofed-over shelter where the cast iron clothes wringer, brushes and brooms were kept. Another corner contained a pile of cinders, picked by us children from factory tips. The pile was sometimes added to by a sack of coke brought by our neighbour Mr. Lambert from the gasworks. These, and peat sods, were used in winter to bank up the kitchen fire and keep it going throughout the night. We called it banking-up. Above the cinders hung a large tin tub which was carried into the kitchen when somebody wanted a bath, which wasn't very often.

There also was a toilet called a petty which was connected to the main sewer; there was no flushing, no lighting, no seat. We used nothing but newspaper there. In summer it stank, in winter you froze to the board. If you stayed too long, one of the family would call from the back door, "Wot yer doin' in't petty? Are ye makin' yer will?" An odd question, because the working class didn't make wills. My sister Jenny would never go out there at night without a lighted candle. If we had no candle somebody had to go out with her and stand outside the petty door until she was done.

Next to the toilet was a brick, roofed-over midden with openings into the yard and the alleyway into which we threw our trash. In due course this was shovelled from the back alley into a horse-drawn cart. In summer, the smell of rotting garbage was everywhere. Flies descended in clouds; hence the upset stomachs. Indoors we had penny flypapers hanging from the ceiling. In warm weather, one could eat and watch the death throes of flies caught on the flypaper above the dining table. Great buzzing bluebottle flies were the only ones to escape, and they not often. Next to the midden was a door leading into the alley. It had a stone gutter in the middle down which rats used to scurry. When I was small the rats frightened me to the point of panic. The yard was enclosed by a rough stone wall. Across the yard was a clothesline which was sometimes used to dry the washing.

Until I was about four my world consisted of our house, the baby sitters' houses, and the Morgan's house next door, where I played with Annie Morgan who was about my own age. I also remember my sister Jenny taking me to the horse trough outside the Griffin pub at the end of our street. The horses were watered there, and how deeply they drank; great draughts that I was sure would empty the trough. Withdrawing their heads, they would shake their wet all over me. People drank from a dented metal cup attached by a chain to the spout from which poured a steady stream of water.

The Morgans never had more than the one child, Annie. Their house was tidy and clean, and smelled as good as it looked. Mrs. Morgan washed dishes at the Bull Hotel in town, where she took Annie; Mr. Morgan hauled coal. They could not have had much money to spare, yet I always felt warm and secure there. I liked the bright red geranium Mrs. Morgan kept in her window.

The Morgans were a strange contrast. He was a dark, muscular fellow, with long, strong arms, and big hands. He used to stand before a little mirror at the kitchen sink and, with the tap running, comb his thick, black hair until it hung in a straight line above his deep-set dark eyes. I used to watch him and wait for him to part his hair, but he never did. I knew Mr. Morgan for many years and he never parted his hair. Everybody else did. He had the darkest side-whiskers which luxuriated down his face like a garden gone wild. Mrs. Morgan was undersized like her daughter Annie. She was as small as her husband was large, as fair as he was dark, and as slim as he was stout. The one thing they did have in common was their sense of humour. They were forever cheery.

All my life I have been able to sense the atmosphere of a house on entering. My senses have never failed me. In the Morgan's house, from my first visit, I sensed the warmest love and affection. In the evening, when Mr. Morgan came home, black as the coal he had carried on his back all day, Mrs. Morgan used to leap up to greet him. As a child, it pleased me the way Mrs. Morgan kept touching her husband. She had a way of reaching up and gently running her hand across his coal-blackened face. Mr. Morgan responded by showing Mrs. Morgan his gleaming white teeth.

Sometimes on a Sunday, Mr. Morgan – his layers of coaldust removed – would take Annie and me to visit Molly, a big black horse with a star on her forehead. It was not really his horse, but he treated it as such. Molly lived in a dark cell in the side of a large building in town. I thought it a

17

dismal hole. I don't know how Molly put with the dirt and the smell and the thick darkness. She always cheered up when we unlocked the door and allowed a flood of light to rush in. Mr. Morgan would place his head against Molly's and soothingly ask her how the night had gone, and how she felt, and how glad he was to see her again. He would then give her a carrot. Molly responded by rubbing her head against Mr. Morgan's waistcoat. She looked at him with knowing eyes and quivering nostrils in a way that she didn't look at us. Before we left, Annie and I were allowed to sit on Molly's back and pat her neck. If it pleased her, the horse would turn round and tickle us with her soft, wet muzzle. The final treat came on the moment of departure. Mr. Morgan would lift us up and allow us to take a handful of oats from Molly's bin. We were allowed to take as much as one hand could grasp. All the way home we chewed on Molly's oats.

I was taught early in life not to talk about Blackburn's all-pervading damp and cold. "It's bad enough without having you gassing about it," my people grumped. I think the damp worried them more than the cold. Mother said that it was much worse than they'd experienced in Fall River, Massachusetts. There was nothing to stop the damp rising from the earth. It got into people's bones. The damp washing hanging from the kitchen ceiling, in which the grown-ups were always getting their heads caught, didn't help.

But then, the cold was sometimes so severe that it made us forget the damp. When the north wind was blowing, and the air was smoking with snow, we went to bed with all the preparations of a military campaign. As the only heat upstairs was that which came through the cracks in the wooden bedroom floors, we didn't walk, we dashed upstairs into bed, taking care not to get splinters in our feet on the wooden staircase. No praying at the bedside for us. Bed warmers, the hot oven shelves covered with flannel, went into bed first, our clothing followed; every garment that could be found was heaped on top. Sometimes we even used thick layers of newspaper as an extra blanket, which rustled when we turned in bed. The kitchen fire was banked up and kept alight with cinders or peat throughout the night. That was father's job. If the man-of-the-house was about, nobody else touched the poker or the fire. I never ceased to wonder how much interest father could take in the fire. You knew his mood from the way he handled the poker, or how he rearranged the coals. I think it gave him great satisfaction and saved him from talking. The house would have been unbearable without keeping the kitchen fire going. Even so, there were nights when it was too cold to sleep. On a really cold morning we had to dress quickly or freeze. We didn't linger in the bedroom, we raced to breakfast. There were no repeated calls to "get up." Cold and hunger were the great persuaders.

Curiously enough, despite the appeals of my sisters, we never lit the bedroom fires except on Christmas Eve to welcome Father Christmas who entered our bedrooms by way of the chimney. Desperate as our condition became, I cannot remember a Christmas as a child without waking in the early hours of Christmas Day to find one or two little gifts at the foot of the bed. What magic to waken and find that Father Christmas had not forgotten us – that somebody cared. Always in my stocking was an apple or an orange, some nuts, and a shining new penny. When presents are rare – I cannot remember us exchanging gifts, not even on birthdays – they are all the more precious. Requests for fires in the bedrooms at times other than Christmas were always met with: "It isn't really cold enough for fires upstairs," or, with the snow-flakes spinning to earth outside, "It's going to get warmer." The answer that settled all arguments was "Coal's done."

One piercingly cold night – with a thick crust of ice and snow covering the bedroom window – father woke up to use the pisspot. He must have been caught unexpectedly. Perhaps he'd been out drinking. Anyway, to his annoyance, he discovered that the pisspots had been left by the drain in the yard and were now buried under deep snow. Before mother could stop him, he'd shot up the window and was pissing into the street. All would have been well had he not pissed on somebody's head. Even better had the passerby not looked up to see who was opening the window. A great howl arose from the cobbles below. With a freezing wind entering the room, a shouting match was soon under way. Mother choked with anger at father. Father choked with fury at the passerby, whose own fury was waking the street. "What right have you," father bawled at the man, "to be wandering the streets at this hour? Why can't you watch where you're going?" With that he slammed the window shut. Next morning there was an unusual tension at the breakfast table.

It took father a long time to live the pissing incident down. In our street such tales quickly got around. I was at a workers' meeting with father some nights later when someone shouted: "Any more bulls eyes, Will?" Everybody roared with laughter, including father, which was not like him. When I told grandmother Bridget about the pissing business she crossed herself.

Although I was first to be put to bed in our family, I was never lonely. I always fell asleep to the drone of voices in the kitchen below. Sometimes I'd fall asleep listening to Jenny twittering and chirping like a bird. She never sang a song right through like mother did. The cracks in the wooden floor beneath the bed were so wide that, except when the adults took an unfair advantage by whispering, I could hear all that was going on. Whether the speakers were in the kitchen or immediately beneath me in the front room, they were never more than a few feet away. Sometimes, when the whispering had gone on too long, I leapt out of bed, and with my ear pressed to the cracks in the floor listened to the local scandal. In our street everybody knew everybody else's business: who was sick, who was well; who was richer, who was poorer; who had "got on", and who had "gone wrong".

The cracks in the wooden floor were large enough for my brother and I to drop metal washers the size of a penny on to those being entertained in the front room below. One night Dan, who was four-and-a-half years older than I, outdid himself by dropping one right down the front of a woman's dress. Convinced that it was a mouse – it was not unknown for mice and bugs to fall from the ceiling, sometimes into your food – the woman grasped her breast and gave a great scream. There was much commotion before the washer was retrieved. It all ended with father bawling at Dan through the ceiling and threatening him with his belt; though father, like the rest, went into fits of laughter once the visitor had left. I think dad had his hands full with my brother. The two of them were always having words. I never knew anyone as prone to giving "old buck" (cheek), or be as stubborn as Dan. He and I had some happy moments together as children, but he later ignored me both at school and on the streets.

I knew from the sounds and smells coming from the kitchen at night what everybody was doing. I could hear my mother and sisters working together. I knew it was washing night because of the amount of water being sloshed about; also because the house became damp; condensation would cover the windows. Next morning the plastered walls were streaked with wet.

Ironing night had its own distinct slightly burning smell. There was also the tell-tale snap of the flat iron lid as a fresh red hot iron was taken from the fire and placed inside.

Baking night was best of all; it offered tidbits. Mother's knocking on the side of the bread tins to get the loaves out, and the rich smell of freshly baked bread, always brought me creeping down the stairs in the hope of claiming my share. Baking was the one activity I really appreciated. I loved to watch mother mix the flour, knead the dough, roll and pat it before putting it in the bread tins which Brenda then placed in the oven. It was my job to prick the tops of the loaves with a fork before they were baked. With mother helping, it was Jenny's job to get the loaves out of the oven once mother said they were done.

When I heard hot coals being pushed under the oven, I knew that roasted potatoes with lots of margarine were in the offing. The most disappointing thing that could happen was to fall asleep before the feast was ready and I had claimed my share.

Many other noises reached me. I knew from the smells and the rattle of pots and pans that mother was cooking the next day's meal. With a double burden of work, the mill and the house, there was always something to do when she returned from the mill after 5:00 p.m. For her, the cooking, scrubbing, washing and cleaning was unending. When all else was done, there were clothes to be patched, socks to be darned. I heard the click of her needles, the kettle whistling on the hob, the scrape of the rockers, the squeak of chairs.

I listened to my family playing games and knew who had won. I heard the cups being tossed, the dice thrown, the dominoes clinking, the shuffling of the cards. Sometimes they would play Find-the-Thimble – giving great gleeful shouts when one of them went from warm to hot. I knew from the way that those huddled round the fire jumped back that a gust of wind had come down the chimney and had driven smoke into their eyes. Chairs being picked up and put down again meant that the family and visitors were changing places in the hope of avoiding drafts. Some found shelter where others found nothing but a gale. On a really cold, windy night everybody was entitled to scrape his chair about the floor as much as he saw fit.

For my sisters to jump and squeal at the same time meant that a mouse had run across their feet. The mice were cheeky because they were hungry. They marched out of the plaster walls as bold as brass. That's why most families, poor as they were, had to keep a cat. We had no fat mice and no fat people. We didn't have a cat in our house; mother said there was no room for a cat. We used mousetraps. They haunted me. The sharp crack of the trap, like the crack of doom, would sometimes waken me at night followed by a momentary squeaking in the corner.

Some of the conversations going on below meant nothing to me. There was a lot of talk about superstitions – superstitions connected with salt, brooms, ladders, warts, the moon, black cats, horses, Gypsies, looking-glasses, spoons, knives, forks – the meaning of which escaped me. Fear of the unknown, which was rampant when I was a child, was acquired gradually through the pores. One day father broke the looking-glass which hung above the kitchen sink. "Mm ... mm," the grown-ups said in a very dark way. "Seven years bad luck!" Father never spoke and he didn't look happy either. I think my people feared the breaking of mirrors more than anything else. They didn't call it superstition. They knew that their spirit was reflected in the glass as well as their face. You couldn't break the reflection of the face without affecting the reflection of the spirit. That took a long time to put right. They didn't lecture each other about it, they just took care not to break mirrors. My sisters and I learnt this fear when young, and it stayed with us. Dan, for some reason, was able to ignore it.

A much more easily understood conversation remains with me to this day.

"Aye, ah'd really like a drink," said father.

"A good glass of stout would make all the difference," answered mother.

"How much money do we have, Maggie?"

"Fourpence."

"Well, that will buy a glass of beer."

"You go and enjoy the fourpence, Will, it will do you good." I heard her put the coins on the table.

"Nay, if we can't afford a glass each, we'll share it," father replied. "Off tha goes t' Griffin and get it."

I heard mother get a mug, put on her clogs and shawl, and leave the house. I heard her footsteps going down the street toward the pub and coming back again.

"Real gradely," father said, smacking his lips, as they savoured half a glass each.

Through the same cracks in the floor I heard my mother's sister, widowed aunt Alice, who was trying to avoid going to the workhouse, express her disgust with the Woodruffs and her own people the Kenyons.

"Well, I'll tell you this: I didn't think you'd put me in't work'ouse. I thowt one of you would take me in. You've got 'earts of stone, that's what." It was the first time I heard the saying "hearts of stone."

I didn't understand the widespread fear of the workhouse until much later. The horror of the poor was not to starve, as one might expect, but to be sent to the workhouse. The conditions in nineteenth-century British workhouses had been so dreadful that they had left a trail of fear which was still very much alive among the poor as late as the 1930's. The workhouses carried this stigma with them even after their name was changed in the 1920s to old age homes or poorhouses. To dissuade the destitute from seeking help, living conditions inside the workhouse were deliberately kept at the lowest possible level. To prevent further breeding, families were broken up. To dissuade able-bodied males from staying longer than they needed, the hardest work, such as stonebreaking or sawing heavy timber, was demanded of them. I was brought up to use the term workhouse – never poorhouse – and to believe that the workhouse was a prison for the poor.

At the time I knew sufficient from the conversation going on under my bed that I ought to feel sorry for aunt Alice. Not least because I knew that she was going blind. When I was older mother told me how Alice had got poorer, older, and more ragged. A spinster, there was no one upon whom she could make a claim, no one to inquire about her, no one prepared to take on the burden of feeding another mouth. Most people looked the other way, their pity for her unstirred. Either to take her mind off her troubles, or to pick up a bit of extra food, she'd started going to funerals. She never missed a good funeral and was always willing to talk about them. She'd got into the habit of sitting in the cemetery. She said she found peace there.

Mother wept when Alice left. Father was not in favour of Alice moving in. "We've got all t' mouths we can feed," he said. "What's wrong with your brothers helping? Eric's got the money and the space. It's scandalous his turning her away."

"He didn't, Pearl did."

"If his wife won't have Alice, then Eric should give Alice t' money. It's scandalous, I say."

It was from my bed that I heard all about the pair of shoes that prevented my sister Brenda from going to Grammar School.

To everyone's surprise, Brenda had done brilliantly in the state examinations for eleven-year-olds. She was right at the top and she'd done it without a book in the house, and with no special coaching. It was a real miracle. Her name was in the newspaper. My sister Jenny showed it to me. It was the first time I'd seen our name in print and it had quite an effect on me. I read the words over and over again. It made me giddy. The next day I expected everyone to stop me in the street and ask me if I was the brother of the girl whose name was in the paper, and who was going to go to the Grammar School in Preston. Nobody did. I became so disappointed that I stopped a number of people to tell them that I was Brenda's brother. I told them how she had won a scholarship to go to a special school for girls at Preston, ten miles away. She was going to ride the train there and back every day without paying. Nobody seemed impressed.

After several days a letter arrived from the school board about Brenda. I heard my parents discussing it in the kitchen.

"Uniforms, including stockings are provided," said father studying a list. "Train fare as well," he continued. "And books and pencils."

"Well, imagine that," said mother, "I reckon they must have money cumin' out of their ears."

There was a pause.

"What's it say about shoes?" asked mother. "Lass can't go to college in clogs."

"Nothing," said father, "nothing."

"It must ... look again."

There was a longer pause.

"Mm, aye, tha reet, Maggie, it does. It says that shoes will be black, of plain design, and of good quality."

"Um, they're fussy."

A long pause followed. "Where wa' it t' come fra?" (Where might it come from?) mother asked.

"We can borrow money to buy shoes, or we can leave her where she is," father said finally. "We might be making a fuss about nothing, Maggie. It's not good to put big ideas into young people's heads. What use is there in this learning when she could be doing real work?"

Although I was very young I knew that something was wrong. I wanted to shout between the cracks beneath my bed, "Brenda's name was in the paper! You can't stop her going to Preston because she hasn't got shoes."

But I didn't shout. Nobody did. To my knowledge, not even members of the school board, which baffles me to this day. Equally baffling is why grandmother Bridget didn't intervene. She was, after all, the most educated among us. She was always on to us about "larning".

Brenda didn't go to Preston. One night when she came back from the lending library, I heard father tell her that they couldn't send her to school because she didn't have shoes, and they couldn't afford to buy them. Brenda didn't throw a fit, which is what I wanted her to do. Apart from a mumbled word or two, she accepted their decision. The matter was never discussed again.

I think father was to blame. Somebody, somewhere would surely have paid for the shoes had he gone and asked, but he was too proud to beg. The truth is he wasn't interested in higher education for his children. It wasn't because Brenda was a girl, I think he would have done exactly the same had it been my brother Dan. He never encouraged any of us to better ourselves or to make the best of our talents by schooling. Education and keeping up the family prestige were never factors in our lives – spinning and weaving were. The mills were our destiny. There was nothing dishonourable in that. What had been good enough for him, and for his father and grandfather, was good enough for us. It's where we belonged. It was our station in life and each should be satisfied with his station. Schooling should not be allowed to get in the way of more important things like spinning and weaving. Instead of going on to higher education, Brenda entered the mill at twelve as a half-timer. She became a piecer, an assistant to a spinner. The brilliant career she might have had was denied her.

Very early, from where I lay above their heads, I became familiar with my people's talk of a "ship coming home." I puzzled about that particular ship for a long time. It must have been the slowest ship on the seas because it never seemed to arrive; it was always arriving. "Aye! Tha'll see when it cums," people shouted, slapping their knees. But it never did come. The only man whose ship came home was mother's brother, uncle Eric.

Nobody believed in Lancashire's future as much as uncle Eric did. He was the success story of the family; he'd gone up in the world. A thin, self-confident man, uncle Eric placed all his belief in science. He played a leading role in the local Mechanics Institute. He made all the speeches there. "Uncle Eric," mother said, "has the gift of the gab."[†] Science, not religion, was the hope of the world for him. He was mesmerized by the latest inventions. He was written up in the newspaper as one of the first in our town to have electricity installed in his house. The rest of us considered it quite an honour.

One night, as a small child, I was taken to celebrate uncle Eric's triumph. Clutching mother's hand, and accompanied by a little knot of muffled-up relatives and a wind that roared over the cold rooftops, we crossed the unmarked boundary which separated the poorer from the richer parts of town. We found uncle Eric waiting for us at his garden gate with a lantern that showed up his bright eyes and the blue veins that ran down his nose. His hair was parted down the middle and shone with oil. As he jumped about with his lamp, shadows flitted among the shrubs and trees. He was very proud to have so many visitors. He led us into a large, dark room where we stood about wondering what was going to happen. Other people followed until the room was quite full.

I didn't share the hearty humour of some of these people. Even the word "eeelectricity" sounded sinister to me. It was a word we had never used before. It didn't come easily to the adults. Perhaps, as the doom-sayers in the room warned, we were about to be blown up! Nervously, I held mother's hand and tried not to fidget.

With a slightly tipsy uncle Eric dragging out the drama, and with everyone else shouting "One, two, three!" the room was suddenly flooded with an entirely new and magical light. The light was soft, yet blinding; it made us blink. It reached everywhere, right into the corners of the room. It came from a large glittering bulb hanging from the ceiling. There was no flame, or spluttering, or hissing; there was no smell as with gaslight. From the look of astonishment on the faces around me there might have been a thousand bulbs above our heads. The air was suddenly filled with a barrage of congratulatory "ahs" and "ums". "It's past talking," they said, looking around; "it beats it all." "Aye, Eric," they chorused, "tha're a one, tha're! Tha should be Mayor!"

"Nay, nay, not Mayor," somebody shouted, "Eric will have to be our mon in Parliament fro' Blackburn." We all clapped. "Speech!" somebody called.

Never stuck for words, a beaming and now perspiring uncle Eric began by saying that "eeelectricity" was going to change all our lives. There was no telling the wonders it would bring. With the help of "eeelectricity", things would buck up for everybody. None of us would have to work any more. Electricity would do it for us. In the golden age of electricity that lay ahead, we'd all be rich. Strikes and lock-outs, hunger and poverty were going to be things of the past. Progress could only come if we all used our 'eads.

Uncle Eric had certainly used his. He had made a lot of money equipping hospitals with furniture and supplies. He didn't make the furniture and supplies – mother said he couldn't tell one end of a hammer from another – he simply took them from one group of people and sold them to another. Compared with our cottage, his house was a richly furnished mansion. He and aunt Pearl had started out quite poor. "Poor as church mice, couldn't afford children," mother told me. I hadn't met aunt Pearl before. Half the size of uncle Eric, she was made up like a clown at the circus. She had blue rings round her eyes; her lips were painted firebucket red; she had bright tinsel on her dress. Even her hair stood on end. She had a strange rasping voice. Her fat, short fingers were laden with jewellery. According to mother, she was wearing a fortune. When I saw how small she was I found it hard to believe the family story that she had once knocked uncle Eric out with a frying pan. He didn't seem any the worse for it.

As if to acclaim the coming of the golden age, uncle Eric and aunt Pearl proceeded to serve hot meat pies, black puddings that scalded one's tongue, and great slabs of cold, potted meat. For "afters" there was hot rhubarb pie smothered with real cream. There was as much beer as one could drink. As the food was heaped on to our plates, the talking stopped. Although everyone set to with a good heart to "brass th' guts," it was some time before everything was gone.

When there was nothing left to eat or drink we picked up sticks and trailed back – some a little unsteadily – to our homes by the mills. Before leaving we all stood and sang "For He's A Jolly Good Fellow!" Uncle Eric stood there blinking, a contented Cheshire-cat look on his face. Everyone agreed that uncle Eric and aunt Pearl had put on a "reeight luvly do". The talk going home was more about black puddings than about science.

Two things stick in my mind about that night: one was the fact that uncle Eric was the only man wearing a suit and tie, the other was the large mantelpiece clock decorated with tiny coloured birds. I'd never seen such a clock before.

Most talk I overheard at night in the rooms below was about work and food, about family and the neighbourhood. Except for talk about Blackburn's dependence upon India, and talk about Fall River, Massachusetts, where my parents had migrated and worked for eight years, nearly all else was about local matters. Barring the mention of other cotton towns, Blackburn was the world. It was one of the first words I learnt to write and spell at school. "Blackburn, Blackburn, Blackburn," I wrote all over my slate. Later on I heard about London and that the King lived there. We didn't talk about him much. We didn't blame him for much either. It was "them" and "they" whom we criticized. "Them" and "they" were always on the workers' tongues.

I was as puzzled by the workers' constant use of "them" and "they" as I was by the ship that never seemed to come home. Who were "them who'd take the bread out of our mouths?" Who were "they who'd see our children starve before lifting a finger?" Later I learnt that "them" and "they" were the bosses, and the bosses men, the toffs, the police, the government, the law, and their many agents – people who, if we didn't watch out, would run our lives for us. Whoever they were, I realized early on that "them" and "they" intended us no good and should be treated as a common enemy. Our relations with "them" and "they" could never be cooperative or peaceful, only combative. Obviously the seeds of class conflict were sown in me at the earliest age. I knew that I belonged to the working class, which was part of the "lower orders." The "upper orders" were "them" and "they."

As a child many other things mystified me, such as "the war," about which my people often spoke. To listen to them, "the war" was the beginning and end of everything. By and large "the war" had changed everything for the worse in their lives. If somebody went into a decline and died, if a man couldn't walk, or a machine wouldn't work, or the harvest failed, or a cow wouldn't give milk, it was always "the war" that was blamed. Much later, I discovered that "the war" was the Great War of 1914–1918 in which my father had fought. Only then did I connect the many limbless men who had hobbled through our streets in my early years with "the war." I'd no idea that "the war" had made our neighbour, Mr. Beatty who lived two doors away, the gibbering idiot he was.

On fine days Mrs. Beatty would put Mr. Beatty outside the front door to air. He lay in a long patched wicker bed on wheels on the narrow pavement, inches away from the street, jabbering and drooling at passers-by. He always had a towel under his chin. When I dared to look at him, I was surprised how strong and big his head was. I never did try to see what was under the blanket. His eyes were open but I think they were largely dead. Like a blind man's, they looked directly ahead but they didn't see. The carters always called and waved their whips at him.

"Up and at 'em," he'd shout back, making his wicker bed shake. He shouted it so often that it became his nick-name.

"And how is old Up and at 'em?" passers-by asked as they took hold of his blanket and waggled one of his stumps. Years had to pass before I learnt that "Up and at 'em" was what British soldiers shouted to each other on the Western Front before going "over the top." Mr. Beatty went on fighting the Great War until he died. His great comfort was for Mrs. Beatty to sit and read the Bible to him. On Jenny's orders, I always crossed the street when she was reading outside her front door so as not to disturb.

Nothing in my childhood, not even downright wickedness, was as bad as "the war". Everybody knew how "the war" had come about. The Germans had caused it. My generation were brought up to believe that the Germans were responsible for most troubles. I think it helped a great deal to have the Germans to blame. Whatever the trouble, if "the war" and "the sickness" couldn't be held responsible, then the Germans must have done it. It came as quite a surprise later on to meet Germans who struck me as ordinary people – people who could smile and have a toothache.

"The sickness" was, of course, the influenza epidemic which followed "the war," and from which so many people died. Whole families lay sick together. The church bells, so I was told later on, never stopped tolling; the undertakers were busy night and day. My mother, my sister Jenny, and my grandmother Bridget were all stricken by it. So great was the fear of contracting the illness that even my mother's sister Alice had refused to come to her aid. My father had gone to fetch her. Little did she realize that one day, when on her way to the workhouse, she would seek my mother's assistance. Help came from Dr. Grieves and a good Samaritan woman who walked in off the street. The woman they told me was plain-faced, plain-dressed, plain-talked and kind. She had seen us in the morning, a dejected group of children huddled in the doorway; we were still there when she passed the house in the late afternoon. "Where's your mother?" she asked Brenda. Brenda said she was sick in bed. So the stranger went in and took care of everything. For two or three weeks she shopped, and cooked, and fed the whole family and kept the house clean until mother and Jenny could get back on their feet. Then, unpaid, she left as mysteriously as she had come and was never seen by us again.

As long as my family had regular work, something to eat, and coal or peat for the fire, they lived in a fairly contented world. Having a good job, keeping a good table and a good fire were the things that really mattered. What disadvantages and hardships they suffered, they offset by an extraordinary capacity for leg-pulling and hilarity. It kept them going. Neighbours who dropped into our house at night – the street door remained unlocked until father went to bed – were always greeted with laughter. For Lancashire folk, exuberance was an inborn trait. So was shouting. I knew when a visitor had entered the house by the great shout of "Y'in?" (Are you in?) which accompanied the lifting of the latch. Some "y'in's" were so loud that they startled me out of my sleep. Having shut the street door behind them, because of drafts, visitors usually stood quite still, head cocked, waiting for an invitation to proceed farther. The answering shouts of the family were equally loud; "Cum in, cum ya." Sometimes I could tell who it was by the smell rather than the voice. Accepted visitors were always told to make themselves "at 'ome".

The habit of shouting sprang partly from a good-natured exuberance; also the constant clatter of the mill machinery had made many of the workers partly deaf. It was common for people to cup their ear with their hand and shout "Eh?". In the mills one used lip-reading or shouted to be heard. Having shouted all day, the workers went on shouting when they got home at night. Shouting in our house was common. It never crossed anybody's mind that I was trying to sleep above their heads. Nobody apologized for making a noise. Except for churches and funerals it was unnatural for us to be quiet.

Quiet or loud, I loved their voices: voices slow and melodious; voices sharp and quick; voices full of sorrow; voices full of joy; sweet voices, like Jenny's, which quite spontaneously – like a bird – could break into song, and break off again just as quickly; voices which, as the night lengthened, sometimes fell silent. Once a subject had been talked to death, custom demanded that the workers should sit back and digest what had been said. I knew when they were ruminating, for the long pauses would be punctuated by isolated remarks like: "By gum! It doesn't bear thinking about," or "Now, what use war that?" or just plain "Eeees!" or "Aiiiis," followed by long meaningful sighs. Minutes later a galaxy of voices would be at it again. My people loved talking; eloquence was their birthright. I loved them for it. I never tired of listening, even when I'd no idea what they were talking about. It was the music of their words that mattered.

Never far from the discussions going on beneath my bed were the technical terms of the industry into which I was born. Such things as wefts and warps, cops and hanks, pirns and picks, sliver and slubber, yarns and combers, were in constant use. Carders, drawers, winders, warpers, beamers, reelers, spinners, piecers, and weavers, all of whom lived in Griffin Street, became part of my everyday life. I learnt about the industry through the pores; by rubbing against it daily.

Later on, as a schoolboy, I learnt about every stage of cotton manu-facture at first hand. It was my job to bring the dinners to each family member in the mills at noon. The meal, a stew of meat, potatoes, and vegetables, was cooked by mother the night before. Each person took their filled basin to work and left it on a large stove in the warehouse. Before noon the basins were hotted up, hence hot-pot. I would leave school at 11:45 a.m., run along the river to the mill and locate my family's dinners. I had a knack of distinguishing our basins from scores of others; which wasn't as simple as it sounds. Everything was fine as long as the bowls had individual patterns. The time to watch out was when everybody brought basins with the same mud-brown glaze. You had to watch your step then or somebody would come chasing after you shouting their head off. Losing one's dinner was a serious matter. I placed each basin in my cap because it was scalding hot, and ran with it through the mill to each family member's work place: first father and Dan, then Jenny, then Brenda. Speed was essential; nobody wanted a cold-pot, not even Jenny and Brenda who always seemed to be lathered with sweat from the heat and humidity of the spinning-room. The last two basins were for mother and me. We ate our dinner balancing ourselves on an overturned round sliver can, our backs wedged against the whitewashed wall. Once I tripped and fell carrying somebody's dinner. It spilled into my cap: meat, potatoes, carrots, peas, gravy, the lot. All I could do was to scoop it out of my hat back into the bowl and say nothing. My hat smelled for days.

Always running in and out of the mills, I had plenty of opportunity to learn about textile manufacture. I watched the bales of cotton being broken up, cleaned, blended, whirled and pounded until a continuous sheet of matted tufts called a lap emerged. This was slubbing, mother's job. Mother showed me how the lap was then fed into the carder which had two rollers covered with fine wire teeth designed to break up the tufts and separate the individual fibres. From the carder the untwisted rope of cotton (a sliver) was coiled in tall cans. The sliver, about an inch in diameter, was then combed to remove the shorter fibres, drawn across smooth leather-covered rollers, twisted into a long, firm thread, after which it was wound on to large spinning bobbins. This was roving. The bobbins went to the spinner where the threads were blended, drawn, and twisted some more. Jenny and Brenda were spinners.

The resulting yarn, including warp and weft, came in all kinds of counts,[†] (threadcounts) or thicknesses. It was then woven. My father was a weaver. His life was spent "kissing the shuttle." He drew the weft thread from the cop by sucking it through a small hole at one end of the shuttle.

The workers, including my own family, took pride in explaining their work. It was like being admitted to a secret society. They were very serious about it. When they talked about cloth, hilarity stopped. Problems that arose in the mill during the day, such as when the weave or pattern was varied, would be discussed at night until a solution was found. Men or women were not judged so much by what they did at home but by what they did in the mill. People respected skill. Pride of work meant a lot in those days. Work was everything.

I have never forgotten my first visit to father in the weaving shed, a long, low, stone-flagged, glass-roofed building. I was five or six at the time. Getting through the great metal-plated door that gave access to his workplace was a nightmare for me. To keep the humidity in the shed, and render the cotton soft and pliable, the door had to be kept shut. To open it you had to haul great weights on chains. The door was too heavy for me to move and I had to wait until somebody helped me. Once through the door, the weights came crashing down behind me as the door slammed to. I went in fear of being crushed.

Once inside I was overwhelmed by the steam, the heat, the clatter, the smell of gas, and the frenzied activity of the machines. Too frightened to move, I froze where I was. Hundreds of looms stretched as far as I could see – all of them crashing frantically. It was the machines I noticed, not the people, most of whom were women and young girls. I was mesmerized by the way the shuttles flew backward and forward: "Lat ti tat. Lat ti tat. Lat ti tat," hundreds of times a minute. A forest of black driving belts hummed up and down between the overhead shaft and the looms. An army of picking sticks[†] were jerking backward and forward, ready to give the unwary a crack on the elbow. Father must have seen me. Sleeves rolled up, he came forward across the sanded floor and took his hot-pot. I could hardly hear him above the racket. "Don't stand theer, gawkin'," he yelled at me "tha'll get used to it." I couldn't get through the door fast enough. I was quite deaf when I got outside.

Lancashire people not only took pride in their work; they were convinced that Lancashire cotton was King. Nobody knew how to make textiles like Lancashire folk. Nobody ever would. My people took it for granted that the industry started with us. Yet the threat posed by outsiders cropped up in the kitchen every now and again. Dad had a different view of the Lancashire cotton industry than those who had never been out of England. He never tired of telling his fellow weavers that the cotton mills in Fall River were more efficient and that they'd better watch out. Mother said he told his Trade Union (the Amalgamated Weavers Association) the same story, but they never thanked him for it. I can remember him going on to our neighbours about automatic looms, "rings," and "mules," and "batteries," and goodness knows what other ingenious devices he'd seen in America. His listeners were astonished when he explained that Fall River weavers did not "kiss the shuttle" to replenish the weft; but that a rotating hopper did it for them. Even more astonished when he told them that in Fall River six, not two, looms were common. "By gum," they'd say when dad had finished. "It doesn't bear thinking about." Having said that, I suspect they dismissed it from their minds. I think they preferred to ignore other people in the world.

The other threat posed to Lancashire came from "t' niggers" whom they sometimes called "t' natives." As far as I could discover, "t' niggers" were poor people who lived in Asia and Africa. My people were simple people, they divided most of the world into "us and t' niggers"; in those days racism was a common ill. As my father had been to China, he was expected to be able to talk about "t' niggers" at first hand.

The workers took "t' niggers" no more seriously than they took the challenge posed by the cotton workers of Fall River. "T' niggers" couldn't match our skill – nobody could. Besides, they were too far away to do us any real harm. The idea that "t' niggers" might have begun the cotton industry and might replace us entirely in the cotton trade never entered anybody's head. Even in the bleakest days of the 1920s and 1930s, when Lancashire was outcompeted, or shut out of European, American, and Asian markets, Lancashire workers never stopped looking on the bright side. Setbacks were always temporary. You didn't grumble about them or show fear; you took them in your stride. Things were "allus" going to get better. There was "allus a silver lining through each dark cloud shining." "You'll see," they'd say, slapping their thighs and putting on a brave front, "things are bound to buck up. It's not t' fost time we've had troubles. I mean, what dun yo think we're made of? ... Toffee, he, he, he. Cum on, lad, it'll be aw reet!"

These things I heard and saw in my early years and took for granted. They moulded my mind.

III   Lights and shadows

My family took food seriously. You might say we had a hunger mentality. In good times, when I was four or five and before the financial crash in cottons in 1920, we began the day by eating a bowl full of scalding hot oatmeal porridge, made with water, served with a little salt. Nothing could fill you up like porridge. "Gives you a lining." Even when mother was working in the mill, no morning passed but what she did not make the breakfast. Jenny and Brenda helped. Porridge was followed by chunks of home-made bread, covered with Maggy Ann (margarine), beef-dripping, syrup, or jam. If fruit was in abundance, the women made their own jam. Shop jam was not as good – there was no telling what you might find in it. Coarse fish was cheap, a week's supply for one person might cost sixpence, and we ate a lot of it. Bought just before it "went off," it could be obtained at rock-bottom prices. Even at breakfast it was customary to gnaw upon a leftover cold haddock or kipper. We children were always being told to watch out for bones. Cockles and mussels, from nearby Fleetwood, were always about. Weak tea was drunk, piping hot, without sugar and milk, in great quantities. I never drank coffee until I was grown up. Other than mother's milk, the only milk I knew until I was in my teens was canned Nestle's milk and blue milk (milk with the cream skimmed off), which was doled into our jug out of a churn brought on a cart from a farm in the country. We knew when the milkman had arrived because he shouted: "Fresh milk, fresh milk," in the street.

Dinners were the hot-pots taken to the mills and eaten between noon and 1:00 p.m. Supper was eaten when the family came home at the end of the day – usually physically drained. It was my job to have the fire lighted and the table set. Mother would decide what to cook or serve cold. Supper could be anything: left-over stew, porridge, fish and chips, toasted crumpets, boiled or baked cod, cold sausage meat, cold tripe doused with lots of vinegar, cheese, pickles – how we loved pickles and beetroot – or a sheep's head boiled in the setpot with barley and peas. The butcher mesmerized me when he split the sheep's head with his cleaver. Crash! ... and out came the brains. If we didn't have a sheep's head, mother might make soup from fish heads and tails, or from a ham bone, or a cowheel, or "bits" of meat, with herbs and lots of potatoes and vegetables. There was always plenty of bread.

Sunday breakfast was always a feast. There was time to cook – either on the gas ring or over the fire – plates of eggs, bacon, sausages, tomatoes, sweetbreads, kidneys, and anything else that could be heaped into the frying pan and on to a plate. In leaner times – from the mid-twenties to the mid-thirties – no such feasts came our way. In the depressed 1930s we ate pickled, desperately anaemic Chinese eggs, thirty for the shilling, which had taken months to cross the world and, for all the good they did us, had better been left in China.

Sunday dinners, like Sunday breakfasts, were very special. It took the concerted efforts of mother, Jenny and Brenda to prepare that meal. In the affluent years, there would be a roast of beef, or a shoulder or a leg of lamb, with several vegetables such as cabbage, peas, beans, and cauliflower. In addition there was pudding, fruit, and balm cakes, dripping with treacle. We weren't fussy about foods that dripped. There was no table linen to be spoiled, only a newspaper. In very cold weather, mother prepared a great cauldron of broth, often with a neck of mutton. I used to watch it cooking on the gas ring, bubbling and popping like an active volcano. I was addicted to its smell. I'd put my head over the side and breathe it in. With a bit of luck, there was no telling what the brimming ladle might bring to the surface. Being the youngest, I got more than my share of the yellow, greasy, delicious dumplings that were fished up. They were so slippery that you had to be careful or they'd jump off your plate on to the sanded floor.

It was usually at this point of the meal that aunt Alice would come down the street and put her gaunt, hungry face around the door. Perhaps she'd smelled the broth. After mother and Alice had made friendly noises at each other, auntie would leave with a brimming jug of hot broth. It always happened this way. I remember aunt Alice well because – except for grandmother Bridget – she was the only relative who regularly came in and out of our house.

The richer we were, the more we ate; when we could afford it, we gorged. I can remember Pancake Tuesdays and Hot-Cross-Bun Good Fridays when we children did nothing but eat. I suppose, in good times, before the bottom dropped out of Lancashire textiles in the early 1920's, that is where our money went. We even bought fancy nuts, which father cracked for us with his granite-like teeth. Nobody was accused of gluttony. Few bothered about their waistlines, not even my sisters. We didn't shy away from fatty meat. If we did, father would quickly eat it. Food that the rest of us might not be able to stomach, he'd swallow at one go. All meals with us were favourite meals. There was an earthy naturalness about our eating. There was a vigour about it that I missed later. ("'unger's t' best sauce"). We champed and chewed with relish. The smacking of lips, belching and sucking of fingers were all ignored, so was slurping hot tea out of a saucer. To eat and drink one's fill was to be blessed.

When there was plenty of good food on the table, those who talked were hushed. "Let food stop your gob," father used to say. We thanked nobody for our meals, except ourselves, silently. Mother was a good cook, but she never expected thanks. "Oh, go on, " she'd say if anybody offered praise. I'm told that the rich were brought up to leave a little on their plates. For us, that would have been sinful. We were taught to polish our plates; using a handful of bread as a wiper, we needed no encouragement. We didn't need a dog in our house to eat the scraps. We ate them, even if they'd been dropped on the floor.

It was while we had money to spare that Mr. Levy, the pawnbroker, who owned t' pop shop a few streets away, persuaded my father to take a large-horned phonograph off his hands. It was called a Victrola. "American – a chance in a lifetime," he'd told father. Although the phonograph was one of the first of its kind, and my two sisters were overwhelmed by it, mother had her misgivings. "It's not like father at all, I don't know what's come over him." Dan's interest was minimal.

The first I knew about the machine was when it startled me out of my sleep. I was spellbound by the strange, panting, whining voice singing in the room below. I'd no idea such things existed. However, as the voice continued to whine and pant for most of that night, and the next, and the next, the spell did not last; especially as there was only one scratched cylinder, and on that only two songs: "Take a Pair of Sparkling Eyes;" and "Just a Little Love, a Little Kiss." The woman who denied the singer "Just a Little Love, a Little Kiss," must have been pretty hard-hearted. Without a little love, the poor fellow died in agony on father's phonograph every night. Soon I knew the words by heart. In spite of the contempt shown by Dan, I often sang myself to sleep with them. "Just a Little Love, a Little Kiss, I'd give my whole life for this ..."

My father took great pride in being the only owner of a phonograph in the street. People put it down to his having lived in America. It must have been unusual to own such a machine, because our house was invaded by strangely silent neighbours all standing and listening. Others put their head round the door hoping to be asked in. There was even talk about buying a second record, or a third. "A penny from each of you will go a long way," father told a crowded house.

There was no telling how many records we might have bought if neighbours had come forward with their money. None did. Friends were prepared to crowd into our cottage, cock their head on one side and listen to the new marvel; nobody was prepared to pay for it. The phonograph was put up for sale. Nobody bought it. At a considerable loss, it went back to t' pop shop.

We seemed to make a habit of taking things back to Mr. Levy. He was always good-natured and cooperative about it. He never held us to the last penny. Some years later, my parents obtained a used banjo from him as a Christmas present for me. I loved it. I played "Little Brown Jug," the only thing I could play, from morning till night until my family was quite ready to throw both me and the banjo through the door. The last time I saw it was in Mr. Levy's window. I've always regretted losing it.

But these were the best of times. In March 1920 the postwar boom of the cotton industry collapsed.

The financial frenzy which had beset the industry during 1919 and the early part of 1920 only made matters worse. Until the balloon burst in March 1920 unmitigated greed had forced dividends higher and higher.[†] So high did profits and dividends rise that there was a loss of all restraint. Speculators borrowed money to buy stocks and shares which they promptly sold at a profit. Shares sold at £10 one day could fetch £15 the next. The more speculation, the higher the inflated values became. From 1918 until March 1920, the manufacturers and the money-spinners – without contributing a single constructive idea to the industry's welfare – enriched themselves. There were accounts in the newspapers of manufacturers playing dice at £5 a throw. Meanwhile, no matter what gains were made in profits and dividends, a weaver's wage remained between one pound and thirty shillings a week. There was no end to the craziness. For a stake of £1,500, three manufacturers ran a motor car race from Blackpool to

East Lancashire. While madness reigned, some manufacturers sold out at absurdly inflated prices and became wealthy country gentlemen. Others hung on, buying up businesses with borrowed money which they could not possibly repay. Much of this money came from the banks. When the crash came the banks found themselves the real owners of much of the Lancashire textile industry – whereupon they refused to pour good money after bad.

To Lancashire's lasting harm, the financial frenzy caused the capital stock of the industry – especially of spinning – to be inflated far beyond any possibility of repayment. An already crippled industry was now overcapitalized.

Neither the employers nor the workers recognized Lancashire's changed position. Both sides believed that they were facing temporary problems; that prosperity would return. The employers blamed the workers and the government; the workers blamed the employers. It didn't occur to anybody that Lancashire's world supremacy in cotton textile production had come to an end. The Lancashire cotton industry had got so used to the idea of industrial growth that it was mentally incapable of dealing with industrial decline. Meanwhile, uncertainty, misery, and bankruptcy grew. Wishing, working, and fighting each other changed nothing.

What the crash meant for the workers was not the loss of profits, but hunger. Some months after the crash in March 1920, father lost his job in the mill. It came as a great shock to him to be thrown out of work; a greater shock when mother and the rest of the family fell out of work too. Keeping a steady job in cottons in the following years became almost impossible. Life for us had always been uncertain; now it became doubly so.

Under the National Insurance Act of 1920, dad received fifteen shillings a week for fifteen weeks; mother, for a shorter period, was paid five shillings. Children were expected to survive on one shilling per week – twelve pennies. But soon these pathetically small amounts were all gone. Any benefits father obtained from his Trade Union also ran out. Things became so bad that mother lost her cut-glass punch bowl to Mr. Levy at t' pop shop. She always called it "my American punch bowl." Standing on a small table in the front room against the whitewashed wall to catch the eye of any visitor, its glass cups hanging on polished silver hooks, the bowl had always enchanted me. The sun didn't often come into our front room, but when it did, the punch bowl magically came alive with a hundred blue-tipped twinkling lights. Although I cannot remember it being used for its true purpose, mother never ceased to lavish care on the bowl. She washed and polished it endlessly. It must have been heart-breaking when she had to surrender it. She never said anything when it was carried from the house, but I knew that with its departure she had lost a symbol of better times. I think the punch bowl was a token of the superior life that she had once lived.

It was a demoralizing blow for father to find himself on the scrapheap, especially as he felt that everybody had a duty, as well as a right, to work. "We mun work," he'd say. I could tell from his sighing in bed at night that the lack of work was affecting his sleep. It gnawed at his heart. It was not like him to turn and toss so. Sometimes, on a moonlit night, I'd waken to see him sitting up in bed staring at the bedroom door, muttering to himself. He simply did not understand why the mills should be standing idle. The town offered to retrain him and other unemployed weavers as shorthand-typists, but he rejected the scheme as a farce, which it was. There was any number of shorthand-typists in town looking for work.

The bottom was reached when, in exchange for a few cigarettes, which he then bartered for food, dad sat in the kitchen and stitched mail bags. He had joined the navy in the age of sail and knew how to use a needle. Even with a piece of leather across his palm, I could tell from watching him that stitching mailbags by hand was a very hard job. He also tried to survive by mending the clogs and shoes of our neighbours. He bought the cokers, soles, pegs, nails, and blacking from Woolworths. His bench was a three-footed last which he held between his knees. Except that he was in his own kitchen, and hungrier, he was doing exactly what the prisoners were doing in the local jail. I never heard him say it, but my sisters said that it was at times like this that he most regretted having left America.

Father never accepted the idea that there were no jobs available. His brand of despair was always tinged with expectation. Sometimes, in the early hours, I would watch his shadowy figure slip out of the bedroom. He was a great believer in the early bird business. For a few minutes he would shuffle about downstairs, taking a long drink from the sink tap. Then I'd hear him unlock and lift the latch of the front door as he went out in the dark to search for work. I heard the echo of his clogs as he hurried down the deserted street. Slowly, the night swallowed up his noise. By seven o'clock he would be standing with a crowd of others outside a mill in one of the surrounding towns, hoping to catch the foreman's eye. Perhaps this would be his lucky day. Many hours later, he would return footsore and hungry, chilled to the bone, a defeated look on his face. On his way home he'd pass equally exhausted workers going the other way, looking for the job that didn't exist. The next morning, wet or fine, he was off again on what mother called his "fool's errand."

His "fool's errand" ended one morning in a dramatic way. He had gone off as usual into the dark night looking for work. We all thought he'd struck it lucky when he didn't return at the usual time. But we were wrong. He came back later that morning looking an awful sight. He'd got himself into a desperate fight with some pickets outside a mill at Padiham where there was a strike. They had taken him for a "knobstick" (a strike breaker), and had almost killed him. Now that was ironic because the only thing he ever belonged to in his long life was a Trade Union. They'd beaten him so hard that he could hardly walk. Thank goodness they didn't break his arms, which they sometimes did. Somebody must have brought him back to town and dropped him off in our street.

He arrived home his hair stiff and matted with dried blood. Jenny was horrified at the sight. She ran to her room. "He was still alive when he got home," mother said, "but only just." His breath was shallow and laboured; his ribs were going in and out like bellows. His face was the size of a large pumpkin; he was black and blue all over where they'd kicked him with their clogs; some of his wounds were gaping. On entering the house, he dripped blood all through the best room, which Brenda had to clean up. Mother wanted him to go to the hospital or to Dr. Grieves. But he refused. So mother and Brenda did what they could for him with iodine and bandages. He never moved or complained when they dabbed his open wounds. It took him weeks to recover. Henceforth, instead of going out on a "fool's errand," he sat by the fire, pale and glowering. I kept well out of his way. Because they should have been stitched, some scars stayed with him for the rest of his days.

Unlike mother, father seemed oblivious of the famine which now stared us in the face. Tight-mouthed, he kept his thoughts to himself and went on doggedly. If anybody asked him in the street how he was, his reply was always the same, "I'm nicely!" It was a lie, of course, but it would have shamed him to tell the truth. He never seemed to realize that his family was getting hungrier and hungrier. It was something that one was not supposed to notice. There was work and there was no work. If you worked you ate. If there was no work you went hungry. You didn't beg and you didn't steal; the unwritten code excluded both. You didn't grumble or complain, whine or whimper. It was a matter of pride. As for the rich, by his lights, it was their job to leave the poor alone. Charity from them would have hurt.

Fortunately for us, it was an attitude that mother didn't share. Although she had been married to father for many years, she had a different code. Come what may, she was not going to see her children starve. Father's unemployment benefits having expired, she kept at him to apply for public relief. He refused. There was a struggle between them and a number of "scenes." "Very well," said mother, putting on her shawl and clogs, "I'll take thi place in t' bread queue and shame thee." Father went. He was angry at being beaten. By the time he got through the door, he was black-faced.

The rest of us sat or stood around the bare table and waited. We didn't have energy for anything else. We were insensitive to anything else except food. Our bellies pained for it. The most affected was Jenny whose twitterings and chirpings had ceased. Robbed of all spirit, she sat there listless. Mother had no energy either, but she forced herself to talk about the wonderful meal that father had gone for, and how delicious it would be. She began by pretending to serve a thick, nourishing broth with many

37

dumplings. She followed this with cutlets of veal – "something special," she said – accompanied by vegetables and roasted potatoes soaked in sizzling fat. She was so convincing the way she heaped our plates and pressed us to have seconds. She also dreamt up side dishes of hard boiled eggs, herrings, sausages, and pig's trotters. Finally, she served cheese, fruit, nuts, dates, and balm cakes dripping with treacle. My, how she made our mouths water!

Much later father returned, carrying a bulky Tate & Lyle sugar sack under his arm. He had the air of a thief. He handed the bundle to mother and left the house. She could make him bring the stuff, but she couldn't make him eat it. "I won't touch it," he said defiantly. How his body carried on without food, none of us knew. Mother worried about him.

With the rest of us watching, mother shook the contents of the sack on to the table. There were two large prison-made loaves of bread that looked as if they'd been dragged through the mud. There were several tins of corned beef, one of which had its side bashed in, a packet of tea, a pound of sugar, a can of condensed milk, some mouldy cheese, a strip of fatty bacon, some margarine that had strands of felt mixed with it, some Lyle's Syrup, a bottle of H.P. sauce, and some salt.

We forgot the feast mother had promised and polished off the lot on the spot. It at least rid us of our aching hollows. The next several days we queued up at the churches and the soup kitchens in the streets. After that father was sent back for more public relief, and still more. The items never varied, they were always horrid, but they kept us alive. Just.

Perhaps it was the shame of going for "charity bread" that made father redouble his efforts to find work. One morning, he came rushing into the house to tell us that he'd been made a town labourer and to ask for my help.

"Ah 've bin told t' wash Victoria," he announced.

"T' Queen?" my mother asked in a startled voice.

"Go on with you, girl. No, t' statue on t' Parade."

Father and I left the house for the centre of town. He led the way carrying a long ladder. I followed with an empty bucket, brushes and rags.

"'Ello! Wert'a goin' wit ladder?" neighbours shouted as we went by.

"T' wash t' Queen."

This response produced a most surprised look on the faces of the passers-by. "By gaw! They're goin' t' wash t' Queen," they shouted to each other.

Father got tired of satisfying people's curiosity and left it to me. I didn't tire. I loved the questions. It made me feel important. To every "Wert'a goin'?" I proudly bawled back: "T' wash t' Queen!" and marched on, head high.

When we arrived beneath the statue we could understand why it needed a wash. Most of the head and dour face were covered with bird droppings. The crown, sceptre, and orb were all filthy. Unveiled in

September 1905, in commemoration of Queen Victoria, who had died in 1901, this was the first good scrubbing the statue had had.

Pestered by a group of unemployed workers who constantly shouted conflicting advice from the foot of the ladder, it took father and me the whole day to make an impression on the dirt. We started from the head and worked down. First we had to scrape off the muck. Then father took a hedgehog brush to the Queen and scrubbed. While I carried endless buckets of water up the ladder from a nearby faucet, he hung on to Victoria's head, back, front, and sides, and continued to scrape, rub, and scrub as if his life depended on it. Yet I knew he hated it. Like his mother Selma, who lived in Fall River, Massachusetts, he'd never liked royalty.

As night came, we left Victoria a glowing green. Father still looked dour; he never said a word in returning the ladder and going home. It's said in the family that he never walked past that statue again. He preferred to go out of his way round the cathedral rather than relive his moment of shame. I have a suspicion that the scrubbing of Victoria was for him the blackest day of the Great Depression.

Alas, there was a limit to the number of statues that needed scrubbing, and father was soon out of work again. So were the rest of the family.

During these lean times, when I was five and my brother Dan was nine, he confided to me that he was not going hungry any more. We were going to steal food together. Tom Tat's grocery shop around the corner was bursting with food. Dan's plan was simple. He revealed it to me in whispers while we were in bed one night. On the first really dark night he'd push me through the window above Tom Tat's shop door. The window was always left slightly ajar. I would jump down inside the shop, open the door and we would help ourselves. "What could be easier?" he demanded.

I was horrified at the suggestion. Stealing with us was associated with going to jail. Caught stealing, you were invariably sent down. Visions of my going to jail passed before my eyes. I lay there in the dark, breathless.

"But that's stealing," I said.

"It's not. It's the toffs that steal. This is taking our due."

"Tom Tat isn't a toff; he's like us."

"Ye're a coward," Dan hissed. "Ye're a yellow belly. If ye don't join me I'll eat yer liver. If ye tell anyone, I'll drown thee in t' canal." He got quite worked up about his proposed raid on Tom Tat's and then fell asleep.

I was too terrified to sleep. Over and over, I asked myself what I should do? Should I tell Brenda? If I did, I might finish up in the canal. Even when I dozed, I woke up sweating. In my fevered imagination I was already in jail. In my dream I didn't seem to have a choice between the jail and the canal.

Dan became obsessed with the idea of robbing Tom Tat's. He kept at me for about a week, his hissing and his threats getting worse all the time.

He even took me round the corner to study the fly-spotted window. It was always left open a crack. "Ye don't have te steal if ye don't want to," Dan reassured me, "but I can't get in unless ye help me open the door. Ye're small enough to be hoisted up there. Only ye can get through the crack." He kept at me so hard that I began to wish that the deed was done and finished with.

The next Sunday night was pitch dark. Our parents were out. Only my sister Jenny and Gordon Weall – one of her young men – were in the house.

"Come on!" ordered Dan, making for the door.

I was on the point of making a desperate, last-minute appeal to Jenny and Gordon; instead I slunk after my brother into the dark street.

Two minutes later we were in the shop doorway. Dan took a look up and down the empty street. All was quiet at the Tat's house next to the shop.

"Quick!" Dan ordered, offering me his back. Although I was choking with fear, I knew what to do; we'd practiced it a dozen times. I also knew from staring at them in the daytime where the lock and the two bolts were at the other side of the door. I'd made up my mind that once I'd opened the door, I'd grab my clogs and run.

I put my stockinged feet on his shoulders and he hoisted me up to the window. Reaching up, I silently pushed the window inward. Still resting on Dan's shoulders, I gingerly began to get my head and shoulders through the opening. My weight now rested on the sill. All that remained was for me to draw back the top bolt, wriggle through the open window, and drop to the floor. I could smell cheese, but couldn't see it.

"Haste!" Dan whispered impatiently. "What are you making?"

"I'm stuck!"

"Stuck?"

With my head and shoulders over one side of the door frame and my legs down the other, I found myself unable to either go forward or backward. Somehow my jersey and grey flannel shirt had become twisted into a hard knot. My back was held in a vice. The more I struggled, the more firmly I was held. I broke into a sweat.

"Get through!" Dan hissed.

"I can't, I'm wedged."

"You've got to," said Dan, reaching up and pushing the soles of my feet as hard as he could.

"I can't," I repeated, my head swimming. "Pull me back," I pleaded. "I'm choking." My body trembled; beads of sweat blinded me.

After hesitating, Dan jumped up and hung on to my feet. The pain was awful. I thought he was going to pull my legs out of joint.

"Ouch, stop it!" I cried. Dan pulled harder. My body never budged.

"Ouch! Ouch!" I sobbed.

"Shut yer gob!" said Dan. Moments later, I heard his clogs echoing down the street. He had deserted me.

Turning and twisting, I made one last panic-driven effort to break free. I expected Tom Tat to come shouting out of his house at any moment.

The next thing I knew, Gordon was standing on a small stool beneath me. He had me by the calves.

"Shush, Billy," he whispered as he undid the knot in my clothing and gently eased me free. Once he had me out of the window, the three of us ran home, double-quick.

That night I lay in bed quaking for ages. I swore I'd never do anything for my brother again. While Gordon and Jenny gave Dan a piece of their mind, they said nothing to father for I heard no more of it. I wonder what the Tat's said when they found their window wide open the next morning. It didn't stay ajar any more.

It was about this time, with things as bad as they could be, and with everybody in the house out of work, that mother and I – miracle of miracles – took the train to Blackpool, twenty-five miles away. I was baffled; I couldn't believe my luck.

I knew about Blackpool as soon as I could stand. It was a pleasure resort on the Lancashire coast which catered to the crowds, especially the Lancashire crowds. In its gaiety, in its conviviality, in its clean, sharp air, in its endless sands, in its joyous freedom, it offered the factory workers and their families relief from monotony, dust, smoke, fog, and damp. Blackpool provided joy in a joyless time. Some of the first greeting cards I ever saw came from there. Against the smoke-filled air of our town, the cards always glittered with sun and colour. The identical cards were in everybody's cottage. We always had pictures of Blackpool and Blackpool Tower on the mantelpiece in our front room. As long as we lived in Griffin Street, the pictures stayed there gathering dust. People were always giving me bits of Blackpool rock.[†] The very mention of Blackpool would stir the imagination of any child in Blackburn.

I can't remember whether we discussed our escape from Blackburn or not. I don't know if father or grandmother Bridget knew what was going on. It was never brought up later in life. All I know is that we were on our way to Blackpool. In the train I couldn't contain myself. I hopped and jumped about with excitement. Until then I'd never seen the sea. I stuck my head out of the window most of the way to catch the first glimpse of Blackpool tower soaring above the flat landscape. Mother was every bit as excited as I. I thought we might have been going to relatives, especially as we had no money – mother said we were going to friends – but I never saw relatives or friends. We did see people from Blackburn, but mother avoided them.

Mother and I shared a single bed which stood in a kind of cupboard on a landing in a lodging house. The place stank of cabbages and haddock. But it was, after all, Blackpool. The only person mother introduced me to was a big-breasted, fish-eyed woman who seemed to own the place. Her face was covered with paint. She wore such a tall, glossy black wig, that I kept my eye on it hoping it would fall off. She also wore a lot of artificial jewellery which hung down to her middle, and which clanked as she moved about. Her earrings were long enough and large enough to swing like the pendulum of a clock. She held my hands on arrival and breathed pickled onions all over me. She grunted, but I don't think she ever spoke to me.

For the first few hours at Blackpool, mother ran me off my feet. I was overwhelmed by Blackpool tower. It gave me a crick in the neck to stare upward at its spire, hundreds and hundreds of feet above our heads. We went to the top and looked down on the ant-like people scurrying through the streets. Before us lay a vast expanse of sand, sea, and sky, all of which ended in a far haze. I'd never seen such unending space. I'd heard about the sea – here it was stretching before me. The ships in the distance were the first I'd ever seen.

I don't know whether it was the excitement of riding an elevator for the first time, or the height of the tower, or the food we'd eaten in the street below, or my fear that anything as tall as the tower must surely fall down – whatever the cause, I became ill. We sat down until my dizzy turn passed.

Having recovered, we raced together across the sand, at first in our bare feet and then on rented donkeys. Mother's donkey captured her spirit and went off at full speed careering toward the sea. My donkey wouldn't budge. The more I shouted at it, the longer it stayed and brayed and showed its teeth. By the time I got it to move, mother was on her way back, her bonny hair streaming in the wind. She was easily the winner. And so we went on, for most of that afternoon, going from one thing to another until we returned to our lodgings exhausted.

The moment we got back I began to feel uneasy. I didn't know why; I just knew that something was not quite right. It began when mother asked me to wait for her on the bench in front of the house. She had to meet someone inside "on business." I was told to stay there until she reappeared. So I sat there alone, swinging my legs, and wondering what it could be that kept her so long. I'd no idea whether something good or bad was happening, and it worried me. When she reappeared, I wondered if I should ask.

I sat there for part of the next day, and the next. I became weary of sitting alone on that horrid bench. I'd never been so lonely. Also, I was puzzled at the men who came out of the house with mother. I'd never seen them before. The strange thing about them was they all wore suits and polished shoes. They weren't weavers, that's for sure. Some were furtive, others hearty. Some would tuck me under the chin and give me a "tanner" (sixpence) or a "dodger" (three-penny bit) which was a lot of money. I was at a loss to know why "dodgers" and "tanners" were being showered upon me. In Blackburn we didn't have any money. What money we had, we knew not to waste. We feared being careless with money; not a light fear, a deep fear. Here everybody was chucking it about.

Mother must have been puzzled too, because after a couple of days she woke up at night and cried her eyes out, hiding her face in a towel. Her sobbing convinced me that she was in real pain. I didn't know what to do. Her crying fit really frightened me. By then I'd come to notice strange smells in the room, and there were half-burned cigarette ends on the floor.

The next morning everything was fine again. The crying was forgotten. Once away from the lodging house, mother's natural happiness returned. She went from being sad, to being intensely happy. She skipped about, made fun, and laughed. She took me everywhere. We visited the circus, the aquarium, and the fairground. We bought knick-knacks, and listened to the Punch and Judy show, and the minstrels on the pier singing: "Oh, I do like to be beside the seaside, Oh, I do like to be beside the sea ..." We listened to the hoarse bawling of the barkers selling boat rides, and went in a boat as far as Morecambe Bay. Having done everything, we sat on top of a tram and rode up and down the sea front, mother's hair blowing in the wind.

We seemed to eat whenever the mood took us. We certainly didn't eat with the fish-eyed woman with the clanking jewellery. I can remember one meal in the Winter Gardens. Mother was excited about it, but I was nervous. Until I grew up, it was the only meal I ever shared with her in a restaurant. There was a great "to do" before we got there. We had to get into better clothes, and wear shoes – all of which we got from a local pop-shop. I had to have my hair slicked down. I've no idea what we ate. I do remember a band playing. There were so many toffs sitting there, crowds of them wearing fancy dresses, and suits, and shoes, that I was too nervous to know what was going on. It was a new experience for me to see so many people dressed up with nothing to do except gorge and laugh. I'd never known mother to dress so well or to be so relaxed. Her face and hair shone. She didn't talk much; she seemed to be in a dream. But when it came to paying the bill, she was obviously uncomfortable. The waiter even bullied a tip out of her. When we came out we stood and watched the coloured fairy lights flicking on and off. What an exciting, colourful world it was! Why wasn't Blackburn like this?

For other meals we went from street cart to street cart, stuffing ourselves. There's nothing we didn't try. We had black puddings, ham sandwiches, jellied eels, herrings, whelks, kippers, sausages, pig's trotters, meat pies, and great Irish roasted potatoes, too hot to hold. We also had apples and oranges, Eccles cakes and lots of cups of tea. Mother fed such quantities of food into me that I could hardly stir. How wonderful it was to be rich!

If only we could have been free of that dreadful lodging house, mother and I would have stayed at Blackpool for ever. Instead, after an unforgettable week, we were back in the train headed for home. How drab Blackburn looked when we arrived. One could smell the poverty, the soot, the muggy, foggy weather, and the troubled times. I can understand why mother went wild.

Things got so bad in the early 1920s that the number of hungry-eyed tramps coming through our street grew. I can see the lucky ones now, their torn clothing black with sweat, their feet in the gutter, fidgeting and scratching while munching on "butties"[†] and swigging tea that some kind soul had given them. Smells were common among the poor, but the tramps had what we called a "ripe" smell; they reeked. Thirst and hunger satisfied, they would throw their string-tied packages over their shoulder and move off with the same steady slouch with which they'd come. I often wondered what their odd-shaped newspaper-wrapped packages contained.

The incredible thing about those years is that the poor began to steal from the poor – something unheard of by us. I have reason to know. One evening as the light from the window was fading, Brenda and I were playing with a new ball on the kitchen floor. The ball rolled from the kitchen into the front room where it came to rest behind a rocking chair in a corner. I ran after it, bent down, and put my outstretched hand round the back of the chair to retrieve the ball. To my horror, my fingers touched what felt like somebody's ankle; in a daze, I felt a trouser leg. Something moved. Fearful, I put my head round the chair and looked directly into the face of a pockmarked scarecrow of a man crouched there. A long, blue scar ran down one side of the stranger's face. His eyes and mouth had a hungry look about them. He smelled abominably. I felt the blood drain from my face. I remember jumping back as if I'd been bitten. With an oath the man flung me aside and ran from the house into the street. Someone ran after him, but he'd gone. We never saw him again. I was left trembling and white; I have never forgotten that pockmarked face with the hungry eyes. As we had nothing worth stealing, he must have been looking for bread, or was hoping to break into and take the pennies from our gas meter.

Deep poverty introduced a degree of fear in the house. Mother worried where the next meal was coming from. We all worried about it. I thought things couldn't get worse. But then something happened which put the problem of food out of our minds.

It began early one morning when I crept after father downstairs. My brother and my sisters were still asleep. By the time I reached the bottom step, father's dishevelled figure was crouched before the kitchen fire. There was a tweedy smell of peat. Although the fire had been banked up all night, the house was bitterly cold. As I drew my flannel shirt closer to my body, my feet froze on the sanded floor. Father was holding something which he was wiping with a towel. It looked like a white doll; but the doll had blood on it. Father's shadowy figure danced on the kitchen wall. "Cum now, cum now," he muttered.

I knew that something was wrong. Mother had been crying in the night. Father had been downstairs several times. I had no idea that a life and death struggle had been going on; even less where the baby had come from. I had by now made up my mind that it was a baby not a doll that father was holding. I found it difficult to believe that the baby had come out of the bedroom. I'd been told that storks brought them, just as Father Christmas brought presents. Jenny believed they were found under flowers; Brenda insisted they arrived in Dr. Grieves' bag. While I watched, I heard Dougdale's factory hooter at the end of the street emit a piercing whistle. I also heard t' knocker-up coming down the row.

"Tell t' knocker-up we're awake," father ordered. He had not failed to see my small figure standing in the shadows. I slipped on my clogs, which were always kept at the foot of the stairs, and ran to the street door. Having turned the key, I opened the door long enough to yell into the wind: "We're up." Mr. Smalley waved his rod and turned away.

By the time I got back to the kitchen, the gas lamp had been lit. It hissed reproachfully. The grinning pot dogs on the mantle reflected its glow. A little wasted thing with a monkey's face lay on one of the rocking chairs. Father was standing with his back to the fire, looking at it dejectedly. "He's a goner," he murmured. I knew that a "goner" meant that the baby was dead. Confused, a cold shiver running down my back, I crept away.

Father didn't go to the mill that day. Nor did mother; she stayed in bed. During the morning Dr. Grieves, wearing his funny Sherlock Holmes cap and cape, drove up with his horse and gig. His brown and white spaniel Joy followed. Joy always jumped into the gig and sat there on guard while the doctor made housecalls. The housecall ended, the dog happily took to the street again.

That afternoon, the dead baby with the monkey's face was placed in a plain wooden box of undressed pine. Until evening the coffin stood on top of the folded sewing machine under the front window. The paper blind had been pulled down. The aspidistra which usually stood there had been placed on the floor. Once I tried to look into the box, but the lid was nailed down.

That evening, after the flood of homeward-bound workers had swept past the house, grandmother Bridget and several neighbours lifted the latch and came in. There was loud whispering upstairs. One of the visitors, Mrs. Fothergill, a woman dressed in black with a solemn face and a mournful voice, who cared for the chapel down the street, had kept on at father about "sprinklin'" (baptism). "Did you sprinkle him?" she kept asking. "Are you sure? You know what happens to an unsprinkled soul, Will." I'm sure that "sprinklin'" never entered my father's head. He certainly didn't "sprinkle" my brother while I was there.

The glances and the whisperings that went on made me think that the grown-ups were hiding something. They seemed furtive. No one could tell me what had happened to my brother except that he'd "died". If he'd had an accident there must surely be someone in the house who could stick him together again, as I did with my toy soldiers. Instead, everybody sat there looking glum and did nothing to help him.

Next morning father disappeared through the door with the coffin under his arm. I was desolated that my brother should have been carried off like that. Where was he being taken? "Straight to heaven," mother assured me. "You'll see him again in the hereafter," my sister Jenny added. "But where is heaven and the hereafter?" I asked. And if we were going to see him again, why was he put in a box and carried off like that? How could he find heaven in a little nailed coffin, without a name, without food, without flowers, and all alone? It took me years to realize that, without insurance, a "proper burial" for him was beyond our means.

His death left me afraid. Death was evidently something that neither Dr. Grieves nor anyone else could fix. It was permanent as nothing else in my life had been before. It was the first time that the truth struck home. It was days before I stopped worrying about my brother. It was just as well that he was never mentioned again.

Later in life I learnt that a "proper burial" – cremation was never considered – was something that the workers took seriously. They were never in doubt what was proper and improper. They did not take the view that what one does with the body after death is not important. On the contrary, they had a horror of being cast into a pauper's or a common grave. It meant humiliation and disgrace. It was all very well to tell them that their spirit would enter into heaven through the pearly gates; they still wanted to know what was going to happen to their bones. That is why most of them paid a penny a week death dues so that the "proper" thing would be done when they died. We paid our pennies to a squirrel-like fellow whom we called t' bump man, but who liked to be called by his full name: Mr. Charlie Hetherington.

The wonder is that the penny death dues were enough to keep Mr. Hetherington in clogs. Collecting pennies for the death club, however, was only one of Mr. Hetherington's occupations. His passion was to study the bumps on people's heads. "Give me your head for a minute or two," he would say, "and a penny, and I'll tell you all that you need to know about yourself." Mr. Hetherington's "reading" of bumps was more reliable than fortune telling, or tossing the cups, or cutting the cards. People said so.

One night father asked Mr. Hetherington to look at our heads. Charlie didn't need persuading. He began with father. He then turned to mother, my sisters, Jenny and Brenda, and my brother Dan. From the look on his face, I could tell that – as far as bumps go – my family were an uninteresting lot. Their mental faculties had not produced any unusual changes on their skulls. He expected even less of me. "As a family, I'm afraid you're a bumpless lot," he said to father. Yet the moment his fingers touched my head he became excited. "Oh, look at this," he began, running his fingers through my long hair, "I say, have you ever seen anything like this?" he went on triumphantly.

The whole family crowded around. By the light of the hissing gas lamp they scrutinized my scalp. They seemed mesmerized by what they saw and felt. "Well," said father, following Charlie's fingers with his own, "now I see what it's all about; the bumps are as plain as can be." The family was greatly impressed when Mr. Hetherington announced that with bumps like that I must surely become Prime Minister of England. "Mm ... mm ...," said mother, "if he'd been born in Fall River he could have become President of the United States."

The news of Lancashire's hard times in the early 1920s must have reached my grandmother Selma in Fall River, Massachusetts, for she periodically sent one or two of her sons to Blackburn to see if her grandchildren, Jenny, Brenda, Dan, and I, were still alive. I don't think grandmother Selma trusted father's letters.

My American uncles, my father's brothers who had emigrated to America with him in 1906, must have given notice of their arrival, for my parents would suddenly go into a frenzy of preparations. Crockery, cutlery, chairs, food, and goodness knows what else were borrowed from relatives and friends. Not until my American uncles arrived did I ever eat ham and tongue at the same meal. On the first visit, father tried to impress his brothers by serving a two shilling bottle of "Barrel Bottom" wine. This last minute idea had sent me scurrying through the streets to the vintner, a florin clasped in my hand. The purchase made – regardless of licensing laws – I ran home with the bottle in a brown paper bag. The wine failed to impress the Americans and it was never served again.

I well remember the stir my uncles caused. Having taken one of the few taxis in town, they arrived in Griffin Street red-faced and hearty. They were full of fun and energy. They were much too florid and much too fat to be textile workers. I don't know to which class they belonged, but they weren't working class; later I discovered that Americans didn't belong to any class. They wore strange straw hats and even stranger clothing. They had shirts with attached collars and loud ties, tiepins, and highly polished shoes. When it got around that the Americans had arrived, our house was flooded with people who took it for granted that my uncles knew every member of Blackburn families who had migrated to Fall River during the past generation. There was such a bustle, it was like having a wedding in the house.

From my American uncles I learnt about America and Fall River. I listened wide-eyed to their talk of such a rich country. I didn't know we were as poor as we were until they started making comparisons with America. "You've got to come," they said. They told me that in Massachusetts they had snow right up to the roof! Jenny and I loved it when they said things like "OK" and "Yeah." Later on my street gang used these words. I didn't know that the Yankees had single-handedly won the Great War of 1914–1918 until my American uncles told me so. I always thought that Dadda had done that.

What grieved me most about these visits, and there were several, was the fact that we children were never allowed to accept money from our American relatives. Each time my uncles were about to depart for Liverpool or London, or to visit their other relatives in town, the same agonizing act was repeated. First they would press into our eager palms a shiny half-crown – on one occasion one of them actually gave me a whole dollar – enough to keep us in affluence for a month. Then, before we could scuttle away with what to us was a fortune, father would reach down and snatch the money back again.

"Nay, nay, Harold" father would protest; as he extracted the coin from our unwilling fingers, "tha mustn't chuck tha money at 'em like that. Tha'll be spoiling 'em. Tha can see, they want for nothing. Tha must be reet out of tha mind, lad." Whereupon, to our profound grief, he handed back the coin.

I knew that there wasn't a word of truth in what father was saying, and the loss of the coin hurt me deeply. Nor was there a word of truth in the inevitable parting scene. When the moment of departure arrived, my uncles would warmly clasp my parents' hands while extending the usual invitation for us to return to Fall River. "You must come back again, Will. Family's roots are at the other side now."

Word for word, father's answer to his brothers was always the same: "That's kindly, that's real kindly of thee. I can't tell thee how much Maggie and I appreciate it. Tell mother that we've just got one or two little things to arrange and then we'll be reet over. Tha'll see!" I never did work out what the little things were that they had to arrange, which they never did.

With the whole of Griffin Street gawking, my uncles would shake hands all round, pat us children on the head, and tuck us under the chin. They would then jump into the rattling taxi, honk the horn repeatedly – which brought the neighbours running – and sway down the street followed by a cloud of blue smoke. After which the family and the neighbours sat around like pricked balloons. Everything in Griffin Street was ordinary again. I never heard my parents speak of it, but in later life I wondered if the coming of my rich uncles had not given them pause for thought. After all, if father had remained a tackler in Fall River, instead of returning to Blackburn in 1914, he too could have visited his relatives in England in a straw hat, a fine suit, a loud tie, polished shoes, and a smoke-wrapped taxi.

In time, I came to resent these visits. They left my parents more in debt than ever. Of course, our American relatives offered to pay for everything, but father wouldn't hear of it. He always put up the same

48

humbug of "nobody wanting for nothing." Worse, every visit was followed by the arrival from grandmother Selma of a great parcel of children's summer clothing. Never money, never food, just clothes – clothes that were too thin for our summers. With their coloured stripes, the shirts contrasted sharply with everybody else's drab grey. Dan and I hated them. They shamed us when we wore them to school or in the streets. Other children envied us for having such rich American uncles, but they went into fits of laughter at the sight of the American shirts and dresses. Because of the stripes, the Woodruff children came to be known as "the Zebra Kids." Even when my uncles stopped coming to Blackburn, grandmother Selma continued to send the clothing. The ordeal went on for years. It got worse as the stripes got larger. Strangely enough the sizes never changed. Jenny, Brenda, and Dan eagerly grew out of them. As I was the smallest member of the family, I regret to say that there was always something that would fit me.

IV Origins

The visits of my American uncles, and the remarks my parents made about the eight years (1906–1914) they'd spent in the United States, aroused in me a desire to know more about my origins. Over the years, mother tried to answer my questions about family history. Because that kind of thing interested her, she'd made it her business to get it all in her head. Father wasn't half as good; he focused on the present, not the past. I don't think family history interested him at all. Sometimes mother answered me in snatches, sometimes at great length. Bit by bit I pieced it together.

I learnt that the Woodruff story began long before I was born in Blackburn in September 1916. It began in the early part of the nineteenth century with my great-great-grandfather George Woodruff, which is as far back as the Woodruff family tree goes. His son Arne was my great-grandfather on father's side. The records of my family are few; there are no outstanding achievements to which I can point. If there were distinguished individuals among the Woodruffs, I have failed to trace them; their deeds have gone unsung. The deeds of the "lower orders" in Britain, to which my family belonged, usually did go unsung. It's the deeds of "them" and "they" that shine brightly in the history of the nation.

According to family lore, my great-grandfather Arne Woodruff was born in the late 1840's in Westmorland. Arne's father, George Woodruff, had had the misfortune to be seized by the army while he was drunk. He fought and died for Britain in Russia in 1856. Mother knew it was 1856 because there was a medal in the family with the date of great-great-grandfather George's death on it.

By the time I was born in 1916, his son Arne had become a family legend. Every now and again my mother, who regarded Arne as a kind of family hero, would tell stories about him.

One day when mother and I were alone, I asked her about great-grandfather Arne.

"He had a hard beginning, that I can tell you," she said.

"What happened?"

"He not only lost his father to the army, he went and lost his mother too. She sickened and died after the death of her husband in Russia. After that Arne stood alone. There were no other members of his family in Westmorland. Nor did anybody come forward to look after him. He was an orphan. He fell into the hands of the parish guardians who sold him to a cotton mill owner whose factory was high on the moors. Fellow called Crankfit. They say he had a stone where his heart should have been."

Days later, in taking up Arne's story again, she talked about his departure from the village. She described an abandoned, forlorn figure waiting by the village green. It was a grey spring day, but the sun was breaking through. Arne's few possessions were tied in a large red handkerchief lying at his feet. He wore a cap – from which tufts of straw-coloured hair protruded – a long dark smock, and clogs. Behind him stood a tall-hatted beadle dressed in sombre black, with black gaiters and black shoes.

Presently the local carrier, Blethley, came along. He was a stocky figure with a clay pipe sticking out from his beard. Arne recognized his red stocking cap. He watched Lucy the bay horse leisurely pull the cart. The cart creaked to a halt.

Removing his pipe, Blethley shouted down, "You Arne, for Crankfit's?"

"That's him," the beadle answered.

"Well then, get up boy," the carter gruffed. "We can't afford to have Lucy standing here all day."

With the beadle pushing and the carter pulling, Arne was hoisted up on to the box next to Blethley behind the horse's tail. On the point of tears, he sat there speechless, clutching his possessions on his knees.

Before the child knew what was happening, the cart with its bundles and packages had rattled around the village Maypole, passed the churchyard where his mother now lay, crossed the stream where the salmon were jumping and the ravens were cawing, and left the village behind. Only then did the boy break down and cry. Blethley pulled on his pipe and studied the back of his horse's head.

Calling at different villages and hamlets, the man and boy travelled together for most of the day, passing from green meadow through ploughland and pasture to fell. Prompted by a grunt from the carrier, Lucy trundled from one place to the next. In time, Blethley warmed to the child, and told him about the great world beyond the moors. It seemed that Mr. James Blethley had been everywhere.

"Have you ever been to Russia?" Arne asked.

"Russia? Now let's see," the carter answered rubbing the side of his nose.

"That's where my father fought and died in a war," the child went on, while fishing around in his bundle to show the carter a medal.

"Oh, that Russia," Blethley said, turning the medal over in his hand. "Bless me, if you had told me it was that Russia that you was talking about ... why ..." the carter went on at great length about Russia, telling the now wide-eyed boy exactly where his father had been killed. In fact, Blethley said he'd fought in the very same battle, on the very same day. And what a battle it had been! Oh, the guns, and the drums, and the flags, and the cries, and the shouts, and the smoke ... " 'Mazin'," the carter ended.

"Do you have such a medal, Mr. Blethley?"

"Why, of course, but it isn't the sort of thing you carries around." Having again declared that it was 'Mazin', which Arne discovered was the carter's final word on everything, Blethley lapsed into silence.

Meantime the hedgerows and fences had given way to dry-stone walls which climbed endlessly across the shrouded fells. Here and there greystone cottages straggled unevenly up a valley. Wild smoke blew from their roofs. Crying curlews and peewits criss-crossed the wagon's trail. The trees gradually became thinner and sparse; the track steeper and stony; the wind stronger and fresher. In the distance a greystone peak stood out like a sentinel in the sky. Arne looked down the fells to see specks scattered like white stones which he knew were sheep. In the valley bottom a winding river glinted in the sun. Sometime during the day they stopped at a small inn where Blethley drank a glass of ale and gave Lucy a nose-bag of oats. Arne had some bread and cheese.

When they came out a whole string of pack horses were tied against the inn wall. They were loaded with textile stuff to be worked up by the handloom weavers who worked in their cottages farther down the slope.

The journey renewed, Blethley talked about a number of things. Yes, he had seen the Queen. Yes, he had seen the new-fangled railways in whose coaches people caught their death of cold. Yes, he knew all about the dreadful accident that had occurred when one steam-driven train had crashed into another. "Railways will never be as good as a horse and cart," he confided to the boy. "God never intended railways."

"You are God-fearin'?" the carrier questioned Arne sharply.

"Oh, yes, Mr. Blethley," the boy replied. His mother had reared him to be God-fearing. She used to say everything was God's will.

"Do you know the town of Blackburn?" Arne asked. "It's where my aunt Beth lives."

"Yes, I know it. It's full of steam-driven cotton factories with tall chimneys spewing foul smoke," Blethley answered pulling on his pipe. "They say this here new-fangled steam business is going to change a lot of things, but I have my doubts. The main thing is that cotton pays well. All the money-hungry people of northern England are making their way to Blackburn. God never intended factories," the carrier went on, shaking his head. "Factories and steam-driven power looms take the work away from the cottage weavers. Fellows lost their lives for burning the first factories down. In 1812 at West-Houghton they hung three men and a boy of fourteen for doin' it. Lad went to the gallows calling for his mother."

Arne shuddered. "Couldn't she save him?"

"Not likely," Blethley answered. "Come to think of it, not long after, in the 1820s I think it was, there was a dreadful rampage at Blackburn itself. Thousands of workers armed with pikes, hammers, and crowbars smashed every power loom they could find. By nightfall there wasn't one left."

"Were there more hangings?"

"Oh my word, yes. Others were sent to Van Dieman's Land."

"Where is that?"

"I can't actually say. All I know is that it's a long way from here and you don't come back." There was a pause. "Factories and power looms were soon back in Blackburn," the carter concluded. "'Mazin'."

The carter knew so much about everything that Arne resolved to tell everyone he met that he'd had the uncommon luck to have travelled with the world-famous Mr. James Blethley.

That afternoon they met a cartload of orphans being delivered to another mill on the fells. There was a wild-eyed idiot among them who stuck his tongue out as he went by.

"Did you ever carry such?" the boy asked.

"The pity I did," the man replied. "They were so young – one was five, the others eight to eleven – and so tired; when I got them to the mill I couldn't waken them. They'd been on the road for days. God never intended that either."

"Why do children have to work in factories, Mr. Blethley?"

"They're cheap and nimble, there's plenty of them, and they don't have anyone to protect them. That's why. God never intended it, I'll swear." Blethley cleared his throat and spat out of the cart.

Arne heard the creaking of Crankfit's waterwheel long before they got there.

"No steam here," said Blethley.

They'd suddenly topped a ridge to see the mill spread out before them. The main building was solidly built in stone and slate. Oblong in shape, it had three levels. Its narrow windows looked out across a pond. Nearby were two other buildings, both of them smaller in size. The windows of one of the buildings were barred. Beyond and around the mill, as far as the eye could see, stretched the lonely, windswept moors. A blue haze rested on the distant hills. There was not a tree in sight.

"Watch your step with Crankfit," Blethley warned as they approached the building, "whatever you say, he's bound to 'av' a fit."

Crankfit was at the gate to meet them. He was dressed in a long black coat and a stove pipe hat. Except for the sharpest eyes, his face was lost in a thicket of beard and hair.

"You're late," he barked at the boy as Arne jumped down from the cart and stood before him.

Remembering Blethley's warning, Arne kept a still tongue.

"Is this all there is of him?" Crankfit asked, while walking round the child and studying him from all sides. "Fat lot of work he'll do. He's stunted, that what he is!"

"He's all I was given," the carter explained, looking at Arne as if he was seeing him for the first time.

"Humph! I suppose I'd better take him," Crankfit said as he peered at Blethley's sheet. He sniffed at it like a bloodhound looking for a scent. "I swear they're getting smaller and smaller all the time," he grumped as he added his signature.

Conditions at Crankfit's were worse than the carrier had predicted. The work force consisted of about fifty young orphans, some of them from as far away as London, who could be worked as the employer saw fit. Although Arne was small in stature, the day after his arrival he was given a large broom and told to sweep the factory from top to bottom. After that, with another boy who was dressed in rags and had broken teeth, he was shown how to rewind twisted ropes of cotton on to bobbins. It was the kind of work that a child could do better than an adult. Power was supplied by a water wheel which groaned and clattered daylong outside the cotton-dusted windows. A large drum at the base of the spinning frame carried drive belts to each side. Once the machine began to operate, with its scores of twisting bobbins, it continued to do so until the drive belts were disengaged at the end of the day. And that not for long. The day-shift was quickly followed by the night-shift.

Discipline at Crankfit's was harsh. One day, as punishment for talking at work, Arne's head was trapped beneath a window sash. With the sill biting his neck, he was forced to remain there for an hour staring at the ground. Another boy got the same punishment for staring out of the window and singing.

After some weeks Arne was put on the night shift, 7:00 p.m. until 6:00 a.m., by which time he was asleep in his clogs. He was spared work on Sundays, but the six church services that he and the other children had to attend in the chapel-like building that stood close to the mill were almost as exhausting as the work itself. How eagerly he listened for the "Now unto the Father, the Son, and the Holy Spirit," which he knew would end the ordeal. It was a relief when the young itinerant preacher climbed on to his donkey and disappeared across the moors.

Food at Crankfit's was as bad as the working conditions. Arne got nothing but gruel, potatoes and scraps, and scant time in which to eat. Things got so bad that he made up his mind to escape. He kept his plans to himself lest one of his companions should betray him. He would go in search of his mother's sister Beth who lived in Blackburn. If he was going to escape, he had better do it before the snows covered the fells.

Arne knew that his only hope lay in slipping away from the other children when they were crossing the yard from the dormitory to the mill. Once inside the building, heavy locks kept them in. His chance came one evening when, on crossing the yard with a number of other children, the foreman was called back to the dormitory. Last in line, Arne looked over his shoulder to watch the man disappear through the doorway. Saying nothing to the others, he turned on his heel, ran round a corner of the dormitory building, sprinted across some open ground, ran past a small graveyard, and vanished along a bridle-path into the heather. With the blood thumping in his ears, he listened for shouts but heard none. He could hardly believe his luck. Darkness was falling. Buffeted by the wind he began his trek across the moors.

Late the next day, by which time he had become desperate for food, he knocked on the door of a lonely cottage. The woman fed him but then tricked him and locked him in a room. "I knew you was from Crankfit's," she shouted through the door. "You're the second runaway I've caught. You're worth two shillings to me. When my man comes 'ome, back you go."

While the woman shouted at him through the door, Arne struggled through a tiny skylight window. From the roof he slid on to some bushes, and ran as fast as his feet would take him to the safety of the moors. Fearful that he would be taken again, he ran until his legs pained him and he could run no more. Fortunately the wind had dropped and with the help of the moon he was able to find shelter and hiding among the gorse. Determined to stay awake, he fell asleep. Several hours later he awoke with a start not knowing where he was. The moon was overlaid by heavy cloud. As he listened, he heard the sound of pebbles being crunched beneath heavy boots. The noise got louder and louder – someone was approaching across a patch of stones. He recognized the voices; they were Crankfit's men. They were men he feared. Terrified, he sprang to his feet and took off like a hare. He didn't dare look back. After a long chase in the darkness along a river bed, he succeeded in giving his pursuers the slip.

The following day Arne came over a rise and saw Blethley's cart coming toward him down a country lane. He ran to it, tearfully begging the carter for help. Blethley recognized him and sensed what was afoot. He took pity on the haggard-looking boy and hid him inside an empty barrel. Arne was ordered to stay as quiet as a mouse. A little farther on Blethley was stopped by two men emerging from the bracken. Deep inside the barrel, Arne listened.

"Good day, Blethley."

"'Day," the carter answered.

"Have you seen a boy in these parts?"

"Well," answered Blethley, thinking deeply, "the truth is, I've seen several since sunup."

"I mean ... a runaway."

"Nope," said Blethley, "can't say as I have."

"Then keep a sharp lookout. It's worth two shillings to you if you catch him."

Arne's hair was standing on end. He was scared that he might cough or sneeze.

"'Mazin'," Blethley muttered as the men fell away and took to the fields.

Arne had become so cramped from crouching in the barrel that Blethley had to help him out. He then took him home where he hid him until the hue and cry had died down. At much expense to himself, he later put Arne on the train for Blackburn. He wasn't happy about using the steam-railway, but he thought they wouldn't look for Arne on a train, not with a ticket.

In time Arne found his aunt Beth in Blackburn. She adopted the boy and taught him how to weave. When he grew up Arne married a mill-girl called Eva Anders. They had a child who became my grandfather William. Grandfather William was killed in the mill long before I was born.

Over the years, mother also told me about her side of the family. From her I learnt about her mother, my grandmother Bridget Gorman[†] Kenyon. My mother's father, Thomas Kenyon, had died when she was very young.

Bridget Gorman was born in County Clare, Ireland, the only daughter of a landed family. We hardly know anything about her people. Her meeting with my grandfather, Thomas Kenyon, was the event that was to shape the rest of her life. Bridget's relatives always held that her meeting with Thomas ruined her. There was little to recommend the Englishman to them. True, he was darkly handsome with a fine moustache. Grandmother Bridget once told me, jokingly, that it was the moustache that made her fall in love with him. He was well-dressed, and dashing. He also had a good job with a large English insurance company, which explains his visit to Ireland. But he was much older than Bridget's seventeen years. He came from a strata of society that had never owned land. He had no "propertee." Bridget was in danger of making a poor marriage in an alien land. Worse, Thomas was a Protestant, Bridget was a Catholic.

Mother said that Bridget's father and brothers – their warnings to the would-be suitor to "pack his bags" having gone unheeded – had chased Thomas from the village. Bridget's father had forbidden her to see the Englishman again. The jovial recklessness he detected in Thomas was not to his liking. But Bridget was a wild, lawless thing; she was tired of piano and singing lessons, and going to church. She had grown weary of good and right. She had found her Prince Charming and was eager to fly away.

There was another motive. Bridget had been "promised" to a neighbour's son – a Catholic boy, rich by County Clare standards – whom she could not abide. The more distance she could put between him and her, the better. Fully aware that to marry Thomas was to sever relations with her family and become a social outcast, Bridget eloped and fled to England as grandfather Thomas Kenyon's Protestant bride.

Revelation followed. Bridget discovered that Thomas already had three children from a previous marriage. Also, although comfortably off, he was much less affluent than he had made himself out to be. The riches she had enjoyed among her own family were unknown to him.

Having made her bed, Bridget Gorman proceeded to lie in it. From the tales I've heard – all this took place long before I was born – she had a happy life with the man of her choice; Thomas was a generous man, easy to live with. She herself was a good wife and a good mother. She had four children of her own, Edward, Eric, Alice, and my mother, Maggie. Maggie, the youngest, was born in Blackburn in May 1884.

Bridget's happiness lasted until Thomas died suddenly ten years later. To her surprise, she was not only a widow but a pauper. The day after her husband's funeral, Bridget found that her total financial resources consisted of whatever money she had in her purse. Generous to a fault, Thomas had always bought presents for his family, and had been an easy touch for any of the wider Kenyon family or anyone else who claimed to be down on their luck. Unknown to Bridget, grandfather Thomas had spent his savings; for some time he had been borrowing against his retirement and pension funds.

Time only added to her troubles. With no money coming in, she scrimped and scraped until all her resources, including her furniture, had gone. She went into cheaper housing. She then appealed to her husband's relatives. Her brother-in-law, John Kenyon at Bamber Bridge, gave her some help, but he had two small daughters of his own and was not as prosperous at that time as he was to become; he couldn't go on helping Bridget forever. From Thomas' boon-companions, some of whom had helped him to spend his money, came nothing.

With no one else to turn to – her frantic appeals to her family in County Clare had gone unanswered – with no funds of her own, and with a dread that her children would finish up in the workhouse, Bridget took the only course open to her: she found foster-homes for her children with people whom she trusted. That is how my mother, after the early death of her father, was "farmed out" to friends of Bridget's who owned a small pasture farm on the edge of town.

Ironically, Bridget found employment looking after the children of a local merchant. She worked hard and saved hard in the hope that she would one day be able to get her family together again. But the merchant's business failed. The merchant's wife, who had become close to Bridget, died. Within a year, Bridget had been thrown back on her own resources.

After many unsuccessful attempts to obtain what she considered suitable work – which was almost anything other than working in a mill – Bridget finished up, as my own mother would do later, as a slubber, cleaning cotton, which was one of the dirtiest and least skilled occupations in textile manufacture. Slubbers or cardroom hands were looked down on. Coarse and degrading, was how Bridget described the work. For a woman as refined as Bridget, who until she was seventeen had wanted for nothing, it must have been a wrench to have had to enter the mill.

Yet Bridget got by. Nobody heard her complain. Brought up soft, she was as tough as steel. I never heard her say a word against the way things had turned out, or against her husband for leaving her destitute. "How was he to know he would die when he did?" she asked me. "He didn't spend the money on himself." Anyway, my grandfather was dead and one never spoke ill of the dead.

One day mother summed up her feelings about Bridget. "She's quality," she said, "royal". "Her trouble is, she's cum down in't world ... right down, I mean."

There was a pause.

"A lot of us have."

On other occasions mother told me more about the Woodruffs. I learnt from her that my father's father, my grandfather William, the child of my great-grandfather Arne and his wife Eva Anders, had been born at Witton, a sub-district of Blackburn in the 1860s. He had been a day-labourer on the land, but had entered the mills to get some ready cash to pay off a debt.

In the mill grandfather William met a weaver, Selma Nilson, whom he later married, and who became my grandmother Selma. They had thirteen children, two of whom died in childhood. Grandmother Selma was to have a far greater influence on the destiny of the Woodruffs than grandmother Bridget was to have on the Kenyons.

Grandfather William had once been invited to take tea with grandmother Bridget. I suppose it was about the marriage of my mother and father. True to her style, Bridget had served a "royal" tea. Grandfather William never stopped talking about it: the snow-white, starched tablecloth and napkins, the lovely china and silver, the delicious feast, which grandmother served in bird-like portions, and which was eaten daintily off the end of a fork, had overwhelmed him. He'd never had such a spoiling. The family story is that grandmother Selma was not impressed with grandfather William's account of the tea party and put a stop to further visits. Grandfather William had a reputation of being chicken-hearted with his wife Selma. Not long afterward grandfather William was killed in the mill.

Mother told me that Selma's father had run foul of the law as a boy and had narrowly missed being one of the last convicts shipped out to Australia in the 1840s. The injustice of the whole thing – the boy was accused of stealing some bedding – the savagery of the sentence, coupled with the hardships he had suffered in jail, left a deep scar on the Nilson family.

During the industrial unrest of the late 1880s, Selma herself had gone to jail for assaulting a policeman during a strike. In the witness-box she had absolutely denied assaulting anybody. She swore that she had never seen the policeman until he appeared in court with the left side of his face covered with bandages. Because of an uproar she caused in court, grandmother Selma had had her sentence raised. The Nilsons were surprised she didn't get three years for carrying on as she did. "It's rotten sods like you," she'd shouted at the magistrate, "who make our life hell. Ah'm just as good as thi are." Guilty or not, her experience in jail soured her of Britain and British authority for the rest of her life. On her release, she would have gladly left the country had she had the money to do so.

Later on, following the death of grandfather William in the mill, grandmother Selma, together with some of her children and my parents, Will and Maggie, did migrate to the United States. I always knew that much, but that's all I did know, an inkling.

V   American interlude

I was in my teens before mother told me in detail about the Woodruff migration to America. "You know, Billy," she said, "your grandmother Selma got her wish to escape from England in a strange and tragic way. In 1905 her husband, your grandfather William of Witton, was killed instantly when a steel-tipped weaving shuttle flew out of the shuttle race and entered his chest. He had been bending down at the side of the loom when it happened. A knife could not have killed him quicker. Your grandmother Selma was left a widow with eleven children, your father was one of them. I don't know how much money Selma received from the mill-owner by way of workmen's compensation and employer's liability,[†] but it was enough to pay for her family's emigration to America. We emigrated with her from Blackburn to Fall River, Massachusetts in 1906."

"How old were you when you went to America?"

"Your father was twenty-three; he was born in 1883 at Witton. I was twenty-two. We sailed in the summer of 1906. We'd been married the previous year (1905) at St. Philip's. Your sister Jenny was about one. Three of grandmother Selma's children remained in Blackburn. They were already married and wanted to stay. Your dad was the oldest of Selma's family to go to America. He'd already been around the world."

"How old were the others?"

"Your grandmother Selma, I think, was in her late forties. Your uncle Peter was six and your aunt Amy was thirteen. Brian, Andrew, Edward, Harold, and Paul were in between. The youngest, Peter, was my favourite. They were true Woodruffs – tough as nails.

"There's no doubt about it," mother went on, "the moment your grandmother Selma knew she was going to receive a lump sum in compensation for her husband's death, she set her face toward America. She'd always been talking about following her brother Mat Nilson who had gone to America years before. Now her chance had come. Grandmother got your father, who had learnt to read and write in the Navy, to write a letter to her brother Mat and his wife Hessie who were working in the cotton mills in Fall River. From there everything led on. Mat encouraged her to come."

Father read Mat's letters from Fall River out loud to Selma who couldn't read. Family and neighbours came together to hear them. Mat wrote that there was plenty of work for Lancashire folk in Fall River, the living was good and the pay much higher.

Selma then got in touch with her nephew Henry Nilson, who worked in a shipping office in Liverpool. He promised to look out for a cheap berth.

Henry came up with a June crossing on an American ship, the *Elizabeth*, out of New York. It had both steam and sail. It offered much better accommodation in steerage class, which was the lowest fare and the only one the Woodruffs could afford, than the larger steamships which were hauling migrants to America like sardines. The *Elizabeth* was a bargain: the best and cheapest thing he could find. The only drawback was that they would have to land in New York and from there go by train to Boston.

When Selma baulked at what the *Elizabeth* was going to cost, Henry had replied, "The only cheaper way to America, Auntie, is to swim." Griffin Street laughed its head off at that!

By borrowing money from a money lender – she got it cheap at fifteen percent – Selma paid her deposit on the June sailing. She never doubted that the employer's liability money would come through; otherwise she would never have approached a money lender. They were avoided like the plague.

Once the sailing tickets had been secured, everybody became excited about going to the New World. They didn't have much to get ready. Selma had almost no furniture to dispose of, little to sell. Most of the clothes the family possessed were already on their backs. Household goods were to be shared between Selma's children remaining behind in Blackburn. Most of the baggage consisted of food and bedding, which would be packed at the last moment.

Except for the bedding, everything was to be carried in straw valises, scores of which the pawnbrokers, Levy & Levy, had obtained as bankrupt stock. On Mr. David Levy's advice, Selma had bought a number of these while they were still going. She also bought a wicker hamper and several clean sacks. She stacked the valises and the hamper in the front room opposite the street door. Visible through the front window, the valises became a topic of conversation in Griffin Street. Everybody talked about the Woodruffs going to America.

Father said that some of the neighbours had tried to dissuade Selma from going. One night his mother and his older brother Joshua had gone on hammer and tong at each other about it.

"You're going to a place you know nothing about," Joshua had argued. "It's plain madness to go off like this with seven young children. Here you've got food and a roof, and you'll have the insurance money. Over there you'll be starving in the streets before you know where you are. It's enough to make dad turn in his grave. Anyway, why do you want to run away? England's the best country there ever was. Even if you hated it, it's plain daft to leave it like you're doing."

"Hush, Joshua, for God's sake, hush," Selma had answered as she walked round the table hacking wedges from a loaf of bread, which she held in her ham-like arms against her chest. "You're prattlin' like a gobbin," she went on, as she threw the wedges of bread to the younger children. "You've never been the one with brains in this family, Joshua. You talk about risk. Your father and I have slaved our guts out here, never knowing anything but risk. There have been times when we've clemmed [starved]. You talk about us becoming beggars at t' other side. Tell me any Blackburn family that's gone over and become beggars. None of them have come back with their tails between their legs. Everybody I've ever heard of who went to America became rich; you know that. Your uncle Mat and your aunt Hessie in Fall River have done very well, thank you. They won't see us starve. And don't give me that old buck about love of country. They didn't show much love for me or my children when they sent me down. That kind of talk is for the toffs. I can't afford it. You expect me to stay awake at night worrying about this country, when it doesn't give a damn for us. You keep the country, Joshua, I'll take the money. Frankly, I don't care whether God saves our gracious King or not. I'm tired of the whole rotten lot. I'm concerned to save my family. I know where our bread is buttered and nothing's going to stop me."

Most of Griffin Street shared Selma's view. "It's a chance in a lifetime," they said. "You're wise to grab it, Selma. We'd be off like a shot if we could."

"I felt like Selma," father told me, "that's why your mother and I agreed to join her, even though your sister Jenny was a baby. America was looked upon by the likes of us as the land of promise. Your mother and especially your grandmother Bridget weren't as keen on the idea as I was, but I thought that it was a chance we shouldn't miss. Grandmother Selma was in charge and she carried the rest of us along with her. She never let up on it."

Dad said that Selma told nobody when she received her husband's death money. He knew she'd got it because she suddenly became bright-eyed. Two weeks before they were due to sail, she left the mill for good. After that she basked in the sun by the front door, arms across her belly, beaming with happiness, and exchanging gossip with all who had the time to stop and talk.

"Then tha's got the money?" passers-by queried, hoping to find out what unheard of sum had come her way. To which question she always responded with a sly look. The more Selma refused to talk about it, the larger the sum became. Rumour made the figure large enough to take the whole of Griffin Street to America.

One day, when mother and I were out for a walk, she took up the American story again. She told me that the whole street had given them a send-off. Despite some talk of Sabbath-breaking, they had it on a Sunday afternoon when the mills were shut. As the weather was fine, tables were brought out into the street. Bunting and coloured streamers were hung from the houses. It was all very pretty. The words "May you Prosper," were chalked in large letters on grandmother Selma's cottage. Cakes, buns, and pies were piled high down the middle of the tables. There were dishes of jelly, and lots of oranges. There was apple juice for the children and beer for the grown-ups.

One of father's friends from the mill, ginger-headed Adam Sims and his wife Emily, who were emigrating with them, turned up at the going away party full of high spirits. Although the Sims had only been married four months, Emily, a mere slip of a girl, was large with her first child. It worried grandmother Selma.

Everybody enjoyed themselves. There were lots of toasts: "To the emigrants ...;" "To our friends across the sea ...;" "To a safe journey ...";
they lost track of them. Sometime during the afternoon, one of the neighbours, pinched-faced Arthur Childers who fancied himself with the ladies, got up to make a speech. "Friends and neighbours," he began in a grave voice. "The ocean may divide us but our spirits will be one." But then somebody pulled his coattail and, with his hand still raised for silence, he slid beneath the table. There were roars of laughter. Adam Sims was the only one sober enough to sing a song right through. In a deep bass voice, with his arm resting on his wife's shoulder, he sang a song they all knew:

> Just like Darby and Joan
> In a world of their own,
> We'll build a nest
> Out in the West.
> Be it so humble,

We'll never grumble,
And when summer has flown
And the grey locks are shown,
Age may betide us,
But love will guide us,
Just like Darby and Joan.

The fellow with the concertina kept on playing while they all sang an encore and cheered and clapped.

Nobody got Selma to her feet. She didn't believe in speeches. Besides, she'd drunk so much that she didn't have any legs. Other than to shout back how grateful the family was, and that she'd never forget her neighbours, Selma drank steadily and kept her seat. By the time it came to sing "We'll take a cup of kindness now for the sake of old lang syne", she had to use both bench and table to prop herself up. That night she slept where she dropped, in her clothes. Selma was never one for losing sleep.

Early the next morning father left for Liverpool. Because time was short, he went by train. He was going to meet his cousin Henry Nilson to make final arrangements for the voyage.

The next day everybody followed. Before sunrise, in the early morning cold, Selma's whitewashed cottage was stripped clean. It looked as if it had never been occupied. The front door swung on its hinges, the inside appeared empty and sad. "It's not much to leave behind," Selma said as she took a last look round. All the seven Woodruff children had been roused long before dawn and were eager to be off. The Sims had arrived and stood in the street with their baggage. Alongside them were the new tenants who had turned up before first light. They were strangers. They sat on their boxes in the street talking in low voices and throwing side-long glances.

Joe Moss turned up with his cart to take the migrants the thirty miles to Liverpool. He was a solid-looking fellow with white hair; not many men carried their years like Joe did. A close friend of the family, his only desire was to do a good turn. As soon as he appeared the baggage and the bedding were loaded up, everybody giving a hand. There was a lot of shouting, hugging and weeping as they climbed on to the cart.

"We'll never see each other again on this earth," grandmother Bridget sobbed, clinging to Jenny. At the end, Maggie had a struggle to get Jenny back from Bridget. Finally they got themselves sorted out. Selma clambered up next to Joe Moss, clutching a flat leather bag fastened to a rope tied round her waist. Maggie sat next to Selma holding Jenny. Behind them sat Emily on a pile of bedding and tarpaulins which they took in case of rain. They wore dark blouses and long dark skirts against dirt. They also had large straw bonnets, a farewell gift of the pawnbroker Mr. Levy. Being a warm morning, their shawls were thrown back on their shoulders.

At a shout of "Giddup" from Joe Moss, the loaded cart began to rumble down Griffin Street. This was the signal for the new tenants to rush into Selma's cottage, dragging their possessions after them. As their departure coincided with the morning rush to the mills, Joe and his horse had to fight against the tide of workers going the other way.

"Lucky old devil you are, Selma," shouted those who knew what was afoot. "Don't forget us." Others just stared, waved vaguely, and shouted: "Ta, Ta!"

Relatives and friends followed until the migrants had passed the Griffin pub. Grandmother Bridget stood on the steps in front of the pub waving and weeping until the cart had passed out of sight.

The freedom to suddenly break a fixed pattern of life, to break out of the ranks of the army of workers and go their own way, made Selma and Maggie want to cry. Neither knew whether it was from grief or joy. They had been used to going to the mills. They'd expected to go there at 7:30 a.m. for ever. Other people had organized their lives. Selma, in a happy daze, asked, "What are we doing going to America, Maggie, when everybody else is going to the mills?" Both women felt easier once the tide of bodies had subsided and the canyons of brick had been left behind. They'd never known such freedom.

An hour later, with the sun peeping over the moors, and the sounds and sights and smells of the countryside bearing in upon them, they reached the top of a hill where they halted to look back at the town they were leaving for good. Despite the smoke haze that hung over the valley, and the wisps of mist the day still retained, they were able to make out the different landmarks. The spire of the parish church of St. Mary stood out most of all. The children were the first to find the tower above the Market Hall. They pointed to the spires of St. Silas' and St. Paul's, and to the railway station on Bolton Road. It was easy to separate the spinning from the weaving sheds because of their flat roofs. The pit heaps and the mining wheels in the far distance were also clear. But the gas works took some finding. The rest was a treeless, dense mass of factories, cottages and smoking factory chimneys. They'd never noticed how many chimneys there were before; the town was peppered with them. If they stood stock-still and strained their ears, they could just hear a church bell pealing far below, the chime rising and falling with the breeze. After everybody had taken a swig of cold tea from one of the jars, they continued their journey.

The children obviously preferred going to America to going to school. Every now and then, with great screams, they'd race through a hole in the hedgerow to pick buttercups, daisies, goldenrod, cornflowers, and poppies. There was nothing to spoil, for the haymaking was done. Here and there they saw small groups of workers stacking the ricks. Sometimes the children would chase a rabbit, or butterflies, or gang up on a dog. Once they caught a hedgehog which Selma ordered them to let go. Another time everybody halted to watch hares playing at the edge of a wood. Higher up on the moors the children raced through the heather and the bracken. Adam enjoyed running with them, but most of the time the boys and Amy kept to themselves. When tired, the children came running back to the cart, climbed aboard and slept on the bedding. Sometimes the grown-ups would burst into song.

Later that morning, by which time the flies had become a nuisance, and they were all feeling the quivering heat, they met a labourer working by himself on the road.

"And where might ye all be goin'?" he asked as he rested on his spade and wiped his brow with his sleeve.

"To America," Selma answered.

"America?" the man replied, swatting the flies. "That's a mighty long way to go with a horse'n cart."

"But we're not," the children laughed. "we're going on a ship."

"Ye are, are ye? Well, by y'r leave, I'll be hoppin' on the cart and joinin' ye." Louder laughter followed.

"Ah well," said the labourer resignedly, "that's the kind of world it is; some mend the roads, others go to America. I'll be thinkin' of ye' all the way. May God watch over ye'."

"And over you too," Adam Sims rejoined.

On looking back, they saw the man waving his cap.

Under a still sky, the migrants wended their way through valleys where the streams ran crystal clear. On they went across gritstone fells and lonely moors where the curlew cried. Other wayfarers passed them on the road. Once they came to a great stone bridge that led them to a sleepy village where friendly people standing in doorways passed the time of day with them. In the late afternoon they rested under a Maypole on a village green still rich with deep silken grass. Whenever they found a really pretty place, Joe Moss would spoil it all with his, "Well, I suppose we should get on." Looking around, Maggie wondered if she was doing the right thing in leaving such a beautiful countryside for good.

They spent the night at a farm near Hesketh with the carter's relatives, the Mosses – red-faced, jovial farming people who not only gave them shelter in one of the barns, but a huge, warming evening meal as well. They could not have been kinder. The Mosses brought a large pot of stew out to the barn on a wheelbarrow. They hurried back and forth 'twixt barn and house, carrying food and drink and doing whatever they could to make them comfortable. They looked upon it as a privilege to be able to help Joe's friends who were travelling across the world. Folks living on the neighbouring farms would never hear the end of it.

After everyone had washed under the pump in the cobbled yard, the stew was served with great lumps of fresh bread and a bucket of fresh milk. There was more than enough for everyone to eat their fill. The children gorged. Fussed by Adam, Emily Sims, who said grace, ate as eagerly as the rest. The meal was accompanied by the sound of thrushes singing their last song of the day.

As soon as the meal was over, the children went to sleep among the hay in the barn. The adults followed. After a day of being bumped about and jolted in the cart, they were all ready for a good night's sleep. There could be no more comfortable bed, and no lovelier smell than fresh hay. As the light faded, bats zig-zagged their way out of the building into the night air.

A cock perched on one of the great beams above their heads woke them with his crowing the next morning. After a huge breakfast of porridge, bacon and eggs, scones, and fresh honey from the Mosses' own hives, the migrants set their backs to the rising sun and their faces to the Irish Sea. The day was yet cool and fresh. Busy as they were, the Mosses took the trouble to walk along a little ways through the early morning mist to wave good-bye.

After a day-long tramp, the travellers were met by Will and his cousin Henry Nilson at an inn outside Liverpool. There were many more carts and vehicles about. Will and Henry had with them the family papers that Henry had cleared at the port. Henry struck them as a bit of a toff. He wore a suit and a tie. He also wore shoes, boasted a watch chain, and carried a hard bowler hat under his arm. The papers were in order, he said. The *Elizabeth* had been delayed, but they'd be off in a day or two. Shelter was waiting for them along the wharf close to where the *Elizabeth* was berthed.

Shortly afterward they climbed a rise and saw an unending sheet of water shimmering in the bright light. For some of them it was the first time they'd seen the sea. They gasped at the sight. The children couldn't get over it. They'd no idea that so much water and sky existed; nor that such huge ships could stay afloat. They expected to see America in the distance. Having avoided the town, they came to a shed by a quiet beach not far from the end of the quay. Seagulls perched on the tin roof. Farther on they could see crowds moving about. Behind the shed was a salt marsh which rang with bird song.

It took some time for Henry to open the warehouse doors, which were fastened by several locks and a large metal hasp. "Can't keep people out," he said as he struggled with a large bunch of keys. With a deep shudder the doors gave way. Tired after two long days on the road, they all poured into the shed intent on finding a place to rest. There were two rooms with straw-stuffed mattresses, a large room for the men and a smaller room for the women. There was a water tap outside and a fenced-in yard with a wood fire for cooking.

Selma and Maggie quickly removed the shutters and threw everything open to the warm breeze. Adam and Will emptied the cart. Joe unhitched his horse and let it crop the grass. The children gathered sticks to cook the evening meal. Soon the smell of cooking was everywhere.

An hour later only Joe, Will and Maggie were awake to watch the great red sun slowly slip into the sea. Swifts and swallows wove a graceful pattern in the fading light. They didn't feel like sleep, instead they sat on the steps, stretching, yawning and yarning, watching the water endlessly rising and falling and listening to the crickets. Now and again they heard the hoot of a ship, and the noises of trains nearby. Spots of light could be seen down the coast. Around them indigo shadows fell.

Joe talked about America. "In a way I envy you," he said. "Plants of your age can still be moved. It's too late for me. Without the right soil, I'd die."

"It's easier for you to stay where you are, Joe," Will answered. "People who have what they need seldom move. Anyway, we'd like a change." At that point Henry Nilson came out of the hut to join them. Maggie lit a candle and went in to lie down.

They were wakened in the early hours by Emily's stifled cries of pain. Selma told Henry to get a doctor quickly.

"No doctor will come here at this hour, Aunt Selma," Henry replied. "It's not safe to be running about the port in the dark."

Selma was silent for a moment. Turning to Will she told him to get extra lights and to get a fire going. "Maggie and I need lots of hot water." She then rearranged the leather bag she carried so that it hung down her back. She needed her arms.

As the time passed, Emily's gasps became more frequent. Two hours later Selma took Maggie outside. "Child's the wrong way," she told her.

Later on the bleeding began. Selma was calm, but helpless to deal with the haemorrhage. Maggie was horrified. By the rays of the lantern, she watched Emily gasping for breath through chattering teeth.

As the first fingers of light crept across the morning sky, Emily's cries became weaker. Adam, who had never left his wife's side, tried to comfort her. Despite all the blankets wrapped around her, she became colder. After fits of shivering, she stiffened in his arms. The light gradually went out of her eyes. A calm stillness prevailed, broken only by Adam's sobs.

At the end, Adam left the warehouse and walked toward the quay alone. Joe joined him. With plaintive cries, a flight of gulls followed.

Selma went to the spigot to wash. With her head wrapped in a towel, she threw herself down on one of the children's mattresses. Silently, her body shook. "Jesus wept," she said.

The next day was madness. All morning, port, city, and funeral officials tiptoed in and out of the shed to obtain a signature from Adam and a mark from Selma. They all said the same thing: "A terrible thing to happen, Mrs. Woodruff. A most unfortunate happening, Mr. Sims." For their services they charged several gold coins which Adam took from a drawstring pouch around his neck.

On the day when they should have had a compulsory bath and been fumigated, Selma, Adam, Joe, and Henry went to the funeral. Will and Maggie stayed behind with the children. In spite of the additional sovereigns which Adam had been obliged to shake out of his purse, the funeral was a shabby affair. "He was fleeced, that's what he was, Maggie,"

Selma said. "Didn't get what he paid for. The way they put her down, tha'd have thought that Emily was a pauper. God knows what would have 'appened if we 'adn't 'ad 'enry 'ere."

That night Selma, Will and Maggie took Adam aside. "What do you intend to do, Adam?" Selma asked. "Ar' te going back with Joe to Blackburn tomorrow, or ar' te going to board the ship with us? Tha'll have to make up thi mind quick."

"I already have. I'm sailing. Emily's gone before me on an earlier tide; she wouldn't want me to turn back now."

"Well, that takes a load off my mind," Selma replied. "Tha can rely on us until we get to Fall River. Tha's had a shock, lad, and tha should put thi 'ead down."

Later that night, Henry beckoned Selma outside. "Listen, when you get to New York you and everybody else are going to be what they call 'processed'. They're going to ask you a lot of questions at the docks about where you've come from and where you're going. Important for you is that they're also going to ask you if you've ever been in jail. You've got to watch that one. It doesn't mean they're going to throw you out, but they could give you a headache. All you have to do is to say no, you haven't been in jail, and for goodness sake, smile. They're not going to stop a widow with seven young uns."

"I 'ope not."

"Another thing, you're supposed to have been fumigated and to have had a bath before boarding. This is all very necessary because a lot of these migrants carry vermin. But you've had other things to do. If they ask you about it when you reach the *Elizabeth* you'd better act daft. You've got to get on that ship. I'd use the Keating's Insect Powder you've brought with you before you board."

Very early the next day Joe drove them down the quayside to where the *Elizabeth* was moored. Although the ship would not leave until the evening tide, it was Henry's idea that they should be available to embark at sun up. "There are hundreds of other people fighting to get a berth," he explained. "Every ship going to America is packed."

Henry pointed out the *Elizabeth* long before they reached it. "There she is," he called out, "the third in line from this end."

"But uncle Henry, you said it was a big ship," the children complained. "You didn't tell us it was the smallest of the lot."

"It'll get bigger as you get closer," Henry assured them.

Accompanied by a stream of horse-drawn cabs, pony traps, and donkey carts, they threaded their way through the throng of migrants who occupied the quayside. The migrants sat about in groups. A few, still wrapped in their blankets, lay fast asleep on the ground. Many were down at heel – their shirts and dresses already black with sweat. Some were dark-haired, foreign-looking people with black curls hanging over their ears. Anxious-looking men hurried from ship to ship, searching for a sailing on the evening tide. A number of bareheaded children ran about in packs calling to each other in shrill excited foreign tongues, as if nobody owned them. Everybody clung to their possessions.

The *Elizabeth* was berthed directly opposite the Customs House. When they reached it, a great shouting was going on. The three-masted ship was throbbing with activity: sailors were in the rigging, cranes screamed as freight was lowered through the hatches, porters swarmed over the gangways carrying luggage. A brightly-coloured, carved figurehead of a woman decorated the prow. This was the 'Elizabeth' after whom the ship was named. With its flags drooping in the heat, the *Elizabeth* looked smaller close-up than she had at a distance; even smaller when compared with the larger vessels alongside her.

"Do you really think that's going to get us to America," Amy asked.

"It's got to," Selma said. "They 'ave our money."

Will was full of questions about the ship. Henry said it was more than 200 feet long, 40 feet across, 30 feet deep. While it was mainly a cargo ship, it could carry 40 passengers – ten first class and thirty steerage. It had been launched as the *Victory* some time during the 1860s from a long-gone British shipyard. Originally it had sailed with cargo and a few passengers between England and the East. Later it had been used to funnel English migrants to Australia and New Zealand. Later still it was transferred to American ownership. Now it was on the Atlantic run.

Sheltered from the sun by a wide awning, which ran along the waterside, they spent a dreary day sitting on their valises waiting to embark. The young children fretted and cried, the older children found it torture to have to sit still. Leaving Henry and Adam to stand guard, Selma and Will dashed across the wide, cobbled road, with its hurrying horses and cabs, to do some last minute shopping on the custom house row. In addition to the large, pillared Custom's House, shops of all kinds lined the street.

Not long before boarding they said good-bye to Joe Moss. He found it hard to take leave of the children. He couldn't get over it that they were about to sail thousands of miles to a new life in America. They watched and waved as his creaking cart turned away from the sea.

Not until the hatches had been battened down, were the passengers allowed to cross a wide gang plank to the main deck. Steerage followed First Class. "With toffs like that aboard we should be safe," Selma commented. Although there were enough bunks for all, the steerage passengers fought their way across the gang plank carrying boxes and baggage. Apart from a few things in a sack, some passengers didn't seem to have any luggage.

Having clambered up to the main deck, the Woodruffs were escorted by sailors past the hatches to the stern. Adam and Will carried the heavy valises. Without Will's energy none of them would have got to America.

68

He could carry the world on his shoulders. The sailors took them down a flight of stairs to the steerage quarters where they entered a cabin large enough for all the steerage passengers. They were given bunks built in a semicircle around the stern of the vessel. The bunks were between the communal kitchen and the toilet, both areas already smelly. Maggie wondered how she was going to make the crossing. Except for sheets placed over string, there was no privacy. Baggage was stowed on the floor. Tickets simply provided for somewhere to sleep, cook, and wash. If this was the 'superior accommodation' that Henry had promised, what must it have been like on the larger ships?

The sound of the ship's windlasses recovering the anchors caused everyone to rush upstairs. Henry was on the quayside. Once he caught sight of them he shouted messages that no one could hear. He continued to wave his hat as the *Elizabeth* – pushed by a battered-looking tug – threaded its way past other vessels out to sea.

Only when the land was disappearing did Maggie wonder if she would ever see England again. She prayed that they'd done the right thing and that all their dreams would come true in America.

Later, from the deck beneath the bellowing sail, Will and Maggie watched the sun sink into the sea. Will, like his mother Selma, was beside himself with excitement at the thought of going to the New World. For a long time they watched the lights of other ships going to and from Liverpool and the stars above. The shrieking gulls had long since fallen astern.

By all accounts, it took the Woodruffs a long time to find their sea legs – longer still to get used to the confined steerage quarters and the unbelievable medley of human beings. Even with fair weather it was usually bedlam below. Except when the sea was rough, which thank God it rarely was, they spent the day on deck. Upstairs they could see the sky. To guard their possessions, the grown-ups took turns below. Although most of the ship was out of bounds to them, there was sufficient room 'Tween Decks for the steerage passengers to take exercise and sit in the open air. Will was in his element to be at sea again. He disregarded the out-of-bounds signs and joined the sailors in their quarters, often returning with tid-bits for the children.

To make sure of a space on the hatches, the migrants either had to stay there all night, or get up before everybody else in the morning. Some people seemed to sit in the same place day after day with a rolled blanket at their backs or across their shoulders. They only moved when the weather turned sour. Scowling looks and hostile mutters were usually enough to dissuade intruders.

Once on board ship, Adam Sims withdrew into himself. He was often seen motionless – hands on rail – gazing across the sea. The grown-ups understood and left him alone.

Maggie used to say that it was the fine weather that saved them. There were days when the sea could not have been smoother. Its mirror-like polished surface stretched in all directions. There were nights when it was warm enough to take a blanket on deck and fall asleep with the wind singing in the rigging and the tapering masts swaying among a canopy of stars. Sometimes, in a calm, the Woodruffs fell asleep against each other listening to the whispering of the sea, the groan and creak of timber and rope, and the helmsman calling out the passing hours by the striking of bells. Nothing bothered them except the odd rat being chased by a squealing pack.

Other passengers didn't take rats lightly. They complained that the ship was a decrepit thing that should never have sailed. When the auxiliary engine had sputtered and died several days out of Liverpool, their concern grew. Fortunately it was put right.

The other blessing for the migrants was the ship's captain. A tall, white-bearded seaman, with a gold-laced cap, and a weather-beaten face, Captain Rogers had taken an interest in the welfare of the steerage passengers from the start. As long as he was about Maggie felt safe.

Her most vivid memory of the journey was the night storm that terrified her and the children, and left most of the passengers prostrate. Almost without warning the vessel had suddenly heeled over. Had the sails not already been furled, it might have capsized. One moment they were lost in the blackest night, the next they were dazzled by a flash of lightning so bright that it blinded them. Deafening thunder followed. Torrents of rain set the decks awash. Ordered below, the migrants hung on as the stern rose in the air and crashed down again with a bone-shattering thump that scattered their possessions. Each moment they went in fear of being sucked down. Utterly dejected, they lay in their bunks and joined the medley of cries and groans that seemed to herald the end of the world. The ship rolled and tossed and pitched throughout the night. The ordeal ended with someone vomiting all over Selma's head; for which she soundly cursed everyone around her.

With the storm gone and the hatches removed, the migrants slowly clambered out on to the deck. Bedding was laid out to dry. Around them was the tired sea, gently hissing and sighing after its ordeal.

Not even the storm affected Selma's appetite. They had taken an enormous amount of food with them, most of which Selma appears to have eaten. Day after day, she sat on deck, at the foot of one of the masts, chewing on something or other, while telling her children, and anyone else willing to listen that there was no storm that was not worth enduring in order to get to America. "We're going to the land of the free," she would shout. "Once across, we'll all be rich." After which she would rub her fat hands gleefully and eat some more.

Selma had always been one for her belly. Will had come home one night when he was in his teens in Blackburn to find his many siblings locked out of the house. Several of them had their hungry faces glued to the kitchen window.

"What's up?" he had asked.

"Mammie's eatin' our dinner," the young ones had complained. "She said, 'Out you go,' and chased us into the street."

Will had joined the others at the window pane to watch Selma cook and eat with relish several chops. She was deaf to the banging of fists on the window. By the time Will got into the house there were no chops left.

"There just wasn't enough chops to go round," Selma explained to Will. "Better a few chops for me than too little for everybody else."

Two nights before they reached New York, Adam Sims disappeared. Although the night was dark, a member of the crew had seen him strolling along the deck toward the stern. Adam was known for standing above the rudder watching the unwinding ribbon of foam below. The seaman had seen him there before, and had thought nothing of it. Earlier, Adam had slept alongside Will by the mizzen mast. They had talked in subdued tones about their future in the New World. When Adam had not returned from his walk, Will had thought nothing of it. After listening to the invisible canvas rattling and beating itself in the sky, and the taught rigging vibrating before the rising breeze, he'd dozed off.

With mounting anxiety, the search for Adam went on all the next morning. The only thing they found was his moleskin purse which Selma and Will were able to identify. Captain Rogers had examined it through narrowed eyes. The incident spread fear throughout the ship.

Selma and Will spent the next two days in the captain's cabin. Endless statements were made by them and others, and signed. Captain Rogers came to the conclusion that Adam had been stunned, robbed, and cast into the sea. "It's happened before," he told them.

Although Adam's empty purse pointed to murder, he was listed as a suicide. Suicide would make it easier for everybody to avoid being held up in New York. It would also make it easier for Captain Rogers, who didn't want to have a murder inquiry hanging round his neck. So suicide it was; after all, with Emily's death, suicide didn't need explaining. Everybody knew how Adam had moped since he put his foot on the ship.

Selma was the first to see the uneven outline of the American coast. On the last night she'd stayed on deck until she saw it. When the pencils of stone began to rise out of the sea, she rushed downstairs shouting and brought up the children. Together they gaped at the sun-kissed city hovering on the horizon. Selma was jubilant at having reached America. Others just stared at the shore disbelievingly, tears streaming down their faces.

Shortly afterwards, like a large bird, the ship folded its wings; the sails were furled; the engines took over. Two men and a woman in uniform clambered aboard from a small boat that had come alongside. They stayed only minutes, after which the *Elizabeth* resumed its course toward the New York docks. It was a sultry day.

Accompanied by a growing number of other vessels, and a burst of whistles and sirens, they approached a large statue of a lady with a lamp. "That's Ellis Island!" someone shouted. Shortly afterward, Captain Rogers brought the *Elizabeth* alongside the quay. With much clanking and clatter the vessel was anchored and made fast. They'd reached the land of promise.

The *Elizabeth* was among the first ships to arrive that day. The first-class passengers quickly disembarked. Henry Nilson had told Selma that if they made a landfall early they'd stand a chance of getting through to Fall River that night.

According to Maggie, there followed a day of agony. Having been tagged with a number, the Woodruffs joined the flood of other steerage passengers hastening toward a large building. The medley of people around them – all shouting in a dozen tongues – was greater than they'd met with at Liverpool. Burdened by children and baggage, and clutching landing papers, everybody rushed forward as if their lives depended upon it. Faces were strained; nobody smiled. Maggie was struck on the shoulder by a wooden trunk carried on the back of a surly man who forced his way past her. She feared the children would get lost in the milling throng. "Everybody's afraid they're going to shut the door," Selma said to Maggie as she urged the children to keep up. Successive waves of humanity pushing from behind flung them forward.

Once through the vast open doors, they climbed a long flight of stairs which led to a great hall. Here they were met by a scene of unbelievable uproar and confusion. In addition to the thousands of milling, bewildered, laden immigrants, there were hundreds of inspectors and officials bellowing out numbers and messages in every language. It was a shock for which Henry Nilson had not prepared them.

In the hall they joined an endless line that, cattle-like, moved between wooden rails. Following Selma and her brood, Will and Maggie, carrying both luggage and a child, tramped from one end of the building to the other. In a storm of noise, doctors with grave looks and blue uniforms gave them cursory examinations as they filed past. While asking questions, they examined hands, face, hair, and eyes. If the official thought it necessary, lungs and heart were listened to. One man was put in a cage to await further inspection. He had a circle with a cross chalked on his lapel, which someone said meant deportation. The ship that brought him would have to take him back. That was when the crying and sobbing began. For a family to be broken up at the last moment was more than they could bear. Others were ordered to sit at one side until their names were called.

There seemed to be no way of knowing why some immigrants were derailed while others went straight on. None of the Woodruffs merited the use of chalk. They passed the medical officials in record time. As cattle go, they were all good stock.

After another long wait, the hasty medical examination was followed by an equally hasty inspection by the immigration authorities. Heading the Woodruffs, Selma proceeded to answer questions read off a board by a slim bespectacled man with an impassive face. His eyes never flickered.

"Where were you born?" he began.

"England."

"Who paid your passage?"

"I did."

"Do you have any money? Let me see it."

Selma fumbled in her bag. As Henry had instructed, she produced the customary five pounds (twenty-five dollars) to prevent her becoming a public charge. For some immigrants such a sum had meant years of saving.

"How many dependents?"

"Seven."

"Ever been in prison?"

"Now, what, I ask you, would a widow with seven children be doing in jail?"

"Yuh, sure. Can you read or write?"

Coached by Henry, Selma knew that there was no legal obligation to be able to do either. Nor would they test her. "I manage," she answered.

"Do you have any relatives here?"

"Yes, in Fall River, where I'm going."

"What skills do you have?"

"I'm a weaver."

"Is there a job waiting for you?" was the last question asked. For reasons which Selma never understood, to have answered "yes" would have been fatal.[†] Henry had told her to say "No," so she said "No," which at least was the truth.

Will and Maggie, who by now knew all the questions and answers, went through the same procedure.

After several gruelling hours, the migrants' names were checked against the ship's manifest. They were given landing cards, after which they pushed open a door marked New York and emerged in the fresh air. While Maggie felt like collapsing, Selma glowed. They'd come through the ordeal without having to spend the night there or stay for a meal in the great dining room. The dining room was double bedlam. One look was enough; nobody wanted to eat there.

Before leaving the building, Selma and Will changed some money. They had been warned from Fall River to make sure that they were not cheated. Selma was puzzled by the strange coins, but rattled them together in her hands to show her delight. They also bought a sandwich and had a cup of tea. As uncle Mat and aunt Hessie had warned them against the many rogues to be found on the docks, some of whom might offer great tracts of non-existent land for ten dollars down, they were doubly careful to whom they spoke.

Having finished his tea, Will went in search of tickets for the ferry from Ellis Island to the mainland and the train to Boston. He returned with a fistful. There was a train, he said, that would take them directly to Boston.

Further confusion awaited them when they got off the ferry. The ticket clerk had told Will that they should go down the platform to catch the Boston train.

"No, no, no," someone who had overheard their conversation intervened. "Show me your tickets," the stranger went on. He was one of those men who seemed to know absolutely everything.

Keeping a tight grip on them, Will showed him.

"You must go a quarter mile up the line," the stranger said.

"Then why did the ticket clerk tell me to go down the line?"

"Why? Because he's crazy, that's why. Wouldn't you be crazy if you had a frantic mob milling round you all day?"

But no sooner had they started going up the line than still other strangers, carrying their belongings in wicker baskets, told them they should be going down the line.

"That fellow's quite wrong," they said. "The ticket clerk is right. Some people will waste your life giving you the wrong advice. Of course, it's down the line. Don't listen to him."

So they all tramped down the line only to be told, as the first man had advised, that it was up the line. Wearily, they turned around and tramped back up the line to a junction where hordes of migrants were sitting about dejectedly waiting for the Boston train. With the smell of sweat and dust upon them, Selma and the rest collapsed upon their possessions. By now, Maggie was in a daze.

They saw the train long before it pulled into the station. It had halted like a great steaming dinosaur among the high weeds and grasses some distance from the platform. It seemed so large. It stood there watching them with a great baleful eye before deciding what to do. Having sounded a deep-throated warning, it crawled toward them. It was the first train whistle that Maggie had heard in the New World. It struck a different chord from English train whistles. She thought it sad. Years later she used to say that all American train whistles sounded sad.

With their possessions slung over their shoulders, some of the migrants had jumped down from the end of the platform and had jostled their way along a cinder track to meet the train. By the time it had shuddered to a stop, it was already half-full.

There followed one of the worst free-for-alls the Woodruffs had ever experienced. With latecomers scurrying up and down the train, and everybody pushing hard from behind, the struggle went on until the long, open carriages were crammed with sweat-stained bodies, mountains of luggage, and crying children.

To get a seat one had to push and jostle somebody else out of the way until every seat was occupied, every aisle filled. Families separated from each other by the crowd shouted with frantic desperation over passengers' heads – often in shrill foreign tongues. Thanks to Selma's inclination to settle any dispute with her muscular arms and thighs – "By your leave, by your leave," she sang out as she toppled people off their feet – and to Will's mule-like ability to carry a mountain of luggage, the Woodruffs obtained seats together.

The journey from New York to Boston was long and weary. It was the longest train journey that Maggie would ever make although it was, in fact, fewer than two hundred miles. It began with the train rolling backward and forward in and out of the station. After that it swayed and creaked its way to a marshalling yard where it sat and wheezed. Meanwhile the day got hotter; flies were everywhere. All the passengers, many of whom they had never seen before, cheered when at long last the train slowly left the yard and got under way. The faster it went the more they benefited from the breeze coming through the open windows.

Maggie was too much in a daze to do anything beyond caring for her baby. Her first impression of America was something of a let-down. There were miles of dilapidated, grimy-looking tenements with people and washing everywhere. It didn't look like the land of promise to her. She'd been wondering for a long time what she was coming to. She hoped it wasn't this. When she wasn't dozing, she watched the passing scene. It became evident that she was looking at a different kind of world. The sky was larger; everything looked twice as big. More of the houses were built with wood than with brick. The roofs were low pitched. The Americans she saw on the different platforms or in the streets didn't walk like Lancashire folk. They bounced along, swinging their arms. "They look as if they own the place," Maggie said to Will. "They do," he replied. People seemed taller and more pale-faced. They had shirts with collars attached, loud clothing, and dresses and suits. How they stood and stared marked them as different. They were surprised at the number of negroes. Nobody had ever seen a black face in Blackburn. In later years they remembered hurrying through a sprawling, tree-lined countryside with the farmers still getting in the hay.

By the time they saw Boston in the afternoon, the crowded coach appeared as if it had been occupied for weeks. Shoes, packages, suitcases, discarded food, banana skins and orange peel, rolling bottles and crawling infants littered the floor. Despite the open windows, a heavy, rancid smell of unwashed humanity filled the swaying car. The view of the backs of the tenements along the railroad track looked like the worst part of Blackburn.

In Boston they left behind the migrants they'd travelled with from New York and caught the train to Newport, which stopped at Fall River, fifty miles away. On this train their valises were carried in the luggage van. The Newport train gave them their first close look at Americans, a surprising number of whom wore suits and shiny shoes. The passengers talked in loud voices as the train jolted along. They also called across the aisles in a rude kind of way. There was nothing cowed about them. They showed an immediate interest in the Woodruff children.

The Woodruffs caught sight of Fall River as the light was fading. "There it is," a Fall River passenger told them, as he pointed to the town's famous landmarks, the double onion domes of St. Anne's Church and the double spires of Notre Dame Church. They caught glimpses of great factory-like buildings topping the wayside trees. Quickly they got their things together. Children were wakened and ordered to hang on to each other.

As the train stopped with a jolt, the Woodruffs poured out on to the platform. Will and the older boys hurried away to retrieve the valises from the luggage van. Selma stood in the middle of a crowded platform with the remainder of her brood around her. Maggie, holding Jenny, stood next to her crying uncontrollably. Her body still swayed with the movement of the vessel left long behind. The journey had been hard. She had found Selma's bossing a great strain. Though tired and numb, it passed through her mind that they had no idea what the Fall River Woodruffs and Nilsons who had promised to meet them really looked like. They did have some pictures, but they were years old.

After standing there for some time and wondering what they should do, a group of five or six strangers approached. "Excuse me, are you from Blackburn?" one of the men asked.

"That we are," Selma replied.

"Well, you've cum at last," Selma's brother Mat said as he shook her hand. "This is my wife Hessie, we've been looking for you all afternoon."

"By gum, am I pleased to see you!" Selma cried, hugging her brother and sister-in-law. Her face became bright red with pleasure.

There were other Nilsons there, as well as several Woodruffs. They were all ages, all of them eager to meet their relatives. Some of them had migrated to Fall River twenty years earlier, most had been born there. There was talk about Blackburn and the sorry fate of the Sims, but not much else. Even Selma, who had born the ordeal of the journey best of all, and who had not once been seasick, was too tired for talk. Nobody asked them if they'd had a pleasant voyage.

From the station they walked beneath a now starry sky to one of the many clapboard tenement buildings which the textile mill had built to house the workers. They were drab-looking buildings, built in the shadow of the mills, with peculiar outside wooden staircases leading to the second and sometimes to the third levels. Here the migrants were split up into small enough groups to be given temporary shelter by the

Nilson and the Woodruff families. By now Maggie was all of a tremble, asleep on her feet. Later on she said that she couldn't have gone much farther without collapsing. Unlike Selma, she felt entirely dispirited. It took her a whole day to decide whether she was going to live or die. She swore that not for all the tea in China would she do that journey again.

From family history I know that my grandmother Selma and her children prospered in Fall River. As she had predicted, America proved to be the place where most of their dreams came true.

My parents also did well. They obtained a living in textiles. For the next eight years, my father earned more money as a "tackler," or overseer, at the Fleetwood Mills in Fall River, than he would ever do again. My parents had their own comfortably furnished apartment in a tenement in County Street. It was there that my sister Brenda was born on 19th September, 1910; the date on her birth certificate was given incorrectly as the 20th. Yet Brenda's birth certificate states that she was born on 28th September. I puzzled over this until my sister explained that mother had changed the 20th to the 28th, so that it would coincide with the date of her wedding anniversary. The date of mother's marriage was important to her. My brother Dan was born in the same house in January 1912.

In the early 1900s when my parents arrived there, Fall River, which stands at the mouth of the Taunton River in southeastern Massachusetts, was the largest concentrated area of cotton textile manufacture in the United States, if not in the entire world. It was called "spindle city," or "the Blackburn of America." Because of the growth of cotton manufactures in the area, Fall River population had soared from about 14,000 in 1800 to more than 100,000 in 1906. There wasn't much else in the way of industry in the town when my parents arrived, except a shoe and a cigar factory. The bulk of the Fall River textile industry had been developed behind high protectionist tariffs which English firms could not pierce. Compared with Fall River, Blackburn and Lancashire in 1906 were second best.

Fall River struck my people as cleaner and dryer. There was more light, more sun, more trees, more water. In addition to the Taunton River, across which was the Brega Bridge, there was the Quequechon River. Falls on the Quequechon had provided the power to turn the water wheels of the factories of an earlier age. There was also a great navigable canal which led to a fine harbour lined with wharves and coalyards. According to my parents, there was more hustle and bustle. Everything was bigger, faster, and noisier.

Their apartment in County Street was better than anything they'd known in Blackburn. It was more spacious, it had great bay windows, hardwood floors, and high ceilings. The roof didn't leak. There was even an indoor toilet. Most of the dwellings consisted of blocks of three-storied, broad-roofed, low-attic tenement houses. They had been built to

77

house the hundreds of young women and girls lured from the land to work in the mills. No such boarding houses existed in Lancashire. In Fall River, because of land values and tax policies, workers' dwellings were dense, tight, and high-rise.

For the rich of Fall River there were spacious and elegant houses. New mansions were going up in the Highland district for most of the time my family was there.

To people coming from England, the ethnic variety of Fall River in the 1900s came as a shock. I think to mother a very great shock. My people were used to English, Irish, and Scots, but not to French Canadians, Poles, Russians, Lithuanians, Syrians, Armenians, Greeks, Portuguese, Puerto Ricans, Canary Islanders, Italians, Spaniards, Germans, and Swedes; all of whom they called "foreigners". Primarily because they had come from Britain and could speak English, my people considered themselves superior to "foreigners." It was not uncommon for "Anglos," such as my parents who had themselves just arrived, to tell "dirty foreigners" to go home. In 1906, most of the population of Fall River must have been foreign born. There was a babel of tongues. To stop people drinking out of the wrong tap in the factory, mother said they had to mark it in several languages: "Don't drink from this tap." Iced-water in the mills came as a pleasant surprise to my parents.

Skill was a factor in getting a job in Fall River; nationality more so. The priorities given to English-speaking operatives explains why mother had no trouble getting a cardroom job as a "doffer," filling and emptying the carding machines. Father became a "tackler" or overseer.

Because each group tried to pull in its own, different functions in the mills were associated with different nationalities: spinning rooms were mostly French, cardrooms mostly Polish, and so on. Because of their long connections with the area, their passivity and their large families, French-Canadians were thought of as the ideal "foreign" workers. They couldn't afford to give any trouble. On the whole, each ethnic group stuck to its own and married its own. The last thing Fall River people wanted to do in the early 1900s was to "melt."

Far from melting, the "foreigners" discriminated against each other. Poles and Greeks were usually thought of as the bottom of the pile; especially by the Irish and the French. But then the Irish and the French were known to use shovels to settle scores against each other in the mills.

Most of the bosses in the mills were native Americans or "Anglos." The higher up they were, the more confidence they displayed in walk and speech. My people could tell a mill boss a mile away.

Whatever the differences in nationality, everybody in Fall River in the early 1900s had one thing in common: they were all struggling to get rich. Most of them were in a hurry. It was a headlong rush to succeed in which money was central. Regardless of the strain, helped by technical devices, some weavers would take on ten, twenty, even thirty looms in an effort to make more money. A "good, steady wage" had been the ideal in Blackburn; to "get rich quick" was the ideal in Fall River. In Blackburn one could not do as one pleased; one could not scramble up the ladder. There was a craft and a class structure which made individual decisions and rapid upward movement within the industry difficult. There were strong ties of loyalty not only to class but also to a particular mill or locality. Order prevailed. In Fall River, in the head-long flight to get rich, kin and ethnic differences were what mattered, not class. Nobody blamed anybody for getting on, for jumping from one job and class to another, even if it was done in a rushed, raucous, and disorderly manner.

One other difference was the great loyalty accorded to the Catholic Church at the beginning of this century in Fall River. Fall River was intensely Catholic. The priests wielded great influence, particularly among the immigrants. The Church provided social cohesion across ethnic lines. Father said that most of the clergy were against trade unions and organized labour. He divided Fall River into two groups: those who laboured and those who owned. The former were chiefly Catholic, the latter were chiefly Anglo-Saxon Protestants.

The outstanding advantage my parents possessed over the other immigrants streaming into Fall River from different parts of the world was not nationality, or language, or religion, but skill. For the others, many of whom were peasants, cotton manufacture was a completely different way of life. For my parents it was the same job they'd been doing in Blackburn. They'd arrived as skilled artisans with a strong sense of pride in their craft and for them nearly all the industrial processes and terms were identical.

It was the size of things that was different . The scale of operations was far greater than they'd been used to; it meant the din of thousands of looms instead of hundreds. The mills had thousands of workers, half of them women and girls. Whereas Blackburn had a large number of small, specialized, fragmented firms, which could meet the needs of all kinds of foreign demands, Fall River, because of the massive, protected home market, had a small number of very large, integrated firms. The manufacturing process from raw cotton to the dyeing of the finished cloth was often under the same roof. The mills, like most dwellings, were built upward: heavy looms on the first and second floors, carding machines on the third floor, spinners on the fourth, with spooling, dressing, and warping above.

Machinery generally was more technically advanced. There were many more automatic looms and more "batteries," a device which changed the weft in the shuttle automatically. Hence workers were expected to handle at least six looms instead of two. Fall River used the faster ring spinning instead of mule spinning. Producing first quality yarn on a "mule" was something of an art. In consequence, the mule spinners had always been the highest paid workers on both sides of the Atlantic. They had led in trade union organization. But the introduction of ring spinning in the United States had put an end to that because it didn't call for the same skill.[†]

There also was a difference in the fabrics woven. Whereas Lancashire was heavily dependent on the export trade, Fall River depended on production of superior print cloth, checks, stripes, and plaids, chiefly for the home market.[†] Because of the use of many colours, weaving in Fall River was more demanding on intelligence and eyesight.

For my family Fall River wages were much higher. For a fifty hour week – from 7 a.m. to 5 p.m. weekdays; half-day Saturday till 1 p.m. – father sometimes earned as much as $18–$20; several times his Blackburn pay of £1 to 30 shillings for almost the same hours.[†] What he got depended on his individual bargaining power. Although Fall River was the backbone of the United Textile Workers of America (founded in 1901, it had organized a large walk-out there in 1904 against wage cuts), most workers were hired and fired on an individual basis.

In Blackburn everybody knew pretty well what they were going to get. Many of the rates of pay had been agreed upon with the trade unions, which in the Lancashire textile industry had always been strong. In Fall River – partly because class solidarity was a difficult thing to achieve when everybody was speaking a different language – conditions were less certain. The unions were bitterly opposed by the employers and infiltrated with company informers and spies. Industrial spies in Lancashire were rare and it wasn't unknown for them to finish up in the canal with their throats cut.

The disadvantage of Fall River from my people's point of view was that the machinery went faster, much faster. My parents were forever trying to catch up. Fall River had more bells and whistles, less give and take. Also offsetting the higher rates of pay was the absence of workers' compensation. Father had one of his weavers drawn into the machinery and lose two fingers. Infection spread and the girl died. Her wages were sent to her family and that was that. Another girl got her hair caught up in a broken belt. She was lucky; she escaped with a deep cut. Patching her up was the extent of the employer's liability.

One thing that my parents could not get over was the amount of theft in the mills. It astonished them. It wasn't just a matter of taking home a few end pieces or filching a faulty bit of work, as one did in Lancashire. It was theft on the grand scale. Yards and yards of cloth disappeared into thin air. In an attempt to reduce it, the factories had been turned into fortresses. There were watchers at every gate and, following a tap on the shoulder by one of the guards, random checks. Body searches were common. Yet cloth continued to be stolen. When thieves were caught they were blacklisted and run out of town. It was cheaper than sending them to jail. The same rule applied to knife play. It was all right to fell a man with a shovel, as the Irish and the French sometimes did, but stabbing a fellow worker brought banishment.

They also talked about the practice of some Fall River mills to keep their windows open; which meant that mother had less dust to contend with in the carding room. In Blackburn they'd stood on damp, stone, oily floors. In Fall River they had dry hardwood floors which mother said was much better. Nor had they ever seen young workers singing and dancing in the aisles during factory breaks. Father said the dancers in the mills didn't have cold English blood; Poles and Italians behaved differently from Lancashire folk. Mother thought that workers in the Fall River mills were no more or less happy than elsewhere; they were just livelier, much better dressed, and money-wise, better off. They weren't as pinched, or as fearful of going broke as Lancashire folk.

In particular, mother remembered the bi-weekly pay delivered by a paymaster who carried a gun! No weaver could have managed to wait two weeks in Blackburn; everything in Lancashire stretched as far as a week and no further. She appreciated the paternalistic benefits provided by the Fall River manufacturers: the subsidized factory housing; the mill playground for children; the school which Jenny attended for four years; the central park not far from their home in County Street where she took Jenny, Brenda, and Dan to play; the free dental care; the parks and sports ground; the work trips and the Christmas parties for the workers' children. She liked knowing the bosses' names, and to whom she was paying the rent. To her dying day, she never forgot the breathtaking views from the steep hillside streets across the Taunton River to the countryside beyond.

One thing is certain: my parents didn't have to fight over pennies in Fall River. For the first time in their lives they were able to save. Relative to what they'd known in Blackburn, they'd become rich. I don't know whether that made them any happier, but it spared them the anguish over money they endured later on.

VI   Return to England

I find it difficult to understand why my parents returned to England in the summer of 1914. Things could not have been going better for them in the United States. Father was earning more money as a tackler than he would ever earn again. By his standards, he was well-off when he landed at Liverpool. Because some of my father's family were still in Blackburn, my parents returned to Griffin Street, the street from which they had migrated eight years earlier. They didn't seem to experience any difficulty slipping back into the groove they had left years before.

The curious thing is that I was never able to get either of my parents to talk about the return journey. I know that in the summer of 1914 they travelled with their three children, Jenny, Brenda, and Dan, on the *Carmania* (Second-Class) to Liverpool. Over the years they talked at great length about the outward journey but almost nothing about the return; one way or another, they avoided the topic. I can only assume that it pained them to mention it. The little I know about their journey back to England I owe to my sisters Jenny and Brenda. They remembered the talk in Fall River about the family's return to Blackburn; the fuss and bother of getting ready to leave; grandmother Selma and several uncles coming to the railway station to see them off; everybody crying; the great liner *Carmania* from whose bowels they hardly ever saw the sea; being met by grandmother Kenyon and several Woodruffs at Blackburn in the pouring rain; being put to bed there on the first night of their arrival and crying their eyes out to go home to Fall River. They didn't realize that they would never see Fall River again.

I suspect that plain homesickness for England on the part of my mother Maggie was the main reason for my family's return. Mother had never been drawn to the New World as grandmother Selma and father had. She never became part of the new land. I don't think she ever came to terms with America. It could not have been for the want of the company of Lancashire folk, for there were plenty of them in Fall River at the time. Indeed, my parents talked Lancashire dialect to Lancashire folk in Fall River so much that they adopted few Americanisms.

I'm sure that father would never have returned to Blackburn on his own. In all the years I knew him, only once did he speak about my future. "Tha'd do well to get across," he said to me one day. "It's better for the likes of us at t' other side." On that occasion I sensed a feeling that he had made a mistake in leaving Fall River. There was a touch of conscience about it. I think mother kept at him about going back to Blackburn so much that he eventually gave in. After all, my parents were rich enough and young enough to migrate again. Father was highly skilled and had the right connections; he could always get a job in Fall River. With cotton textiles booming on both sides of the Atlantic Ocean, he felt free to come and go. They had plenty of money and plenty of time. There would always be work for skilled Lancashire folk.

Grandmother Selma may have been another reason for their leaving – perhaps a major reason. I never heard mother express any warmth toward her. While she admired Selma's toughness and resolution in migrating as a widow with so many children, she couldn't stand her domineering ways. Selma was always interfering. There were times when mother wondered whether Jenny, Brenda, and Dan were her children or Selma's. Selma also got on mother's nerves with her constant criticism of England.

When Selma heard rumours of my parents' decision to return to Britain in 1914, she couldn't believe it. Having taken all the trouble to escape from what she called 'Babylon,' here was her eldest son, of his own free will, going back again.

Father knew what Selma's reactions would be. That is why he told mother to break the news. Many years later I asked mother what Selma had said.

"Nothing," mother answered quietly. "She simply took hold of my hair with one hand and flattened me with the other." One blow from Selma's enormous arms was enough. "Then she spat on the ground and walked away."

Until his death, father remained the black sheep of the Fall River Woodruffs. Selma never forgave him for taking her three grandchildren back to England. As a boy he had given her a lot of trouble. She had never forgotten his running away to sea. Until she found out where he was, she worried a great deal. Eventually she bailed him out of the Navy because he was under age. He came home in high feather, as brazen as could be. He must have liked the sea because when he grew up he had another stint as a seaman travelling the world.

I have often wondered why father ran off to the war after he reached Blackburn in 1914. Perhaps the same trait was at work that had caused him to run off to the Navy. Of course, he acted no more strangely than many other men at the time. In 1914 madness prevailed. Shamefaced, he had come in one day shortly after their arrival in Blackburn to announce that he had joined up. Mother was dumbstruck. He was running away. Not so much as by your leave, either. She argued with him; pleaded with him. He had no need to get involved, she told him. The war was not for his age. Heavens name, he was thirty-one. He had a family to think of. Instead of his going to France they should take the first ship back to America.[†] President Wilson had pledged that America would stay out of the war. How could she manage without him? Silently he had stared past her and persisted. His silence had choked her. She had not managed to budge him. His worry was that he might not get to France in time. Like the rest of England he turned a deaf ear to Lord Kitchener's warning that the war would last three years.

A week later, in front of the Town Hall, she attended some kind of ceremony for those who had volunteered to go to the front. She took the three children, Jenny, Brenda, and Dan. There were lots of flags and bunting. She remembered the large Union Jack, fastened to a pole on the Town Hall roof, flapping above their heads. The mayor, a red-faced man wearing an ermine-trimmed robe, a cocked hat, and his chain of office, made a speech about the wickedness of the Hun and the need to fight for freedom and liberty. To the children's delight, a band played. And then, with orders ringing out, and with much stamping of feet and slapping of rifle butts, the men marched off to the railway station.

On the way home, the children waved small Union Jack flags they had been given. Tears blinded Maggie to what was going on. The world, her world at least, had gone stark raving mad. After six weeks training in England, dad was sent to France.

Father may have used the war as an excuse to get away from mother who felt she had made a great mistake in returning to Blackburn. She said the truth had struck her like someone hitting her in the face. She suddenly realized that the Blackburn she had left years before had not changed. She found herself ensnared in the very life from which they had escaped. In comparison to Fall River, Blackburn was small, straggling, dowdy and run down.

"Then why," I asked her, "after so many years in America did you return to England?"

"I wanted to smell the lilies of the valley," she replied, which I suppose was a symbolic way of saying that she wanted to return to her roots in Lancashire. I know she would never have left America had she known that father was going to run off to fight in France.

I once asked my sister Brenda how she explained father's returning to England and his running off to the war.

"Father always was a 'gormless' [witless] creature," she said. "He had the head and brains of a brass knob. He didn't foresee anything because he never thought about anything. He was a grand worker, nobody better, but where brains were concerned he was lost."

Dad's dashing off to war made things much more difficult for mother. The war years, 1914–1918, must have been hard for her. She had three children to care for. When her savings ran out, as they did, she was forced to go and work in the mills.

Mother rarely saw father for the next four years. When he came home on leave, he had changed – the old jauntiness had gone; he was thinner and there was a troubled look about him. "There's going to be nobody left to fight," he had said. My father's coming home on leave in 1916 had meant a second honeymoon for my parents. My birth on 12 September 1916, and the fact that I was named William after him, spoke of the joy they had known.

Until I was about ten I always believed that I had been born in our cottage in Griffin Street.

"Ah, no, Billy," my sister Brenda said one day, "that's where tha wrang; tha was born in t' mill."

My interest aroused, I discovered that I was born prematurely in the carding-room of Hornby's cotton mill, which was only a few minutes from our home in Griffin Street. Day long, mother cleaned cotton there. She told me how – on the morning of my birth – she had fainted before one of the cotton grinders.

"It was the telegrams."

"What telegrams?"

"From t' War Office. The first one they brought to t' mill. The foreman read it to me. It said that your dad was killed and that the War Office regretted it. Just a line to change your life. Everybody was real nice. Told me to go home and rest, and to come back when I was ready."

"Did you?"

"Well, when you don't have any money and your husband is dead and you've got four mouths to feed, including your own and your unborn child, you'd better be ready all the time or you'll starve."

"But dad wasn't dead."

"No, that's right, he wasn't. A week later another telegram came to the mill saying that the first telegram had all been a mistake. Two hours after that you arrived. Patrick Murphy, Hornby's foreman, delivered you on a heap of cotton against a wall in a corner of the shed. Dr. Grieves should have done the job, but he arrived too late. I was in my own bed by the time he got there. With or without Grieves, it was a fine birth. No commotion. Of course, there was the din of the carding machines and the veil of cotton dust, but no bother, all went well. When he'd delivered you, Mr. Murphy dipped his thumb into one of the fire buckets and baptized you, 'Father, Son, and Holy Ghost.' He wrapped you in a sheet and shouted to the other cardroom hands: 'Cum and look! Have you ever seen sich? It's a boy, and a sturdy one at that; worth a drink o' rum and tay, he is.' They came running. 'Oh, a grand bairn, a really grand bairn,' they clucked as they crowded around. 'It's not every day it happens in't shed. Tha can be reet proud of thiself, Maggie, tha can. Spitten image of his dad.' 'Lucky his dad's alive!'

"Later that morning grandmother Bridget came across from Dougdale's mill. The three of us were bundled on to one of the factory's horse-drawn flatbed carts. With you held in my arms, we rattled our way through the streets until we reached our cottage. Two days after you were born, I was back at work, slubbing in the mill; cooking, washing, and cleaning at home."

With mother in the mill during the war years, the job of caring for me fell to my sister Jenny who was eleven years older than me. I think she brought me up more than my mother did. Staying home and keeping house meant the end of her own childhood, and the end also of whatever little schooling she had had. Several times daily she took me from the wooden box which served as my cradle, wrapped me in a blanket and ran to the mill where mother was waiting to suckle me. The suckling done, she then ran back again and rocked me to sleep. When I think of how small my sister must have been, and how hazardous the cobbled streets were with their wet stones, and jostling, horse-drawn carts, the more remarkable it seems.

Once, when Jenny was unwell and could not take me to the mill, mother ignored the factory regulations and left her work. On slipping out of the mill, she had the misfortune to run headlong into the timekeeper at the gate.

"Here, where t' goin'?" he demanded

"Home, t' feed child, it's clemmin' [starving]."

"If tha goes out now, tha stays out!"

Mother returned to the cardroom.

Whatever the drawbacks, being in Jenny's care didn't do me any harm; I thrived. I'm told my sister handled me as well as a grown woman. Indeed, one might say that I had a privileged childhood, for Jenny, whom I later called Gaga, loved me and sang to me all day long. She loved me even more when I began to creep about and play with her. Not many infants can have been loved with such warmth. It is the warmth of love she bestowed on me that I remember best. She never thought of me as a burden. Only reluctantly did she surrender me to mother at the end of the day. Jenny was always pleased when morning came, and mother departed, and she could reclaim me as her own.

When in later years I suggested that I'd robbed her of her schooling, she countered: "Playing with a baby brother was much better than going to school, especially here." She didn't like English schools. She never forgave the Blackburn school children for ripping the buttons off her brand-new American coat. She'd never known anything but America and felt alienated. After four years in an American school, her accent was almost entirely American. She never saw America again, but she never forgot it. Later on in life when I met her on the streets and asked "Where to, Jenny?" she'd always grin and reply, "America." One day she told me that she had had a dream in which she had travelled back to America in a beautiful gondola.

I don't know whether it was a common practice for a child of eleven to keep house and care for a newborn infant, but Jenny did. After 4 p.m. when my sister Brenda and my brother Dan came home from school, she had to care for them, too. She kept order by putting on a show. Wearing one of mother's wide-brimmed hats – held on with a long hat pin – and long dresses, she clowned and acted for us until mother came home. Then she helped mother to cook and wash and prepare for still another day.

The wonder is that mother and grandmother Bridget should have gone on working in the mill all day while the Woodruff children ran loose. With father away at war, and her savings exhausted, mother had no choice. Her war allowance from father was not enough to keep her going. Her earnings as a slubber in the mill when I was born in 1916 were fifteen shillings per week. Wage increases during the war were offset by ever-rising food prices. Grandmother's savings had gone too, and she had to work to stay alive. She had a tiny cottage not far from Griffin Street. For some reason she never lived with us or her other children – not even during the war. She clung to her independence till the end. Not once can I remember her sharing our house or our board. Later my siblings and I talked about this. Dimly, we felt that there was something wrong. We were never able to explain Bridget's strange stand-offishness. Working-class families were usually close. I was the only one – other than mother – who could reach out to Bridget. Father, Dan, Brenda, and even sweet Jenny found grandma difficult to understand. Bridget simply didn't welcome attention. I sometimes wondered if that was the reason why she didn't remarry. The fact is she lived in a world of her own.

There were times during the war when mother felt that the whole world was crazy. There'd never been such slaughter. She told me how the first casualty lists from the 1916 battle of the Somme had stunned the whole of Blackburn. The tragedy was on such a scale that the common people simply couldn't comprehend it. Everybody felt they'd been kicked in the belly. "You couldn't go out, without having to stop and hold somebody's hand," she said. "Death was common. Black clothing was everywhere. The best went to France and got killed, the rubbish stayed home. It frayed everybody's nerves; put everybody's temper on edge." One day she'd gone out and bumped into Mrs. Ball who had lost her three sons on the Somme. "I held her by the hand and nearly died," mother told me. Like many others, mother wondered whether the war was a scourge sent by God. Some people took to religion, others to drink, squandering their money away. Fortune-tellers had a heyday; licentiousness grew; a coarse life became coarser. Mother remembered vividly the excitement in Britain when German Zeppelins first bombed London in May 1915. Innocent people had been killed asleep in bed. What was the world coming to?

Like so many of her generation, mother blamed the war for everything. Whatever misfortunes followed 1914, she put them down to the war. She always held that it had changed father for the worse. The man who left her to fight in France in 1914 was not the man who returned in 1918. "My Will never really came home again," she said. "Fellow who did come home was somebody else. He'd had t' stuffin' knocked out of him."

Father certainly paid a price for his actions. Like so many others, dad came home from the war disillusioned. His experiences must have shattered his earlier desire for change and adventure. He fought for three years as a private with the infantry on the western front until he was wounded late in 1917, and was invalided out of the Army in 1918. He returned to Griffin Street, Blackburn, a sick man.

Both body and mind were affected. For years he had a racking cough from the gassing he'd suffered at the third battle of Ypres late in 1917. It was the first time the Germans had used mustard gas, and the first time they had deployed it by gunfire. Earlier they had used large canisters from which the gas was released when the wind was favourable. Releasing gas by shellfire had caught the British unawares. The soldiers had panicked when they saw the clouds of gas; clutching their throats and screaming with pain, they had fallen where they stood. Father was a great runner and had taken to his heels. He was one of the last to fall, one of the first to be picked up and treated.

It was when father was in hospital in France recovering from his gassing that he saw the King. It was a great honour to see the King. One day, when he was in a talking mood, he told me about it.

"You never saw such a cleaning up as went on," he said. "One day, the place looked like a slaughterhouse; the next, there were flowers everywhere. They brought a giant orderly into the ward who picked up the bodies and shuffled them about like dolls. Some of the patients cursed him, but anybody who stank or looked horrible had to go. I recognized the small grey-bearded, khaki-clad figure as he entered the ward. 'That's him,' somebody called. Poor devil rushed past my bed as if he had a train to catch. There was such a long crocodile of people chasing after him that anybody standing on crutches had to hobble noisily out of the way. Here and there he'd stop, pin a medal on to somebody's shirt, and mumble something. At least he had the gumption not to stick his nose behind the curtains where the German wounded lay. Once he'd gone with 'Three cheers for the King,' the giant orderly shuffled the bodies back again. The next day the ward was its usual bloody self."

"Did you feel bucked up by the visit?" I asked.

"I felt the same after he left as when he came. I felt sorrier for him, I suppose, than he felt for me. He never lost his bewildered look."

The small disability pension they gave father when they invalided him out of the Army in 1918 was soon cut off. Except for the war, he enjoyed supreme health throughout his life.

On another occasion father told me that by the time he left the front late in 1917, a great disillusionment had settled on the battlefield. Phrases like self-sacrifice and sacred duty were not heard any more. No longer was there the fraternizing with German troops that there had been on that first Christmas in 1914. Anybody who fraternized was brought up sharp – very sharp. Bellyachers were silenced. To get a 'Blighty' – a wound that would take one home out of the carnage – or to be killed were the only ways out. His mob came close to mutiny. Hardly a week passed without a deserter being shot. They sent a staff colonel with a red band on his hat to talk them round. Told them they should be ashamed of themselves; asked them 'Where is your love of country?' Gave them a good raking over, he did; said they didn't give a damn for freedom. Dad felt like telling him that the only freedom they had was the freedom to get killed. First whiff of cordite and the red hat was gone. When they gave dad a rifle in 1914, he had felt like two men, he said. Like being on a horse. By 1918 he was glad to be rid of the gun and the uniform. After that he had to learn the hard way that the politicians' promise of a 'Land Fit for Heroes' was pie-crust thick.

Father's recklessness in volunteering to fight for Britain in 1914 was the last straw for grandmother Selma. Yet she had not hesitated to encourage her other sons to fight for the United States once America had entered the war. There used to be a newspaper cutting in the family showing a picture of Selma with her sons in uniform sitting on her porch in Fall River under the stars and stripes. The accompanying article, which I read as a boy in Lancashire, claimed that she had more sons serving in the United States Army and Navy than any other mother in Massachusetts.

Grandmother Selma lived into her mid-nineties.

I can remember nothing of my father's homecoming or of the rejoicing that signalled the end of the greatest war there had ever been. My first dim memory of him is the glee he took in throwing me against the ceiling. It was a short distance, but to me it seemed quite far. "One, two, three, whoops!" he called out, against mother's protests. I also remember him rasping my soft cheek with his coarse beard. The more I squirmed to escape, the harder he rasped. It was not a game that I enjoyed, yet it was preferable to the strangely silent, withdrawn man that I was to know later on. Always his name to me was Dadda. Like grandmother Selma, mother called him Will.

At least there was a job for him when he returned to Griffin Street after the war. As far as profits were concerned, nothing had helped the Lancashire textile industry as much as the war. Despite the sky-rocketing price of cotton, brought on by speculators once the United States had entered the war in 1917, the last year of the war (1918) was the most prosperous year in the industry's history. More money was made in Lancashire cotton textiles that year than in any previous twelve months.[†]

With such an immediate demand for his skills, I think the idea of returning to Fall River gradually fell out of father's reckoning. The state of his finances didn't give him that option. He must have been poor on coming home from the war. Moreover, the longer he delayed returning to America, the less chance he had. By 1920, beset by the severe competition of the newly-established South Carolina cotton mills, Fall River was experiencing the same decline Blackburn and the other cotton towns in Lancashire had undergone earlier. Letters from his brothers in Fall River told him so. Naturally, Fall River, like Blackburn, thought the industry was suffering a temporary setback. My father's brothers in America were no more able to forecast the decline of the industry in Fall River than father could in Blackburn. In the following year (1921) two other events took place that further discouraged father's return to the United States. President Harding signed the nation's first generally restrictive immigration act. Emigrating to America was no longer just a matter of catching a boat. Also, in 1921 a recession beset the American economy.

Jenny continued to care for me until she entered the factory at the age of thirteen.[†] By then the Great War had almost run its course. Thenceforth I was farmed out to baby-sitters who lived in the vicinity. This went on for several years until I went to school when I was almost five. The only baby-sitters I can remember were Mrs. Beddle and Mrs. Allison who took care of me shortly before I went to school.

Mrs. Beddle was a short, red-faced, warm-hearted barrel of a woman, with an unpleasant smell, who seemed to roll about the house rather than walk. As her skirt touched the ground, I could never decide whether she moved on wheels or feet. Her only inheritance from her husband, who had been lost at sea, was a large green parrot called Toby. Mrs. Beddle always spoke to the parrot as if she were talking to her dead husband.

"What do you think we should do now, Mr. Beddle?" she would ask, turning to the bird.

Peering through the wires of the cage, Toby would blink a lot before answering; sometimes scratching his head gravely. Finally, he would pull his head back and ruffle his feathers as if he was about to say something of the utmost importance. He must have had a lot of advice to give, for once started, he would squawk and screech on and on like a cotton grinder. Toby had been to sea for long periods in the course of which he had picked up words which the barrel-like woman said would have been better left behind. Words like "Well, damn my eyes!" always threw her into fits.

One morning when I arrived, the bird was hidden beneath a cloth where he remained silent and unrepentant throughout the day. I never did find out what he'd done.

Mrs. Beddle was always strict about my eating habits, and was ever ready to sit down and help if my bread and cheese, or hot-pot, proved to be too much for me.

"More harm," she cautioned, "comes from eating too much, than from eating too little. We mustn't overeat, must we," she warned, as her fork repeatedly stabbed and carried off what I thought was a disproportionate part of my dinner. But then she had almost no resources of her own. Eating my dinner was the only way Mrs. Beddle could gain relief from the stomach growlings which went on all the time.

The other baby-sitter, Mrs. Allison, had a strange way of running to the door while calling "Is that you, Jack? Is that you?" In her haste to get to the street, she would drop whatever she was holding. The odd thing about it was that Jack was never there. Nor was anybody else.

"I thow't it was 'im," she'd say sadly on returning from the door; "I thow't it was 'im."

Then she'd carry on as though nothing had happened.

The longer I stayed with Mrs. Allison, whose heavy eyebrows and large nose gave her a frightening appearance, and whose ammonia smell was no better than Mrs. Beddle's, the more she ran to the door. One day I told mother about it.

"She's lost her only son," mother explained.

"Is he dead?"

"He just disappeared. Nobody knows where. It's left her a bit queer in t' head. Mrs. Allison is a good woman," she assured me.

It's just as well she was, for I was left in her care for hours on end.

90

VII   World outside my door

Apart from going with Jenny to see the horses at the trough outside the Griffin pub, close to our house, I saw little of the streets in my early days. The streets were considered an unsuitable place for a young child, and my parents were always too busy to take me to a park or to the countryside. Sometimes they took me to the open air market in town. Unless we went on the tram, which cost a penny, and which we never used if father was in charge, we were faced by what a child thought was an endless march through all kinds of weather.

Once when father and I were coming home through a blizzard, which had struck unusually late in the year and had fallen upon us suddenly, I shouted to him that we should take the penny tram ride home. He didn't even turn round. "Tha won't melt" he shouted into the wind, as he continued to clump his way along the snow-covered pavement. With the bitter snow-laden wind stinging my eyes and pricking my face, I followed as best I could. Alongside us, steaming horses and snow-covered carts, piled high with empty beer barrels, plunged through the dirty puddles and the growing slush. My heart sank as I watched the tram, on which I had set all my hopes, lurch past. Screaming its protest at the weather, and I hope at father, it disappeared into the surrounding gloom where its yellow eye flickered and died. In desperation, I followed the snowman who trudged on before me. The usual crowds of people had disappeared.

By the time we reached home, father and I were covered from head to foot with snow. The sidewalks had long since disappeared from view. Other than to stamp our feet and shake ourselves like dogs, we entered the cottage as if nothing had happened. Until our clothing dried, we stood on newspapers before a roaring fire drinking hot tea. My sisters had been bundled upstairs. Despite the fact that we were both steaming like sheets taken out of the boiling set pot, nothing was said about our nakedness or the weather.

I saw a great deal of my father when I was a child, but I rarely got close to him. Other than mother, nobody did. When I was small, he would talk at great length to me, especially about the Woodruffs and their adventures in America, for which he had a lasting love. By the time I was born he'd not only lived in America, he'd been round the world. As a boy he had run away to sea and had got as far as China. Later he had gone to sea again. People used to point at him and say, "Will Woodruff's been to China and to America." He it was who taught me what a big place the world was. He had many strange tales to tell. He'd seen volcanoes erupting into the sky; he'd seen whales and seals and many creatures of the sea. As a sailor he'd visited lands where there were lions and tigers and giraffes and elephants. He knew what it was to climb the ship's rigging and take in the sail in a mounting storm. In far-eastern waters he'd seen ships scattered by a typhoon. He'd seen so many different things and had met so many different people that I came to the conclusion that he'd been everywhere, and had seen and heard everything. When he told me that we go to bed when the Chinese are waking up, the effect upon me was electrifying. I can still hear him saying it. The Chinese intrigued him.

As the years passed, he became ever more silent and heavy of mood. Sometimes he was almost dumb. As everybody else's father liked to talk, his silence struck me as odd. I've trudged miles with him through the streets of Blackburn, loaded with bags, without exchanging a word. I always wished it would happen but I can never remember him holding my hand or carrying me on his back or patting my head. Although he kissed mother good night before going to sleep, he never kissed me or anyone else in public. Kissing was not a Woodruff trait. Even when he stood me on a box in front of one of his looms to teach me the rudiments of weaving he didn't say much.

I not only went shopping with my parents, I went drinking with them too. Every Saturday night, when they were in work, was spent at their favourite pub. Sober from Monday to Saturday, they would break out and make up for lost time. Sometimes with other young children, mostly by myself, I'd wear out the night sitting in the pub kitchen. It was a dreary experience. The smell of stale beer and cigarette smoke was everywhere. Worse, I was warned by the pub-keeper's wife to sit still and keep my hands off everything. Nor was my loneliness relieved by the pub-keeper's cat or dog. The moment I appeared in the kitchen they fled to some hidden corner from which they hissed and growled at me for the rest of the night. Their noise was drowned by the clash of glasses, the shouts, the wild laughter, and the snatches of song coming from the bar. "Meet me in love's sweet garden, down where the roses grow…" "Oh, you beautiful doll, you great, big beautiful doll…" People drank more if they sang. A pub bar late on a Saturday night was not the place for inhibitions.

Occasionally I was able to escape into a picture book which the pub-keeper's wife thrust into my hands. She didn't growl at me or hiss, but I knew better than to say that she had given me the same book for the past three weeks. I also whiled away the hours by listening to the bar piano. When all else failed, I made a dream world of the fire, or watched the second hand twitch its way across the face of the inevitable Westminster Chime clock standing in the corner. However the night passed, it came as a relief when I heard the cry "Time, gentlemen, please." After that, amid muttered farewells to those who had left the pub with us, and who seemed reluctant to go home, we walked through the dark streets, my parents discussing the latest gossip. There was always something or other that had caught their fancy. In time, as they often changed their "favourite" pub, I came to know most of the pub kitchens in Blackburn.

One night all monotony vanished when a fight broke out in the bar. I knew from the dreadful things being shouted that somebody had run off with somebody else's wife. There was such bawling and screaming and smashing of glasses and furniture that I feared for my parents' lives. With distraught faces they rushed into the kitchen, scooped me up and fled into the night. We never drank there again.

I have happier memories as a small child of going with my parents to the music hall at the Theatre Royal. I used to peer down from the gods – which cost 3d. – on the most exciting scenes. The music, the flood-lit stage, the sparkle, and the glitter intoxicated me. Never before had I seen so many well-dressed, beautiful, rich people. Everything they did belonged to another world. Nobody in our street talked like that, nobody dressed like that, nobody was so cheeky or so swaggering. They would come right up to the edge of the stage and talk to you as if they'd known you all your life. Then they'd get everybody to sing "Ta-ra-ra-boom-de-ay" until the windows rattled. I liked the comedians least of all; they spoke so quickly that I had no idea what they were talking about. It was at the music hall that I saw a man with elastic skin and a dog-faced child; I saw a lady cut in half, a man swallow fire, billiard balls multiply on command, and a magician take a pigeon out of his hat. It was quite common for the performers' hats to rise in the air and for their hair to stand on end. I was entranced. I believed everything I saw. I felt cheated when the audience booed the performers or threw rotten tomatoes at them. I've known the curtain be rung down to protect a particularly bad actor from having the life pelted out of him. That's when the mystery and the magic fled; the theatre became commonplace. At such times, I began to notice the fleas. I was also taken to magic lantern slide shows and to one of the first silent films which was accompanied by a pianist; talkies came later. Here again there was always someone who was dissatisfied; at the films the audience took it out on the pianist by pelting him with refuse. Eventually the piano player was forced to take cover behind a tall ivy-covered trellis – whereupon the protesters proceeded to fight among themselves. If you couldn't have a fight, it wasn't worth going.

When money was short we went to "penny readings," where, having paid a penny, we sat quite still on a hard bench in a cold warehouse. The reader was a grey-haired, gaunt-faced elderly gentleman who wore a threadbare suit and a winged collar. His name was Mr. Peck and his false teeth kept slipping. Unable to remember what Mr. Peck had read to us – I recall only the hard seat and the cold – I asked my sister Brenda. She said that he read only classics. From him she had heard abbreviated versions of the works of the Brontë sisters, Dickens, and Robert Louis Stevenson. It was from Mr. Peck that she heard of *Uncle Tom's Cabin*. I gather he first told us in his own words what the story was about, and then filled in by reading from the text.

Some of the happiest moments I had away from home as a child were spent with my sister Jenny. She looked after me, even after she started working in the mills. She was the first to take me on community outings into the countryside. Several Sunday mornings we boarded a horse-drawn coal barge which leisurely made its way on the local canal past the crowded housing, the mills and the slag heaps into the open countryside. We sat on newspapers to protect our clothing from the grime. We made light of dead fish and rats and the odd dog or cat that floated by with distended belly. Mostly we ignored such things; the grown-ups had a way of seeing only what they wanted to.

Once we had left the vile smell of the town and the black poisonous water behind, we were surrounded by meadows alive with birds and bees. The water became clear enough to watch the pike hunt their prey. Breathing deeply, we filled our lungs with the smell of the summer's new-mown hay. Always the meadow larks called. The distinct call of the cuckoo was heard from distant woods. One listened for the answering cry. Listless, flat-topped brown hills touched with shreds of clouds sat all around us. Wild flowers filled the banks. We never passed anybody on the towpath without a shouting match taking place. A boisterous repartee between boat passengers and whoever was on the path was expected. It was part of the fun. The trick was to make sure you got in the last word.

The outings took all day. We'd eat and drink at noon at a pub in the countryside – the horse knew where to find it. From the sips of beer I got on such occasions, I learnt to drink. It was high-spirited self-entertainment all the way. It was taken for granted that anybody who possessed a banjo, or a concertina, a harmonica, or a tin whistle would bring it with him. Everybody was expected to do something, even if it was just to join in the singing, or cheer and clap.

My sister's young man Gordon Weall was one of the better clowns. He would bring a false nose, moustache, teeth, or a wig, and in no time at all he would have the whole barge shaking with laughter. He was a master at disguise. He'd go out of his way to start people laughing, which with Lancashire people was infectious. Once they started laughing, you couldn't stop them. They would laugh and laugh until they gasped for breath and tears ran down their cheeks. The men laughed with a determination to wring the last bit of pleasure out of it. "A good laugh beats all thi medicine," they'd say. The day gone, we'd wend our way home again as the lowing cattle left the fields.

Best of all were the horse-drawn "sharabang" (char-à-banc) trips which also took parties of workers into the countryside. The "sharabang" was a long, open cart in which we sat on benches with our backs to the sides. There was a wide step at the rear. Behind us, down the length of the wagon, was a rolled tarpaulin which could be pulled over our heads in case of rain. The driver sat up on a box behind his two horses, his whip standing in its rest against the sky. It was never used. Mr. Beatty in his wicker bed, this time without the wheels, was placed in the middle of the cart against our legs. Everybody had his place, nobody was neglected. With so many giving a hand, there was never any trouble getting the basket in and out. If we went into a pub, Mr. Beatty went with us.

We started these trips at dawn, coming together in front of the "Griffin." The younger women wore colourful dresses with wide brimmed straw hats held on with ribbons. The older women had a kerchief wrapped tightly around their heads and fastened under the chin. The men wore trousers, shirts, and caps; every head was covered. Everybody brought their own food. There was always a lot of shouting and laughter before we got away. There were no religious barriers.

We spent the whole summer's day in country lanes, sometimes passing through woods with the bright sun piercing the boughs; other times crossing open fields; still other times experiencing the great silence of the moors, a silence broken only by the cries of the pewits and the curlews, and the chatter of rushing streams. Every now and again, as we jolted through the ruts, we'd be bounced about a bit, or be thrown backward and forward as if we were riding a wave. "Whoa!" everybody would yell, as we lurched forward: "Whoa!" when we were thrown back again, while laughing ourselves sick. No setback was allowed to interfere with our merrymaking. If we struck an especially deep hole or root, we'd hang on to Mr. Beatty's basket and roll with him while he drooled. In the hilliest parts, the young got out and pushed. Mrs. Beatty was for ever attentive to Mr. Beatty, wiping his face, feeding him, and sheltering him from the sun. You'd wonder how she could have been as happy as she was.

As a result of my sister's pleading, I was allowed to sit up front on a high box next to Mr. Fisher, the driver. I was proud to be sat up there next to Mr. Fisher, but I'm not sure that he had the same feelings toward me. He sat like a stone at my side, towering above me. He was the only man wearing a bowler hat. The grown-ups called it his "badge of office." He never took his eyes off the road, never turned round to see what was going on behind him, never acknowledged that I was there. At least he seemed deaf to anything I had to say; especially when I asked if I could hold the reins. Later on he gave me the reins and told me to start the cart. I swelled with pride at the idea. However, his two horses, Polly and George, both reddish-brown giants, ignored my "Giddups!" They wouldn't budge. Finally, they looked round at me so pitifully that I could do little else but hand the reins back.

What fascinated me about Mr. Fisher was his ability to carry on a conversation with his horses and his passengers at the same time. As Mr. Fisher never looked back I was never sure if he was talking to the horses or the passengers.

"You're a sly one, you are, you want it your way." And then without moving his head or his body, or even taking a breath, he'd go on: "No there's been no change in Sarah's condition. One says it's rheumatics, another says its water. I'll tell ye one thing, that there medicine she's got now is sheer poison. I know, because I tried a drop. If that doesn't do it, nothing will. What did I tell you," he continued without a pause, "I knew you'd leave it to him." I could only think that "you" was Polly, the horse. "For all the good you're doing, you might as well sit up here with us." And then without any sign that he was changing the conversation: "No it's the red, murky stuff; bottle should be marked kill or cure; can't say I'm drawn to it."

And so the day went on until we'd visited our last pub and everyone was warm and merry back in the "sharabang." The horses always knew when the homeward journey had begun – they pulled harder. Everybody took it for granted that we'd sing ourselves home. As the light faded and the "sharabang" rattled on we sang:

> Come lasses and lads, get leave of your dads,
> And away to the Maypole hie,
> For ev'ry fair has a sweetheart there,
> And the fiddler's standing by ...

and

> Buy my caller herrin. They're bonnie fish and halesome farin'.
> Buy my caller herrin. Just new-drawn frae the Forth.
> When ye were sleepin' on your pillows, dream'd ye aught of our
> poor fellows,
> Darklin' as they faced the billows, all to fill our woven willows? ...

and

> In Dublin's fair city, where the girls are so pretty,
> I first set my eyes on sweet Molly Malone.
> As she wheeled her wheelbarrow through streets broad and narrow,
> Crying, 'Cockles and mussels, alive, alive, oh!'...

We sang the songs we all knew. Although it was Sunday, we sang few hymns; though one day, when crossing a large moor wreathed in mist, we sang "Out on an Ocean all Boundless We Ride." Sometimes the men would lead, sometimes the women; sometimes there was two-part harmony, sometimes three- or four-part. Whoever was moved to sing, sang. I noticed how still everyone in the "sharabang" became when the rich voices fell silent.

In the stillness I listened to the jingle of the harness and the whispering sounds in the darkening hedgerows and meadows around us. I watched Mr. Fisher's lamps of flickering yellow patches light our way.

And then, after a mile or two, unheralded, soaring to the sky, came Patrick Mulroony's voice singing Oh Danny Boy.

> Oh Danny boy, the pipes, the pipes are calling
> From glen to glen, and down the mountain side.
> The summer's gone, and all the leaves are falling
> 'T is you, 't is you must go and I must bide.

Out of the dusk, his brother Mike joined in from the other end of the cart.

> But come ye back when summer's in the meadow
> Or all the valley's hushed and white with snow
> 'T is I'll be here in sunshine or in shadow
> Oh Danny boy, oh Danny boy, I love you so.

> But when ye come and all the flowers are dying,
> And I am dead, as all the flowers must die,
> Ye come and find the place where I am lying,
> And kneel and say an ave where I lie.

> And I shall hear, though soft you tread above me,
> And in the dark my soul will wake and see.
> For you'll bend down and tell me that you love me.
> And I shall sleep in peace for all eternity.

There was no strain; no difficulty keeping the other's pace. The two men just opened their mouths and in high, soft, flowing voices sang like birds. Everybody joined in toward the end. By the light of the stars I saw Mrs. Mulroony and my sister Jenny weeping, though I knew I should not have looked. Few things can be as beautiful as a cart full of simple people harmoniously singing their way home through the gloaming with gladness in their hearts.

Later I watched Mr. Fisher play a game in the dark with Mr. Beatty. Without moving his seat, Mr. Fisher reached back until he could grab some part of Mr. Beatty. Having got hold of him, he pretended to shake him like a terrier shakes a rat. "Grrrr," he went. Mr. Beatty must have known who it was, for he gave the same squeal of delight every time it happened.

Mrs. Beatty enjoyed it too. "Oh! Oh!" she cried every time Mr. Fisher's hand approached, "we must stop him, Eric, mustn't we?" Between these attacks, she wiped her husband's dribble and played with his hair.

The grown-ups said that Mr. Beatty and Mr. Fisher had gone off as young men in 1914 to fight the war in France. Mr. Beatty had been hit with a shell. He would have bled to death had Mr. Fisher not scooped up what was left of him and, risking his own life, run back through the mud looking for help. Mr. Fisher, they said, had saved Mr. Beatty's life. Some said that was a good thing; others didn't seem so sure. They looked down their noses and studied their clogs and said, "Mm ... mm," in a very serious grown-up way.

97

By the time we got back to the "Griffin," I was fast asleep across Mr. Fisher's knees. I don't know how long I had been there. I can remember him holding me up while everybody stood and sang:

Praise God, from whom all blessings flow.
Praise Him all creatures here below;
Praise Him above, ye heav'nly host;
Praise Father, Son, and Holy Ghost.

VIII   Schooling

Because my parents did not want to go on paying a baby-sitter, at the age of four I was sent to St. Philip's school round the corner from where we lived. As I was to turn five several weeks later, nobody commented on my age. The law was ignored. On my first schoolday Brenda took me by the hand and left me in my classroom. I think I was smaller than most of my companions, and I remember feeling afraid. I had good reason to be.

My schoolmates were a wild lot. They were forever digging each other with dirty pen nibs, bumping and elbowing each other, farting, spitting at each other, drenching each other with water pistols, or dragging each other down to the floor. Scores that could not be settled in the classroom were settled amid yelling and screaming in the school yard. Newcomers were always roughed up by bullies who ran in a pack.

One day, shortly after I began my school career, I was playing in the school yard when I had my first taste of cruelty. Without any warning, a pack of bullies knocked me down. I expected my brother who was also there to defend me. He didn't. Yet Dan was quick with his fists. His walking away from me on that occasion coloured my view of him for the rest of my life.

With my ears ringing from the first blows, I appealed to the older children in the playground to help me. Instead they took pleasure in watching me get bashed. As I was too small to fight my attackers on equal terms, I tried to seize their legs and topple them. One or two kicks in the face with steel-capped clogs put a stop to that. By then, with stars dancing before my eyes, I didn't know where I was, or where the school was. In a blind, crying rage all I could do was to hang on to one of my opponents and, in a tangle and a tussle, have the wind knocked out of me. Every time I broke free and managed to get to my feet, weeping and gasping for breath, I was thrown down again.

Only when my face was covered with blood was I allowed to scramble through the pack and run in search of my sister Brenda who I knew was playing in the girl's yard next door. She was horrified when she saw my

98

already swollen lips and puffed-up face. "I'll murder them for this, Billy," she hissed as she took me home. Despite her bathing my face, I must have been a ghastly sight when my parents came home that night. Mother was shocked. "Tha's been at it agin," was dad's only comment.

Back to school I went the next day.

A week or so later, before my wounds had healed, three bullies grabbed me in the playground again. My earlier terror was renewed. At first I managed to break away, but they recaptured me and dragged me down. At that moment a fury landed in our midst. It was Brenda. "I'll show you," she shouted, "hurting our Billy! Take that ... and that ... and that!" Like a wild animal she rained blows upon them until they pleaded for mercy. They got none. Scores were settled without the unforgivable act of running to the teachers to tell tales. At my schools, tell-tale tits always got their tongues slit, or something equally dreadful. Everybody in the school yard was deeply impressed with Brenda. Henceforth, for as long as I stayed at St. Philip's, I may not have been popular – which priggish-like I sought to be – but at least no one dreamed of touching me. Even so, my early schooling was not a happy experience and I can remember the relief I felt when the school day was done and Brenda came to take me home.

The more I think of my first schoolroom at St. Philip's, the more improbable it seems. I remember our teacher Mr. Manners as a small man with a thin waist. He had large, thoughtful grey eyes and a hollow face concealed behind a pepper and salt moustache. He wore a stiff, high collar and a dark suit that, like his bald head, shone with age. More than anything else I remember Joe, the idiot, Mr. Manners' nephew, a little grey figure with a swollen, misshapen face, and a cast in one eye, who sat on the front row directly in front of his uncle with nothing better to do than to pick his nose. That was bad. Eating the stuff was revolting. Hardly a day went by without Mr. Manners breaking off lessons to give Joe a slap on the head for his antics.

Joe and Mr. Manners seemed to be tied to each other with an invisible rope. When one stood, the other stood. When one sat down, the other sat down. When one left the room, the other followed him, even to the toilet. They came together in the morning; on and off they fought until noon when they sat in the classroom and had their dinner together. The battles were renewed in the afternoon. They left together at night, a weary Mr. Manners muttering to himself in an absentminded sort of way, a radiant Joe. Joe must have thought that life was a funny business, for he was always laughing. When he wasn't laughing he looked older than his years. He was the only child there in a suit, shirt, tie, and shoes. Now and again he would jab one of us with a pen nib to let us know he was still about.

The decorations in Mr. Manners' classroom were meager. There was a stained print of Boadicea, an ancient British queen, and a torn map of the world. Most of the map was painted red, "The British Empire, our Empire," Mr. Manners assured us. I had no idea why we had such a big empire except that it was taken for granted that we were better than anybody else. Of the song we sang every year on Empire Day (24th May), I remember only the first two lines: "What is the meaning of Empire Day, why do the cannon roar?" The meaning to me was that we got free buns and half a day off school. There was also a large Lever Brother's Lifeboy Soap poster. The rest of the room was covered with our caps and coats hanging on hooks. Because of the occasional outbreak of head lice, one took care to keep one's cap separate from the others. The soap poster covered most of the wall at my side; it showed a bar of lathered Lifeboy Soap with a finger which pointed directly at me. Beneath the finger in great letters were the words "WHERE THERE'S DIRT, THERE'S DANGER!"

That poster worried me. I took it personally – after all the finger did point at me. Why had Mr. Manners sat me there? My neck was no dirtier than the others'. Nor did the poster lead me to wash my neck anymore than I was doing. Washing in such a cold, wet climate didn't come easy with us. I never knew anyone in my early years who believed that cleanliness was next to godliness. I think we believed in being comfortably dirty.

Oddly enough, it was Lifeboy Soap coupons that obtained for me the first book I ever owned. It was a one-volume encyclopedia called *The Wonderland of Knowledge*. I took the trouble to save the coupons. My letter to Lever Brothers was the first letter I ever wrote and I haunted the postman every day after I posted it. I was so excited when the package arrived. It was addressed to me. I wouldn't let anyone touch it. I refused to have the string cut and preferred to struggle to untie the knots. After some minutes, I extracted the book from its cardboard box and laid it on the table. It smelled so new and clean. You wouldn't believe it but it was 10½" long by 7½" wide by 1½" thick. I know because I measured it. It must have weighed several pounds. The cover was a treat for the eyes; it was dark blue; in the centre was a man reaching out for the sun, the moon, and the stars.

I must have obtained the book several years after I had learnt to read, for I gorged myself on it. It was never out of my hands. I never dreamt that a book could contain so much knowledge. And not only knowledge, but inspiration. "You are now standing," it said on the title page, "at the Gateway to the Wonderland of Knowledge ... the key to your future and the future of the World. For you will learn by the past deeds of Men and Nations what good things to do and what bad things not to do. You will be inspired by the nobility and perseverance of those who rose from humble birth to sway by Thought or Deed the destiny of Man. And what they did, you too may do."

At the time I wondered why the author kept stressing the "humble birth" bit.

"Anybody who buys books with soap coupons, Billy," my sister Brenda concluded, "would have to be of humble birth."

The book started by tracing the history of the world. I'd never heard about Ancient Egypt, or the Chaldeans, or the Jews, or the Cretans, but it told me. The Ancient Egyptians and the Jews ranked higher than the rest because they had more than one section each. I'd no idea How Music Began, or of the Seven Giants of Music, or the need for Mighty Music of Our Modern Age, but it told me that too.

There was nothing the book didn't tell me. Having read Music Through the Ages, I plunged into The Romance of Exploration from Marco Polo onward. I didn't realize the world was so big.

After that I tackled the Great Names in English Literature – thirty-two of them. Of the thirty-two I had heard of only two – Shakespeare and Milton, and not much of them either. Writers like the Venerable Bede and Samuel Pepys were eye-openers for me.

There followed the Marvels of Invention. There was even a section on Spinning and Weaving. Then came Wonders of the Insect World. This was the only part of the book that I couldn't get excited about, though I did enjoy the section headed Ogres of the Insect World.

I think by the time the editor had got through with the Ogres, he was ready to pitch anything in and take his pay. Under Miscellaneous I learnt How to Build a House, Where Our Pearls Come From, and The Story of Buttons.

From The Story of Buttons under the heading Stories Retold, the book made a strange diversion to The Story of Beowulf. I never did understand what Buttons had to do with Beowulf.

My attention was then engaged with Things to Make and Do. This section was full of useful ideas. It taught me, if I needed to know, how to make a Clothes Hanger, a Sled, a Hockey stick, a Barrel Stave, Skis, and a Dutch Jumper. From this point the ambitious were encouraged to try their hand at making a Whistle, a Passe-partout Frame, Batiked Glass, an Alligator, an Igloo, an Algernon Peanut – which took some doing – a Kangaroo, and a Dodo.

The book ended with Puzzles and Tricks – which I learnt by heart – and, best of all, a section on Magic.

I suppose that next to the Bible, the *Wonderland of Knowledge* was the most important book I ever possessed. Being the only book I owned, I read it and re-read it until I knew it backwards. I created my own adventure in learning. The book was my most valuable possession and I possess it still.

Father was not struck by it. Mother opened her eyes with awe when I began to rattle off my knowledge. "Imagine you knowing everything," she said.

Anyway, back to school and Mr. Manners. I think the poor man must have worked himself to death. He sat at a bare table on a platform in front of us. He stayed with us from morning till night. Behind him was the blackboard. Above his head hung an electric light bulb with a plain shade.

Working on the blackboard he taught us the alphabet, arithmetic, and the names of our kings and queens from King Canute on. He also taught us the names of distinguished Englishmen and the battles they had won. We copied these things on our slates and then erased them with a rag. We rarely used ink and paper which cost more. He taught us the names of the local rivers and towns; not to mention lots of other things that many of us thought nobody needed to know. He also taught us how to spell. We learnt by chanting in a sing-song voice, sometimes swaying to the letters, words, or numbers. I found it easy to learn by jingles: "Two pints make one quart, four quarts make one gallon ..." Or, "Thirty days hath September, April, June, and November. All the rest ..." I have dozens of these jingles in my head. If I can remember them after seventy years, then I did learn something in school after all.

For me, St. Philip's was a bleak place except at Christmas when the whole school was transformed into a magic castle. I must have been very impressionable for, when my first Christmas at school came round, I watched transfixed while teachers and students converted dark, crowded classrooms into glittering caves. Fluttering coloured paper streamers, pom-poms, Chinese lanterns, and decorations were hung everywhere. Helped by the ever-present drafts, the great silver bells swung leisurely above our heads. When the gas lamps were lit in the afternoon, the sense of magic grew.

Everything at school was transformed at Christmas. A feeling of festivity filled the air. There was no thrashing. The cruel use of the Dunce's hat – which I feared more than anything – was temporarily discontinued. Even Mr. Manners and Joe took a rest from fighting. We didn't do a stitch of work. We played leap frog and had snowball fights in the school yard. We formed choirs and produced plays. For the plays we created scenery, properties and costumes out of nothing. We rehearsed the plays several times. I remember the fun I got out of doing these things. I also learnt about language and elocution in the process.

In one of the plays I was chosen to tip-toe into an artist's studio and place my head in the hole another student had made in the artist's canvas. The whole idea was that the artist would fail to notice that his canvas had been damaged and would go on touching up the face – my face – with paint. All I had to do was to put my head into the hole and keep absolutely still.

When the great night came and most of our parents were in attendance, I crept into the artist's studio. Having made sure that the artist was not there I placed my head into the hole in the canvas. At that point the artist returned with his paints. This was the part we had never rehearsed properly. Instead of applying a dab of paint to my face – as he had been instructed – he began to plaster me with the stuff. Howls of laughter came from the audience. When I opened my mouth to protest, he popped the paint brush right down my throat. By now the audience was uncontrollable. The play was considered a great success, but the taste of paint stayed with me for days.

Just before Christmas the older boys carried in a Christmas tree dusted with snow. It was so high and so wide that they had difficulty getting it through the doors. I was intoxicated when they hung the tree with decorations and candles. It became a mass of colour and light. I had never seen such a beautiful thing. How it contrasted with the dark day! They also brought in the crib with statues of Mary and Joseph, and the Infant Jesus, and the Three Wise Men from the East. There also was a cow eating from the manger. Thus did I first learn of the joy and peace of Christmas.

While we were singing carols around the tree, a horse-drawn cart arrived at the school laden with wooden crates filled with boxes of chocolates. The news spread like wildfire. Some kind soul, whose name has long since been forgotten, had donated a box for every child. In those days of poverty and shortages, such a gift was overwhelming. We shrieked with delight as box after box was extricated from the wood shavings. Each chocolate box lid was a delight in itself. My box showed a boy and a girl skating down a frozen river with snow-covered cottages lining the banks. It was sheer magic for me to possess such a prize. I kept the lid for ages.

Somebody at this time gave me a Chinese paper lantern with a candle inside which I lit when my brother and sisters took me round the darkened streets singing carols. "Christmas is coming," we all chanted,

> The geese are getting fat,
> Please to put a penny in the old man's hat;
> If you haven't got a penny, a ha'penny will do.
> If you haven't got a ha'penny, God bless you."

I seem to remember that we gave a lot of blessings and received some ha'pennies.

In time, I made many friends at school. We never called each other by the names our parents had given us. We called each other "Woody," or "Fatty," or "Freckles" or "Skinny." Children were also known by the colour of their hair, "Red," or "Blackie," or because of some remark or attribute associated with them. Sometimes the friendships lasted for years; sometimes they were short-lived.

On occasions the friendships were placed under great strain. I remember a good friend of mine, Harold Watkins, turning to me in the classroom for help one day. The teacher had asked Harold a question which he obviously couldn't answer. Nor could I. Without thinking, I whispered a phrase which grandmother Bridget had taught me the previous evening and which was still jumping about in my head. Words fascinated me. Tell him that "Discretion is the better part of valour," I whispered. I was surprised at the speed with which Harold fastened on to the phrase, and repeated it out loud. Neither of us really knew what discretion was or valour. All I know is that Harold got a clout over the ear for it. He always held it against me.

If I cannot remember learning much at school in my early years, it is because my energies were directed elsewhere. After school and on Saturdays, from the age of six, I ran errands – one never walked errands – for a neighbour of ours, Mr. Tinworth, who had turned his front room into a grocer's shop. I was so small that I found it impossible to lift the laden delivery baskets off the floor. Once the grocer had managed to get my arm through the handle, I was able to stagger off down the street. I became expert at carrying the basket on my hip. The grocer paid my parents one shilling and six-pence per week, of which I received one penny. Sometimes, customers would give me a half-penny for carrying their groceries, so I didn't do too badly.

Invariably, I spent the penny I received for my labors on a gob-stopper – a coloured ball of toffee on a stick about the size of a golf ball – which I bought at Mrs. Hudson's tiny sweet shop down the street. She kept the gob-stoppers – upon which her small customers repeatedly choked when the toffee came off the stick – in a big glass jar. I always felt very important when the jar was brought to the counter and I was allowed to dip my grubby hand inside to choose the colour I wanted. Mrs. Hudson's shop was one of the brightest lights in the otherwise grim surroundings. I liked everything about it. I liked the tremendous doorbell that announced my entrance; I liked the warm, sugary, toasty smell that greeted me; I liked all the shiny good things that were there to be eaten. Most of all I liked Mrs. Hudson because hers was the only shop where my opinion counted. In Mrs. Hudson's shop, the customer, however small, was in charge. Spending my penny was the most important decision of the week.

I must have shopped with Mrs. Hudson for several years. We came to know each other quite well. She never changed; she was the same sweet, grey-haired old woman when I met her as when I left. I owe it to her that I know so much about the confectionery industry. When I became more affluent, she introduced me to all kinds of chocolate and sugary delights which she kept in her rows of jars. I think I must have eaten my way through her store. She also taught me to be discerning. Gob-stoppers were all very well when you were a child, but not when you were growing up. Under her guidance, as the weeks and months passed, I moved on through a whole gamut of licorice delights, aniseed balls, and teeth-locking toffee, each piece of which had a different animal on the wrapper, until I reached what Mrs. Hudson thought was the industry's masterpiece: colorful packets of candy cigarettes which looked just like the real thing. I never did reach the chocolate pipe and cigar stage. One Christmas I bought from her a great black chocolate minstrel playing a banjo. It was a

"Christmas special," not available at any other time. I remember eating it
– cannibal-like, banjo and all – in one go from head to foot.

Whatever serious learning I did between the ages of six and ten, I did
at the knee of my sister Brenda and my grandmother Bridget. Brenda was
not only at her best in tough spots, she was also highly intelligent. Other
than father, she was the only one among us who could handle arithmetic.
Sums were a closed book to grandmother Bridget, mother, Jenny, Dan,
and me. It mystified me how Brenda could order figures about the way
she did. No matter how many she wrote down they always did exactly
what she told them to do. Nor did she ever tire of doing completely dull
things with them. Unlike her, I didn't care how long it would take to fill
a water-butt with a hole in the bottom. With a sum here and a sum there,
she was quite happy filling the leaking water-butt for ages. I wondered
why the butt should have had a hole in it in the first place. Why didn't
somebody fix it? Then she would work out how many freight cars were
needed on a train that could stretch from London to Edinburgh.
Everybody knew there couldn't be such a train. It was ridiculous.

Daft as all this seemed to me, she always came up with the right
answers. "You see how easy it is, Billy," she'd say as she arranged the
figures as she wanted them. Well, it did look easy the way she did it, but,
with me, the figures went crazy. The moment I touched them they
stampeded in every direction; they did awful things; they rebelled –
anarchy reigned.

"What on earth are you doing, Billy," Brenda would say, taking over.
"You've made a dreadful hash of it. It's quite simple, really. You just have
to keep your head." Then she lined up the figures again and off they
went. They never failed to obey her. The annoying thing was that she
didn't seem to try. She was like a good collie dog with sheep. Without any
fuss, all the figures finished up in the right pen. "There's nothing to it at
all, Billy," she kept saying as she disposed of the last sheep. There was no
end to the problems she could handle. Indeed, she was always making
problems harder than they need be. Once I managed to get a problem
right. For a moment she was quite startled. "Ah, but that's the answer in
yards," she gloated, "what would it be in feet, Billy? Come on!" That
floored me.

My debt to grandmother Bridget is even greater than that which I owe
to my sister Brenda. Nightly she taught me something my parents never
did: to read and write. I think she had a conscience about mother's
upbringing, and gave me the attention she ought to have given her. She
stood over me while I wrote the letters of the alphabet on a slate and
struggled to link word to word, sentence to sentence. Her wrinkled finger
followed mine along the lines of a children's English grammar she had
borrowed from the public library. My memory says it was Baines
Grammar, but I could be wrong. "Practice makes perfect," she kept
saying. Like me, she had no stomach for figures: "soulless," she called

them. She told me about the library books she had read. She didn't go for the classics like the Penny Reader, Mr. Peck. She liked to read the novels of the time. She was fond of the books of a writer called Warwick Deeping. I suspect she liked him because he had written a successful book about an Irish girl called *Kitty*.

Bridget often talked about America. Like my Fall River uncles, she left me with the impression that America was the largest, richest country in the world. Beyond the packed cities and skyscrapers of the American eastern seaboard were endless grasslands reaching to high mountains. Everything was big. Sometimes she'd talk about the different people who lived there, some of whom carried a gun – a practice I found wildly exciting. "One day you will go to America, Billy Boy," she said, as if it had all been arranged. As I got older she used to worry about my future. "You can go a long way, Billy Boy," she would say, shaking her lace cap at me. "That's if you wish to. But you won't go without "larning" [learning]. It's the key that opens all doors. You're behind, and you'll have to make up. Now get out your slate."

Because mother could never make up her mind which church she belonged to – someone said she shopped for a new religion like shopping for a new hat – we children had the unusual experience of being tossed between St. Philip's (Church of England) and St. Peter's (Roman Catholic) schools.

Father didn't care to which church he belonged, provided he could stay away from it. Mother said that father had believed in a God of love before the war but not after it. The slaughter in France had left him without a mooring. "He floats," mother said. Father Prendergast of St. Peter's, whom father always disrespectfully called "Father Spend-the-Brass," once took him aside for backsliding as a Christian.

"Do you believe in God, Will?" he asked.

"I did until the war," father answered. "Tha'd be surprised if tha'd sin what Ah've sin." After which they shook hands. But they shook hands like two wrestlers: a touch of the hands without any warmth. I felt there was a gulf between them which neither could cross.

Unlike mother, father was almost devoid of religious feeling. Mother once took him to a great revival meeting. She thought it would restore his old faith, but he was just as impassive about religion when he returned as he had been when he left the house.

I have the faintest memory of mother taking me to such a meeting. I remember the short train journey to a station outside Blackburn where we were met by hundreds of other men, women, and children. At the station all was stir and bustle. I can still see the banners and flags bobbing up and down above the heads of the pilgrims as we inched our way along a narrow country lane toward a turreted church at the top of a hill. The well-trodden ground was carpeted with autumn leaves of every hue.

At the sound of a command from the front of the procession we repeatedly fell upon our knees into the mud – the wise ones crouched – and sang a hymn about sin. We sang loudly so that our words were not only heard across the fields but at heaven's gate. I can recall only the last three lines of each verse:

> ... All my sins, I now confess them,
> Never will I sin again,
> Never will I sin again.

As we shuffled forward, the more fervent pilgrims struck their breasts while pouring out their confessions, protestations, fears, and hopes.

> Lord have mercy upon us,
> Christ have mercy upon us.

Only when I caught the eye of a girl about my own age who crouched beside me did I see the funny side of what we were doing. For a moment we had the giggles; she pinched my arm, I pulled her plaits. Meanwhile, like an incoming tide, the procession surged onward until we reached the entrance to the church. Slowly we mounted the steps and passed through the great doors, our eyes adjusting to the dark inside. The sweet smell of incense and the warm scent of burning wax greeted us there. One and all dipped their fingers in the font of Holy Water, crossing themselves in the name of the Father, the Son, and the Holy Ghost before going forward into the church.

The building was ice-cold when we entered, but was "set on fire" by a small, dark-eyed monk in the pulpit. He was dressed in a brown robe tied by a white cord at the waist. His cowl was thrown back and lay about his shoulders. He wore leather sandals on his bare feet. His stubs of hair reminded me of a hedgehog. Except for the flickering red eye of the altar lamp, and the burning candles and tapers, the church was lit only by the dim light which filtered through the windows.

The priest began his sermon by making the sign of the Cross and kissing the Crucifix which hung at his side. While I cannot remember a word of what he said, I shall never forget his powerful voice echoing strangely throughout the church, his words bouncing off the walls and the distant rafters. He had a peculiar habit of thundering and then whispering. Throwing his weight from one foot to the other, stretching out his arms, he mesmerized me. He must have said some very important things for he was constantly interrupted with heartfelt cries from the congregation: "Alleluia! Alleluia!" The service ended by our reciting the Confiteor, the Our Father, and the Hail Mary. We left with the monk's blessing.

We did not have to kneel in the mud on the way back to the station. With the church bells tolling above our heads, we simply formed up outside the building and sang our way down the hill now bathed in sunshine. Everybody was relaxed in the train. People were brighter-faced; they said they felt better for coming. I suppose they'd purged their sins; the wrongs they'd done were forgiven them; they'd won a new beginning.

Anyway, back to Father Prendergast and St. Peter's. Father Prendergast was a fat, jolly man of undoubted sincere piety, who seemed to get fatter as times got worse. Everybody liked him, especially for his short sermons. I liked him too, but I took a dislike to St. Peter's from the start. I remember it as a forlorn building with a large bell in a belfry; the grey stone walls had blackened with age and dirt. A bare cindered yard at the side, from which dust blew most of the time, was the playground.

The best thing about St. Peter's was that Rosie Gill went there. She was my six-year-old sweetheart who always wore the same old brown woolen hat pulled down at the back, and a grey coat much too long for her. One day she showed me an amulet of Mary and the crucified Christ, which hung on a cord around her neck under her blouse. It was a dazzlingly beautiful thing of the brightest colours and had been specially blessed. I knew from the way she drew it up so slowly from out of her dress that I was somebody special. At that time Rosie and I considered ourselves engaged; we always held hands. We didn't have much to say to each other, but we were happiest when we were together.

We were holding hands one day on our way home from school when I had a sudden impulse to look over the stone parapet which flanked the span over the Blakewater River. The parapet was about five feet high and was not meant to be climbed by small children. Removing my bulky woollen gloves and disregarding Rosie's protests, I jumped and clawed my way up the wall until I was able to look down on the dark river rushing over boulders below.

Before I realized what was happening, one of the bigger boys took me by the heels and heaved me over the parapet into the river. Stark terror possessed me as I fell head first. I remember striking the water with a loud splash; my face struck the rocks.

Rosie was the only one to come to my help. Dripping with blood, I fought my way to her at the side of the river. Leaning on her, with my teeth chattering, I drunkenly made my way home. Fortunately mother was there. She nearly fainted when she saw me. She didn't console me as Rosie had done but she washed and bandaged my wounds.

My face remained grossly swollen for weeks. When the swelling had subsided and the scars had gone, I was left with an entirely different-shaped nose. Rosie Gill was a great comfort to me in the days that followed. Father extended no sympathy. The way he went on about it, you would have thought that I made a practice of jumping off bridges and breaking my nose. No effort was made, either by teachers or parents, to find the bully and punish him.

In my early days, when I was five or six, I used to call for Rosie on my way to school. Her home was in the next street to mine. On my arrival Mr. Gill was always standing with his back to the fire, drinking tea. He drank it sip by sip, tasting it with great care before swallowing it. His bottom was so large that no heat reached any other part of the room. He always had on the same oatmeal-coloured woollen undervest, with three buttons at the top, and the same balloon-like trousers. The vest and pants both looked slept in. His feet were wrapped in slippers made out of an old coat. Mr. Gill must have eaten a lot of eggs, for there were egg stains from his neck to his waist. Rosie said her father was a sloppy eater and that her mother had given up worrying.

What did arouse my curiosity about Mr. Gill was the strange way he kept peering down the inside of his trousers. He would push the front of his pants away from him as far as his braces would go. Then he'd look down into the dark hole he'd made as if there was something moving about there. As I watched him I wondered if he was trying to discover how much room he had to spare; or whether he had got too hot. After a while I made up my mind that Mr. Gill had a pet rabbit in his pants, and was curious to see what it was up to. I would not have been the least surprised if a rabbit's head had suddenly popped up over the top of Mr. Gill's trousers. I never did ask Rosie what she thought.

In time I came to realize that there were few men as lovable, or as big-hearted as Willie Gill. He was a thoroughly good-natured man, with a good-humored face, who was never happy unless he was helping others. I never knew a man with better intentions. Little wonder that his fellow-Catholics thought so highly of him. His size made him all the more lovable. He was so large that he never entered our house without it becoming crowded. In a genteel way he had reached the last state of shabbiness. Unwashed, he always wore the same undervest, the same old coat stained with snuff that had come apart under his armpits, the same trousers that were so thin that his knees showed through, and the same cracked shoes which revealed his bare feet. Above his big, friendly, puffy, red face, with its rheumy eyes and large whiskers, he wore a crushed, bent hat made of wool and bits of fur. It added further distinction to an already odd appearance. His hair had never seen a comb. He smelled suspiciously of urine.

Mr. Gill had long since given up working for a living. Any money the Gills had came from Hessie, his thin little wife, whose weak, staring eyes didn't seem to like what she was seeing. Those eyes troubled me as a child. There was a story that Mr. Gill had worked in the mills but had given it up. Some said life had been unkind to him; others said he lacked backbone. Most said he was broke because he spent his time looking after others.

Meanwhile he survived by thinking up the most preposterous schemes to make money. One of these was to sell as fresh tobacco the fag (cigarette) ends which we children retrieved for him from the gutters.

Having taken the paper off the fag ends, he placed the tobacco in a dish in his window. It was sold as "Fresh Virginia." I cannot think how many diseases he must have spread. The really good fag ends we found in the streets we smoked ourselves.

Mr. Gill first aroused in me the joy of going to Blackpool. It was long before my visit there with mother. One day – wonder of wonders – he suddenly proposed to take ten of us, including me, to Blackpool. Pied-piper fashion, we eagerly followed his waddling, fat figure to the railway station unable to believe our luck. He had our parents' consent to take us, but we would have followed him anyway. Armed with buckets and spades, we trooped after him. We cheered as the train moved off. We heaped praise on Mr. Gill until his cheeks shone.

We'd gone only two or three stops when Mr. Gill said we had to get out. Puzzled, for we had no idea that Blackpool was so close, we leapt out of the train ready to run into the sea. But while there was plenty of sand, there was no sea. "Tide's out," said Mr. Gill, wrinkling his nose. Nor was there a tower; nor were there any people.

"Where's the tower?" everybody demanded.

"They've just moved it," Mr. Gill said, stuffing his shirt back into his baggy trousers.

"Where are the people?" we pressed.

"Gone home."

"Are you sure, this is Blackpool?" I asked.

"Eh?" he countered.

"Mr. Gill," I demanded, "where are we?"

"Little Blackpool. Big Blackpool is farther on."

"But you said you'd take us to Blackpool," I protested.

"You promised us," some of the children began to cry. The crying got louder and louder.

What with the threatening weather and the children, I thought that Mr. Gill was going to break down and weep. Instead, he shuffled in place like an elephant fastened to a stake. "Oh dear," he kept saying, his face past hope. His good-hearted plan to take us off our parents' hands and spend the day digging in a sandpit had misfired.

Had he told us that he was taking us to a sandpit we would have gone with him gladly. But he'd said Blackpool, and Blackpool was a very different thing. Every suggestion he made, including building sand castles – after all, we had brought buckets and spades – was rejected. By now the children were making quite a din.

Threatened by our spades, Mr. Gill became desperate. "Follow me," he called as he quickly shuffled off, his sail-like trousers flapping in the breeze. "I've just remembered, Blackpool is round the corner." We speedily pursued his disappearing figure. Walking directly behind him, I felt the whole sky was covered by the seat of Mr. Gill's pants.

But the real Blackpool was not round that or any other corner. Turning corners only revealed more broken ground, more empty acres of sand. Tired of searching for the real Blackpool, our protests were renewed.

A vanquished, snuff-stained Mr. Gill led us back to the railway station. Some of the children cried all the way home. It was raining hard by the time we got back to Blackburn. Not knowing what to do with us – our people were still in the mills – he sat us all in his front room, half of which he occupied, and followed our movements with watchful eyes and a nervous cough. He was, after all, surrounded by ten discontented children brandishing spades. At the first mill whistle, which told him that our parents were on their way home, Mr. Gill rushed us out of the house. He never played the role of Pied Piper again.

To return to St. Peter's, I thought the school was as cheerless inside as it was out. Indoors it was like St. Philip's: the rooms were dark and had little else but rows of wooden desks and benches – the latter polished by the seats of past generations. The walls bristled with wooden pegs on which hung caps and coats. There were the same lights, the same table for the teacher; the same blackboard. Both schools also shared a distinguished war record of former students.[†]

In addition to Father Prendergast there was a young curate called Smail. He had come from a rich parish in London and had a hump on his back, hence his nickname Humpty Dumpty. He must have wondered what he'd fallen into at St. Peter's. He seemed to play no part in school life. Whenever I saw him in the streets he had his head down reading a heavy leather-bound prayer-book. He always had downcast eyes. I don't know whether he was a real priest or not. What I do know is that he had a quick temper. Give him cheek – "Smail, Smail, ate a whale," we used to call after him – and the prayer-book would hit you like a stone. Everybody I knew gave him a wide berth. Mother said he was "a fish out of water". There were also two nuns: the twinkling, big-boned, rose-flushed, innocent Sister Lucy whose face was like a polished apple, whom everybody loved, and the gnarled, black-eyed, thin-lipped Sister Loyola whom everybody feared, and to whom I took an instant dislike. I always felt a shrinking from her.

When Sister Lucy entered our room everybody looked up, everybody smiled. She had a delightful way of reaching down and gently – ever so gently – pinching your cheek. She was so sweet and cherubic that I always felt like standing up and pinching her back again. When Sister Loyola entered the room, the class froze. At the end of the day Sister Loyola took merry-eyed Sister Lucy home as though she were dragging her on a halter.

At St. Peter's they were forever talking about sin and hellfire which gave me nightmares. There were dreadful pictures in our classroom showing all kinds of human suffering. Whereas the Lifeboy Soap poster had been my constant companion on the wall at St. Philip's, at St. Peter's

111

I sat next to a large picture of Christ with hard, staring eyes, pointing to his exposed, bleeding heart. There was a Cross on the middle of the heart and a fire on top of it. I never lost my fear of the blood. Although I felt a childish loyalty to Christ – Sister Lucy had said that Jesus had suffered terrible things to help us – I found the picture oppressive and avoided Christ's eyes and his pointing finger as much as I could. Elsewhere in the room were pictures of Christ being scourged at the pillar, and Christian martyrs being fed to the lions. The only peaceful thing in the room was a blue statue of the Madonna which stood on a windowsill with its back to the light.

The Catholics were expected to pray all the time. We prayed and prayed. Sometimes we would make the Stations of the Cross in the chapel at the top of the stairs next to our classroom, to which we had a communicating door. We banged and bumped and snickered as we went down on our knees and got up again, making our way from Station to Station. I was too small to know what the Stations of the Cross were all about. Christ's passion and death interested me but I was always bored by the time we reached the last Station. Obviously I lacked reverence and devotion.

When the door leading from our classroom to the chapel was left open I could see as far as the altar. Compared with our drab room, it was like looking into another world – a world of blue skies studded with golden stars, of gleaming metal and stone, of rich tapestries, polished wood, and a mysterious, flickering red light hanging before the tabernacle. Mass was said there to a crowded congregation every Sunday.

In or out of the chapel we were forever crossing ourselves and getting down on our knees. Our teacher, Miss Little – she was in fact very large – would always ask us to pray before class to help us in our work. Not that much work was done.

The happiest moments were when Father Prendergast wandered into our classroom making the sign of the Cross. He was a kind man who didn't seem to have any purpose other than to tell stories in a slow mellow voice and make fun. His stories always had happy endings, like Noah and the Ark, or the fellow who was swallowed by a whale. The pictures of suffering around the room never affected his spirits. He had a hearty laugh which caused the folds of flesh on his neck to glisten. He laughed so much that I feared that his shaking belly would escape from beneath the black belt which held his paunch in place.

One day, during one of his visits, Father Prendergast playfully asked us what we'd like to be when we grew up. I knew it was only meant for fun because we were all destined to work in the mills. However, I boldly said I'd like to be a tinker. The tinkers – most of them Gypsies – who mended our pots and pans struck me as wonderfully free; they never worked in the mills; they came and went as they wished.

For some reason my answer threw Father Prendergast into fits of laughter. Every student in the room joined in. Even Miss Little, who found Father Prendergast's visits a strain, laughed. I could tell from the trouble Father Prendergast had in adjusting his belt that his rippling belly had broken loose.

There was no laughter when Sister Loyola visited the class. She was as earnest about suffering and sacrifice as Father Prendergast was jolly. She had suffering and sacrifice on the brain. She rolled the word suffering off her tongue as if she took pleasure in it. Sometimes I wondered if her idea of love wasn't to thrash us all. "Only through suffering will you know love," was one of her favourite sayings. By her lights there was need of a vengeful God. She left me with a life-long fear of God. I didn't fear Christ. He had given His life for others, and as far as I could tell, was a good man who was now quite dead. Paintings and statues of Him were all around us. He was the Good Shepherd: He was real; I knew Him. God was different; He was full of mystery; He was a strange figure who could pop up anywhere at any time. My mind could grasp the idea of Christ, but not of God. I never understood why God had sacrificed His son instead of Himself.

Sister Loyola knew all there was to know about God and Christ and she did not like her views challenged, not even by Father Prendergast. Whenever he tried to assert himself: "Oh, come now Sister, not everybody must suffer," Sister Loyola's eyes would flash and she would withdraw into a dark, offended silence. There was an iron rigidity about Sister Loyola that was alien to both Sister Lucy and Father Prendergast.

One had to watch out for Sister Loyola. She'd spring a question on you without any warning. "Who is God?" she'd ask. By rote we'd answer "God is the Supreme Spirit, who alone exists of Himself, and is infinite in all perfections." "Who is Jesus Christ?" she'd follow. "Jesus Christ is God the son made man for us," we'd chant back. "Why did God make you?" was one of her specials. Everybody in the class knew the answer. "God," we'd jingle, "made me to know Him, love Him, and serve Him in this world, and to be happy for ever with Him in the next." "And sin?" she would ask. "Sin," we would answer, "is an offense against God." Before she left the room she would ask, "What will Christ say to the wicked?" We could jingle the answer without thinking: "Christ will say to the wicked, 'Depart from me, ye cursed, into everlasting fire'." Hell was final; from everlasting to everlasting. The threat sowed a seed of fear in me which remained.

I loved the words, I loved the imagery, the mystery, and the rhythm. I loved parading my knowledge. But I didn't understand a single thing. I never worked out how three gods – God the Father, God the Son, and God the Holy Ghost – could be one. The nature of God the Father I simply could not grasp. I was especially confused about the use of the word God. To say "God" was all right, but to say "By God" in a loud voice was all wrong. I could tell from the distrustful look in Sister Loyola's eyes that she didn't hold out much hope for me. "These things you must learn, child," she insisted, "understanding will come later."

I have never forgotten Sister Loyola's sermon on the crucifixion and death of Christ given to the whole school one Good Friday. We were all assembled in the main hall which contained a large plaster statue of St. Michael spearing a horned serpent that had a man's head – the Devil; at St. Peter's everybody knew about the Devil. Hypnotized by Sister Loyola's words, we relived Christ's Passion. We shared His Agony in the Garden. We saw His Scourging at the Pillar. We watched as a Crown of Thorns was pressed against His brow. Together we walked with Him as He carried His blood-spattered Cross along the Street of Sorrows. Eventually we reached Calvary, where we bided while His feet and hands were pierced most cruelly. With Sister Loyola we saw the Cross being heaved up against the sky. As we looked upon the sagging figure with its bowed head, its haggard face, and its stiff, outstretched arms, our sorrow was complete.

While she was talking, a storm had blown up. Papers were scattered and a cloud of dust came through the windows before we could shut them. The blackened sky was split by flashes of lightning. Sister Loyola had just cried out: "And the curtain of the temple was rent from top to bottom," when the whole school was shaken by a crash of thunder. I felt the building rock, my chair shake. I heard the windows rattle. I didn't need convincing that Jesus had just given up the ghost. I was too terrified to believe anything else. To me this was the God of wrath; the God of vengeance; God on the grand scale; only this God could have shaken the school down to its foundations.

Sister Loyola never let the Woodruff children forget that we had come from St. Philip's. She was wary of us on that score. "All Protestants are heretics," she repeated with a dark look that went right through me. I wasn't sure what a heretic was so one day I screwed up enough courage to ask her: "What is a heretic, please Sister?" As always, the answer was on her lips before I'd finished asking. "A heretic," she intoned, "is someone who has offended God and has been abandoned by Him." That left me more puzzled than ever.

In Sister Loyola's eyes the Woodruff heretics were lucky to have made the change from St. Philip's to St. Peter's. "God is in our church," she said proudly, "not in their's." Her unshakable faith in the right God ensured certainty. I knew enough from Sister Lucy's comments that only a fool would not have God on his side. "God," Sister Lucy had assured me, "is all-powerful, all-watching, all-seeing, all-vengeful. No one can fool God." Sister Lucy's religion was simple: fear the Lord and glorify Him every day. "Hold fast to the Cross," she urged me. It was not only the right thing to do, it was the wise thing to do. I don't know what others thought about God, but I kept a still tongue and followed Sister Lucy.

Of course, there was more to St. Peter's than the severity of Sister Loyola. There were the smells. As the chapel was next door to our classroom upstairs, the air was always sweet with incense and the smell of candles. Sometimes we heard from there the gentle tinkling of a bell. I also liked the colourful ceremonies and the sense of mystery and excitement that prevailed. What went on at St. Peter's overwhelmed my imagination. As long as I went to that school I was literally besieged by sacraments and miracles: seas parted, the dying were healed, ghosts rose, chariots of fire soared through the skies followed by burning winds, worlds moved; there was no end to it. The imagery of it all impressed me; even sustained me. At St. Peter's we were eternally being "washed in the blood of the lamb." At St. Philip's you never saw a drop of blood; you were washed in Lever Brother's Lifeboy Soap.

Nothing stirred me as much as the great Easter procession held by St. Peter's, St. Alban's, Corpus Christi, and other Catholic groups. Massed Bands came from all over the district. The importance of a procession was always measured by the number of its bands; in those days brass and silver bands were everything. There were so many bands that they could make "Faith of Our Fathers" resound across the entire town. When the bands passed by, the noise was deafening. With their polished brasses and their different coloured tunics, and their leaders strutting proudly with a long silver stick with a brass ball on top, the bands thumped, and pounded, and boomed, and crashed until you couldn't hear yourself speak. Whether marking time with their polished boots on the cobbles, or on the march, the bandsmen blew their horns and beat their drums until the veins stood out on their necks and the windows rattled. The crowd would make way for the procession, count the number of bands, and cross themselves.

I preferred the hymn:

> O Mary, we crown thee with blossoms today,
> Queen of the angels and Queen of the May ...

to the more militant "Faith of our Fathers" with its deaths "in dungeons dark."

It would take a hard heart not to be moved by the spectacle of Mary's garlanded figure rocking above a sea of wide-eyed, young girls carrying bouquets of sweet-smelling lilies of the valley. Dressed in the purest white, stumbling along at their own pace, they contrasted sharply with the soot-stained walls and the grimy streets.

It was especially moving when the crowds sang and the massed bands crashed out their praise to Mary, Queen of the May:

> To live and not to love thee, would fill my heart with shame.
> When wicked men blaspheme thee, I'll love and bless thy name ...

Alas, there were wicked men about who not only blasphemed Mary's name, but who sometimes did their best to disrupt the procession. Some Protestants were touchy about the route taken by the "Cat-lickers." The violence went in cycles. Most years were peaceful, but then the fighting would break out again like a rash. Rotten eggs were thrown, banners seized, poles smashed. Catholics and Protestants fought all over the street, with nothing to show for it.

While the battle raged, the bands continued to march in place, crashing out still another hymn. Disregarding the fact that the faithful, and the not so faithful, were being beaten over the head, and little girls sent screaming – with drums thumping, horns blaring, and cymbals crashing – the bands played on. After all, they were being paid.

Because of recurring violence, the Chief of Police, Protestant or Catholic, with his medals, his bright belt, and his white gloves, always headed the procession. It was meant to be a warning to those who wanted a fight.

Sometimes when a wind got up the marchers had enough trouble on their hands without protesters. People's attention was diverted from the Eucharist to whether the wind was going to blow over the banners. It wasn't unknown for those who carried the big banners that stretched across the street to be lifted off their feet and flung aside.

One moment the image of God Almighty, resplendent in the reddest of robes, would be soaring above our heads and our hearts, the next, He would be wrapped around somebody's head. It was a fate that could befall any of the radiant holy men and women whose portraits rode past at roof level on a full sail. Befittingly, I never knew the banner bearing the blue, glittering figure of the Virgin Mary, the Mother of God, with its inlaid profusion of lilies and roses, and its golden crown, suffer such ignominy. As the wind rose, a shouting match would develop between those holding the poles and those, front and aft, who held the guide ropes. "Nay, nay, pull on it tha clown," someone would shout, "pull to t' right; can't tha see what's wanted?" Because of his strength, not his religion, father was sometimes asked to help with the big banner. I knew when they'd slipped the pole into the leather holder which hung between his thighs, that that was one banner that would not blow over.

Accompanying the Chief of Police at the head of the line was a resplendent figure who far outshone the arm of the law. He wore a long scarlet, gold-trimmed cloak with a fur collar, striped, sail-like trousers, an Admiral's hat, pointed fore and aft, and polished shoes covered with spats. In his right hand he carried a silver baton. This was the Grand Knight of Columbus, Willie Gill. No longer dishevelled, no longer with broken shoes, no longer with an old coat bursting at the seams, a bent and battered hat, this was the real Willie Gill. Even his step had changed; he no longer slouched. Everybody knew him and they never failed to express their surprise at the transformation.

"My, what a toff tha are, Willie," they'd call out. "Tha're a one, tha're."

Twirling his silver stick, Willie reveled in the praise. Such a day took years off his life. Not everything, certainly not the important things in the life of Willie Gill could be expressed in terms of cottons and money.

There was happiness and dignity and glory to think about. It caused one to blink when you saw him the next day. It was like a mirage: the emperor had gone, the tramp had returned.

The best thing about the Easter processions was the eating and drinking that followed, weather permitting. Some Easter picnics became a soggy, treacherous, fight against the driving rain. If the weather was fine, having declared their faith with might and main to the entire town, the Catholics would file into somebody's meadow where large tents and food awaited them. Led by Mr. Gill, the bands would march through the farm gate, taking care not to step in the cow dung, and then stop playing. Chin straps were loosened, box hats removed, sweat wiped off puffed-out red cheeks, banners lowered and placed against the trees. For a few minutes people would stand around wiping their foreheads and talking. A clap of the hands from the priests was the signal to stop talking and begin eating. Accompanied by the tinkle of glass, the clatter of plates, and the rattle of cutlery, it was a free-for-all.

The tents seemed full of refreshments. There were plates of bread and margarine. There were pies and cakes, jellies and preserves, and buckets of hot water for the teapots. For those who could get to the barrels quick enough, there also was cider.

The first time I ever felt tipsy was after drinking a glass of that cider. Either my mates and I had got in the wrong queue or the people doling it out didn't realize that the drink was inordinately intoxicating. I knew something was wrong when the features of those around me began to quiver and quake and their speech thickened. It took a long time for the priests to catch on to what was happening. They thought our weaving about on the grass was funny. Not Father Prendergast. He was too old at the game. The moment he arrived, he took one shocked look at us and boomed: "Serve no more cider! Satan is in the barrel!"

You wondered where such mountains of food for those Easter treats came from and how they could all be eaten. Despite the lean times a lot of it was provided by the parishioners, the women trying to outdo each other. Each woman watched her own and other people's food to see which was eaten first. Pies and cakes that lingered were no honour to anybody and were quickly disowned.

We children slipped underneath the broad tables, hidden from sight by the long table clothes that reached to the ground. We crawled about there against the shuffling feet and ate like horses. To obtain our share we periodically reached up, grabbed what we could, and disappeared from view.

When the serious business of eating and drinking was finished, everybody turned to gossiping with kinsfolk and friends or to playing games. We had races, tug-of-war, and, while the fiddlers scraped, clog dances by a group called the Cloggers, who laughed shyly as they danced. And when that was done, and night had fallen, we sat on benches or on the grass outside the tents and sang. When the light failed and the fiddles were stilled, my family had a way of reuniting and wandering home together.

After my fight with Sister Loyola, I knew these times no more. I shall never know how I came to be so stupid as to allow myself to fall into her grasp.

One day Miss Little had sent me with a message to another teacher. It was 11:30 and I'd soon be off to the mills to deliver my family's midday meal. When I looked down the massive oak banisters on the main staircase, there wasn't a soul in sight. Apart from the drone of distant voices, all was still. I threw myself headfirst on to the banister and shot down toward the ground floor.

I arrived at the feet of Sister Loyola. There was no mistaking the shiny black shoes, the black gown with its black rosary that hung from waist to knees, or the wooden cross that swung pendulum-like from side to side. Sister Loyola was a small figure but from the angle I observed her she appeared enormous. I was seized with terror.

While she held me with her cold eyes, I wished I might fall through a crack. I was so frightened that I could neither move nor breathe. After one of the students had broken his arm sliding down the banisters, Sister Loyola had let it be known that anyone else found sliding down the banisters would suffer dire consequences.

"Don't you know it is forbidden to slide down the banister?" she demanded austerely.

"Yes," I stammered. My lips and tongue felt dry.

"So you have done it willfully?" she said, her black eyes boring a hole into my face.

"Yes," I faltered; yet I felt no remorse.

Before I could escape, she had grabbed me by the ear and was dragging me back up the stairs to my classroom. She twisted my ear so savagely that she made me cry.

The moment Miss Little saw Sister Loyola she took off her spectacles.

"Oh, dear," she said. Miss Little did not like crises; she did not like violence. If she was forced to punish us, she did so reluctantly and with a light hand. For this she was respected.

"Stop what you're doing!" Sister Loyola ordered the class, "I am about to make an example of someone who willfully disobeys school regulations. Your cane!" she demanded of Miss Little.

"Oh, dear," Miss Little repeated, constantly adjusting her pince-nez spectacles.

Still held by the ear, I watched Miss Little go to the cupboard for her bamboo rod. Each teacher had such a cane and used it regularly. In my early education there were many sticks but no carrots. Even in the Catholic school there was no time wasted discussing guilty consciences. If you broke the rules, you were for it. No argument. The cane was administered either on the seat of the pants or on the hands. The rod on the seat of the pants was less painful. With Sister Loyola there was no choice. She always went for the hands.

Having let go of my ear, Sister Loyola began to push back her wide sleeves. With my heart thumping, I stood there watching her, fearing the worst. She tested the rod, bending it with her hands. Then to get the feel of the cane, she struck the air several times. "Whoosh, whoosh," it went.

"Put up your hand!" she ordered. Her unusually pale face had reddened. Her lips were set in a hard strength of will.

I raised one of my arms, offering my palm.

"Higher!" she ordered, lifting the hand with the tip of the cane.

Every eye in the classroom was on the cane. Where thrashings were concerned, Sister Loyola had a reputation second to none. It was something worth watching.

I waited, biting my lip.

Suddenly she brought the stick down across my palm and fingers with all her strength. There was a whoosh, a rattle of her cross and beads, and a sudden stinging of pain as if my hand had been laid open. The cane had become a rod of iron. I stifled a howl.

She cut me five more times on that hand, each cut worse than the last. I saw and felt the red weals. I also saw a shocked Miss Little standing there, hand over her mouth.

Breathing heavily, Sister Loyola demanded the other hand.

"No!" I screamed "No!" Three cuts were the regular punishment. I'd already had six.

Sister Loyola reacted as if I'd struck her across the face. There was a murmur from the class which suddenly shifted position like a sea in change.

"You wicked, wicked boy!" she called threatening me with her stick.

"No!" I repeated defiantly. Shaking with anger and shamed before the class, I felt rebellious, even violent. Before Sister Loyola could recover from her surprise, I lunged forward, struggled with her, and wrenched the cane out of her hand. I then rushed to the open window and flung the stick into the street. Avoiding Sister Loyola's outstretched hands, I ran from the room. I left my cap and coat behind; I didn't stop running until I reached my mother in the mill. Between tending the clattering machines, she heard me out.

"So much for St. Peter's," she said, doffing another can of cotton.

This traipsing backwards and forwards between St. Philip's and St. Peter's did not do the Woodruff children any harm. Other than to be given strange looks, and to be the subject of nods and whispers, which suggested that the Woodruffs had escaped from a zoo, we were never ostracized because of it. Father Prendergast and the Reverend Reeves, who was as lean as Father Prendergast was fat, probably took the view that the Woodruffs were not worth fighting over. The Reverend Reeves once asked me: "Do you have the faith, my child?" I cannot remember how I replied, but I must have said something awful for the Reverend lapsed into shocked silence and never bothered me again.

All I cared about was how my street friends would take this crossing of religious boundaries. Fortunately, they ignored it. What did it matter which school the Woodruffs attended? We all ran together on the streets at night; we shared the same conditions; we lined up together at the soup kitchens; we joined each other's gangs; in football we joined each other's teams; we went scavenging together; explored the countryside together; fought and quarreled together; went to week-night prayer meetings together; and sang each other's hymns without paying any attention to the words. Together, without having any idea what it was all about, we annually burnt an effigy of Guy Fawkes while chanting "Remember, remember, the Fifth of November, Gunpowder, Treason, and Plot". How the fleas jumped from the old straw mattresses we threw on the flames.

For those who sickened and died before they had tasted life, we attended funerals in any church. Funerals of young friends carried off by tuberculosis, diphtheria, whooping cough, scarlet fever, and typhoid were quite common in those days. Diphtheria was the most feared. The first funeral I ever attended was that of a six-year old classmate, Enid Small, who had died from diphtheria. Her wan-faced corpse was kept on a bed in a corner of the front room of her cottage with a candle at her head and feet. I can remember the ill-lit room with drawn blinds and a sweet, sickly smell where white-faced people whispered, and everything was stiff and white and dead. The lips I'd seen chattering were now frozen. Little wax-white hands lay on the counterpane. Even as a child, the stiffness and the whiteness bothered me. It was so final, so still. I'd seen my baby brother die in my father's hands. Death frightened me.

Whatever convention demanded was provided. Death always brought a release from want. We were offered food and drink while we were there. Rubbed and scrubbed, we followed her hearse to the grave.

Enid was followed by John Bell who died of tuberculosis. My sister Jenny was always on to me about keeping my head away from him; she knew the signs. John was forever laughing, forever telling funny stories, and forever coughing. I visited John when he lay as a corpse. His body was unusually straight. His face made me catch my breath, for it looked as if it had been molded out of the same lifeless putty which sealed and fastened the glass in the window behind him.

Regardless of the church we attended, those of us who survived the childhood sicknesses would grow up and go to the mills together; collect the dole together; go to choir practice together; fight the war together; make love, and marry together. Mixed marriages were common. There was plenty of bigotry about in Lancashire when I was young, but never among children.

It says a lot about the early 1920s that my brother and I were prepared to attend the church or chapel that offered most food. We cast our net widely: Catholic, Church of England, Congregational, Presbyterian, Methodist, Independent, Unitarian, Baptist; we tried them all. Dan had a nose for these things. All one had to do was to follow him. He would dart from chapel to chapel, church to church, with a sure knowledge of who was offering what.

We were completely unscrupulous about it. We'd sing anybody's hymns, provided tea and rock buns followed. Accompanied by the organist, and the earnest young preachers with good looks and sonorous voices, we'd sing "Now thank we all our God," or "Count your blessings, name them one by one, count your blessings, see what God has done," with copious insincerity. We thundered out the words, "I know not, Oh! I know not, what joys await us there, what radiance of glory, what bliss beyond compare," but it meant nothing. Our sole concern was food.

I thought that some of the churches and chapels we visited were severe and dark. There was no delight or beauty in them – no strange lights, no radiance, no mystery. It made it easier if there were paintings on the walls; then, while the preacher preached, I could join Moses or Isaiah, or Abraham, or some other Old Testament prophet, or lose myself in the maxims painted on the walls, such as: "In everything give thanks," or "Abstain from evil," or "Cast all your care upon Him, for He careth for you," and many more.

Both church and chapel smelled of hymnals, camphor, wax, and carbolic soap. I don't know why but everything in my childhood had to be scrubbed, rubbed, and polished. Scrubbing brushes were everywhere. They were called hedgehogs and would take the skin off you if you didn't watch out. If a thing didn't shine, as all doorknobs and brasses did, or smell of carbolic soap, as most floors did, it wouldn't do. The constant rubbing, scrubbing, and small-tooth combing was the only way to cope with the dirt.

In our search for food, my brother and I were compelled to listen to innumerable sermons on sin, mortify ourselves in the long, polished pews, and endlessly repeat the Lord's Prayer. The sermon, usually delivered from a pulpit high above our heads, was literally and physically the price we paid for the refreshments, which at times seemed so far away. Sometimes I suspected that the preacher was trying out his sermon on us before he gave it at the Sunday service. I really resented it when, on top of everything else, he announced: "We will now lower our heads and examine our conscience." That was all very well for a minute or two, but some of the preachers had a conscience the length of your arm. I think they were stretching it out before handing out the buns. It wasn't my conscience that was troubling me – it was my belly.

I hope there wasn't as much sin in town as the preachers said there was. According to them, the place was awash with big and little sins. The big sins, they warned us, were the ones to watch. If you dropped dead with one of those chalked up against you, you went straight to hell and stayed there – forever. It struck me odd that one of the big sins should have been

121

gluttony. I didn't think my brother and I should stay awake at night watching for that one; not when we couldn't get enough to eat.

Not only did there seem to be a surfeit of sin about; there were so many ways in which the Devil could trap you – even without you knowing it. I was worried when I learnt that you could even sin by silence. According to the preachers, you needed eyes in the back of your head to keep up with Satan. If you didn't watch out, he'd nab you and you'd be in hellfire before you knew it.

These sermons not only made you feel hot round the collar, they also puzzled you a lot. I never understood why you would go straight to hell for gluttony, but pull down a fairly light sentence for drunkenness. Nor did I understand how God and the Devil could keep a proper tally of all the petty and mortal sins that were about.

I expect the preachers knew. I suspect that they also knew what we were up to. They never distributed food and drink until the sermon was over. Although the rock buns they handed out were too hard to be eaten quickly, we speeded things up by dunking them in the hot tea. One afternoon, with Dan's help, a gang of us collected eight buns and eight cups of tea each from different places of worship. As a count was kept by the ministers and their prim wives of our comings and goings, our multiple appearances must have caused a staggering increase in church and chapel attendance.

When I look back over my school years, I don't remember learning much more than how to survive. I suspect that that is all that was expected of me. School was a holding pen until I entered the mills. No teacher ever wasted time talking to me about the love of learning, or the fact that education mattered. Nobody emphasized what good friends books can be. Curiosity was not encouraged. Now that I sit down and try to recall my schooling, I am shocked by the few memories I possess concerning my formal education.

I can, of course, remember teachers other than Mr. Manners and Miss Little, but I have only dim impressions of what they taught. Teachers at my elementary schools were interchangeable. They taught a bit of everything. I know I must have taken the eleven-year-old examination – the one in which my sister Brenda had earlier distinguished herself – but I cannot recall it. Obviously my efforts did not attract anybody's attention. No one – grandmother Bridget was dead by then – ever impressed upon me the importance of this particular examination.

There must have been textbooks in my late years at school, yet I cannot remember a single one – not in Mathematics, not in English, not in Geography, not in History. Certainly no book ever went home with me. My family never bought school books. At my school there was no home-work and no report cards. I never owned a school satchel. What would I have done with it? Nor did I ever understand the grounds on which children passed from one grade to another. Seemingly without rhyme or reason, some children would go on to the next class, others would stay behind.

From the age of ten onward school for me was incidental. I was up at 5:00 a.m. to deliver newspapers. I always got to school as the bell rang. From 9:00 a.m. until 11:45 a.m. I dozed; worse still, I think I slept. At 11:45 a.m. the teacher gave me a signal, and I ran from school to deliver my family's dinners in the mills. Dinner hour was from 12:00 till 1:00 p.m. I had to move quickly because, as spinners, my sisters did not work in the same mill as my parents. If there were groups of workers standing or squatting against the mill walls when I arrived, I knew I was late. I had my dinner with mother in the cardroom, one hand covering the hot-pot from the fine dust that sometimes fell like a gentle rain.

It wasn't difficult to know when the dinner hour was done. Precisely at 1:00 p.m. somebody threw a lever and with a creak, crack, thump and clatter the whole room began to tremble and shake. Once the machinery became alive and the myriad wheels began to turn, you either jumped up smartly ("turned to") and set about your business, or you found yourself in trouble. The machine was the boss, it wouldn't wait, and it took no excuses. Glad to escape the din, I raced back to school. From 1:30 to 4:00 p.m. I must have dozed again. After 4:00 p.m. I ran the streets with the evening edition of the local newspaper. Then I came home and ran errands.

No wonder I didn't have time for schooling. I suspect I used the classroom as a place where I could rest before tackling the tasks that awaited me in the real world. My teachers knew I was physically exhausted and were kind enough to leave me alone. None of them ever asked me to go chasing prizes. I cannot remember ever being put under severe mental strain; which, later on, I recognized was all to the good. Nor was I ever encouraged by my parents to take school seriously. When in later years the seed of learning was planted in me, it found a fertile, unworked soil in which to grow. Yet the fact remains that when I left school at thirteen, I had learnt little about my heritage; nothing about my body and the way it functioned. Even with the help I'd received from grandmother Bridget, I couldn't write a simple letter applying for a job. Not that it mattered; there were no jobs available.

ix Blackpool rock

Looking back, I think the years from the early twenties to the mid-thirties were rather like Lancashire weather: generally awful, with bright periods. One such bright period occurred a year or two after my visit to Blackpool with mother. The whole family suddenly packed up and went to Blackpool together for the first and last time.

It must have been in 1924 or 1925, when the textile industry had made a partial recovery from the crash of 1920 and was preparing to take another fall. Anyway, my people were in jobs, otherwise we wouldn't have had the money to go.

We went during Wakes Week, a traditional holiday originally linked with the Church. Each cotton town had its own particular Wakes Week when everything shut down. It was used by the mill owners for maintenance and stocktaking. The workers used it – if they had the money – to escape to the hills or the sea. If they didn't have the money – most didn't because holidays with pay were unheard of – they would cover up by saying, "No, we've decided against it" – going to the seaside for Wakes Week – "We're just going for days. There's nothing like your own bed." Everybody knew "days" was humbug, but the pretence was kept up.

It was agreed that we'd all get away at the crack of dawn on the Saturday morning after the week's work had ceased. Every hour mattered. Until then we children talked and slept Blackpool. Somehow money was provided for new buckets and spades. When the day came we were up at dawn straining to go. We searched the sky for the sun. The family's one and only straw valise was got out and filled with food. The price of food at Blackpool was too high. We took bread, oats, a large can of Lyle's syrup, margarine, cans of milk, fish, and pineapple chunks, tea, sugar, eggs marked with our name, a jar of jam, a jar of piccalilli relish, salt, and sauce. The clothes we took were chiefly those on our back. Having left two shillings under the pot dogs on the mantelpiece for food on our return, we locked the door and left the house. The week's rent we took with us to spend in Blackpool.

Father went first, carrying the valise with a leather strap, then mother, then us. Our first stop was the "King's Arms," where our parents vanished. Jenny, Brenda, Dan, and I were left to amuse ourselves on the pub step. Fortunately, the "King's Arms" had two enormous marble pillars at the entrance that looked just like potted meat. Jenny at once took charge. She pretended that the doorway was her shop. The rest of us lined up before an imaginary counter and placed our orders. Whereupon with an equally imaginary knife, Jenny, with the pub regulars constantly stepping over us to get in and out, proceeded to cut slices off the pillars to meet our needs.

One pub customer, a twinkle in his eye, stopped and talked to us.

"What you up to?" he asked.

"We've opened a potted meat shop," said Jenny.

"Oh, you 'ave, 'ave you? Where's your folks?"

"Inside."

"Going to Blackpool, are you?" the stranger went on, eyeing our buckets and spades.

"Yis," said Brenda.

"How much did you say your potted meat was?"

"It's very special today," said Jenny. "Sixpence a pound."

124

"Well, I'll take two bob's worth."

With our eyes popping, Jenny "cut" four pounds of meat according to the customer's instructions. She "weighed" it, "wrapped" it, and "handed" it to him carefully. The man pretended to put the packet in his pocket. After that he handed Jenny a real two shilling piece.

"That'll be a 'tanner' each," he said.

"Oh, thank you," we rejoiced.

"Ta, Ta!" he said. "Remember me when you're on't sands."

"Oh, we will," we chorused.

We'd "eaten" an enormous amount of potted meat by the time our parents emerged. By now they were full of the holiday spirit. There followed further stops at the "Lord Derby" and "The Plough." Each stop increased our fears. What if our parents drank so much that we might never get to Blackpool? What if we had to drag them back to the house drunk? We need not have worried.

I'd noticed for some time that something was dribbling from the valise that father was carrying, but had kept a still tongue. Nothing must prevent us getting to the station and getting on that train. Eventually even father noticed that something was wrong. The procession was halted, the strap undone, the top of the valise lifted.

"It's the bloody syrup," father muttered, scratching his head while staring at the confused heap of syrup-saturated clothes and provisions at his feet. "You wouldn't believe it, the damned stuff's everywhere."

With us all looking on he separated the can and its lid from the other items in the suitcase. Staring at the empty, two pound tin in disbelief, he said the most awful things about syrup in general and Lyle's syrup in particular. Then he kicked the empty can into the street, slammed the valise shut, fastened the strap, and marched off in a towering rage toward the station. His foul mutterings could be heard yards away.

We children followed, breathing an enormous sigh of relief.

Still dripping syrup, we climbed aboard the train. It was an excursion train and it was packed. It was good humour all the way. Everybody had broken loose. If anybody had talked about cotton on that train he'd have been thrown out on to the track, headfirst.

On arrival in Blackpool we were told that the ticket collectors would not bother us, and they didn't. "If caught, act daft," father advised. An unwritten rule existed whereby children of the working class didn't pay. Following Dan and my sisters – Jenny although fifteen was so small that she always passed as a child – I dashed past the ticket collector and waited for our parents at the station entrance which was clogged with people. It was easy to tell rich from poor children. The rich children were clean and tidy, wore respectable clothes, and had clean noses. They shouted respectability. No dashing past the ticket collectors for them.

From the station we walked to a lodging house in the back streets where we stayed for a week. Father paid on arrival. I cannot remember much about the lodging house except that we all slept together in one room and that there were lots of other Blackburn children with whom we could play. We loved crowds and, in or out of the house, crowds were everywhere.

I think we abandoned our parents on arrival and, except for food and sleep, joined them again only when it was time to go home. Sitting on benches, sometimes in sand-streaked bathing suits, we ate twice a day with all the other families in a large room downstairs. Everybody squeezed in where they could. Nobody dreamt of grumbling. We'd come from the same town, some from the same street. We belonged together. There wasn't a sad face among us. Old and young, we'd promised ourselves a treat in Wakes Week, and we were not going to be done out of it. The dining-room table and benches rocked with our laughter. Every meal was a joyful shouting match.

Aside from the smells, and the queuing for the toilet, everything was bliss. In the dining room the landlady's word was law; nobody contradicted her; nobody answered her back. She was skilled at her job; even more skilled at getting us out of the house when she wanted to. The only subdued person was the landlady's husband who seemed to do most of the work.

If I cannot remember much about the house, it is because we were rarely there. As long as the weather was fine – and it was with us – we were on the beach or paddling in the sea. As always, we ran wild. What the adults did was their business.

A week later, with long faces, and our mouths stuffed with Blackpool rock, we caught the train home. It seemed to go faster on the return journey. There was no stopping at pubs, or pretending to eat potted meat. Our week of make-believe was over.

After Blackpool, Blackburn air was like lead.

X   Running wild

I began to run wild from about the age of seven. After that I rarely sat at home in Griffin Street. Our house was so small that my brother and I were happier on the streets. To sit around at home was to get in people's way, or run the risk of being given a job. Clogs had to be taken to the cobbler, meat scraps or a soup bone had to be obtained from the butcher. Fish heads and tails had to be collected from the fishmonger. As I was the youngest, and Dan had a way of disappearing, I was invariably assigned these jobs. When I went to the butcher I always carried a "dodger" in case my pleading eyes failed to break down his resistance to part with scraps for nothing. Usually, with the "dodger" still in my pocket, I would return with a bundle of meat scraps and bones wrapped in newspaper. Same with the fish heads. We must have eaten a lot of printer's ink.

Going to the cobbler or clogger was another job allotted to me. The cobbler lived a few doors away. He sat in his front room, bent over his work, with a powerful gas lamp at his side. The lamp had a number of mirrors around it which provided an unusually bright light. The whole place smelled of sweaty feet and wood shavings. Front cokers, metal runners attached to the wooden sole, cost eightpence; heels fourpence; a toe cap twopence. With his tools and wood in easy reach, the cobbler cut and shaped new clogs to size on the spot. While my family sat at home in their stockinged feet, I sat with other children on a bench by the cobbler's last. We slid along the polished bench until our turn came. Grown-ups were always served first.

I marvelled how the cobbler filled his mouth with nails and wooden fillings, and how he seemed to fire them from his mouth at the clogs – like bullets from a gun. He never missed. When he stood up to shake the shavings off his leather apron, I noticed the stoop of his shoulders. Perhaps because his mouth was always full of pegs and nails, I can never remember him talking.

Chores finished, I would dash away to join a gang of boys in the often rain-darkened streets. When the paper blinds were drawn, each cottage became a shiny, orange-patched island in the dark. Street gangs were usually eight to twelve strong. Ages ranged roughly through the same numbers: eight to twelve years. Girls did not run with us, nor did the feeble-minded; they were kept at home. Each district in the poorer parts of town had its own gang and resented inroads made by others. Religious denomination didn't matter. On the streets, we were all pagans. Our gang met at corners, locked shop doors, and mill sheds. Huddled together in the dark, we talked about and planned everything – well, almost everything. I can't ever remember us talking about sin and virtue; such topics never entered our heads. Our favourite topics were sport, murders, robberies, suicides, battery and assault cases, lockouts and strikes. A run of victories for the town's football team, the Rovers, would keep us talking for weeks. It was impossible to run out of things to say about the Rovers. In the football season we lived and dreamt about them.

A good murder – especially a child murder – would also keep us agog. We were well informed about murderers like Jack the Ripper and Charles Crippen. If we ran out of murders, there were always more to be found in a newspaper called *Thompson's Weekly*. Sometimes one of the gang would bring a juicy bit from *Thompson's*, which was read out and reveled in by the light of a flashlight. Hardly good reading, but I don't think it did us any harm, and it helped to prepare us for the larger world. As children, we were astonished at the dreadful things grown-ups could get up to.

If all else failed, we would sit entranced while Shorty Cooke – one of the gang – told us a story which we all knew was a whopping lie. Yet he told his tale so naturally and so convincingly that you wanted to believe him. One of his best was the visit he and his father had made to the Cup Final at Wembley in London. He had it all off pat, including the arrival of the King and Queen, yet we knew that he and his dad had never been beyond the tram ride to Whalley Bridge. Shorty ran a firewood business out of an old pram. He sold penny bundles of firewood, which he bought from a dealer in bulk, extracting a stick from each bundle and selling it again. If he hadn't got himself killed in the Second World War, he would have become a millionaire.

Until we reached our teens, sex was almost a non-subject. We knew what "cunts" and "pricks" were. We knew where babies came from. Occasionally, we'd swap stories about the sexual life of our parents; sometimes a show-off type would display his penis; other times we'd prey on courting couples for the fun of it. Our flashlights were detested by them as they clung to each other against dark mill walls. But such activities did not hold us for long. Sex was dull. Girls were not wanted. Food and adventure were our overriding interests. Among the gang it would have served me ill to have talked about my earlier affection for Rosie Gill. Such a confession would have been considered a sign of weakness.

In the nipping cold of winter we kept ourselves warm with portable winter warmers – empty Oxo beef tins which we first perforated with a nail and then filled with slow-burning cotton waste. We carried the flat tin – half as big as our hand – inside our shirts. Periodically, to keep it nice and hot, we'd take the can out of our shirt and whirl it around on the end of a string. We rarely set ourselves alight. Often we'd share a cigarette, passing it from mouth to mouth. Harry Barnes was never without a fag. We suspected he had pilfered them, but we never pressed him. We thought it very manly to smoke and, of course, we were men. We inhaled deeply and took pride in blowing the smoke down our noses. When the mood took us, we'd carry out raids on neighbouring territory. Knives were never used, we couldn't afford them, but we did carry catapults, marbles as ammunition, peashooters, stones, and sticks. For a few bruises we'd rid ourselves of all our aggression.

On Wednesday nights – market night – we ran across the stall-covered town square snatching whatever fruit and vegetables we could. There were scores of naphtha-lit stalls, all of them selling the same produce; all of them considered to be quite different by those who shopped there. Our target was the discarded produce thrown into the trash bins standing between the stalls. A fine point, to be sure, but to take fresh produce, especially if one sold it, would have been stealing. We followed the rules. Some things you could take without feeling shame or guilt; others you couldn't. Barbarians we may have been, outright thieves – by our lights – we were not. Speed was vital. One had to run, jump, hang on to the bin, reach down, sort out the rotten produce in the half-dark, fill one's pockets, and make one's escape before a rod descended across the exposed seat of one's pants – accompanied by a "sod off" or two. It was quite a challenge. Afterwards we'd crouch in a heap beneath a hissing gas lamp and compare our spoils. On Wednesday night we ate enough fruit and vegetables to last the week.

Saturday morning, before I took to going to the reading room in the town library, was usually spent at the stockyards. For a penny or two, groups of us would struggle across a bog of steaming manure to help the red-faced farmers drive the protesting cattle they'd bought to their farms in the surrounding hills. When business was slow we sat on top of a wall gaping through the barred windows of the Summer Street Abattoir to watch the slaughter going on within. It puzzled me how such formidably powerful bulls could be felled with a single blow to their lowered head. One moment there was a fearful, pulsating mountain of muscle, the next a carcass of bones and flesh. Pigs had their throats cut, squealing all the time; after that they were thrown into great tubs of boiling water.

I agonized over the lambs and sheep. With frightened eyes they climbed a death walk directly in front of where I was sitting, at the end of which they were stabbed through the head. Blood was everywhere. No matter how many warnings I shouted, I never saved one. I never understood why they died so meekly; why they accepted their fate. As long as I was a child, staring through that window, I never accepted the inevitability of death. I wanted the animals to kick and fight.

Sometimes on a Saturday morning on our way back from the stock-yards we'd look in on the open-air market on the town square. It was usually packed with slow-moving, slow-buying casual passers-by. There were fruit stalls there, but we never pinched damaged fruit on a Saturday – broad daylight and too many people. We just wanted to look. If you had pennies to spare you could buy a "thoroughbred" puppy, a hen, a rabbit, a ferret (to catch the rabbit), a singing bird in a cage, a pocketful of tame mice, or a goldfish in a bowl. "Real diamonds" cost sixpence each; a "gold watch" made of brass and tin a shilling; "new" false teeth or spectacles, whose owners were in the graveyard, two shillings and sixpence. Second-hand shoes, suits, and hats, third-hand silk stockings, fifth-hand books and magazines were all available at give-away prices. Ill-fitting used shoes were a constant source of corns. There were also "miracle" soaps and toothpastes, and furniture polishes, and methylated spirits which some people drank for whiskey. For threepence you could buy a bottle of medicine that would cure anything, including corns. For nothing at all, unless you wanted to give a penny, you could watch a man almost kill himself lifting impossible weights. Another fellow broke bricks with his fists, or snapped thick chains from his wrists and legs. Still another repeatedly swallowed fire while the merchants clamoured, bawled, and wheedled: "Who'll give me sixpence for this luvly silk dress? What am I offered: sixpence?... fivepence?... threepence?... Must I go to the workhouse?" Silence may be golden, but it was useless for selling used anything on Blackburn square. We heard the shouting and the barrel-organs long after we had left.

From the 1920s onward, with the coming of the talking pictures, many Saturday afternoons were spent at the cinema, with peanut shells and orange peel all over the floor. The matinee, solely for children, was a wild affair where order was kept by a man who carried a long bamboo pole. Those caught blowing rice or rock-hard peas at the pianist, or spitting orange pips from the balcony, or whistling too long at the kissing scenes, ran the risk of getting whacked over the head – a real hard whack. Entrance was gained by handing over two empty, clean, two-pound jam jars. With two such jars, I saw Charlie Chaplin in the first silent films, and Al Jolson in the first talking motion picture "The Jazz Singer." In celluloid form Buster Keaton and Mary Pickford also came to town. Although the sound of the early "talkies", or "pictures", was atrocious, I was spellbound.

Talking pictures opened up a new, exciting kind of world. It is impossible to convey the impression the earliest films made upon me. It was like seeing the first electric lamp, or the first automobile. In exchange for two empty jam jars my spirit could soar across the great plains of America as far as the Rockies. With the pianist thumping out a tune, I jolted along in a convoy of covered wagons, gun on knee. I helped to clear the forests and build a log house on the American frontier. Keeping an eye open for Indian braves, I put the plow to the virgin land. There were times when, glued to my seat, I feared the red Indian warriors as much as any white settler had done. The "talkies" caused an uproar in my imagination – enough to keep my young mind occupied until the following week.

When we children were not at the films we were watching the town's football team, the Rovers. We slid across a neighbouring roof and never paid to get in. Once in the ground we scattered; better one thrown out than the lot. We boys were crazy about football (soccer); cricket we hardly knew, tennis even less. The first time I heard thousands of people – caps in hand – sing "Abide with Me" was late one afternoon at the Rover's ground. The words were printed on enormous screens. To keep time with the bands, one simply followed a little ball that jumped from word to word.

> Abide with me; fast falls the eventide;
> The darkness deepens; Lord, with me abide;
> When other helpers fail, and comforts flee,
> Help of the helpless, O, abide with me.
>
> Swift to its close ebbs out life's little day;
> Earth's joys grow dim, its glories pass away;
> Change and decay in all around I see;
> O thou who changest not, abide with me.

The massed singing gave me gooseflesh; religion was real in those days.

Everybody but the dead and the dying watched the Rovers. Nothing was allowed to interfere with a game, not even a snowstorm. Fellows would rush off to a match as if their lives depended on it. When the Rovers played, the town's honour was at stake. Only Aston Villa had won the Football Association Cup more times than Blackburn – six times against our five. The workers spent Saturday afternoon at the game and the rest of the week arguing over the outcome. Next Saturday the madness would begin all over again. If a player left Blackburn to get better pay elsewhere, the town took it as an insult. He had put money above the game, wealth before civic allegiance. One year, by illicitly raffling the same two pound bag of sugar over and over again, our street gang equipped our own boy's football team with Rover colours. A fraudulent street raffle was fair; begging was outlawed by ourselves. We played – shove, push, kick, run – on the nearby tip, using caps for goal posts.

I was eleven when the Rovers won the Football Association Cup at Wembley Stadium in 1928. Few things have provided me with such excitement. The match against Huddersfield was broadcast all over town. My mates and I listened to every word. It was the first time the final had been broadcast by radio from London. We heard the King and Queen arrive and the singing and the playing of the massed bands. It came over the radio as real as being on the field with the ninety thousand fans.

It was amazing what Blackburn did. Everybody said we were in for a licking. After all, Huddersfield had a far better record in League football that year than we had. They had a far better team. Their forward line was the best in the country; their centre forward, Jackson, the bane of all goalkeepers. Some said he was as good as Stanley Matthews, the greatest of our football idols. But our eleven finished up beating theirs by three goals to one, just the same.

How did we do it? Well, in the first minute our centre-forward, Roscamp, scored a goal by bundling Huddersfield's goalkeeper Mercer, ball and all, into the net. It took our breath away. You could hear the roar of the Blackburn fans all the way from London. After that it was our game. By half-time we had a lead of two goals to none. Huddersfield fought back in the second half, but our half-back, Campbell, bottled up their forward time and again. Only Jackson got past him to score Huddersfield's single goal. Roscamp offset that by scoring the third goal for Blackburn. Puddefoot, another of our heroes, just missed scoring a fourth.

When the final whistle blew, we all danced for joy. The town went mad. It remained mad until long after the victors came home bearing the precious trophy. At the station the team was mobbed. All traffic was brought to a standstill. We followed the players around the town with free beer flowing everywhere. It had been 37 years since our last win. Six times we'd won the cup. We'd equaled Aston Villa's record. Our town may have been in bad shape, but where Association Football was concerned, we were top of the pile.

Most Saturday nights we haunted St. Philip's church hall, close to the school, where they held a weekly sixpenny dance. At the interval hot tea and meat pies were served. The dance hall never lost its pork pie smell. Any member of the gang who hadn't eaten two meat pies by the end of the interval just wasn't trying. Two was the limit; to take three was stealing. If we ran into trouble in getting our share we simply appealed to family and friends who were dancing there. Some dancers seemed to enjoy slipping us hot meat pies as much as we enjoyed eating them. Once, when we were absolutely stuck, we set some mice free during the spotlight dance when most of the room was in darkness. We helped ourselves during the confusion, and ran for our lives. Next week there were two large cats there.

To escape from the murky darkness of the streets into the lighted dance hall was the highlight of my week. Unlike some of my companions, who were concerned solely to obtain meat pies, I loved the lights, the music and the air of romance which filled the room and warmed me through. To see all the mill girls powdered and prettied up with their curled hair and white dresses, and all the boys in their tight-fitting suits, their hair slicked down with brilliantine, never failed to raise my spirits. There wasn't really room for such a crowd but everybody knew everybody else, and it was all very friendly. The dancers shared the chairs and their laps. There was always something or somebody to sit on. It was so intimate and intense that there was no room for wallflowers.

Being there every Saturday night, I knew all the dances. My two sisters danced as well as anybody; especially Jenny who danced as light as a feather. If she hadn't had a partner to hang on to, I think she might have flown round the dance hall.

The Spot-dance, especially when it was a waltz, was my favourite. The moment the main lights were switched off, and the spotlight was switched on, a hush fell on the room. The ceiling became a mass of tiny twinkling lights, like stars revolving in the sky. The girls' necklaces, bangles, and earrings – all glass – winked in the flashes of light. Everything became remote. With the spotlight darting about the room, I watched the dancers swaying effortlessly like a gentle wave, to the muffled tap of the drum. "Moonlight and roses bring wonderful memories of you ..." Sitting under one of the tables, peeping through the tablecloth, I went on hearing the music long after the band was stilled.

It was always a great let-down when the lights were turned on again. The moonlight and roses, the princes and princesses had all departed; a laughing, milling, sometimes overdressed, shoving, pushing, perspiring crowd of cotton workers had returned.

Another centre of attention for us children was the Theatre Royal, which was sometimes used as a music hall. The theatre had rosy plush seats. As they didn't barter seats for jam jars, our gang either had to furtively make its way in via the endless concrete back steps, from which

132

we tried to slip into the gods, or find a relative or friend to pay for us or smuggle us in. Two adults, wearing long coats, could easily smuggle in a child between them. It was not considered stealing to wangle your way into any form of entertainment. Begging directly from people in the theatre queue, however, always ended with being chased down the street. The grown-ups wouldn't stand for it. If we failed to penetrate the theatre's defences, and it was music hall that week, we'd find out where the freaks and curiosities were lodging, and carry out a vigil outside the house in order to watch them for free.

The first of such vigils was before a row of houses in Talbot Street several streets away from the theatre. We arrived there about forty minutes before curtain time. It was winter, dark, and misty. We didn't know which house contained The Tallest Man in the World, The Smallest Man in the World, and The Wild Man from Borneo, but we knew they were there. We decided to divide our forces: each one of us would patrol several houses and give a shout if anything happened. I was told to walk up and down before three large black-stoned houses at the end of the street.

I was staring at the front of one of these houses when I felt my hair rising. A pang of terror shot through me. Peering through the window above the doorway was a man's face. A man would have to stand on a ladder to peer through there. He fixed me with his eyes. I was looking at The Tallest Man in the World.

Instead of raising the alarm, I just froze and stared back. Moments later a taxi pulled up at the curb; it was without a roof. The door of the house opened, The Tallest Man in the World lowered his head, hurried down the stone steps, opened the iron gate, crossed the sidewalk without looking to the left or right, climbed into the open taxi and sat bolt upright. I might never have been standing there.

He was followed by The Smallest Man in the World who didn't reach as high as The Tallest Man's knee; yet from the way he bore himself, I knew he was a man not a child. The look he gave me suggested that he did not like being seen for free. Behind him came The Wild Man from Borneo, complete with skins, feathers, shield, and spear. He showed me his teeth, but I was too scared to respond.

By the time my mates had run from the other end of the street they saw only the back of the car surmounted by the head and shoulders of The Tallest Man in the World. The music hall's greatest attractions were swallowed up by the mist. We went back there the next night and the next, until we had had our fill.

Theatre, rather than music hall, was my greatest experience. I remember my first curtain rising. Somehow I'd got the money and had been allowed to go on my own to a children's matinee of Robert Louis Stevenson's "Treasure Island." It was like looking into a lighted, magic kingdom. No man – not even a Red Indian or The Wild Man from

Borneo – has ever frightened me as Long John Silver did. When it was over I rushed into the street and grabbed the first person I saw – in this case a nice old gentleman – to tell him all about it. I felt it vital that I should warn him about Silver's treachery. The old man must have understood children. He rested himself on his walking stick and, with a benign look, and the odd "Well!" or "You don't say," heard me out. He seemed as revolted by the perfidy of Long John as I. In later years, I wondered what the old gentleman said to his wife when he got home.

For me, the fictitious, floodlit world of the theatre was far more real than reality. One entered into it, took part in it; even to the extent of shouting warnings to the heroine and hissing the villain. In the gods the audience was completely uninhibited. "Bloody scoundrel thi are, knocking 't lass about like that," somebody would bawl. If we shouted too much, or too loudly relayed the play to a deaf companion, or overindulged in having a good cry, a stentorian voice would shout "Shut thi gob!"

The trouble with some people is that they would go on nursing their grievances long after the play was over. They stood outside the stage door and hissed the actors they didn't like. The villain – however striking – had to watch his step when returning to his lodgings. "Ah could teach thee a lesson or two," they'd call after him. "A thorough bad 'un thi are."

If we had no money for music hall or theatre, nor jam jars for the "talkies," we could always fall back on flying our linen kites. The wind was always waiting for us. I never knew a wind that could change its mind so capriciously. To me the wind was a mischievous being, ready to trick you and take your kite. You needed to plot and plan against him. I often wondered where he came from and where he was bound. I envied the wind his freedom to come roaring over the hills and go his way.

Playing buck and stick on the mill tips was another great standby. The buck (also called a piggy) was a small piece of wood about the size of an adult's thumb. It had a nose at one end. The stick was a picking stick from the mill. The object was to raise the buck, by striking it on the nose, and hit it as far as possible. The one who hit the buck farthest won – that is unless a stray dog reached the buck first and made off with it. Next to football and marbles, and pitch and toss played with buttons, buck and stick was our most popular game. Sometimes we'd share the tip with groups of unemployed who, desperate for something to do, would play marbles or pitch and toss by the hour. When I think of the yelling and the bawling we did, it's just as well that we had disused cinder-tips to play on. Occasionally, interrupted by an unreasonable parent who dragged his kicking, screaming offspring home, we played buck and stick as long as the light lasted.

Occasionally all games were stopped short by a group of men who took over the tip for a dog and rat fight. After the laying of bets, the dogs would be matched against rats. The man whose dog killed most rats was the winner. There was no sport in it. The rats never had a chance. Nor did they want to fight. From the moment they were let out of the cage, they sensed they were in deadly peril and tried to get away. Far from fighting, when the dog went after them they'd crouch and squeal with fear. I never saw a dog bitten, but I saw a lot of rats killed. Those that escaped and sought refuge in the outer tip were despatched by men carrying picking sticks. It was a cruel sport.

As we grew older, we took to chasing each other in and out of the town's clay pits. One day we'd fight with clay balls, another day we'd join the girls to mold clay into the most marvelous bread and cakes and play shop. We even devised a clay currency. Other days would find us running through disused quarries filled with nettles and dandelions. In summer we preferred to go barefoot but one had to keep a sharp look-out for broken glass. Alone, or with other gangs, we'd fight pitched battles along the canals and, if there were no courting couples there, or tramps setting up house, defend the railway tunnels from attack.

Sometimes, oblivious of danger, we'd chase each other across single-line railway bridges where it was strictly forbidden to go. Three friends and I were once caught on such a bridge. It was winter. A coal train was upon us before we knew it. Its red and black nose swayed toward us at an alarming speed. Puffs of blue smoke belched forth rhythmically above its head. We knew that the only safety bay was farther on, beyond our reach. It was too late to run back; not least because the track was frozen and slippery. Terrified, we took the only course open to us: we scrambled over a metal screen and, fully dressed, fell into the icy canal below – that is all except Wilfred Green who fled before the oncoming train. As I fell, I felt the train thunder past above my head.

With the other two boys I dragged myself out of the canal. Our teeth were chattering, our lips were turning blue; fragments of ice were forming on our clothing. We lay on the bank for several minutes gasping for breath, quivering at the jump. In the distance the train rattled and rumbled on its way.

"We'd better find out where Wilf's got to," one of us said.

We clambered up the steep bank until we reached the track again. Wilfred Green had disappeared.

"Wilf!" we shouted, "Wilf!"

There was no reply. Shivering with cold, we began to walk back across the bridge, puzzled where Wilf had got to.

We found a lumpy object at the end of the bridge. It was Wilf. He was lying on his belly, at the side of the track. He didn't look like Wilf Green anymore. Not like the Wilf Green who always came out on top of our fights. He looked like a crumpled, blood-stained sack, or some other refuse tossed out of the train. His legs lay on the track. They had been severed at the knees. Speechless, we stood there and stared.

None of us approached the body. We had the wind up too much for that. We backed away and fled back across the bridge to a signal box we knew was there. Breathlessly, tearfully, we told the man in the box what had happened. Then we all ran home, going our separate ways slantwise across the fields. For some odd reason we had suddenly become afraid of each other.

For a long time Wilfred Green's life hung in the balance. Youth, strength, luck, to say nothing of medical care, pulled him through. In time he was fitted with false legs with which he began life anew. In the hospital, and in the streets later on, he avoided those of us who had been with him when he lost his legs. He wasn't blaming us – at least I don't think so; it was just that he'd begun a new life which, for reasons that he knew best, he didn't want to share with us. Mother said his pride was at stake.

After several weeks of sitting around and wondering whether Wilf would live or die, life went on as before. Undeterred by the near fatality, whole evenings were given up to playing king of the mountain on a slag heap near Nig Lane. The slag heaps were pyramid-shaped piles from disused mines in the Dells End district, well outside the town. Hundreds of feet high, they were a blight on the skyline. Nobody wanted them; nobody knew what to do with them. Meanwhile they rotted, fumed, and fouled up the local canal (cut) and everything else in the vicinity. No grown-up went near them, so they were a perfect place for gang warfare. The coloured pools of stagnant water that stood at the foot of the tailings fascinated us. They were every colour of the rainbow. The nettles that proliferated there provided us with no hazard. Reciting the words: "Gently stroke a nettle and it will sting you for your pain; grasp it like a man of mettle and it soft as silk will remain," we'd grab a handful and hope for the best. Everybody had to pass the "nettle test". The outcome was always as the jingle foretold.

Slipping and sliding about among the rubble, one gang would defend the summit, while the others – no holds barred – tried to dislodge them. It was hard work dragging oneself up to the summit and then slithering down again. It also had its dangers, for landslides happened on the steep slopes. In summer, if we got too dirty and too hot, and the light was still good, we'd strip off and "One, two, three", throw each other into the canal. When the seasons changed and winter followed autumn and summer, we'd desert the slag heaps and go sledding. Our breath a steaming mist, we'd come whizzing down the frosty hillsides headfirst, disregarding the trees and the great clods of heavy wet snow that sometimes fell from the branches. The closer to the trees we came, the more exhilarating the ride. Other than by chance, I cannot explain how we managed to survive.

With water everywhere – teeth-chattering cold water even in the summer – we learnt to swim young. The canal was a dirty colour, but the river Blakewater or Blackwater that ran through town was worse. Its walled banks by the mills were stained black and brown with mill dyes. Although forbidden to children, we one day went wading in the black, murky river by the factories looking for fish. "You shouldn't be in there.

It's dangerous!" a woman shouted over a low wall. We took no notice of her. We turned over stone after stone without finding a fish. The river was dead.

In all our wild escapades we seldom ran foul of the police whom we called coppers. Except during strikes and lockouts, we rarely saw them in the poorer districts. When we did see them we always felt watched. Come to think of it, no matter how poor we were, there was very little crime. Crime and poverty in our society did not run together. We may not have respected the toffs' law, but it was not in our nature to break it. Most of those I heard of going to jail were arrested during a commotion outside the factory gates. That's when the police always appeared. For us they had a stigma; we were brought up to distrust and avoid them. We distrusted them because they defended the rich; also because many of them were strangers from other towns. We avoided them because they used their batons rather than words. We always got the "short end of the stick."

We had a similar fear and distrust of the courts. We felt the law was to protect the rich, not the poor. It was up to us to keep out of the way of the law and to take care of ourselves. Many is the tale of so-called justice I heard in the mill among mother's working companions. That of a crumpled, dwarf-like Irish woman who used to eat her dinner with mother and me in the carding room sticks in my mind. When I first saw her she had just returned from jail. While we balanced ourselves on an overturned sliver can against the wall, and swallowed our meal, she told me how she had become a guest of His Majesty's Government. One evening, when crossing the centre of town, she had run into a group of demonstrators being chased by the police. She had sought the protection of a wall while those fleeing had raced past her. The next thing she knew was that she had been struck over the head, handcuffed, and thrown into the Black Maria.

Despite her pleas of innocence, she spent the night in jail. The next morning, with many others, she was hastily brought before a magistrate whose only purpose it seemed was to establish her identity and determine the length of incarceration. All her tears got her nowhere; she got three weeks: "A week for each crime," she said. "I was in the way, I'm Irish, and I'd no money. I had everything against me," she finished. "Justice isn't for the likes of us."

The old woman had no reason to deceive a child. She was warning me to watch out. I felt the incident was so unjust that it has remained clear in my memory. As I grew older, accounts of similar injustice confirmed my belief that the law was for the toffs. Any poor man or woman who thought that the law was there to help and protect them was in for a shock.

For us children, the long summer school holiday was the period of greatest freedom. It was then that we fled the grimy factories and the high smoking chimneys for the lanes, fields, hills, and empty, wind-swept moorlands which lay outside the town. Whenever the weather was fine, we fled like farm animals escaping from a long hard winter indoors. Having been shut up, we discovered the sun, the moon, and the stars again. The vast expanse of the countryside made us feel free. Our parents didn't bother that we might get lost, or drowned, or gored by a bull, or fall out of a tree, or break our necks. Children were not the focus of their life, work was. Oddly enough, on these occasions girls and boys went together. Rosie Gill and Annie Morgan would always come on these outings. Dan avoided them, Jenny and Brenda were by now too old.

With a little food under our shirts, and accompanied by birdsong, we ranged the countryside in a straggling procession from morning to night, getting hotter and hotter as the day wore on. I remember long summer days that never seemed to end. We explored the surrounding villages such as Feniscowles, Riley Green, Copster Green, Tockholes, and Ribchester. Every Lancashire child knows that "chester" means the site of an old Roman camp. Ribchester was not just another village. To us it was the ancient crossroads of Roman communications, one arm of which went from Ilkley Moor in the east to the Fylde in the west; the other arm from Manchester, twenty-five miles to the south, to Carlisle, ninety miles to the north. We were proud of our link with the Romans. Nobody could tell us much about centurions, or the Roman heavy cavalry, or which legion was where. We relived our Roman history, walking the ancient roads, storming the ancient walls, stirring the pigeons out of the Roman ruins, and with exultant war-whoops, slaying the fiercest of Roman soldiers before they had time to seize their swords or sound their horns. One thing we all knew was that the Romans had built a wall – the Wall of Hadrian – seventy-three miles long across northern Britain, one hundred miles to our north. After keeping guard there for three hundred years, they got tired of our weather and went home. A lot of different people must have followed the Romans in Britain. The Normans did in A.D. 1066. Yet it is the Romans we remember best.

When we were not killing Romans, we robbed bird's nests, mimicked their calls, plucked berries, chased butterflies, fished, rabbited, skimmed pebbles across the water, and ran down the turf-clad banks to swim in the Ribble, at one time the boundary between England and Scotland. That part of our sex education which we had not already acquired in our homes we obtained by following the activities of the stallions and mares, the bulls and cows, the cocks and hens we chanced upon in the fields. Steeped in local lore, we were ever watchful for witches and fairies, especially if a mist was about. We knew that at certain times of the year witches were quite common on Pendle Hill; also that eaves-dropping elves lived in caves, or in the roots of trees, or under large rocks and were best left alone. We knew the eerie stories connected with certain farms. We expected every ruin to have a ghost and always took it for granted that unseen eyes were watching us as we hurried by. One field we avoided was where a milkmaid had been murdered. Some grown-ups swore that on dark nights she could be heard walking in the meadow, weeping and bemoaning her fate. We knew every grim detail. We also avoided old church yards with their sloping, moss-covered stones, lest we should be caught unawares. Having run ourselves to a standstill we'd make a bed on the turf and sleep among the daisies, buttercups, and fluffy dandelion balls.

All summer long, we ran as free as the wind. Provided we closed all farm gates behind us and never interfered with the grazing cattle and sheep, we were free to follow a path or a rushing beck wherever it led. Nobody bothered us. Sometimes we'd look in at a farmhouse to watch them milk. I thought the way the milk squirted from the udders into the pail was magical. I loved all the sloshing about of milk that went on from one pail to another. To be given a mug of warm milk with cream on top, whose sweet smell was equal to its taste, was to know what paradise was all about. It certainly tasted better than blue (skimmed) milk or canned milk. Our best bet for a free drink – even the girls among us believed it – were men milkers, not women. Naturally, we all drank from the same mug.

The only authority we recognized was that of the older children. If the oldest was a girl, she ruled; it was her job to bring us home safely. In town each child was responsible for its own acts; when roving the countryside we acted as a group. We depended upon each other. Everything had to be shared. There was no "iffing" and "butting", no sticking out. You kept the rules or you didn't go next time.

Before dark we'd be home again, achingly hungry, with grazed knees and elbows, and perhaps a sunburn. Sometimes we'd bring bundles of nettles for nettle-beer, cresses, and docks; sometimes armfuls of flowers; sometimes stained linen bags filled with berries; the older children knew which berries to take and which, like the Baneberry, to leave alone. Sometimes we'd come home with nothing: sodden, wet through, icy-cold, and our clothes full of clinging, prickly burrs. Always our energies were spent, our instincts and our imagination satisfied. Life may have been dangerous – jagged rocks and seemingly bottomless holes in the river were the greatest hazard – but for us children it was never dull. We lived in a world of intense activity; a world in which there was never enough time to fit everything in.

The sights, smells, and feelings of those long summer days remain with me. I can still see the cloud shadows moving smoke-like across hill and dale. I have never forgotten the green bulk of the hills, where the soil lay barren; nor the sea of bluebells, daffodils, violets, and primroses surrounding Whalley Abbey. I've never lost the smell of fields carpeted with lilies of the valley or new mown hay; or the peculiar dry smell of heather at the end of a long hot day. I can still remember hedgerows covered with flowering currants and white hawthorn; damson trees white with blossom; smoky-faced lambs skittering behind the drystone walls which climbed endlessly across the fells into a windy sky. In my ear the song of the pewit, the curlew, and the lark never dies; nor does the lilt of the singing stream. I shall always hear the shrill clear whistle of the shepherd calling his dogs.

If the weather went against us, we'd play king of the mountain in one of the cottages after the adults had gone to work. Girls were banished from these games. Armed with pillows, one gang would defend the top of the wooden staircase leading to the bedrooms while another tried to dislodge it. Repeatedly, somebody would fall from the top to the bottom of the stairs without coming to any harm. More damage was done to the pillows than to us.

Sometimes foul weather was disregarded. We went out just the same. During my unfortunate, short-term career as a Wolf Cub Scout, I won a competition by lighting a fire on an island in the Ribble in the pouring rain. I think I was tougher and more resourceful than many of the other cubs. I'd joined the Scouts not because my parents said I should, but because scouting seemed to me such a good idea. It was what I was looking for.

If I excelled on that occasion it was because I was determined to show them who was the best Cub Scout. I was the only one who had lit a fire on that island in the rain before. I had no uniform to spoil and I was used to getting wet.

When the signal to begin was given, I ransacked the island for the driest twigs and the driest dead grass. My fire was crackling and sending up clouds of sparks before the other fires were lighted. I'd lit it with one of the two matches we'd been given; no rubbing sticks together in that weather. I must say the Scout Master didn't like it when I gave him the other match back.

I loved every minute I spent with the Scouts. I loved the knot-tying, the First Aid, and all the rest. I really believed in it. I left for the sole reason that I could not afford to buy a uniform. My nemesis was the Scout master's mother who used to attend our meetings in St. Alban's Church Hall at the other side of town. There was no Scout troop at St. Peter's or St. Philip's. She and I never hit it off. She was always tidying me up, which I resented. She didn't have to keep saying how odd I looked in my ragamuffin outfit. I was tired of her treating me as a kind of ugly duckling. It irked me so. She made it plain that I just didn't belong there, that I was a hanger-on, and the sooner I left the better. I suppose I'd jumped into somebody else's pond.

"Oh," was all my parents said when I broached the question of buying a scout outfit "Oh." I did raise tenpence to purchase the Scout necktie and a leather-studded fastener, but that wasn't good enough. I was issued an ultimatum by the serious young man who led us: "Cub Scout cap and a uniform, or out! A stained cap, patched pants, and torn jersey won't do. It's letting the side down."

I was sad and humiliated when they threw me out. I just didn't feel it was fair, especially as I was enjoying it, and I had won the firelighting contest. "Oh," was all my parents said when I told them that I no longer was a Cub Scout "Oh." For a long time afterward when moving about the town, I followed my troop's way of alternating running with walking. Run a hundred steps, walk a hundred steps, and so on. It made me feel that I was still part of the group.

On an earlier occasion, before I joined the Scouts, a mate and I had borrowed a bike and cycled down to the Ribble to camp there. I rode on the carrier with a borrowed tent, food, blankets and a pot wedged between me and the saddle. The ride was endless and very bumpy. I gripped the metal seat springs in front of me so hard, and for so long, that I couldn't release my fingers when we got there. They were frozen to the springs. I also had severe cramp in my bottom and my legs. Fly-troubled cows, with swishing tails, gazed incredulously as I ran up and down the river bank, flapping my arms about, trying to restore my circulation. Swallows skimmed the foaming river, feasting on clouds of gnats. Rings showed the currents' flow.

My mate and I must have been very hungry, because we ate our two day's rations during the first long twilight. Food gone, our troubles began. Unlike the warm day that had preceded it, the night became astonishingly cold with a chilly breeze. The damp rose from the ground and penetrated our limbs. Our discomfort grew. Unable to sleep, we sat up at every sound. One moment we were absolutely certain that someone was being strangled to death at the water's edge; the next moment somebody seemed to be crying for help from the black rock-studded river. Periodically, an owl hooted close by.

Shaking with cold and fear, we stuck our heads through the tent flap, and looked around. Nothing looked as it had done in daylight. The ground was a wet, misty grey. Mysterious shapes were everywhere. We had a feeling of being completely lost. I wondered out loud whose silly idea it had been for us to be there at all. My friend guardedly suggested that the idea had been mine. I really wasn't up to fighting him so I let his silly comment pass. Blankets round our shoulders, we struggled from beneath the tent fly and walked up and down the river bank, talking to each other in strange, muffled voices. We agreed that when light came, we'd go home. Only when the blood was flowing again – we'd been walking about as stiff as posts – did we notice the starlit beauty of the sky. Our interest in stars, however, was fleeting. We crept back into our damp tent and slept.

Several hours later, before daybreak, we were wakened by a cow lowing. From the noise it was making it might have been an elephant in mortal agony. Unable to sleep with that din in our ears, we got up to investigate. It was a black and white Jersey lying on the bank closeby. With her big, sad eyes, she seemed to welcome us. While bellowing across the valley, she heaved and strained. When a calf's head popped out from her rear end, I knew why she wailed so.

I'd seen a calf born before but this birth was no less magical. I stood there awestruck. Despite the early hour, the flies began to swarm. We tried to help the cow by driving them off with our caps. The cow didn't mind. By now she had stopped her lowing and was purring like a large contented cat. We marveled at the way she cleaned her calf with wet, sloppy licks. Nobody had to tell the calf what to do. It struggled to its wobbly legs from a bed of buttercups and began to feed from its mother's udder. It made us feel glad that we'd come.

Though still before daybreak, I thought we should tell the farmer that he'd got a calf. With the soft light changing from grey to silver, we tramped down the misty bank in the direction of the farm house. The river sang at our side, toppling and turning in the dark shadows. Chewing their cud, other cows placidly ignored our passing. Glittering, dew-soaked cobwebs lay on the tufted grass. Across the fields the plaintive curlew had begun to call. The last bats of the night flickered by. At the house there were plenty of dogs barking, but no lights. We had to throw stones at the windows to waken him. After several throws, a wild-looking head appeared.

"What's t' want?" the farmer demanded sharply.

"Tha's got a calf," I shouted, disregarding his ugly look.

"Oh, Ah 'av, 'av ah?"

"Tha 'as."

"Wheer?"

"Down t' bank. He woke us up."

"Tha's woke me up. Cudn't ya 've cum 'n told me after cockcrow?"

"We thowt tha'd want te know."

"Ya did, did ya?"

"Ai, besides, we're goin' oom."

"Well, that's summat," said the farmer as he slammed down the window.

"Cheeky bugger," I said to my mate. "He didn't seem to appreciate us tellin' 'im."

With the sky becoming lighter, we went home, riding through the soft early morning light. As I was riding pillion again, it was as hard riding back as it had been getting there. On arrival, we shamefacedly confessed to having eaten our two days' food. The only thing we talked about at home was the birth of the calf. Seeing that was worth all the trouble we'd had.

XI Bamber Bridge

Once I had found my street legs and could wander off from home on my own I spent some of my summers with my mother's kinsfolk, my two maiden aunts, Betsy and Grace, who lived in a rambling old converted farmhouse in a quiet country lane at Bamber Bridge, close to Preston. They were Kenyons, and except for heaping love on to my sister Brenda and me, assiduously avoided the Woodruffs. The only link my family had with them, as far as I knew, was through the mail. Brenda, who had spent some time with them recovering from a sickness, was the one who made the initial arrangements for me to go there. Their father had helped grandmother Bridget after the death of her husband, grandfather Thomas. We all knew that.

Betsy was the hearty, red-faced, fat one. The folds of flesh on her face almost concealed her small nose and her ever-merry eyes. She was sheer bulk and must have weighed a ton. She moved about slowly. She never walked across a room without making the floor creak. Her feet left an imprint wherever she walked. I was always apprehensive that she might step on me. To a child's eye she had a gigantic bosom. When she hugged me, I felt myself disappearing between her breasts. She had large powerful hands; the largest I had seen among the Kenyons and the Woodruffs.

Aunt Grace was just the opposite. She was Grace by name and grace by nature. She was shy, pale and slim. Her small, fine head, wispy fair hair, pale blue eyes, and tiny hands and feet gave her a delicate look. Whereas Betsy flattened everything that got in her way, Grace seemed to float above it. She was sprightly. She enjoyed life just as much as Betsy, but was always restrained. Betsy was forever going into fits of laughter which shook her whole frame; which in turn shook the room. Grace never went beyond a sweet smile. Betsy was what you saw. With aunt Grace you always felt she was holding back on you. If a pig, hen or duck fell sick, Grace was the one who nursed it. Betsy said that Grace had had many suitors when younger, but had neglected her own interests in favour of their widowed father whom, together, they had cared for. When I knew them I suppose they were both in their forties.

Regardless of their different traits, my aunts loved each other deeply. They were never apart. I came to love them with all my heart.

The third member of the family at Bamber Bridge was Whiskey, a salt and pepper, wire-haired fox terrier. I cannot imagine why they called him Whiskey for my aunts were strict teetotalers. It didn't take me long to realize that Whiskey was the boss of the house. I never knew a dog which took less notice of his mistresses. Regardless of my aunts' cries, "Oh Whiskey this and oh Whiskey that," unperturbed, the dog went his own way. He knew exactly how to handle them. Battles of will between the women and the dog always ended up with Whiskey lying fast asleep on their knee. When the four of us came home from our daily walk, ignoring aunt Betsy's loud protests, Whiskey always took the big upholstered chair by the fire. They'd long since given up any attempt to dislodge him. Any effort to bother him was always met with a low growl.

Whiskey must have tired of female company. From the moment I arrived at Bamber Bridge he attached himself to me. He took my arrival as sufficient excuse to avoid his weekly bath which he hated. I never slept there without having him across the foot of my bed. A large Bible lay on a heavy table in my room. At its centre was a steel roller with spikes on it. There also was a tiny key which when turned caused the book to play "Faith of our Fathers." It was fascinating to watch the turning barrel playing. Whiskey and I played it so often that my aunts feared we'd wear it out. He rarely went to sleep before me and took great interest in the long stories I told him before sleep claimed us both. On those occasions when he fell asleep first, I used to watch my candle flicker and splutter. Sometimes moths would come through the open window and charge the flame before I had the chance to blow it out. Because of the dog and the kindness of my aunts I rarely missed my gang once I left Blackburn for Bamber Bridge.

Betsy and Grace Kenyon were very well off. Mother told me that their father, a builder, and a shrewd man in all his undertakings, had left them more than enough money to last the rest of their lives. Mr. John Kenyon's portrait hung in a gilded frame above a marble-encased clock in the lounge. He had obviously dressed up for the occasion. He wore an old-fashioned, black, Prince Albert coat which reached down to his knees. He had a turned up collar with the corners turned down and a black tie. He didn't look very comfortable, yet his face and his long white beard exuded kindness and good will. His life had evidently been successful and was drawing to a close in a manner he had wished. I suppose he must have been the brother of my grandfather Thomas who had left my grandmother Bridget destitute. His daughters were the only link the Woodruffs had with the Kenyons and that a tenuous one.

He had bequeathed to my aunts the large house in which they lived. It had several levels with a sharply pitched, red tiled roof, a permanently locked attic at the top of the stairs, and large, bright windows which had recently been added. It must have been an old building because I could scratch out the crumbling mortar from between the bricks with my fingers. At the front – part of which was plastered – was a large white-painted doorway with a roof above it. On the door was a huge black knocker with a lion's head. One reached the front door by way of a heavy wrought iron gate which gave access to a front garden always awash with flowers.

Most exciting of all, the house, with its flagged corridors and its heavy oak furniture, had a secret door built into the side of one of the steep paneled staircases. The thin, flat piece of wood which served as a door was opened by sliding a piece of the beading on the paneling. This released a bolt and allowed the panel to swing inward. Behind the panel was a hiding place, what was called a Priest's hole, where Catholic priests had taken refuge when fleeing their Protestant persecutors in earlier times. Once I was allowed to hide in the Priest's hole while aunt Betsy, pretending to be an Elizabethan soldier, tried to find me. The hullabaloo she put up when climbing the stairs was enough to terrify any priest.

Aunt Betsy was funny about religion. She thought that everybody in the world, at least those in their right minds, was Catholic. That's because Bamber Bridge and nearby Preston were chiefly Catholic. But I knew that Blackburn was chiefly Protestant. She never listened to me when I tried to put her straight. I don't know what she would have said if I'd called her a "Cat-licker", or had repeated the derisive parody of the time: "Catholic, Catholic, quack, quack, quack. Go to the devil and never come back."

Compared with life in Blackburn, my aunts lived in the best of all possible worlds. Whereas in Blackburn we trod on each other's toes, Betsy and Grace had enough room to rattle around. Whereas our house smelt of cotton and fish, my aunts' house was alive with bright, sweet-smelling blooms picked from the garden. Grace used to spend lots of time each morning cutting and arranging the flowers. She also cared for innumerable indoor plants and ferns. When she wasn't messing about with the flowers and plants she was interminably polishing the heavy furniture which already shone like a polished apple. When that was done she would sometimes change the lace covers on the backs and arms of the chairs. Because of the large windows, there was light everywhere. The dark, serious faces staring at me from the black-edged, brown photos hanging on the walls in the different rooms never bothered me. I presumed they were Kenyons but I never had the interest to find out. I knew from the flowing dresses, the tight suits, and the hair styles that those Kenyons, like Mr. Kenyon who kept his eyes on everything from above the clock in the lounge, were long since dead.

My aunts were lucky because they never had to worry about money. We worried about nothing else. Mill whistles didn't bother them. They ate regularly and well. Biscuits, dates, grapes, oranges, apples, or bananas were always sitting about on a sideboard waiting to be eaten. There was an orchard, several hen coops, and ducks in a pond at the end of a field. In the early days I used to throw a stick in the pond in the hope that Whiskey would retrieve it. He spurned the idea. Some of the produce they grew was given to a middle-aged couple, Jim and Effie Bairns, who came in to help every day. Some of it was sold in Bamber Bridge and Preston. More to keep themselves busy than to earn money, for which they had no real need, my aunts also fattened a pig or two.

In the evenings they read to each other, played their gramophone with its large green horn, sewed, cut out table mats, played Snakes and

Ladders with me, or made stockings – which they sold to a dealer in Preston – on a stocking frame. If the gramophone became too loud Betsy would muffle it by stuffing a stocking into the horn. Grace spent a lot of time at night pressing flowers in a large book which never left the lounge table. She was a collector like her father. As he had collected stuffed birds, she collected flowers. Sometimes my aunts chose to do nothing more than rock in their chairs. Slowly the hush of the night would deepen. When they were rocking, they avoided conversation. Their lives were just as regular, secure, and stable as my family's life was haphazard, uncertain, threatening. They might have been living in a castle with a drawbridge.

Every afternoon, wet or fine, we all went for a walk. Betsy was always in charge and the procedure never varied.

"Grace," aunt Betsy would yell, "have we got the sticks?"

"Yes, sister," Grace would answer, unperturbed.

"Billy, you ready?"

"Yes, aunt Betsy," I would reply.

"Grace, do we have the coats?"

"Yes," Grace would respond, her arms full of them.

"Grace! Where's Whiskey?"

Only when everybody had the right stick, the right coat, the right shoes – clogs were not worn – the right umbrella, and the right hat did the procession begin. Betsy went first, grasping a heavy cane, moving slowly. She bore herself like some large animal venturing into perilous territory. I walked immediately behind her, carrying the umbrellas, followed by Grace. On these occasions my aunts wore poke bonnets or straw hats with a thick wide red band tied at the back. Wet or fine, I wore a Sou'wester storm hat which, with other apparel, including innumerable pairs of hand-made stockings, was always kept ready for me.

Once in the fields, Whiskey never failed to streak off as if he'd seen a rabbit.

"Come back! Come back!" Betsy bawled, raising her stick. "Oh, that dog, he'll be the death of me."

Ignoring Betsy's calls, Whiskey by now had wriggled through the hedgerow. Betsy shouted after him as if he were misbehaving himself for the very first time, "You bad dog; you bad dog!" she complained. "We never want to see you again."

Covered with mud, Whiskey always reappeared when we were on the homeward stretch. He fell in line with us as if he'd never been away. Nothing was said. By then, aunt Betsy only had wind enough to trundle home.

Year after year, the walks took the same route. Nothing changed – not even the demonstration that Betsy put on almost daily in summer at the side of a deep pond which lay on our route where boys sunbathed and swam in the nude. Betsy always got worked up about the nude bathers long before we reached the pond.

"Just look at that, Grace," she shouted over her shoulder, while pointing with her stick. "Did you ever see such?" she continued in a shocked voice. "What are we coming to? That's what I ask you, what are we coming to? There's no shame."

On and on she went, her red, moist face becoming scarlet. By the time we reached the pond, her stick was raised like the sword of an avenging angel. By then the swimmers had slithered down the wet, muddy bank into the water. Whereupon Betsy marched to the water's edge to deliver her usual sermon about indecency, shame, disgrace, and immodesty. She always ended on the same note: "You're a bunch of hooligans, that's what you are; you brazen, disgusting ragamuffins. There's no decency in you. You're a disgrace to Bamber Bridge."

All of which sent the swimmers into fits of laughter.

"Silly old bugger!" they'd shout back while splashing water at her. "Why don't you fall in?"

After a summer or two I took all this in my stride. Aunt Betsy didn't mean what she said. It was her way of enjoying herself. She would have been mortified if the hooligans had suddenly worn pants. Quiet, gentle aunt Grace never intervened – she stood at some distance, her face wrapped in smiles. She enjoyed her sister's daily tirade more than the swimmers did.

Aunt Betsy was obviously destined to run into male nudes. She once took me to the Natural History Museum in Preston where she was halted in her tracks at the entrance by a large bronze statue of an ancient Greek male. "Well," said Betsy, staring at the metal penis and testicles, "I'll be blessed; if this is what we get at the door, Billy, what will we get inside?"

Each summer I used to fret until my parents gave me the necessary ten pennies for the train ride to Bamber Bridge. The fare was all I needed. I went just as I stood, wearing a jersey, a thick flannel shirt, corduroy pants, stockings, clogs, coat and cap. Apart from a penknife and some string and one or two other odds and ends in my pockets, I didn't take another thing. I took no underwear, no change of clothes, not even a toothbrush or a handkerchief. Everything awaited me in the heavy wardrobes and drawers in my room at Bamber Bridge.

The first time I ever went there I went alone. I was told where to find and leave the train; I was given an address and ten pence for the fare, and that was that. Other than that I knew that my sister Brenda had been there before me, I have no idea what prior arrangements were made. I'd met my aunts once before in Blackburn and I'm sure my father had sent them a note before I went there. Nothing was said about my return. It was all done in such a matter-of-fact way that I cannot remember being confused or frightened. Nobody at the station thought it odd that I should be travelling alone. I was much too concerned to stick my head out of the carriage window and drink in all that I could see than to worry whether I should get lost or come to any harm. The journey was only a few miles, but I was as excited as if I were going to the moon. I could see my aunts were puzzled when I arrived, but I'm sure it never entered their heads to send me back again. Nobody mentioned Blackburn until the summer was done and it was time to go home.

Unless my aunts were out for a walk, I never had any difficulty finding them. They were always there, fussing about in the field, or in one of the out-houses with their livestock. They never fell ill, or went away. Each time I arrived they were exactly as I had left them the time before. If they were working in the fields they'd be wearing the same funnel-like hats, the same fingerless gloves, and the same clogs. Aunt Grace always wore the same white lace collar; aunt Betsy the same black bow on a white shirt that crackled with starch and was as hard as rock. The aprons and the heavy skirts were always the same. My room, which looked down to the duck pond, was always ready, and always as I had left it. As if I'd arrived from an epic journey, on the first night I was always expected to give them an account of what I'd seen out of the carriage window. At Bamber Bridge nothing changed.

Whiskey invariably warned everybody of my coming. With piercing yelps he flung himself against the back of the door. Then he jumped up to the glass panel to make quite sure it was me. The moment I got the door open he'd be all over me, licking my face and behind my ears. Then he howled his way through the house and across the field announcing my arrival.

Because of an unspoken agreement between us, my aunts invariably ignored my approach. The procedure never varied. They went on fussing with their ducks and hens as if Whiskey and I did not exist. Meanwhile I crept up silently behind aunt Betsy's enormous figure and suddenly shouted out as loudly as I could, "Auntie, Ah've cum!" Whereupon Betsy dropped whatever she was holding, pretending that she'd had the shock of her life. She slowly swung her immense figure around. Her hands shaking, she stared at me with laughing eyes. "Why, so tha has, luv," she said. "He's cum, he's cum, Grace," she bawled across the field as if Grace didn't already know. Then she took me in a tight embrace, crushing me against her crackling, starched bosom.

Continuing to hug me warmly, Betsy ran her hands over my frame. "Grace," she shouted, "Grace," her voice now filled with urgency, "the poor bairn's starving. His bones are sticking out, Grace. Come and feel."

By now, Grace had come running. "Why, so they are," she'd say, running her fingers over my arms and legs, while clucking her tongue disapprovingly.

At that point Betsy always looked at me as if I were a lost cause. "They've let him go too far this time," she would say, darkly. "They've left it too late. He's skinnier than last time; there's nowt we can do."

"We can but try, Betsy," Grace sighed, her fingers running over my spine. "The skeleton's there; we've got the frame to work on."

This talk never bothered me. I knew I wasn't dying. It was my aunts' way of preparing themselves for the challenge that lay ahead. If I appeared undernourished when I arrived, they were determined that I would not leave in the same condition. The challenge was to get as much fat on my bones as possible before my summer holiday came to an end. As eating was my possessing passion, I could hardly complain.

For weeks on end, they stuffed me with food. No matter how I protested, "seconds" and "thirds" were piled on to my plate. I was encouraged to gobble. I lost count of the many hens and ducks I consumed, or how much fresh milk I drank. Sometimes I ate so much at noon that I could hardly stand. If I didn't respond to the treatment, I was given a second dinner at night. There were occasions when I found myself almost too taut to totter to bed. The more flesh I put on – and it was impossible not to gain weight with that kind of care – the greater their satisfaction. I was weighed nightly and they beamed at every extra ounce. Even Whiskey seemed to take a delight in it.

When the time came for my departure – my family took it for granted that my aunts would pay my return fare – they would weigh me for the last time. By the look on their faces, that last weighing was a life and death matter. If the figure was not to Betsy's liking, the weighing was repeated. "Now, Billy, tha must try a little harder this time, luv," she'd say, while surreptitiously putting her hand on my shoulder.

The weighing having been brought to a satisfactory conclusion, the women ran their hands over me once more to make quite sure they'd done their job. They always told the platform man at the railway station what miracles they'd worked on me during my stay. "Billy's still on the skinny side," they'd say, looking at me critically, "but he'll pass. He might just last the winter. We couldn't do more in the time." At that point they lifted my cap and ruffled my hair.

It was expected of me that I would weep when leaving them at the station, and I always did. They wept too. They took turns hugging me till the very last moment before letting me go. With my pockets full of apples, and my arms full of food – all of which I was ordered to consume during the half-hour's journey home – and my hot hand clutching a shining half-crown which was always pressed on me at this point, I somehow managed to clamber aboard.

As aunt Betsy was too large to climb into the train after me, she always beckoned me down again so that she could give me one last squeeze. She used to squeeze me so long and so hard that it took the platform man, with his neb cap and his shining buttons and shoes, to get me back into the carriage. To forestall any further squeezes, he quickly slammed the carriage door behind me. I barely got in before the train began to lurch out of the station. Brushing my tears aside, I waved good-bye until the two bonneted faces, handkerchiefs to noses, passed out of sight. Then I settled down and began to gorge as I had been bidden.

Few summers passed without my spending some time with my aunts at Bamber Bridge. They never came to our house in Blackburn. If I didn't appear they would send the whole of my railway fare to mother so that there could be no excuse for my not coming. Every visit was joyful. Always they were happy and unchanged. I felt that nothing could affect their world. Yet something did.

One summer's day a stranger came to my aunts' house. The stranger had a large cardboard folder under his arm tied with a bow. I met him at the front door talking to Betsy. He was such an odd-looking fellow that I could not help staring at him. He wore a dark-blue suit with faded grey stripes. The garment was threadbare; the arms and legs were far too short. His shirt and tie were equally worn but clean. On his head he had a tattered blue trilby hat that shone with grease at the sides. He had cracked shoes laced with hooks instead of eyes.

"This is Mr. Simon Gripper, Billy," my aunt said, introducing me. I jerked my head in greeting.

Mr. Gripper put a cold, wet hand around mine, while observing me sharply. Neither of us spoke. I suddenly felt an instinctive dislike for him. Whiskey must have felt the same, for he growled. The hair along his back stood up, which was always a bad sign.

Mr. Gripper was the nearest thing to a gorilla in a suit that I could imagine. He had the same wide shoulders, the same flat face, the same fish eyes, the same flat nose, the same protruding bottom lip, the same wet, steamy brow. When he left, he walked like a gorilla rocking from side to side. As he disappeared down the lane I decided to forget all about him.

Imagine my surprise, therefore, a week or two later, when running into the living room with Whiskey for tea, I found him sitting on Whiskey's favourite chair talking to my aunts. His suit seemed to have shrunk since the last visit. Apart from a grunt and a wave of the hand, he wasted no time on me. Having been given several thin cucumber sandwiches and some sticky fruitcake, I chose a chair among Mr. Kenyon's stuffed birds which lined one side of the room, as far away from the visitor as I could. Whiskey sat under my chair with a baleful eye on the stranger. We had never been unhappy at tea before.

While eating as much as he could, Mr. Gripper never stopped talking. As far as I could make out he was telling my aunts how he had come by his present job; which, of all things, was selling religious pictures from door to door. Hence the large folder he carried.

"It's the Lord's will," he intoned, in what I thought was a slushy voice; then he paused and gave a long sigh. Whiskey growled; I felt like growling too.

Meanwhile Mr. Gripper drew from his folder one vivid picture after

150

another. There was Jesus as a child, Jesus as a man, Jesus crucified. There was the sacrificial lamb. There was the Holy Mother Mary, dressed in the richest silks. Pictures of the Sacred Heart and the Saints followed. Some of the Saints wore halos and floated through the sky, others were covered with blood and gore. There was no end to the pictures. The furniture in the living room was covered with them.

"One cannot make a living this way," Mr. Gripper conceded, "but it gives me the chance to earn my daily bread and spread the gospel of love at the same time. What better task?"

I shall never understand why my aunts allowed Mr. Gripper to cross their threshold. Perhaps he didn't look as ugly to them as he did to me. Perhaps it was downright jealousy on my part which made him seem so greasy and servile. I felt threatened by him. What I found really objectionable was the way aunt Grace had eyes and ears only for Mr. Gripper. Aunt Betsy, Whiskey and I might never have existed.

One week later, Mr. Gripper was back. The next week he was back again. Once, out of the corner of my eye, I saw him take auntie Grace's hand, which really upset me.

Later that night, when I was on my way to join my aunts in the kitchen, I heard the only cross words that I ever heard between them. They must have been arguing for some time, for they were both worked up.

"Grace," said Betsy, who had been plucking and trussing some ducks for the church, "I don't know what's come over you, luv. We've come this far. Let's go on together. I'm not happy, luv, for your sake."

I was shocked at Grace's reply.

"You're not happy," Grace responded in an unusually hard tone. "The truth is, Betsy, you don't want me to be happy. You'd rather boss me for the rest of my life."

Those words made me catch my breath. How unfair to aunt Betsy! She worshipped her younger sister. I was not surprised to hear aunt Betsy burst into tears. Her sobbing shook the room.

"May you be forgiven, Grace Kenyon," she sobbed. "You know, I don't want anyone to hurt you."

"No one's going to hurt me, Betsy. I'm not marrying Simon. There's nothing going on between Simon and myself if that's what you're hinting at. We're just friends. He's a good man out on his luck who needs help."

The next thing I knew was that aunt Grace had also burst into tears. "Oh Betsy," she cried as she flung herself into her sister's outstretched arms. I crept away with a heavy heart.

The next day I decided to have it out with aunt Betsy about Mr. Gripper. "I don't like him, aunt Betsy," I said. "Nor does Whiskey. We hate him."

"You shouldn't talk like that, Billy. You're jumping to conclusions. You don't know anything about him. As Christians we must love Mr. Gripper, forgive him from our hearts, and pray for him." But her voice betrayed her. She obviously didn't like Mr. Gripper any more than I did.

When I returned the following summer, I was dumbfounded to be met by Mr. Gripper. I ran right into him. Whiskey was nowhere to be seen.

"Oh, it's you again, is it," he said, holding my arm tightly and staring through me.

When I went down the field to give aunt Betsy a surprise she hardly responded to my creeping up on her. She seemed a bit thinner and tired. Her eyes were worried, even haunted-looking. Aunt Grace looked better. She had twice the life she had had previously. Instead of following Betsy's moves as she had always done in the past, she seemed to be leading. I hadn't been there several hours before I realized that Grace had transferred her affections from me to Mr. Gripper. On her suggestion, he had moved into the house; worse, he had taken my room. Grace seemed to have lost her head over him. Nothing was too much trouble. Mr. Gripper was in charge.

That summer was the only unhappy one I spent at Bamber Bridge. With Mr. Gripper giving orders through Grace, the peace and laughter went out of the place. Gripper's shrewd, mottled brown eyes seemed to follow me everywhere. He showed no interest in fattening me up as my aunts had done in the past. He'd given up selling holy pictures. Instead he marketed the stockings my aunts made. Each now had her own stocking frame. When they weren't looking after the livestock and the orchard they knitted stockings; Jim and Effie no longer came. While Mr. Gripper didn't do any work himself – he had a chest complaint that demanded rest – he was forever on about wasting time. "The Lord never wastes time," was one of his favourite sayings. Even our afternoon walk had been sacrificed to Simon Gripper's need for more stockings.

Yet Mr. Gripper never bullied them. "I quite understand," he would say when Betsy objected to something. "How foolish of me. You are right and I am wrong. I was only trying to do what is best for us all." I used to watch Betsy's reactions. Her face would go from red to scarlet. Then it would set on fire. Yet she managed to hold her tongue.

Mr. Gripper never sat in the evening without telling his rosary. He kept it in an old snuff box which he carried in his waistcoat pocket. It was a very poor thing compared with the one aunt Grace had. Hers was made of ivory beads with a silver chain and a golden cross. As my aunts were devout Catholics, they would sometimes join him in saying a few Hail Mary's and Our Father's – something they'd never done before. Whenever we could, Whiskey and I fled the house for the fields. We were both heavy-hearted.

Although I attended a Protestant school at that time, my aunts always insisted on my going to St. Augustine's Catholic Church with them. In an undemonstrative way, the church was the centre of their life. There was always something being "got up" by them for the church. Open-handedly, they gave innumerable hens and ducks to the never-ending bazaars.

What I could not stand about Mr. Gripper was his behavior in church. When he genuflected before the altar, I thought he would never get up.

He struck his breast three times during the Confiteor, hitting himself hard enough to break his ribs. "Through my fault," thump. "Through my fault," louder thump. "Through my most grievous fault," crash! The half empty church echoed to the thumps. At the elevation of the Host, he would groan. He relished the words "miserable sinner," and beat himself as he repeated them. When he groveled before the altar rails to receive communion, I wished that the vaulted ceiling of the church would fall on him.

To my aunts' obvious displeasure I couldn't help staring at him. "Aunt Betsy," I whispered, "why does Mr. Gripper have to beat himself like that? You don't."

"Sh-sh. Stop talking, Billy, you can't talk here. What will people think?"

Not only did Mr. Gripper thump himself in church more than anybody else; when the congregation recited the eight Beatitudes – blessed are the poor; blessed are the meek; blessed are they that mourn; blessed are they that hunger and thirst after justice; blessed are the merciful; blessed are the clean of heart; blessed are the peacemakers; blessed are they that suffer persecution for justice's sake – Mr. Gripper's voice was louder than all the rest. At Benediction one Sunday evening he sang a solo "The day that Thou gavest, Oh Lord, now is ending" which almost took out the windows. Grace thought it was marvelous. I thought it awful. Only Betsy's shushing stopped me from saying so.

I have reason to remember that particular summer. It was the summer Mr. Gripper robbed me of a tooth. I'd had the misfortune to develop toothache. The pain was awful.

"Simon, take lad beyond t' bridge to Henry's," aunt Betsy had asked Mr. Gripper. "He's a young man just starting out. He'll put it right. They say he's got a new-fangled American drill that does the job in half the time. Tell him to do a good job on t' lad. Mustn't lose tooth at his age. I'll pay when you tell me how much it is."

So off we went to Henry's. Mr. Gripper didn't have to tell me that I and my tooth were a complete nuisance and that he wasn't enjoying the excursion one bit.

Our arrival at Mr. Henry's was announced by a large doorbell. A threateningly, ominously empty chair occupied the surgery. There were no other patients. Mr. Henry emerged from a back room.

"He's got a bit of a toothache," Mr. Gripper grumped at Mr. Henry. "Can yo put it right?"

I was put in the chair. With the aid of a great light, Mr. Henry studied the offending tooth. His poking made it worse.

"He needs a small filling," Mr. Henry concluded. "Take a few minutes, that's all. He won't feel a thing. It'll take out all the pain."

I watched Mr. Gripper eye the dentist slyly. "Wot's cost?" he asked.

"Three and sixpence."

There was a pause. "Wot's an extraction cost?"

"Two shillings."

"Take it out," said Mr. Gripper.

"But I can save the tooth," Mr. Henry said. "It's a straightforward job. A perfectly good tooth."

"Take it out," said Mr. Gripper.

"But..." the dentist faltered.

"Young man," said Mr. Gripper, "yo're wasting my time. Dost t' want to earn two shillings or dostn't thee?"

Mr. Henry made a pathetic gesture. "All right," he said. "I've heard yer."

I returned to aunt Betsy without my tooth.

"Had to come out," said Mr. Gripper. "Nothing else for it."

The next time I went to Bamber Bridge I was surprised to find my aunts' house occupied by strangers. The door was locked and I had to use the knocker to rouse them. A tall oldish couple came to the door.

"Ah've cum te stay with my aunts," I said. "Ah cum every year."

"Tha won't be staying this year," the man said.

"Why not?"

"Because thi aunts don't live here any more. They sold t' house. It's an old folks' 'ome now. Didn't ye know? Thi aunt Grace has got herself wed."

"To Mr. Gripper?" I asked, my heart sinking.

"The same," the woman said. She was about to go on, but the man gave her a reproachful glance, whereupon she fell silent.

I stood looking vacantly from one to the other. "Where are they now?" I asked.

"They're running a general store with Mr. Gripper in Preston," the man answered. He went back into the house to find the address which he wrote on a slip of paper for me. He also gave me instructions on how to get there. His eyes told me that I was in for a shock.

An hour later I found a grocer's store in one of the back streets of Preston. The shop faced an ancient aqueduct, the black, greasy stones of which ran with moisture. All around was a bleak industrial area with the railroad and factories only yards away. Dirt and peeling paint were everywhere. If anybody had told me a year earlier that I should find my aunts living in such an unattractive and unlikely place I would have thought them mad.

The shop was empty of customers when I entered. With their backs to the entrance, Betsy and Grace were busy unwrapping and emptying boxes. They got such a surprise when they saw me. They flapped their hands to show their discomfort.

"Oh, Billy," they said, "why did you come here?"

They proceeded to hug me, but it was in an absent-minded, apprehensive sort of way. They didn't have the life and strength of earlier times. Betsy moved stiffly in a way I'd never known. I was startled at aunt

Grace's appearance. She looked crushed. She had great black rings under her eyes, which I'd never seen before. She could hardly breathe from asthma – something she had never had at Bamber Bridge. She told me Whiskey was dead.

While we were talking, Mr. Gripper came up from the cellar. He looked extremely well and prosperous. He'd got himself a better suit. His hair glistened with oil. He wore a gold watch-chain. From the moment he saw me, he was hostile.

"Oh, it's you is it?" he said as he came forward. "Thought we'd got rid of you, we did. Well, you've come to t' wrong place for a free summer this time. Tha'd better go back where tha cum fra. Can't have thee interferin' with our business."

"Simon!" Grace said angrily.

But Simon was not to be put off. He pointed to the door through which I had just entered. The message was clear. He wanted me back in the street. My aunts stared at me with empty eyes. There was time only to squeeze their hands. We didn't speak. We just clung to each other pathetically. None of us cried, but our eyes were wet. I knew in my heart that we all wanted to sob and sob.

I never saw my aunts again. I did write a letter to them when I got home asking them if I could help them in any way, but it was returned to me by Mr. Gripper. Mother came in one day and told me in a sad voice that Grace was dead. The news gave me a lump in my throat. My eyes welled with tears. Betsy had gone to live with friends in Scotland. I thought mother was going to go on about Mr. Gripper – all the Kenyons and Woodruffs knew about Simon Gripper by now – but she didn't. I don't know what became of him. I hope he did ill. He left me with a life-long distrust of unctuous people.

XII   Grandmother Bridget

From about 1922, when I was six, to 1926, when I was ten, I became closer to grandmother Bridget than to my own family. I had never met my other grandmother, Selma, who lived in America. Both my grandfathers had died before I was born. Hardly a day went by when I was not in grandma's house. With Jenny and Brenda in the mills, it fell to me to help her to keep it clean. I chopped the sticks for the fire that heated the washtub standing in an alcove of the downstairs room. I ran errands. Sometimes, when things were especially bad, I'd bring a shilling or a half-crown from mother to buy food.

It was during these years that grandmother fell on bitterly hard times again. She was living in a doll-like house at the end of a row of cottages in

Astley Street – five minutes walk from Griffin Street. The house was shaped like the tip of a flat iron. It had one tiny room downstairs and an equally small room upstairs. Apart from the street door, two windows (one up, one down), a corner in which to cook and another in which to wash, a broken rocking chair, two stools, a rough, bench-like table, a fireplace, and a bed with a wooden chest at its foot, there was little else. All the starched linen, the silver, and the fine china, with which years before she had beguiled grandfather William on his one and only visit to her, had long since gone to the pawnshop. Apart from my intrusions, which she welcomed, she always kept herself to herself. I think she did so because fate had dispossessed her. It had cast her into a society for which she was ill-suited. She didn't avoid people because she was "stuck-up"; she stayed aloof because it was the only way to protect her sanity. Maggie was right when she said her mother had "cum right down".

Next door to grandmother's cottage at the end of the row was a high-walled cobbled yard. At one time grandmother had kept her brooms, tin bath and laundry tub there. When I knew it, the lock grandmother had put on the door had been broken and the yard had become a steaming manure dump used by the town's street cleaning crews as well as by several horse stables in the vicinity. Although Bridget's house wall hid the manure, there was no mistaking the smell. Because of it her two windows and her door were always kept shut. The final irony was that the police were pressing grandmother to get rid of the manure.

Desperate, Bridget asked me if I would go to the police station and try to sort out how she was to stop people dumping manure outside her door. I wasn't happy about going to the police – it was probably not the place to go – but I went. I suppose I must have been about nine.

Having run through the streets I reached the station and began to lay Bridget's troubles before the sergeant in charge. He was a tall, burly individual with a clipped moustache. I was very nervous because I'd never been in a police station before, and I had been raised to fear and avoid the police. From the word go, I sensed that my visit was, to say the least, inopportune. Perhaps it was my luck to meet with the most officious sergeant on the force, but the chap in charge left me in no doubt that my sudden unannounced ragged appearance to discuss steaming manure was not to his liking. He had more important things to do.

"The coppers have complained to grandmother about the manure in her yard. But she's not the one who puts it there," I said.

"Who has complained?" he asked, his red face reddening.

"The coppers."

"And who might the coppers be?" he threatened, taking up a heavy, black ruler, and leaning down menacingly from his desk.

"You're a copper, aren't you?" I said, my eyes glued to the stick.

"Bert, Charley," the sergeant called to two policemen who were listening from the other room, "There's a young gentleman here who thinks we're coppers. Not officers, not sergeants, not constables, just plain coppers."

"Well, you are, aren't you?" I said, displaying monumental stupidity.

At that moment the topic of manure went through the window. For the next several minutes I was given the worst dressing down of my life. With his face aflame, the sergeant threatened me with a fate worse than that suffered by the Christian martyrs. I suspect he had a whale of a time working me over. He said he would have the whole Blackburn police force down on my head and I believed him. Jauntily, he swung the ruler close to my head so that I would be left in no doubt. I'd be in the "clink" for the rest of my life. He put the fear of hell into me. With my eye on the ruler, I edged back to the door and fled.

"Well?" asked grandmother, when I returned, breathless from running. "What are they going to do about it?"

"Nothing, Grandma," I answered. "They didn't want to talk about manure."

Grandmother not only had to tolerate the manure; directly opposite her house lived the town executioner. I was horrified when she told me about the hangman. Not that I ever heard anyone speak against hanging; tooth for tooth, eye for eye was the general feeling of the time. I spent hours gingerly peeping through her curtains in the hope of catching a glimpse of the hangman hurrying off with his rope to Lancaster, Manchester, or Liverpool. I tried to draw out of Bridget the fine details of how the poor wretches died. "It's not a subject for 'dacent' conversation," she silenced me. Father knew the hangman; he often met him in the pub. He spoke highly of him. He said he was the happiest of men. The only strange thing about him, father said, was his ice-cold hands.

As grandmother got older she often talked about Ireland; about her birthplace, County Clare, with its ruined castles and the ghosts that haunted the broken walls; and about her life as a teenage girl before she met grandfather Thomas. Sometimes she'd tell me about the great balls she'd been to. Like my mother and my sister Jenny, she had had a passion for dancing. No matter how much she tried to conceal it, I detected a wistfulness, if not a downright sadness, when she recalled her maiden days at home. She also talked about the history of her people. What I know about the feud that has raged between Ireland and England for centuries, I learnt from her. "The trouble with the English," she said one day, "is that they can never remember what the Irish can never forget. In a quiet, but rich voice, she sometimes sang a song about Robert Emmet, the Irish martyr:

> The struggle is over, the boys are defeated,
> Old Ireland's surrounded with sadness and gloom;
> We were betrayed and shamefully treated,
> And I, Robert Emmet, awaiting my doom.

She sang it as a dirge, not as a call to arms; she was never bitter: not against fate, not against the British. Grudges were no part of her.

She also told me about the great famine in Ireland in the 1840s in which millions had died or fled to America. "It was not a famine, Billy Boy," she said. "There was plenty of grain, but it was sent to England to pay the rents. It was a great 'starvin'. And it was to England's shame!"

She taught me to be courageous, loyal, and honest. Falseness she couldn't abide. "If you give your word, Billy Boy, keep it." Especially did she teach me to be upstanding. "You must never grovel, Billy Boy. And never beg. Stand on your own feet. And don't whine." While she provided me with an education, she never stopped stressing character. "Don't become a clever devil, Billy Boy. There are too many of them about." Whatever manners and courtesies I learnt, I learnt from her.

She never mentioned God. The only concession she made to the saints was to wear a large sprig of shamrock on the 17th March, St. Patrick's Day. In her opinion St. Patrick was a "foin Saint, a very foin Saint," and that was good enough for me. One of her favourite ballads was about St. Patrick's Day:

> O Paddy dear, an' did ye hear the news that's goin' round?
> The shamrock is by law forbid to grow on Irish ground!
> No more St. Patrick's Day we'll keep, his colour can't be seen,
> For there's a cruel law agin the wearin' o' the Green!

One night when we were sitting before the embers she told me how in 1920 some 20,000 Irish had appeared outside a London jail where almost two hundred Irish political prisoners were fasting unto death. As darkness fell across the roofs of London, someone called for silence. Faintly they heard the sound of voices singing inside the jail. Then a great thunder rose from the square into the night sky as the Irish – in and outside the jail – sang "The Wearin' o' the Green." "It stunned everybody who heard it," Grandma said. "Papers were full of it. Not long afterward the prisoners were freed."

Grandmother lived to see southern Ireland become the Irish Free State.

When my lessons were done, she turned down the glass-funnelled paraffin lamp and relapsed into quiet contentment before the fire. Often she gently rocked herself, while humming a tune or gravely sipping a cup of tea. I never knew her to touch alcohol. Although she had few visitors, she always tidied herself up at night. By the time I reached her cottage, she had changed into a long, dark garment which contrasted with the lace cap which came down to her shoulders. Sometimes she wore a blouse with big, shiny buttons. Usually I found her before the fire, her feet on a stool, her hands on her knees. There was always an open book – her escape from wretchedness – on the cornice next to her wire-framed spectacles. I often wondered how she could sit there by herself for hours on end staring at the flames. Sometimes I'd catch her carrying on a conversation with the embers and her memories.

On occasions I managed to persuade her to take a short walk. With her hat and her jacket and her silver-topped cane and her cracked, polished shoes, all of them relics of her better days, she looked quite a toff. Even when she was a slubber in the mills she never wore a weaver's shawl or clogs. Poor or not, she never lost her dignified bearing, the Kenyon air of gentility. There were times when her neighbours found her difficult to understand but they all called her "royal."

"And where do you think you're going?" she'd ask if I walked too fast. "I can't keep up with you." Only once did I see her truly worried and sad. Shortly before I arrived, a hog of a rent collector had threatened to throw her into the street. Tears were rolling silently down her wrinkled face. Her long, thin neck seemed to have contracted. She wasn't crushed – she was too tough for that – just badly wounded.

In retrospect, regardless of her growing poverty, regardless of the fact that the surrounding misery never seemed to abate, I remember grandmother Bridget as always happy and cheerful. The hardness of her lot never hardened her soul. She had a gentle voice with an Irish lilt. Like her late husband, she was completely unselfish. When as things got worse she lost her job in the mills, she tried to survive by doing people's washing and was never satisfied until it was whiter than snow. It used to infuriate me the way some of the workers robbed her. "Tell her I'll give her the money next week," they'd say when I delivered the laundry beautifully wrapped in clean newspaper. I knew they were lying; there were times when I felt like telling them so. I knew how desperately grandmother needed the money; sixpence, ninepence, or a shilling would have kept her going.

"These people don't speak with a plain tongue, Grandma," I complained.

"They're poor too, Billy Boy," she said, clasping her wasted hands, "they don't know which way to turn."

By the time she was in her early sixties, about the time of the General Strike in 1926, she was destitute. She had no income at all. I cannot believe that some of the Kenyons did not try to help her, but I saw little evidence of it. Everybody was desparately trying to survive. Also I suspect that Bridget put them off in her own innocent, refined way, as she did the offers of help from her neighbours. Except from me, she never accepted help gracefully.

For a period at least, grandmother was eligible for outdoor relief from the town. Like others, she could have queued up for one of the Lord Mayor's parcels, which every now and again were distributed in front of the Town Hall. But the idea of queuing with hundreds of others seeking public charity was an anathema to her. She would not make an exhibition of her need. The churches provided food – in helping to stem the tide of want, Blackburn churches and clergy had a long and honorable tradition – but some churches adhered to the maxim "support only those that are of the faith." It grieved mother that Bridget would not apply for the dole. To refuse the dole was refusing good money. Nor did she resort to the Poor Law Guardians. That would have been the final blow to her self-respect. Bridget preferred to keep her pride and to genteelly starve to death. Pride was all she had left.

Living from hand to mouth ourselves, there was little we could do for such a proud woman. I suppose my family must have helped her with the rent. I couldn't give her anything from what I earned running errands; my people took it. I sometimes brought her a basin of broth from the street kitchens run by the Salvation Army, or the Catholic Sisters of Mercy and Charity. Some of the Protestant churches also handed out free soup or a piece of potato pie. Grandmother wasn't easy. She ate the food I brought her, but she refused to go and get it. That was begging.

The trouble came when she began to lose interest in food altogether; not only in food but in life as well. She became increasingly listless. Etched by a nest of lines, her deep-set blue eyes became deeper still. The light in them was lowered. She didn't seem to care what happened to her. She got so weak that I began to do all her cleaning. That's how, one Saturday evening when grandmother had gone to mother's, I came to open the box that stood at the foot of her bed. I lifted the lid gingerly knowing that I was prying. I was astonished to find a whole lot of fine clothes there. Among them was a beautiful blue ball dress decorated with imitation pearls. There also was a little book with a list of names in it.

As the clothes meant food, I brought up the subject when grandmother returned. I confessed I'd been prying into her trunk.

"You didn't tell me about all the fine clothes you're hiding," I said to her. "That's money. Why don't you pawn them?"

"They're not for pawning, Billy Boy," she answered quietly. "Not my best feathers," she added with a bright, quick smile. "Not those!"

After a long silence, she spoke up. "Would you like to see me in my best feathers?" she asked, an unusual note of mischief in her voice.

"Yes," I said, for I knew it would please her.

Before I could stop her, she had jumped up, taken the glass-funneled lamp from the cornice, and was on her way upstairs. I was left with the firelight.

After a few minutes she called down: "Are you ready, Billy Boy?"

"Yes," I called back, "I'm ready."

I looked up as I heard her feet on the stairway. What I saw made me catch my breath. Grandmother was wearing the ball dress I'd seen in the trunk. The pearls glowed softly as they caught the firelight. Around her neck she wore a long fluffy boa made of feathers and delicate fabric. On her feet were the elegant slippers. A tiny patch of lace covered her hair. From her wrist hung the little book. Her face was lit by the paraffin lamp which she held before her. I noticed that the deep lines and wrinkles had gone. Her face had changed. It seemed much younger and smoother.

"Grandma," I gasped.

As she stepped lightly on to the sanded floor she pretended to consult her little book. "I believe you asked me to dance this one with you," she said as she extended her hand toward me gracefully.

Kicking off my clogs, I hurriedly pushed whatever furniture there was out of the way. Resting her hands on my shoulders, for she was taller than I, we began to turn slowly in the confined space. The lamp on the cornice, which she had replaced, flickered a dim light. It threw our shadows against the wall. Increasing our speed we danced round and round, grinding the grit with our toes. Grandma's eyes were almost shut.

In time, I tired. Bridget didn't. She moved effortlessly, like someone possessed; she never wanted to stop.

"Oh, Billy Boy," she scolded when I stumbled, and then we were off again, faster than ever. My head spun.

I don't know how long we danced. The dance ended when I fell over a stool and could go on no more.

I didn't know what to do when I got up off the floor, so I stood there breathless and clapped as I'd seen dancers do at the edge of the ballroom floor. "Grandma," I said, "you danced beautifully."

She smiled, made a slight bow, and went upstairs. Shortly afterward, she came down again, coughing harshly. This time she wore her usual black dress, with her lace cap hanging to her shoulders. The flushed cheeks had paled; the deep lines had returned; dark rings surrounded her reddened eyes; she was strangely cast down; there was a tiredness in her voice – a grating in her throat. She had difficulty breathing. When she stepped into the room I could hear her bare feet on the sand. Her step was halting and unsteady.

I didn't see anything of grandmother the next day. Two nights later I entered her darkened cottage. There was no sign of her. Having struck a light, I saw her empty purse on the table. It lay there wide open as if it had been thrown from the door. My eyes took in the faded pictures on the wall, the setpot, the frayed curtains, the broken rocking chair, the glass-funneled lamp on the mantelpiece, and the gutted candle on the table. I knew something was wrong. I ran upstairs. There was no one there. When I lifted the lid of the trunk at the foot of her bed it was empty. I ran home and told mother.

Two days later uncle Edward walked in to tell us that grandmother Bridget was dead and buried.

Wearing her ball dress, she had stumbled all the way to the workhouse and had died there a few hours after being admitted. She had declared herself "without next of kin," which had made it all the more difficult for the workhouse authorities to get in touch with us. It was the police who had informed uncle Edward.

A week or so later, Mr. Hetherington, t' bump man who had studied my head years before, told us he'd seen grandmother on the day she was missing. She was resting on a bench at the edge of town. He'd walked past her and had wondered what she was up to dressed like that. "Ah've never seen anythin' like it," he said. "You might have thought she was frozen to't bench. She was sat straight up, back like a ramrod, head held high, oh, so high, feathers aflutter. She had her silver-topped cane in her outstretched right hand. Her t' other hand lay on her lap. Cheeks were sunken, but t' nose and chin were out there. I could have sworn t' eyes were closed. She was like something on t' parade. Well, I didn't know what to say. I felt right bamboozled. I almost stopped and asked her what she was up to. But then I had second thoughts. It was none of my business. It was summer, and t' old lady was known for taking walks. As for t' funny dress and scarf and slippers, who was I to judge? There's no telling what an old woman will get up to. So, I doffed mi cap, held mi tongue, and went mi way."

Several days later, the workhouse returned Bridget's belongings. There was the silver-tipped cane, the dress, the scarf, the lace cap, and the now torn slippers. They also sent a faded photograph of grandfather Thomas, and the little book that contained Bridget's list of dancing partners.

Out of it all came my first great heartbreak. For the first time in my life I knew what it was to be scalded with grief. I was more upset than when I heard aunt Grace was dead. On and off, I wept for days. Several times I cried myself to sleep. I not only wept, I loathed myself for not having done more. I loathed the grown-ups, especially uncle Eric and uncle Edward, when they came together in our house to brood over stewed tea, while they accused and mocked each other for having "driven t' poor owd woman in t' workhouse." Silently, I listened to their every mealy-mouthed word. Rage possessed me; they were all to blame. For the first time the idea of running away from Blackburn and Lancashire entered my head. Grandmother had had to die before they recognized her existence. With all their fine talk they had managed to inflict on grandmother Bridget the two things we all feared most: the workhouse and a pauper's grave.

Between them they'd driven Bridget Gorman Kenyon "over t' hill."

XIII Strike!

Something must have been sadly wrong with Britain when people had to "genteelly" starve to death as grandmother Bridget had done. Living through the 1920s was like sitting in a boiling pot of broth. There was never any peace. By 1926 things had got so bad that the workers began to talk of bringing the country to a standstill through a General Strike. The idea had been mooted a couple of years before; it gave the workers something to live for. Unrest was everywhere. A show-down had at last become unavoidable. The working class was going to make one last big effort to set everything right. In April 1926 the mine owners posted new wage offers that were tantamount to a lockout. With that, matters were brought to a head. On 1 May 1926 the Government declared a State of Emergency. The fight was on.

I was nine at the time. I'd almost no idea of what was going on, but I remember being thrilled at the prospect of a decisive fight with the bosses. Young as I was, I knew that right was on our side. Not for a moment did I doubt the complete justice of the workers' cause. Before the strike there was to be a meeting in the Blackburn Trade Hall. Father's Trade Union had asked him to go. Everyone talked about it – even at school.

I was so excited and interested in what was going on that I asked father to take me with him to the Trade Hall meeting. When we entered the crowded hall you could feel the sparks. People were really worked up. The place hummed with voices. Messengers were running about. Delegates from all the major industries – mining, transport, railways, engineering, and textiles – were present. They all had their banners. To loud applause the meeting began with one of the miners' delegates taking the platform and appealing to his "brothers and sisters" to come to the miners' aid. "The hour of decision has struck!" he shouted to wild applause. "Defend us in our fight for a living wage."

What followed came as a surprise. I thought the Amalgamated Weavers and the Spinners and Twiners trade unions would all line up behind the miners, the railway and other transport workers to fight the bosses. Instead a shouting match began between our own textile people in which all order broke down. Nobody seemed to know if we were going to have a General Strike or a National Strike, though I couldn't see the difference. Tall, angular Patrick Murphy thought that a General Strike would make matters worse, and he advised against joining the miners. He was shouted down as "a capitalist lackey and a running dog." Those who wanted a General Strike were shouted down as "Bolshies and Reds in the pay of Russia."

"Revolution's out of the question," Mr. Murphy argued, jumping up on his chair. "It's purposeless to talk about a workers' state. The country is not with you. Of course we must continue the struggle, but there is a right way of going about it and a wrong way. There are two sides to this question. Why come out now, when you've already lost so much through strikes and lockouts? I ask you, what can you gain? Nothing. On that you have to agree. Half a loaf is better than none."

While many workers booed Mr. Murphy, half a dozen other speakers stood on their chairs bawling at each other at the top of their voices. One of them shouted, "Half a loaf rubbish. Next thing you'll be telling us that a crumb is better than nothing. What I say is not a penny off the pay, not a second on the day! One out, all out!" By now everybody was clamoring and uneasy.

As far as I could make out all the speakers were proposing something different. Some were bawling for revolution; some were calling for peace; some were yelling for help for the miners; others were shouting to leave the miners to their fate. Everybody was rude to each other. Expressions like "Hold thi trap," "shut thi gob," and "shut up," were hurled across the room. They stung each other like wasps.

Once the meeting got out of hand, the chairman's shouts of "Gentlemen, please! Gentlemen, recognize the chair!" were ignored. So were the appeals of many others who called for "Silence, please. Silence!" The drum beat of the chairman's gavel on the table only added to the din. I'd never been to a workers' meeting as unruly as this. Father's trade union meetings were all solemn affairs, like going to church.

As the noise got worse, father said, "Let's go home. Too many crackpots." Until then he hadn't opened his mouth. Others must have agreed with him, for lots of people were streaming out of the hall. They smelled danger. I remember looking back as we left. There were more people standing on chairs than ever.

The next day father read from the paper that "Because of the lively differences of opinion expressed at the Trade Hall meeting, a decision to join the other unions calling for a General Strike, has been deferred." Later that week, another meeting was convoked, but that didn't get anywhere either.

Two days after that father came home looking glum. "We're coomin' oot," he said, "a sympathy strike, and a damned lot of good it will do; especially as the TUC (Trades Union Congress) doesn't want us out yet. Anyway, the decision has been made. It is only the timing that's in t' air." Murphy and other moderates had been overruled; the crackpots had won. Father was obviously worried. He began to talk about what was at stake; who would finish up having to give up what. He wanted to get it off his chest. Then he relapsed into silence.

I was with mother in the mill when the strike began. "Where are you going?" mother asked workers who were hastening past her.

"Going? Why, on strike, of course. Didn't you hear the call 'All out?' Why, you must be deaf? Y' either starve outside in t' fresh air with us, luv, or starve in here covered with dust. Which do you want?"

Mother was bewildered. She had a deadly fear of violence. Reluctantly she threw her shawl round her shoulders, shut down her machine, and walked out. The strike was on. It was 3 May 1926.[†]

"Fight! Fight! Action! Action!" people were shouting in the streets. A river of workers was streaming home. There were bursts of cheering.

I've never forgotten how the whole world fell silent the next day. Even the factory engines were stopped. It was the deep, strange silence of the high moors. No shouting, no roughness, no disorder, no lawlessness in Blackburn. Soldiers were guarding public offices. The newspapers, including the *Daily Herald*, went off the streets. The trains, buses and trams were still. The iron and steel industry was brought to a halt. The mills, mines and engineering shops were all shut down. Some merchants shuttered their stores. For all the work done the schools might as well have been closed too.

My family sat in silence in our gloomy kitchen in Griffin Street, holding our breath, waiting for the revolution to begin. The streets were full of rumors: special constables were being sworn in; extra police had been brought in from Burnley and Preston; the mails were being censored; the telegraphs were controlled; the Manchester demonstrators had been fired on; there had been arson at Bank Top Mill; troops were in charge of all roads; there'd been clashes between them and groups of "Reds;" a police spy had been taken out of the canal near Whalley Bridge with his throat cut; at Walton-le-Dale, near Preston, the police had baton-charged strikers interfering with the buses; the docks at Liverpool were paralyzed. No tale lost anything in the telling. Uncle Eric was the only one we knew who owned a radio. He could have told us what was going on. But I cannot remember that he did, or that we asked him.

After eight days the papers were back on the streets with banner headlines: GENERAL STRIKE BROKEN. ENGLAND STANDS FAST. The first general strike in the history of the country had failed.

Oh what a let down! People cried. No tongue could tell their tale. If they had been beaten, it would have been one thing. But they hadn't. The strike wasn't broken; it was abandoned. There never was any fighting on any scale. Those at the top, like Jimmy Thomas of the Railway Workers' Union, had betrayed us. Dad said the labour leaders had played with fire and then run for cover. Maybe, but Prime Minister Stanley Baldwin and the bosses had won. There wasn't going to be a revolution after all.

We didn't starve after the General Strike but we were humiliated. Conditions were worse. Despite all the honeyed words, victimization was common. The bosses did what they liked. They kept those they wanted and threw out those they didn't. Ringleaders were blackballed. Little pity was shown. Hours were increased, wages cut. The factory owners never shared the good times with us, only the bad. When there was cake, they ate it; when there was sorrow, they lumped it on to us. Under the Trade Disputes and Trade Unions Act of 1927, which was passed almost overnight, many rights that the workers had fought for over long periods were abolished. General strikes and sympathetic strikes were outlawed. New laws sent workers to jail for picketing. Any excuse would do: "The accused was lurking in a doorway." "The accused had his foot over the factory threshold" during a lockout. Labour Party finances – and hence the strength of the Labour Party – were deliberately undermined. Political activity on the part of the Trade Unions was curtailed. The policy of fining workers also became harsher. In 1928, Nelson (it was called "Red" Nelson) was brought to a standstill for seven weeks because of what the workers felt was an unjust weaver's fine. In Nelson a lot of workers and their families went hungry. Henceforth, you toed the employers' line or you were for it.

What the textile workers suffered was nothing compared to the miners who had started the row. Over one million mineworkers, together with their womenfolk and children, were abandoned to the mercy of the mineowners. The miners stayed out on strike for seven bitter months. "We'll starve before going back," they said. By the time they went back they were starving. They took a heavy beating: hours, wages, the lot. There hadn't been a strike like it before and there hasn't been one like it since. It was soulless capitalism at its worst. Mother's only comment, when father told her of the miners' plight was, "Why do people have to be so cruel to each other?" She never realized that her God of mercy was not widely known; it was the God of wrath, the vindictive God that ruled.

So bad did conditions become that a proposed visit of the King to Lancashire at this time was canceled.

The ever-darkening scene in Lancashire after the General Strike of 1926 prompted a shift in emphasis from trade union to political action. There was a new interest in winning seats on the Town Council and in Parliament. If the workers could replace the toffs in Parliament a new day might dawn.

Blackburn began at the local level. We tried to get Patrick Murphy on to the Town Council. His sunken, snub-nosed face was well-known in town politics. His fairness and candour made him well-liked. The workers trusted him. His honesty was apparent. His opponent was an absentee conservative factory owner, Henry Hen. Hen's slogan was: "Vote for Hen, the man who lays the golden eggs."

I was ten at the time. With Harold Watkins, Rosie Gill, Annie Morgan and others, I gladly helped Mr. Murphy by distributing handbills in the streets and at the factory gates. I got cross at workers who called him an Irish mongrel. Murphy had been kind to me since I was born. What did being Irish matter? Grandmother Bridget was Irish.

Anyway, as was to happen time and again, Labour lost the election. Despite all our shouts of "Vote, vote, vote for Mr. Murphy, Murphy's sure to win the day...", most workers preferred to vote for the Tory bosses, who, with the Anglican Church, were all-powerful in our town. The people Labour wanted to help proved to be their worst enemies. Too many of the workers didn't want to change. They had a mental block which prevented them from putting their own people in charge. Like father, they were not radical at heart. Also, the mill bosses were generous in doling out free beer in a roundabout way.

All Patrick Murphy could afford to give his election helpers – when his predicted defeat was announced – was twopenny worth of fish and chips in a white paper bag with as much vinegar as we wanted. Mr. Murphy stood at the fish and chip counter – the strain of the election showing on his face – doling out twopence for each of us. When we'd finished eating we all sang "For He's A Jolly Good Fellow!" It must have touched him for he had difficulty holding back his tears.

As the contraction of the industry continued and wage levels fell, industrial action became paramount again. Strikes and lockouts became endemic. There was no stopping them. From the General Strike of 1926 until the mid-thirties, two-thirds of all working days lost in strikes in Britain were in textiles. Things got so bad that agitators worked on people's feelings to bring about a clash between the workers and the police at the factory gates. For boys of my age the prospect of such clashes offered excitement. Mother told me to stay away from these meetings. "They're dangerous," she warned, gently rubbing the sides of my head with her hands.

I ignored her warning. Riotous meetings before factory gates drew Harold Watkins and me like a magnet. The more dangerous, the more we were drawn. I'd never heard such fiery speakers. Harold said they'd been brought in specially. One day we were in the middle of such a crowd when somebody shouted "Coppers!" Panic-stricken, Harold and I fled with the rest. Suddenly, I tripped and fell. A tidal wave of workers passed over me. As I struggled to my feet, I caught a glimpse of the horses and the raised batons. The horses were almost on top of me when I felt a stunning blow to the head. There was no "In the name of the law, I order you to disperse," just a crack on the skull. Stars jumped before my eyes. I suddenly felt dizzy and weak. I nearly fell again. Somehow we got away. Despite my thick woollen cap, I had an egg on my head, which I tried to conceal for weeks.

Father never turned up at any of these factory gate meetings. He was always suspicious of anybody letting off steam. It embarrassed him. Yet he was ever loyal to his union. When the union said "Strike!" he struck; when they said "March!" he marched – though like a lot of factory folk he didn't enjoy it – if they asked him to carry a banner, he carried it. When his fellow unionists sang:

> You should rally round our banner in a true and loyal manner,
> And be eager in the fight that's being waged …

he sang as hard as the rest. He had his own opinions about strikes, which he sometimes shared with the family, but he never let the side down. The Trade Union was the only thing my father ever joined and he remained loyal to it.

Dad's staunch loyalty to his union almost proved to be his undoing. The occasion was a strike meeting before the Town Hall. The time was the late 1920s. Almost everybody in town was on strike. There were to be a number of speakers including Patrick Murphy. There wasn't a "Red" on the programme. Like many others, just for the fun of it, Harold Watkins and I decided to go with dad to hear what the speakers had to say. The rest of the family showed no interest.

It all began peacefully enough. No one expected the procession to become as large as it did. It wasn't meant to be a procession at all. We were supposed to go in handfuls, which is how we started out. But soon there were scores, then hundreds. Drums, flags and banners appeared from nowhere. Some said we were going to the Town Hall, others said the meeting had been changed to the Trade Hall, and that's where we should go. Still others had no idea where we were going. They didn't care. They'd seen a crowd and joined it. They loved a parade; some even brought their dogs.

Drawn along by the drumbeats, the procession wound its way toward the centre of town. Caps pulled down, most of the men were buttoned up to the neck. Here and there the women had thrown their shawls back on to their shoulders. There was mist in their hair. There were a lot of red faces from the cold. With the factories stopped, the air was free of soot; the leaden sky had not yet turned into rain. Odd shouts and snatches of song echoed in the street. Children skipped in and out of the crowd. As the procession moved along, the crowd joked, chattered, and exchanged gossip.

The farther we got, the more people joined us. Others waved to us from teashops and the Ambulance Drill Hall and wished us "Good Luck!" When we got to the "Royal" there was a crowd standing in the doorway trying to find out what was up. They must have rushed from where they'd been sitting, enjoying their lunch. Some were carrying glasses of beer; others still had a napkin round their neck. Those with money could still eat well. They didn't respond to our shouts to join in. They stood there wordless, looking on. There were lights inside and glints of glassware.

It was just beyond the "Royal", close to Spries the undertaker, that a column of mounted police slowly emerged from a side street and blocked our path. A silence fell upon the procession; the crowd stiffened; there was a confused murmur; the dogs at the front began to bark. Harold and I thought it was just another group of police going about their business. They'd nothing to do with us. We weren't outside factory gates threatening violence, or kicking "scabs," or stirring an angry mob to burn down the mill. We weren't hurting or threatening anybody. Ours was an entirely peaceful procession.

I remember being impressed by the horses. They were in first-class condition: sleek, spotlessly clean, and groomed as on parade. I noticed the piping on the officers' coats, the highly polished shoes. The silver pieces on the harness glinted in the light. I'd never seen so many police horses in Blackburn before. They must have been brought in from outside.

I continued to be fascinated by the horses as they jingled toward us in a slow canter, their hoofs ringing on the stones. There were shouts: "Get out of bloody way! It's our bloody street!" Boos followed. Everyone began to talk at once. For a moment the column slowed down, but people pushed from behind causing the procession to sway forward again.

Only when the canter changed to a gallop, and the police drew their long batons, did I become afraid. The terror I'd felt once before, when I'd fallen in the middle of a mob, returned.

As the crowd turned to flee, a shot rang out. Pop! it went. It sounded like a firework. Somebody shouted "They're firing on us! It's bloody murder!" Panic seized the crowd which now tried to fall back, shouting, swearing, swaying, struggling, and screaming in fear. People ran in all directions to get out of the horses way.

Running along the sidewalk, father, Harold, and I clashed with a group running the other way. They were led by a man who was still carrying a banner "UNITED WE STAND, DIVIDED WE FALL." A group of us was swept into a furniture shop doorway. The door was locked. With the battle going on all around, we huddled there.

Baton-swinging riders repeatedly swept past our shelter. Lashed now by cold gusts of rain, the horses galloped, turned, reformed, and galloped again. They were led by an officer who rode at great speed, shouting commands. The street was full of cries for help. The windows of the barber's shop and the bakery across the street were being smashed. People were making concerted if confused rushes in an attempt to escape and save their heads. The sound of batons on flesh – a dull whack – made me wince. Flags, clothing, food were scattered all over the cobbles.

A few feet from where we were crouching, Patrick Murphy lay on the ground. One of the horses, snorting, its harness jingling, pranced all around him. Telling us to stay where we were – we were too terrified to do anything else – father and another man ran out and, with blows raining down on their backs, dragged Mr. Murphy from under the horses' hooves into the doorway. Mr. Murphy had blood on his bald head. His eyes were glassy and unseeing, his face pallid. "They've cracked his skull like an eggshell," father said. Dad was calm, as firm as a rock, Harold and I were shaking.

Once the police had moved farther down the street, the shopkeeper opened the door and offered us an escape through a back alley. He was obviously on the workers' side. "Bloody murderers," he called the police. He refused to have Mr. Murphy carried into his store, but promised to call an ambulance. We'd be sure to be arrested if we tried to carry him through the streets.

Leaving Mr. Murphy on the step, the shopkeeper led us at a fast pace through several rooms piled high with merchandise. As he'd turned off all the lights, we couldn't help bumping into each other. The rear entrance – to which he led us – opened on to a back alley from which we hurriedly made our way home. Father came out of the affair with a nasty welt across his back. "What a gobbin you are," mother scolded. "Might have got the child killed." The experience left me shaken.

The town was in an uproar after the police attack. The newspapers called it a "rampage" and demanded heads. The cavalry charge was about the most stupid thing the police had ever done. Had they been local police they would never have done it. Everybody who was anybody in town came down on the side of the workers. Some preachers made sermons about it. It was all right to make a baton charge against troublemakers, they said, but this was a savage attack against a peaceful procession. No one had the right to drive law-abiding people off the streets. It was a disgrace.

If there were people in town who supported the police, they kept quiet. The mounted police who had dispersed the crowd were quickly sent back to where they'd come from. The chief of police explained that most of the injuries had been caused not by batons but by people falling on the cobbles. The police had not charged until they had been fired upon. Fortunately, no one had been hit. An inquiry would be held. It would take time but he promised that the investigation would be thorough.

"It will all die down," father admonished those of us who heatedly discussed the event. "Nothing will come of it. You'll see."

Which is what would have happened had Mr. Murphy's condition in the infirmary not taken a turn for the worse. The news that his condition had deteriorated stirred the whole town up again. Vigils were held outside the hospital. Carrying lanterns, church choirs, aided by a muted cornet, sang hymns outside his window. There were more articles in the paper, still more sermons. Murphy became a symbol of the town's troubled conscience.

I came home one day to find mother crying. "Patrick has gone," she said. We were all stunned. I felt close to Mr. Murphy not least because he had helped to bring me into the world.

There followed one of the greatest funeral processions our town had known. Mother and I joined in; we felt we owed it to him. We got to the church service at St. Michael's too late. It was crowded out. Every church, mine, mill, and factory was represented; even the Chief of Police was there. Willie Gill, with his cocked hat and his long robe, was up front with the Knights of Columbus. With him were many of the town's priests, and preachers. The clergy wore sombre black. Behind them came the altar boys dressed in white, swinging pots of incense. The coffin was carried on a horse-drawn hearse. The horses wore black velvet capes and black waving plumed headdresses. Shuffling crowds went before and behind the cortege. There were several bands. They played hymns, including "The day Thou gavest" and "Nearer my God to Thee". Everybody tightened up when all the bands played Handel's "Dead March." The dirge mingled with the grinding of the carriage wheels, the clink of the horses' hoofs, and the shuffling of the crowd. There were so many flowers that they had to be carried on carts. Mr. Beatty's friend, Mr. Fisher was there, his char-à-banc covered with wreaths. Wreaths were always sent; they were expected. The whole route to the cemetery was lined with sad, red faces. They wore the lost, vague look that people wear at funerals. Not all were hushed. "It's a

170

fine funeral," someone said. "He deserves it. Pity he can't see it. Upright in 'eart he was. Ah well, pray for his soul." Between-times, the appealing supplications of the priests were heard above the crowd: "Kyrie eleison; Christe eleison."

Mother and I couldn't get near the grave. Father Prendergast said a few words. He used the text "Blessed are they which do hunger and thirst for righteousness." He said that Patrick had led a blameless life and had gone to his reward. We saw the flowers, the piles of sods; and the surrounding granite headstones. We saw Father Prendergast reach down and scatter earth over the lowered coffin.

"Ashes to ashes, and dust to dust, to the consummation of the world."

Then Mrs. Murphy bent down, her white hair blowing in the wind, her wan face marked with grief. We heard the click of spades. We watched as Mrs. Murphy stumbled out of the graveyard, helped by her children. She seemed to be in a stupor. We waited until the solemn crowd dispersed along the cemetery paths – many with a handkerchief to their face. As their voices died away into the streets, we went forward to pay our last respects and to see the mountain of flowers whose scent was overwhelming. In time, except for the harsh note of the raven, the graveyard fell silent again.

XIV   Siblings

The special link formed with my sister Jenny when I was an infant strengthened as the years passed. We were always close. She was a Kenyon rather than a Woodruff. She had the Kenyon's good looks and sweet disposition; though her sensitive face was longish rather than oval. It was a delicate, bird-like face of perfect proportions. She had the Kenyon's rich, dark hair. I remember most of all her wide-open, brown eyes that shone like buttons; brown was not a Woodruff colour. They were the brightest eyes in the family. They were ever watchful. Any commotion would scare her off. If she got really angry with father or her sister Brenda, she would simply go and live with friends until the storm had passed and all was love and forgiveness again.

By the time I was eight or nine Jenny was entering adulthood. She had started courting. As she had bestowed so much love and care on me, I looked on her young men with jealous eyes. I used to think that some of them were not good enough for her. I kept in touch with their comings and goings – usually through the cracks in the floor beneath my bed. Whenever one of them came to the house, my brother and I were sent to bed. The rest of the family used to go out to keep out of the way. There was John whose hair shone with brilliantine; there was Alec who wooed her

171

with Black Magic chocolates or with fish and chips; finally there was Mike who did nothing but sigh. I couldn't work out why Mike came at all. When the sighs became unbearable, my brother and I would shout down: "Go and put a sock in it," which kind of spoiled the atmosphere. Sometimes Dan and I got into such fits of laughter that we had to pull the blankets over our heads. It was when there was nothing but silence that we felt impelled to hop out of bed and peer through the cracks in the floor to see what was going on.

I preferred it when my sisters invited their young friends to dance in our front room. They were crazy about dancing. There wasn't exactly a lot of space in which to dance – even though what furniture there was had been removed – but nobody worried. Somebody would bring a concertina or a banjo and away we'd go. It was one of the occasions when Dan was willing to join in. We jerked, twisted, and spun to the latest tunes in that confined space until it made us dizzy.

I learnt to dance the Charleston and the Black Bottom in that little room. American dances were popular with us. The Charleston was the big hit. As fashion dictated, my sisters had their hair bobbed, wore short skirts and gartered stockings. When the dancers got too hot they just leaned against the walls or stepped out of the front door and cooled off in the street. Everybody was good-hearted; those were happy times.

But I am forgetting the one occasion when the dance ended in a fight. I don't know how it began. One moment all was bliss; the next moment the girls were screaming and the boys were knocking each other down – Dan in the middle of it. Jenny disappeared upstairs from the first blow. I knew it was serious when I saw mother grab the rolling pin, the frying pan and the poker – the three deadly weapons in cottage fights – and run upstairs, too. My job was to open and shut the front door, lock and unlock it, as the bodies, some of them with bloodied noses and torn suits, were tossed into the street. The fight wound down with two of the boys wrestling on the sanded floor. Kind of spoiled their shirt and pants.

Being the youngest in the family and the most readily available, I often served as Jenny's courier. It baffled me why I had to keep running with notes between Jenny and her current suitor when they were only several streets apart. I not only had to carry notes, I had to describe in detail to Jenny what her young man looked like when I delivered the note. "Did he look well?" Jenny would ask. "Are you sure? Think carefully, Billy, don't rush it. Was there any last word?" There usually was: "Tell her, I'm allus thinking of her neet and day." If I thought a fellow was not really worthy of my sister, I stuck a dart in him whenever I could.

This courier business could go on for weeks with Jenny going into a kind of decline. There were times when she didn't sleep or touch her food. "You're letting your courtin' get the better of you," mother scolded. The courier business, as far as I could see, didn't have the slightest effect on anything or anybody. It was just a waste of time, paper, and my clog cokers.

I was glad when Jenny settled for Gordon Weall and the courier business stopped. There was nobody better than Gordon. He was lucky to get Jenny; she was equally lucky to get him. I gave the romance a push whenever I could. Mother was thrilled with him. He had a happy disposition, strong face and body, a fresh complexion, and a crew cut, which must have been one of the first in town. When he walked into our house with the top of his hair shaved off, we went into fits. He looked just like a Red Indian brave.

I never knew anyone who enjoyed life as much as Gordon. People said he laughed right down to his heels.

Jenny and he had a wonderful courtship. They were a sunny-tempered pair. When they were both in work and could afford it, they'd dash off on a train to Blackpool to dance all night in the Tower Ballroom. They'd come back at dawn and go straight to work. Fifty miles for a dance! Now that was really living it up. Poor they may have been, but none so joyful.

Like Jenny, Gordon was a giver. In return for my help in his job as a painter he was generous to a fault. Every Easter, when he was in work, he took me to the Easter Fair. The news spread when the long convoy of lorries, carts, one-horse caravans with a dog tied underneath, animal cages, and massive steam engines piled high with scaffolding, poles, and canvas arrived. Overnight, the whole square was covered with tents, canvas booths, roundabouts, and lookers-on. All was din and bustle.

Paradoxically the fair got bigger, better, and brighter as times got worse. The bleaker our world, the greater our need of diversion. No depression in trade and industry was allowed to mar it. People flocked to it in such numbers that you had to lock arms and jostle your way through the crowds. It was not uncommon to see groups of five or six people linked together. All was happy shouting and lovely disturbance.

One year Gordon spent a whole three shillings on me. Thirty-six pennies! I rode on everything. I think I ate everything too: ice-cream, roasted potatoes, sticks of sugar. I can see him now, waving to me excitedly, as my papier-mâché horse rose and fell to the accompaniment of piped music from the brightly coloured and elaborately decorated steam organs. Later on we went on the Big Dipper (a kind of roller coaster), the Cakewalk (a walkway that moved up and down), the perilous chairboat swings, and the Big Wheel, and shrieked like everybody else.

Gordon considered the sideshows of freaks and caged wild animals a real "swiz" (cheat), so we avoided them; we also avoided the contortionists, the fortunetellers, the black-faced pill and potion sellers who for "tuppence" would cure you of the most dreadful illnesses, as well as all the other catch and roll-down-the-penny men and deceivers, who stood ready to pick the spare pennies from the pockets of the gullible. We made exceptions only for the coconut-shies and the Aunt Sally stands where, with hard wooden balls at a penny a go and to the light of a naked flame, we tried to dislodge a coconut or knock down a wooden effigy of a woman.

One year we almost went into a booth marked: MODERN AMERICAN ENTERPRISE. REFINED ENTERTAINMENT. "What is refined entertainment, Billy?" Gordon asked me. Having scratched our heads, we decided against it.

At the end of the day, there was always the added joy of going home through the littered, crowded streets hanging on to a coconut and a large balloon. A day or two later, with equal bustle, the fair disappeared as quickly as it had come. With it went the wet, trodden paper and the orange peel. Watercarts washed the cobbles free of sweat and stale beer. Normality returned.

It was Gordon who introduced me to speed. One day he roared up to our front door on a used motorcycle he'd just bought. The big buckskin gloves and goggles he was wearing made him look very daring.

"I was lucky to get it," he said, his face flushed and happy. "It was already sold to a chap who couldn't take delivery. The coppers had other plans for him. I got it just at the right moment."

I must have been somebody special, for I was the first to be invited to ride on the pillion seat. Jenny wouldn't go near the machine. It terrified her.

"What's that strange knocking sound?" I asked, as I clambered aboard.

"Nothing, Billy. Minor adjustment of the carburetor is all it needs. Goes like a bird."

This flying like a bird past houses and park railings was an entirely new experience for both of us. The faster we went, the happier we were. Gordon went so fast that things became a blur. I learnt to hang on with my knees and hands as we roared round the bends. We raced across town; we thundered down quiet country lanes leaving a cloud of dust behind us. On occasions Gordon avoided obstacles by whizzing around them at the last moment. Another "minor adjustment," this time to the brakes, was obviously needed. Meanwhile the strange knocking sound got louder and louder.

Gordon was not satisfied just with speed; he had to do antics. With me off the pillion and the bike in motion, he hung on to the handlebars while jumping from one side of the bike to the other – like he had seen cowboys do with horses in western films. He also rode while standing on the seat. It was hair-raising. He became known as the daredevil of the district. It was Jenny's belief that he would finish up killing himself and her brother. He didn't, but looking back – especially when one considers the potholes and ruts that pitted the roads in those days – she had every reason to be afraid.

The knocking sound, which Gordon was always going to fix but never did, one day brought our wild riding career to a close. Giving a particularly explosive knock, the engine died. Later the bike was sold for little more than scrap.

Brenda was entirely different from Jenny. She took after father, she was a Woodruff: stocky, silent, tough. She didn't flutter about like Jenny did, she stomped. She didn't have Jenny's good looks. She had a Woodruff face: strong, square, with the broad brow and thoughtful eyes. She didn't indulge in fairy stories like mother; she dealt with immediate problems. Nor did she sing. She could no more sing than father. One thing was certain: she was utterly reliable.

When at seventeen she joined the Salvation Army it came as a great surprise to my parents. Father was not against the Salvation Army, no working man was, but he didn't like her going off like that. There were words in the kitchen. The dispute between Brenda and father started innocently enough, but one thing led to another. Neither could bear to hear the other one out. The shouting match ended with father bawling: "Goddamit, go 'n join t' Army if tha must, but stay theer. I've 'ad enough of thee."

"I will," Brenda flared defiantly. Then she burst into tears, ran upstairs, and slammed her bedroom door. It was so tense and quiet in the kitchen that I could hear father's watch ticking on the fireplace. Moments later, Brenda came storming down the stairs clutching her belongings. Mother tried to grab her as she crashed through the kitchen but Brenda pushed her aside and was gone.

"See what tha's dun," mother screamed at father, tears running down her face. "I 'ope tha satisfied."

Some days later, driven by mother, father went in search of Brenda. I think he bitterly regretted having thrown her out. He found her and they made their peace.

Brenda came home with dad carrying her brown paper package, and we all sat together again in our stockinged feet in the kitchen and ate roasted potatoes.

"It's like old times," said mother. It wasn't. Everybody was tense. But time passed and wounds healed. Brenda joined the Salvation Army.

With her scrubbed face, her black bonnet and her red sash, Brenda now attacked sin as fiercely as she had attacked those who had bullied me at school when I was four.

I found her conversion overwhelming. "Billy," she said to me one day while pressing my hand against her bosom. "Billy, you must declare yourself. Are you for God or for Satan?"

More than anything else I was for Brenda so the first thing I did was to stop the harassment our street gang had been giving the Salvation Army. Keeping our distance, so as to avoid being clouted by an overzealous Soldier of Christ, we urchins used to march after the Salvation Army band and parody the Army's favourite hymns:

> You won't go to heaven when you die, Mary Ann,
> Yes you will, no you won't, yes you will, Mary Ann …

We also mocked them with the lines:

> Sally Army sells fish,
> Three-half-pence a dish.
> If you don't like it, don't try it.
> If you don't want it, don't buy it.
> Sally Army sells fish.

We'd end with:

> Oh, you're in the Sally Army
> And safe from sin.
> You'll all go to heaven,
> In a corn beef tin.

The worst kind of nonsense, yet we indulged in it repeatedly. Odd that we should have picked on the Salvation Army which did so much to help the poor. Our conduct was a mixture of mischief and hooliganism. Anyway, largely because of me, these attacks by our gang on the Sally Army ceased after Brenda joined up.

One of the first things Brenda did after joining – to the obvious discomfort of father – was to launch a holy war against drink. The trouble was she went overboard about it. Unlike her usual steady self, she worked herself up into a frenzy against alcohol. She was indefatigable in persuading people to sign the pledge of abstinence. She was also expert at working the crowd for copper and silver. She was very brave the way she stood with her group under the flag in front of the Griffin pub at the end of our street, rattling her tambourine and selling the Salvation Army newspaper *The War Cry*.

Those drinking in the Griffin took a different view. The pub was one of the few places where the workers could relax. Drink meant conviviality and friendship. For some it meant oblivion from a bleak existence; their only armour against despair. It was one of the few escape valves the workers had. They didn't want anybody spoiling it by reminding them of sin, or by singing temperance songs in the bar.

At first the pub-keepers were good-hearted about it. They saw the funny side. But then they came round to the view that Brenda was trying to rob them of their living; especially with her talk about banishing barmaids. It was embarrassing to father. The pub-keepers were especially sore with her when she brought in other contingents of the Sally Army from Preston, where the English temperance movement had begun.

Yet Brenda made many converts. She did, after all, labour in a fertile field. Drink was one of the besetting sins of the time. Everybody forgave a drunk. At some weddings and funerals people used to drink so much that they forgot why they'd come. Money that should have been going into people's bellies, or on their backs, went down their throats. I often saw shawl-covered mothers, with infants in their arms and toddlers hanging on to their skirts, trying to get their husbands out of a dingy pub late on a Friday night before the weekly earnings had all gone.

One man Brenda saved was Mr. Lambert who lived with his wife next door. Until Brenda got at him, Mr. Lambert spent most of his time working as a laborer at the Gas Works or drinking in the pubs. His consumption of alcohol was prodigious. He was known as an irredeemable tosspot. Mrs. Lambert, a bright-eyed badger of a woman, was forever throwing her shawl over her head and running to his rescue. Having picked him up off the pavement somewhere in town, she'd reel to and fro with him, doing her best to get him home. She'd come back up the street, staggering under his weight, propping him against the wall while she took a breather. The ordeal was habitual.

It was just as well that Mr. Lambert was a silent rather than a fighting drunk, otherwise, being drunk so often, he would have been killed. We children were rather cruel about it. If Mrs. Lambert had not got to the rescue in time, we'd follow the old man through the streets as he struggled home, teasing him, and going into gales of laughter when he went sprawling or clung to one of the gas lamps. He would reward our unforgivable behavior with a gurgle or two and a silly grin. He never harmed anybody and was far better than a lot of nasty people I knew.

I've forgotten how long Brenda worked on him before he agreed to sign the pledge. But sign it he did, and a very different man he was. He became one of the stalwarts of the Nazarene Chapel. He was one of Brenda's favourite redemptions. She used to say that if she could save Joe Lambert, she could save anybody. "Ate out of my hand, he did."

As long as she remained a Soldier of Christ, Brenda never relaxed in the battle against alcohol. Yet she never converted my parents. Despite her unending call for penitence, they remained faithful to the pub. As long as they had money, they frequented the pubs, especially on a Friday or a Saturday night.

There were others who didn't rely upon Brenda and the Salvation Army to help them in their fight against the demon drink. They took direct action. My friend Harold Watkins and I one day witnessed his mother being beaten by his father for being drunk. Somebody had run in to tell Mr. Watkins that his wife was coming up the street, tipsy. He ran to meet her and proceeded to beat her on the head and shoulders until, with a bleeding face, she managed to struggle through her door.

Nobody would have dreamt of intervening; they might have intervened had he not done something about it. "If I wor in your place..." they would have started. In such a close society, trollops and drunks among the women had to be contained. What you did in your own cottage was your business; what you did in the street – especially what a woman did in the street – was something else. I knew the Watkins family as well as my own, and I know that Mrs. Watkins never got drunk again.

I never did learn all the unwritten laws that told you what you could and could not do with alcohol, or anything else, in such a tightly knit community. There were fine lines which you must not cross, and about which you could learn only over time. You simply had to watch for the signals. Sometimes I found them conflicting. Why did we react so harshly to a drunken trollop in the street, but did little, if anything, to stop two drunken women beating each other to death? I could watch two men fighting and have little reaction; a man and a woman fighting didn't upset me much; but two women fighting, their mouths full of anger and foul words, filled me with disgust. Not so for many people; such a fight had a laughing, jeering crowd around it in no time. It was the only time I would have been happy to see a policeman in our street. One day I asked grandmother Bridget what she thought of women fighting in the street. "It's not a subject for 'dacent' conversation," she silenced me.

Partly because of such harmless alternatives as the bicycle, the radio, the cinema, and organized sport, drunkenness declined as I passed from childhood to youth. Drunks didn't lie about the street as they used to. Nor were they the source of jokes as they had been.

I was closer to my sisters than to my brother Dan. He was a real Woodruff, with all the looks of dad. The one thing I remember about him as a boy was the trouble he caused. Trouble attracted him like a magnet. He was tough and aggressive and had something of the rebel in him. For all the attention he gave me, I might not have existed. In the house he could be very difficult. I never knew whether or not I was going to get a "lander" (a blow to the head) from him. But for Brenda who used to take my side, he might have bullied me more than he did.

Sometime in the mid-twenties, when he was twelve or thirteen, he'd had brushes with the police. They'd been to the house twice with complaints. Once they flushed him out of the indoor market in town after it had been locked up for the night. Fortunately he had not broken into the premises, nor by the time they got to him, had he had time to eat anything. He was let off with a warning. Next time they picked him up in the railway clearing yard. Again they could not pin anything on him except trespass which wasn't worth pressing.

With his headstrong nature there was no telling what trouble Dan might cause. On an earlier occasion, when he was eight or nine, he went on strike against food and school. He sat in a corner of the house where my father left him, his childish, red face contorted with rage. Nothing shifted his obstinacy. Mother was out of work at the time. Dan's teacher was grey-headed Miss Grieves who passed our door daily. I don't know how long his hunger strike continued, and under what terms it was settled, but daily bulletins were issued to Miss Grieves as she went by.

"He 'asn't eaten his porridge from yesterday," mother would call from the front door.

"Give it to him tomorrow," Miss Grieves would call back, hardly breaking her stride.

Mother worried about Dan. She worried about him so much that she would sometimes burst into tears. He caused her the most sorrow, yet Dan was her favourite.

On leaving school at fourteen, Dan became a tenter (an assistant) to father in the mill. His destiny was to be a weaver. But he hated weaving; he hated the mill and its foul air, its smell of gas and its clouds of steam; he hated being tied to a machine; he hated being trapped for fifty hours a week; he hated the discipline; he hated breathing the fluff that fell like snow; he hated the nerve-shattering din. He had been reared on cotton; cotton was in his blood, but he had no love for it.

Whenever I ran into the weaving shed with father's and Dan's dinner, dad was always on to him.

"That's not the way to put cob on t' shuttle, you gobbin," father would scold.

Dan bristled.

"Look," father went on, "tha's got a mash. That's because tha wasn't watchin'. Tha's goin' to break warp the way tha goin' on. Nah, tha'll have to start afresh. See, pull t' cloth back. Comb it out gently, there's nothing to it. Piece it from t' back and pull it through. Titivate it. All it needs is for thee to use tha gumption."

Dan usually gave as good as he got. "Ah didn't touch cob, it all happened on its own," he would bawl back. The last thing he wanted to do was to please father.

I think Dan was right. Perhaps he was strangely wooden-handed and clumsy as a weaver, but sometimes these things happened on their own. Dan got mashes like nobody else; really interesting mashes that caught everybody's attention. They'd cross the weaving shed to see them. I've stood with him awestruck before a loom as the threads went wild before our eyes. In no time at all, hidden gremlins had torn the threads right across the loom.

Dan and I were too mesmerized by the growing rent in the cloth to know what to do. Eventually dad came across to see what we were staring at. Appealing to the Holy Trinity, he leapt to stop the loom.

"Tha goin' to get a prize for this one, Dan, tha are," father shouted, eyeing the damage.

Dan sulked back.

"Nobody can weave cotton and hate it at the same time," muttered an old weaver who worked next to dad. "Loom won't stand for it."

From what father told mother, I knew that Dan was always being "fetched up" in the warehouse and fined for bad work by the "cut looker", the cloth inspector. As weaving was paid by the piece, it meant a cut in pay. It made Dan sullen and angry.

After my brother had suffered about a year of purgatory, father one day found the weft and warp threads on Dan's loom a tangle of mashes. Dan was nowhere to be seen.

"He's buggered t' job up," father told mother that evening. To mother's growing concern there was no sight or sound of Dan. He didn't come home that night, or the next. Days later we discovered that he had run all the way from the mill to the army recruiting sergeant in Blackburn. Dan having lied about his age – he said that he was sixteen the minimum recruiting age, whereas he was only fifteen – the sergeant enlisted him and despatched him within hours to a remote part of Scotland. A day or two later Dan entered the barracks of the Argyle and Sutherland Highlanders Regiment in Inverness. It was about as far from Blackburn as the recruiting sergeant could have sent him. As distances went in those days, he might as well have sent him to the moon.

When I heard about this, I secretly hoped that Dan had found his niche, and that I might never see him again. My immediate concern was to recover all the tin soldiers he'd extorted from me over the years.

My hopes were soon dashed. Far from finding his niche in the Army, the barracks at Inverness proved to be worse for him than the weaving shed. But then Dan didn't see much of the barracks. Not long after he arrived there he was confined to the army jail – on grounds of insubordination. For most of the time he was in Scotland he was rarely out of jail. It left Dan with a totally prejudiced view of the military.

The army held a similar view of Dan. His obstinate and unruly nature gave them nothing but trouble; though he was not the "wild savage" they said he was.

The impassioned, desperate, scrawled notes we received from Dan – some of them in the official mail, others smuggled out – certainly aroused our sympathy. However badly written, they revealed the mind of a confused boy whose only desire was to come home. I remember Dan telling us how cold his cell was, and that he could see a great loch and empty mud flats from his jail window. The more time passed, the colder it got, the more frantic the messages became.

Father's first letters to Inverness, claiming that his son had been recruited under age and under false pretenses, were ignored. But, urged by mother, he kept at it. Eventually he received a reply:

"I have to inform you," the adjutant of the Argyle and Sutherland Highlanders wrote, "that your son, Dan, has willingly undertaken to serve His Majesty for the next twenty years. This is where the matter now stands. It is purposeless to discuss it further." There was a handwritten postscript about Dan having crablice.

Mother became very excited when the letter arrived. She kept turning it, trying to decipher it. When father came home he sat down to read it. He read it to himself several times.

"Well," said mother, tapping her foot, "for goodness sake, stop dilly-dallying. What does it say?"

"It says he's got crablice," said father, refusing to be bullied.

Prodded by mother, who seemed to have forgotten all the trouble Dan had given her before he disappeared to Inverness, father continued to besiege the regiment with letters. There had never been so many letters to and from our house.

Worn down by both father and son, the colonel of the regiment began to have second thoughts about Dan. If father would send thirty pounds, the colonel wrote, he would send Dan home. Thirty pounds was two-thirds of father's annual wage when he was in work.

Shortly afterwards another letter came saying that the colonel would settle for twenty pounds. Dan, he said, was giving them a lot of trouble.

"They've bitten off more than they can chew," said father, studying the letter. "If we hang on long enough, Maggie, they'll pay us to take him back."

But mother was not prepared to wait. She took her troubles to Dr. Grieves. Failing Grieves, she intended to approach uncle Eric, or the moneylender. As always, Dr. Grieves helped. He knew what he was doing. The Army didn't try any snotty business with him. Mother said the Army's reply to Grieves when he sent the twenty pounds was all "please and thank you, and here's your money back."

A week later, Dan came home. It was a Saturday. Mother was busy taking freshly baked bread out of the oven. She stood speechless with emotion when the latch was raised and he entered the house. He'd lost weight; he was thinner than I remembered him; his head was shaven; he looked crushed. With a hoarse cry, mother dropped the loaf on the kitchen floor and ran to Dan. They hugged each other and cried.

Instead of Dan's luck taking a turn for the better, he began to tread an even harder path. A friend of father's at the Bank Top Boiler Works hired Dan as a "devil." A "devil" was a boy who tightened and untightened the bolts inside mill boilers when they were being repaired. Dan was lowered through one of the boiler openings – usually too small for a man – carrying a wrench and a lamp. Except for a loincloth, he went naked. While his mates shouted and pounded on the outside of the boiler, he struggled with the wrench on the inside. When he emerged he was covered with soot. The only thing white about him were his teeth and his eyeballs.

Whether he was working locally, or for weeks at a time in other towns, he always came home as black as coal, and dead beat. He came through the back alley to our cobbled yard. Here, wet or fine, he stripped off. With his dirty clothes lying on the cobbles, he stood naked while mother rubbed and scrubbed him, trying to get him clean. It was as well that water was free, for she poured dozens of warm and cold buckets of water over him. Then she lathered him again and again with soap until all the soot was driven from his rippling body and had settled on his feet. The rubbing and the scrubbing went on until Dan's skin gradually changed from black to grey, grey to pink. Mother never tired. By then the backyard was awash with clothing, soapsuds, and soot. I never saw Dan so docile. Apart from catching his breath when the cold water was thrown over him, he never murmured. He was too tired to talk. I felt truly sorry for him and said so.

"Tha gets used to it," he replied.

XV   Parents

I was in my teens before I stopped taking my parents for granted and began to realize how different they were.

My father was a man of extraordinary routine. Throughout his life he was a man you could count on. Whatever hour of the day, we all knew where he was and roughly what he was doing. The factory and his home were his world. He was the first up in the house. When there was work, he was the first to reach the mills. I think he loved the mills; he loved the humming, clattering machinery, the oil, and the dirt. He started each week with a clean, mended, collarless cotton shirt, always buttoned at the neck, and cheap, blue overalls. The sleeves of his shirt were rolled up to the elbow. When he was a tackler and overlooker, he wore a natty red neckerchief and a fustian waistcoat, which we thought dandy. We were disappointed when he stopped wearing them. When he went drinking he wore a narrow white scarf criss-crossed around his neck. As long as he lived, he scorned English braces for his American belt. He would threaten us children with his belt, but never used it. There were no brutal beatings in our house.

I saw father each noon when I ran from one mill to another delivering the family dinners. When I handed him his hot-pot he never thanked me. He never joked with me or made fun. Yet his fellow workers understood him and thought well of him. "Yo dad's aw reet," they'd shout as I tried to slip between the thundering looms.

I was proud of him when he was a tackler. The way he'd set up a loom always fascinated me. He'd bring an enormous beam holding the warp threads on a two-wheeled sled to the back of the loom. He'd not only manhandle the beam into the loom, he'd then thread hundreds, if not thousands, of warp ends through the eyes of a heald or heddle board, which was as wide as the loom. From the heald board he'd then pass the warp ends through the teeth of a fine comb called a reed, after which he'd come to the front of the loom and tie all the new warp ends to the ends of the previous warp. Then he'd make various adjustments which tacklers called tuning. Most times the warp threads would be arranged by a "drawer-in" and a "reacher"; sometimes he'd struggle on alone. I came to the conclusion that he and I were people of consequence in the mill. After all, if I hadn't brought his dinner every day, he couldn't have done all those things.

Ritual-like, he'd bring his empty basin home at night, fifteen minutes after the five o'clock whistle, and put it in exactly the same place on the sink. He also brought the local newspaper, *The Blackburn Telegraph*, which he read to mother. He had no interest in books but would now and again borrow one and read it to Maggie. With the life he put into it, he could have been reading a funeral notice. One night a week he'd give a hand with the heavier washing. Another night he'd get down on his knees to pummel a large bowl of dough in preparation for mother's baking. I marveled at the way in which, with one blow, he could bury his arm up to the elbow. Plop! plop! went his fists. It sounded like something heavy being dropped into water. When the mood took him he would shave at the kitchen sink before a small looking-glass. Sometimes he'd go for a week or more without shaving. Among the workers, nobody took any notice of an unshaved face.

Each Friday night dad came through the door and placed his pay packet on the table in the front room. Mother would retrieve it. He may have doubted his wife's accounting abilities, but financial responsibility in the house was hers. Other than to pay his trade union fees and shop for groceries with mother, he never coveted money. I never heard him say that somebody at work was being paid more or less than he. Even his cheap Woodbine cigarettes – he called them coffin nails – were bought by mother. She stacked them on the mantelpiece above the kitchen fire. Day by day the stack was reduced until it was renewed the following Friday night. Despite all the trouble he had had with his lungs – as a result of being gassed – as long as he had money, he never stopped smoking.

The only time he showed an interest in the amount of his pay was when a co-worker cheated him out of his one-third share of two shillings and sixpence. I am the one who saw it happen and later in the day told dad about it.

The joint earnings of father and two other men had been placed on the kitchen table awaiting division. The three of them had been working together in the factory on a special job, for which they'd been paid quite a heap of silver. With my head the height of the table, I saw Mr. Lamp flick half-a-crown under a fold of the newspaper that covered the board. He did it so quickly that father and Mr. Clay didn't see it happen, but I did.

Why would Mr. Lamp want to do that, I wondered? I was doubly puzzled when I watched Mr. Lamp secretly retrieve the coin before he left the house. His eyes met mine; he looked troubled. Later that night I asked dad why Mr. Lamp had played such a game. Father paled. "Are you sure, he did that, Billy?" he asked me. "Oh, yes, Dadda, I'm quite sure." Father put on his cap and went out and came back clutching ten pennies.

When the weather was fine, father spent Sunday mornings wrestling on the moors. All sport was forbidden inside the town on Sundays; the day was meant for rest, meditation, and church. In the Blackburn of my childhood, religious life was intense. Games, fighting, dancing, singing, drinking, and all forms of public entertainment were banished. It was the only day when the factory clocks could be ignored. Nothing was allowed to disturb the Sabbath stillness, or compete with the church and chapel bells.

Woe to those who disregarded this unwritten code! One Sunday morning I and other heathens were playing football behind St. Philip's Church hall when a group of black-clad women, wielding umbrellas and sticks, attacked us. Until I received a whack across the head, I thought they were making fun. Far from it, the wrath of God was in their eyes. We'd fouled the Holy Day and they were after blood. We never played football on a Sunday morning in town again. Outside the town, in the hills, we could play to our hearts' content.

Father and the other grown-ups had long since learnt the unwritten code. Men and boys met at a wrestling site somewhere on the moors, "up top". Sometimes we'd be accompanied by the pitmen racing their whippets. Women and girls were never there. My brother and I rarely missed a match. In time we became familiar with the jargon of wrestling and could talk about chips and backheels, hanks, clicks, hypes and hitches just like anybody else. The procedure was always the same: a ring was formed, two men stripped to the waist, trouser legs rolled up, clogs and stockings were removed, small bets were placed, the fighters squared up to each other, a touch of the hands, and the fight was on.

One minute father was crouched down, facing his opponent; the next the two of them were slipping about on the gouged grass. The fight ended when both shoulders of one of the wrestlers touched the ground, or when one of the men conceded defeat. While Lancashire had a reputation for fights where no holds were barred – even for fights making use of steel-tipped clogs – our Sunday morning fights were not looked upon as war or gambling, but as sport – as wrestling for its own sake. It was meant to add to the spice of life. With us, kicking, gouging, biting, and tripping were all forbidden.

Father was an outstanding wrestler. He knew all the holds and falls. He was all muscle. As the workers said, for a man in his thirties "he stripped well." His wrestler's arms were tattooed with a mermaid on one arm and an anchor on the other. About medium height, he had a barrel chest covered with hair, a massive ox-like neck, wide-spread shoulders, a well-muscled body, and hairy legs like the trunks of trees. He had an unusually large head covered with straight, brown hair, a Roman nose that was in proportion to the rest of his face, a firm mouth, the strongest teeth, the dark blue eyes of his mother, and a clear, healthy-looking skin. It was the first time I saw him as a man rather than my father. I was proud of him because physical strength was admired by us. For his age, having recovered from his wartime wounds, he must have been one of the fittest men about. He could lift, push, or pound anything. Few wrestlers managed to floor him. I never understood how anyone who could fight for hours on end could be as gentle with flowers and birds as he was.

Usually the wrestling contests went on until the smells of Sunday dinner wafted across the moor. At that point the fighting stopped as quickly as it had started, bets were settled, and everybody hurried off for the best meal of the week. Often father would be congratulated by the other workers. It made no difference to him; he was never elated or downhearted. He'd had a good "punch-up" and that's all that he cared about. It must have been a wonderful escape from what seemed to me a routinely monotonous life. Having struggled into his shirt and jacket, he would leave the field as calmly as he had entered it.

Father's quiet ways never deceived me. I learnt early in life when to keep out of his way; lurking beneath that still, quiet nature was what we called his Viking temper. It was that same Viking temper that had sent his mother Selma to jail. When aroused it was an anger that would stop at nothing. One Sunday morning on the moors I saw it almost kill two men.

It happened like this. Father had wrestled and beaten one of the Calvert brothers fairly and squarely. It was the brother who was always boasting about his strength and prowess. He was then challenged by the other brother, an equally solid man. In this match father was tripped from behind by the first Calvert and was sent sprawling. The movement had been so quick that most of the onlookers didn't catch it. As father got up one of the Calverts called him a "half-breed Yank." At that, dad suddenly went wild – this time with his bare fists. I saw the flash of his fists in the sun. I heard the click of them as they struck his opponents' jaws. Suddenly there were three men rolling on the ground.

I'm convinced that father would have killed the two Calverts had the crowd not rushed in to separate them. The three men were dragged to their feet: gasping for breath, heads down, wet foreheads almost touching, pale with anger, the blood beating in the neck veins, they glowered at each other through bloodshot eyes. His arms gripped firmly from behind, father made several efforts to break free. In a display of self-destructive fury, he twisted and turned, reeled and staggered, dragging the three men who were hanging on to him across the turf. By now everybody was shouting at the top of their voices and falling over each other.

With a superhuman effort, father shook off those who held him. Hitching up his pants, he walked away. I knew from the way he walked that he was in a fearful rage, and that the brawl might be renewed. With the crowd in uproar, the Calverts followed him, but then had second thoughts. Father may not have had many brains, but when it came to fearlessness and brawn he was up front.

Except for the intensity of this particular fight, it had followed the customary procedure of using fists to settle disputes. There was nothing wrong in punching someone on the nose, or threatening to "knock yer bloody 'ead off". Workers did it all the time. The other workers intervened only when there was danger of someone being killed. That would complicate matters. The society of my childhood was no place for people with weak stomachs.

Oftentimes, supper over and the light still good, my brother and I would accompany father to the cindered wasteland outside the walls of Dougdale's factory where he had a small plot of land. He grew flowers there and kept a cabin with a score of homing pigeons. The allotments, of which there were many, were rented by the mill for a minimal sum. They were usually used for growing vegetables. They were no more than five minutes walk from our house across the open factory tip. Ritual-like, we trudged behind father who carried a bucket of water in either hand.

Usually Dan and I released the pigeons. We undid a catch on the pigeon cote's window and raised a wooden screen. With a great frantic, noisy flapping of wings, the birds were gone. Occasionally, as a special treat, we were allowed to hold one. They'd peck each other, but they never pecked us. Having scraped the hut clean of muck, we would then sit on an upturned bucket and watch the birds in flight. Dad never sat on a bucket; he could squat on his haunches for hours on end.

Cooped up all day, the pigeons expressed great joy at being free again. Endlessly they banked and turned, wheeled and whirled in the sky. The wonder is they never collided. Sometimes the birds watched us from neighbouring roofs, but mostly they stayed aloft, dancing in the evening sky. They had an uncanny way of knowing when their food was ready. The moment the grain was put in their trough they returned with the same eagerness they'd shown on departure. Supper done, they'd flutter up noisily to the rooftops. Father seemed to fly with them.

Mother always said that father talked to the pigeons more than to us. So he did. He talked to them the whole time he was there. When the time came for the birds to be fastened up for the night – not he but they decided when that was – they'd glide down from the roofs. He used to lure those nodding and strutting about on the cabin roof by rattling the food can or calling their names from inside the cote. He went on muttering at the birds until the last one was in and the safety hatches had been dropped into place.

He also talked to his flowers which he grew behind protective wire against the pigeon-shed. Bending over his blooms, he was deaf to whatever was said to him. Mother would have preferred "greens" to flowers, but "greens" to father meant "rabbit food." He had no interest in growing them.

How he grew anything at all was a miracle. Every ounce of soil had to be carried in and enriched with diluted pigeon droppings. The climate with its flooding and its heavy frosts presented a constant challenge.

One vicious hailstorm could devastate his garden. In thirty minutes magnificent blooms became broken stalks. Yet for years he had the best chrysanthemums for miles around. Some years they were ridiculously large and reminded me of Jack and the Beanstalk.

Time and again I watched him rebuild his garden after it had been washed away. On his hands and knees, with a trowel, he'd replant everything that had been lost. As the light faded, he'd go on tilling, mulching, and watering until his garden was restored. I suppose that's where I learnt about patience long before I knew what the word meant.

Father was not alone in clinging to nature and a bit of earth. All across the cindered wasteland, nightly and at weekends, workers struggled to grow potatoes, cabbages, carrots, radishes, beets, turnips, peas, and beans. They needed the vegetables; even more, they needed to be out of doors, close to the earth, growing things. In later life, it occurred to me that a cinder tip could not have been the healthiest soil in which to grow vegetables, but I can't recall anybody having died of it.

With the light almost gone, father banged the empty buckets together to signal that it was time to go home. No words. He crossed the cindered waste with a bunch of flowers in his hand and several pigeon eggs in his overall pockets. We followed, carrying the empty buckets. On arrival home, he always put the eggs into a basin on the sink. Awkwardly, almost abruptly, he would then hand the flowers to mother. No words, no glances, just a muffled grunt that seemed to say all that needed saying.

The only occasion when father threw all routine to the winds was at the time of the annual pigeon race from France to Britain. Every year, until the race was over, the family lived on the edge of a precipice. Madness reigned. The chosen birds, sometimes as many as six, were placed in a special box which was taken to the railway station and, with dozens of other such boxes, sent to France. I used to go with father to see the birds on to the train and to wish them farewell and good luck. Although he never said a word to me, he never stopped talking to the pigeons.

"Tha mustn't loiter this year, Harry," he'd tell one of his favorites, as we went along. And to another: "Bernie, if tha finishes up in t' wrong cote this time, tha goes in t' pot."

Silently, with other equally somber bird fanciers, we stood together on the platform until the train departed.

Because of his war service, father knew every station the train stopped at in France until the birds reached their destination. He kept a list of the stations on the cupboard door at home. Once it came time for the birds to be released in France, the tension in the house became unbearable. A great excitement swallowed up all other activities. So that the whole family – and everybody else in the vicinity – could be free to search the sky, meals were forgotten, baking was postponed, clothes stayed dirty. Everybody went on to the tip to watch.

The moment a tiny dot was spotted darting in and out of the low clouds, a cry would go up from the workers occupying the hilly ground. Then would come the sweating: was it our pigeon or somebody else's? Only father could tell. Only father could recognize a pigeon at that distance. With everybody frozen to the spot, the pigeon would fall out of the sky on to one of the cabin roofs. A sigh of relief would go up. In a race like this seconds counted.

One year father's favourite bird, Charlie, had raced from France to the north of England leaving the other pigeons behind. Father saw him long before he was visible to the rest of us. In time, we spotted the bird swooping through the clouds, tacking this way then that; breaking his heart to get home first. There wasn't another pigeon in the sky. Blessedly, the wind had died down. We all knew Charlie and we swelled with pride for him. By now a perspiring father was inside the hut waiting to clock in the winner. Everybody in the surrounding pens and on the hillside kept so still they might have been carved of stone. We were certain that, for the first time in the history of the race, Charlie and Blackburn had won the coveted prize.

Hypnotized, we watched as a flapping, fluttering Charlie came in low over the house tops toward the cabin roof. He flared, braked and was down.

Then to our horror, instead of hurrying inside as he had been trained, Charlie proceeded to strut about on the roof. The more he strutted, and bowed, and cooed, the louder the oaths coming from father inside the hut. While others resorted to prayer, father swore, whistled, and rattled the feed can. All to no avail.

The reason for Charlie's delinquency was not long in finding. Against all rules, a female bird was strutting about on Mr. Pindle's cabin roof next door. In a moment, Charlie had hopped across and joined her. With everybody holding their breath, Charlie began to make little pretended dashes at Mr. Pindle's pigeon. He hopped and bowed and cooed, and puffed up his chest and spread his tail. What on earth was Charlie thinking about? Didn't he realize he was on the edge of fame? Obviously, he had forgotten the race.

When father realized what was going on, he came roaring out of the cabin like a mad bull. He was so infuriated that he ran to Mr. Pindle's fence shaking his fist. Seizing the dividing fence, he almost wrenched it out of the ground. Mr. Pindle and father began to hurl insults at each other; relations between the two men had always been strained. Father accused Mr. Pindle of deliberately sabotaging Charlie's victory. From Mr. Pindle's side there was a cry of outraged innocence. Father must have said even worse things than that, for the next thing I knew an enraged Mr. Pindle had climbed the fence and was aiming blows at dad's head. Father exploded with anger. Before anyone could stop him, he had grabbed Mr. Pindle by the scruff of the neck and the seat of his pants and had hurled him back over the fence. Mr. Pindle sailed through the air, arms and legs outstretched, an astonished look on his face, to fall with a great bone-shattering bump at the other side. The wonder is he wasn't killed.

Mother was the youngest of Bridget Gorman Kenyon's four children. She had her mother's fine features: the lovely blue eyes, the long eyelashes, the fine hands, the lovely, thick, centre-parted, dark hair, the soft, sensuous oval face, the warm unaffected gaze. Of medium height, she was neither thickset nor slim; she was in between.

The early death of her father, and her being orphaned off as a child, undoubtedly contributed to her life-long feeling of uncertainty and insecurity. "No" and "yes" were always followed by "but-er-I ..." Although Bridget had assumed that the rough-mannered farmer who had "adopted" Maggie was kind and honourable, there is a mystery about what happened. I suspect that she was brutalized. Certainly she was neglected and it seems that she was not sent to school. Eventually, in desperation, she fled from her foster parents back to her mother. They didn't come after her. Bridget said they would not have dared.

Of greater consequence, her childhood experience left her with a fear of not being wanted. Mother must have been glad to marry the strong and resolute young man that by all accounts father was before the war. The marriage gave her a feeling of security which she so badly needed. My sister Jenny told me that mother had once said that only after her marriage did she recover the sense of belonging she had known before her father's death. That's why father's running off to war in 1914 came as such a shock. She felt vulnerable again.

I was always at a loss to understand Maggie's relations with her mother. For someone who had been orphaned off and neglected at an early age, it is a wonder that Maggie had any relations with Bridget at all. How could Maggie be so illiterate when Bridget was so schooled? Why would Bridget spend all the time she did educating me when she had neglected her own child? Mother was ever tight-lipped about it. Bridget was equally silent. In all the time I knew Grandmother Bridget, I cannot remember a single occasion when she talked about her daughter's early life. The only comment that Bridget ever made about mother's life-long illiteracy was that "Maggie was not one for 'larning'." Mother never did overcome her lack of schooling.

When I look back and think about my parents, I remember one as dull and grey, the other as a brightly flashing, sometimes blinding light. Whereas father was placid, mother was mercurial; he was a plodder, she a romantic. Mother was forever vibrant and passionate. She was sponta-neous, expansive, impulsive. She needed to touch, to pat, to kiss. Nobody ever doubted her warmth of heart or generosity of spirit. Her talk jumped about, but she was never dull. On the contrary, she crackled with life, living each moment intensely. She couldn't stand silence and inactivity.

With her, laughter and tears were the real thing, and never far apart. It didn't take much for her to have a good cry. Sad or glad, she was always singing. She had a melodious, fine voice. I never heard father sing, except at his Trade Union meetings. Mother was always doing something different; she had to; she was easily bored. She tired when father read the newspaper to her at night. She wanted to jump to the end. To her a newspaper was a kind of fairy tale. He droned on monotonously reading every single word, page after page, with no sign of tiring or, for that matter, of interest either, unless perchance he came across some news from America.

When the newspaper bored her, she'd stop listening and tell us children a story. What kind of story? Well, every kind – some of which she had collected in her head, others created as she went along. Believing in fairies, as she did, there were stories about little creatures with magical charm; stories in which you would never want for anything; stories where you could be invisible; stories where you sailed away inside a bubble to a kingdom in the sky; stories of a boy and girl who followed a star to the edge of the world. One of her favourite stories was about a bird which always came to her rescue at the very last moment. She really believed in luck. Some of her stories were difficult to follow, "up in t' air," as we would say.

Sometimes she told a story in which she was the queen and I the king. She had lots of coloured ribbons and dressed up with elaborate care. Halfway through this particular story I had to temporarily swap roles: I ceased to be the king and, much to my delight, became the villain. A dab or two of soot on my face from the back of the chimney, and a hat which mother quickly made out of a newspaper, turned me into a marvelous-looking scoundrel.

Mother thought and spoke in terms of imagery. With her it was a gift. She could create magic with scissors and paper; she could snip whole groups of people or animals into existence. With a clay pipe filled with soap and water she did even more astonishing things. In no time she'd give you a shining new world. One of my earliest memories was blowing bubbles with her. She concocted bubbles of every hue. She sang a song about them:

> I'm forever blowing bubbles, pretty bubbles in the air;
> Oh they fly so high, nearly reach the sky,
> Then, like my dreams, they fade and die.
> Fortune's always hiding. I've looked everywhere.
> I'm forever blowing bubbles, pretty bubbles in the air.

Invariably she sang the words lightly while skipping about. When it came to dancing, she was, like my sister Jenny, as light as a feather. She would suddenly grab your hands and dance you off your feet. When she played "Ring-a-ring-o'-roses, all fall down," she didn't pretend to fall, she fell as a child does; "All fall down" – bump. She clapped her hands the same way. I can see her falling among the daisies and the bluebells, her lovely, dark hair streaming in the wind. It was like watching an actor on a stage, with the lights and colours changing all the time.

With mother you never knew what she would get up to next. Father was concerned with each day; with getting by, with the immediate and the present; mother was concerned with change, with eternity. She was a stargazer; she not only knew there was life after death, she looked forward to it. Dad didn't give a thought to the unknown; she never stopped thinking about it. He didn't expect much of life; mother knew that sooner or later it would be glorious. She had visions and hopes. "No 'arm in 'opin'," she would say. Her God was always a merciful God. While she knew nothing about religion, she was a firm believer in the "Kingdom come" idea, "of the glory there's to be"; of a world where everybody would be judged and punished or rewarded. She never mentioned the punishments; she stressed the rewards, and the peace and rest there was to be. For her, a God of vengeance, a vindictive God, could not exist. Her God of Mercy would reign for ever and ever. Amen. She believed that love made the world go round. She expressed herself with such conviction that you got carried away. You didn't worry about the details.

Details never troubled her. She was deaf, dumb and blind to details. To talk about ends and means to her was to take an unfair advantage. I remember the look of amazement and dismay that appeared on father's face one day when mother began to chuck money into a beggar's cup. While father was worrying how to find enough money to feed the family, mother was throwing it away. One day, with no money to spare, she went and bought a new hat for which she could have had little use. "Why did you buy it?" father asked incredulously. "Because I laked it," she answered innocently. Father almost had a fit. Usually, she didn't respond to his anger.

Mother's dislike of detail gave her an entirely different attitude to money than the one held by father. Money baffled her. I remember standing at my mother's knee while she emptied her purse on her lap. She proceeded to make several little heaps of coins to meet her bills. I watched while she moved the piles from one knee to the other. It was like moving pawns on a chessboard. Except that the more she moved her coins, the more bewildered she became. Fear entered her eyes. Then she broke down and cried. The sobs were heartfelt; they conceded total defeat. There was no way that she could manage.

She did not have any idea of the nature of the industrial changes going on around her. Her protest about living conditions – marked by so much squalor and ugliness – came from the heart rather than the head. Because her sensitivity and her imagination were so strong, ugliness hurt her more than the rest of us. The ugly surroundings in which we lived offended her eye. The saying "where there's muck, there's brass [money]," made no impression on her. Certainly, she had no idea how prices and wages were arrived at. The reasons for the ongoing fight between factory owners and workers escaped her. She simply hungered for the decent conditions she'd known as a child while her father was alive. Had he lived, she would never have been a slubber in a mill – that's for certain. Like her mother, she didn't blame anybody for the way things had turned out. She didn't dislike or hate anybody for it. She wasn't militant about anything. She just wanted to live decently; to be rid of the constant anxiety about money. Like grandmother Bridget she feared the violence going on around her. That is why she feared strikes and lockouts. They frightened her to death. They not only introduced violence into her life, the outcome was always the same: less to eat. "What's the use?" she would ask. At heart she was a pacifist.

The Kenyon pacifism almost cost her her life. One afternoon she and I were coming home from the market. We'd almost reached our door when our path was suddenly blocked by a giant of a woman who wore a black shawl fastened tightly at the neck. Neither of us had noticed her approach. Although I assumed that the woman was an acquaintance of mother's, I was repelled by the pockmarked face, the staring, bloodshot eyes, and the strong smell of drink.

Before anyone could stop her, the woman had seized mother by the throat and had begun to shake the life out of her. Mother's screams were stifled by one of the woman's hands; my shouts were ignored. By now mother's shawl and parcels were on the ground; her long, dark hair had come undone and was hanging down her back. Deep, bloodlined scratches marked her face. She didn't strike back or struggle. She was too terrified. "Oh my God," was all she said. I stood there paralyzed. All I managed to do was to drag the woman's shawl off her head.

Having struck mother in the face several times, the woman picked her up and tossed her on to the cobbles as if she were a rag doll. Mother lay there groaning. With every kick from the woman's steel-capped clogs her groans grew. "Oh, my God," she kept saying. By now bright red blood was on the stones. Every time mother tried to get to her feet, the woman knocked her down again with a vicious kick. Screaming with pain, mother recoiled from each blow, twisting and turning like an eel trying to escape.

Panic-stricken, I ran into the house. Brenda was the only one at home. "Mother's being murdered!" I screamed. "She's being kicked to death in the street!"

Brenda's response was to grab the long broom and dash out. I ran after her.

By now, a ring of jeering, shouting passersby had formed, making it difficult for mother to escape. Such a group always assembled for a street fight. Some of them loved it. The woman was on top of mother pummeling her for all she was worth. Any efforts being made by the onlookers to stop the woman's blows were half-hearted.

Brenda didn't wait for their help. She dashed through the spectators' legs dragging the broom after her. I followed. Before anybody could stop her, she had swung the broom head into the air and brought it down on the woman's head with a sickening thud. The blow was so hard that it broke the broom handle. Squealing like a stuck pig, the woman slid off mother's chest on to the cobbles where she lay unconscious.

With the help of a neighbour, we got mother to her feet. Head down, face covered with blood, she tottered toward our door. I picked up her shawl and the torn packages. Nobody interfered. Had they done so, they would have been impaled on the splintered shaft that Brenda held spear-like before her.

I never discovered why mother was attacked.

Sometimes Maggie seemed to attract trouble. Her simple, unaffected, credulous outlook was just not up to life. It landed her in one pickle after another. The gold coin episode was one of them. It was one of the few occasions when father was uncontrollably angry at mother before us children.

It began with a knock on the door. Only mother and I were in the house. She was ironing. She was using a box iron which was kept hot by exchanging the luke-warm iron bar inside the box for a red hot one out of the fire. Having exercised great care not to drop the red hot piece on to the hearthrug, she had just clicked the iron's trap door shut when there was a rap on the door. As it was unusual for people to knock, we peeped through the curtains to see who it was. We couldn't see anyone. When we opened the door, a small, dark-eyed stranger stood there, grinning. He had peculiar long, black, curly hair that fell down the sides of his face. I could not help noticing the many gold rings he had on his fingers. He also had several gold teeth. In a twinkling he had his foot in the door. Mother thought him a Gypsy. There were always tan-coloured Gypsies about in those days with their covered wagons, pegged-out horses, foals, dogs, stewpots, and swarthy children. My people feared them. From missing children to missing washing, it was always the Gypsies who got the blame.

"We want no Gypsies here," mother said, as she struggled to get the door shut.

"Do Gypsies come as well dressed as I?" the man asked in a hurt tone, "With gold on their hands?" he went on, flourishing his fingers. He was wearing a dark suit – a little worn and greasy, but still a suit. He also wore a collar and tie, a black trilby, and polished shoes. Whatever he was, he certainly didn't look like a Gypsy.

"What do you want?" mother asked.

"I want to make you rich," the man replied.

"And how do you think you're going to do that?"

"It's easy, you give me your gold and I'll give you more money than you've ever had." At this point the man produced a role of bank notes such as neither of us had seen before. Holding the bundle before our eyes, he flipped his thumb through the notes several times. It was enough to make our eyes pop out.

"We don't have any," mother said, making to shut the door again.

"You know that's not true," the man said in an oily voice. "There's always a ring somewhere, or a trinket, or a coin that you're hanging on to. Now I ask you, what good are you doing locking them away in the house, gathering dust? Use your gumption, woman, get rid of your dust catchers and get some real money. You can't buy food with dust catchers, but you can buy food with these." Whereupon he flipped through the bundle of banknotes again. The notes made a comforting, swishing sound. "This is your one and only chance. For your gold I will give you enough money to pay all your debts. Think what your husband will say when he comes home: enough money to pay all the bills, and some to spare!"

I could tell that mother was dithering. She started her "but-er-I..." business.

"Well, that's it," the man said as he stuffed the money in his jacket pocket and took his foot out of the door. "You don't know a good thing when you see it. Ta, Ta!" he said, touching his trilby. His gold teeth flashed a smile.

I knew that, in addition to mother's wedding ring, there was one piece of gold in the house. It was a gold coin, an heirloom from father's side. Mother said it had belonged to great-grandfather Arne. Thus far, it had survived all the ups and downs of the family fortune. It was hidden in a crack of the wall upstairs.

"Hang on," said mother, as she ran from the door, through the house and up the stairs.

In seconds she had returned with father's heirloom.

The moment the gold coin was in the man's hand he was all business. There was no more laughter, no more chatter about making mother rich. Ignoring mother's "but-er-I," remarks that she had decided against selling the coin, after all, he popped a piece of glass over one of his eyes and studied the gold piece carefully.

"Oh well," he said, "if this is all you've got, I suppose it will have to do. It's inferior, that's what it is. I'm in two minds to take it."

He then counted out some paper money, placed it in mother's palm and was gone. Before mother could shut the door, the man was half-way down the street. "But-er-I," said mother, "I do hope I've done the right thing."

I shall never forget the look on father's face when he came home and mother told him what she had done. He stood and grasped the back of a chair, his face inflamed with anger. His knuckles were white. "Tha's done what?" he murmured. "Tha's done what?" He couldn't grasp it. Then, flinging the chair aside, he exploded. "Tha's a gobbin! A damned fool gobbin, that's what thi are!" he roared. That was as close as father ever came to striking mother. We children stood there, helpless, wide-eyed.

194

Mother having stammered out a description of the man, father put on his cap and went in search of him. "Ah'll kill him! Ah'll kill him!" he yelled, as he banged the front door behind him with enough force to shake the house. I silently hoped he wouldn't find him. I knew that in a temper like that father would beat him to a pulp.

Father was gone for hours. We sat around waiting, imagining all kinds of horrible things. Eventually he came home still looking like black thunder.

It was a long time before we learnt what had happened. He'd traced the fellow across town as far as the station bar. By the time he'd got to the bar and made inquiries, the man had been and gone. Just left to catch the Manchester train, they told him. Dad had rushed off to the Manchester platform only to see the peddler disappear into the last coach of the already moving train. In a towering rage he'd stood as the train whistled its way into the dark tunnel, its red lights glowing, then fading.

He never saw his coin again.

Father was never sure what surprise mother would spring on him next. The only thing about which he could be fairly certain was that mother would pay the rent. The rent was one of the few money transactions that even she respected. Every Friday night, before any other spending was done, three shining half-crowns (seven shillings and sixpence) were placed in a little wooden coffin-shaped box that hung on a nail behind the front door. There had to be three coins – it made it easier for the collector. You didn't argue. You paid the lot in three half-crowns.

The rent was collected every Saturday afternoon by a burly, red-faced chap who burst into the house from the street. He never knocked, he never took off his cap, he rarely spoke. When he did, he was surly and abrupt. If you said that the roof leaked, or something else, and would he please ask the landlord to fix it, he'd give an especially loud grunt and disappear through the door. Complaints got us nowhere. Most times he simply pocketed the three coins, made an entry in the blue, penny rent-book that stuck out of the box and left. Our feelings toward t' bump man or t' knocker-up were entirely different from those we held for the rent collector. He was feared; he was also despised. The dislike we felt for our landlord, who was unknown to us, we turned on to him.

There were occasions, however, when mother violated even the all-important rent-rule. The danger signals were a penitent look on her face or new hats on my sisters' heads. I knew from the growing tension in the house, as the time for the rent collector's visit approached, that the rent had gone. Sometimes I'd reach up and shake the box myself to make quite sure the money was there. It made me feel better when I heard the coins clinking against each other.

I've never forgotten the first occasion when the coins didn't roll into the collector's hand. He stood on the doormat, shoulders arched, clutching the upturned box, an incredulous look on his face. He never moved. I was hypnotized by him. Mother, who believed in miracles, kept her eyes glued to the empty box. She wouldn't have been the least surprised to see a little bird fly in and three shining coins roll out.

Alas, the little bird which always saved her in her fairy stories failed to intervene. Instead, the collector began to shake the box like a terrier shakes a rat. Finally, he threw it and the rent-book down. "Well, tha knows what it means," he said, scowling at us, "three times and ye're oot." Then he slammed the door behind him so hard that mother's punch bowl tinkled.

My parents feared the rent collector because of the power he wielded. He could not only put us in the street, he could ruin our credit. We always bought "on tick" at Tom Tat's grocery store round the corner. I ran for different things during the week, mother and Tom Tat made a reckoning every Friday night. What she couldn't pay she would "carry over" until the following week. What the bank-book was to the toffs – uncle Eric would actually show us his bank-book to impress us – the rent-book was to the working class. A clean rent-book meant that you could get a loan from a moneylender, or do business with the pawnbroker. It gave the poor respectability as nothing else did. In a community where most things were bought "on tick" during the week, and settled for at the weekend, a "clean" rent-book without delinquencies could be the difference between eating and going hungry. No wonder we put the rent in the box behind the door on a Friday night before we bought food or went drinking.

Following one of these scenes with the rent collector, mother vowed to get rid of him. "And how will you do that, pray?" father asked. "I'll follow a rainbow," mother answered, "and get a better house elsewhere." Which is precisely what she did.

One night father came home, tired out, to learn that we were moving.

"Will," she announced triumphantly, "I've taken a house on Livingston Road close to Eric. It's where the toffs live. We're going to leave the grime behind. We've lived too long in a house in which you can't swing a cat. That horrible rent collector can keep it."

Father was dumbfounded. He stood there and blew out his cheeks as if recovering from a blow. He seemed to have difficulty breathing. Mother never gave him a chance to recover. "It's the most perfect house," she assured him. "Think of it, Will. There's room for everybody, four bedrooms." Ignoring father's "but," and "in heaven's name," and "have you taken leave of your senses, woman?" she raced on.

Mother had suddenly become wonderfully eloquent. The dykes had burst. There was no stuttering, no "but-er-I", no hesitation about what she wanted to say. She poured out what she felt, suffered, and thought about living in dirt. She described the new house better than any rental agent could have done. "There's an indoor toilet," she said, "one that flushes, and a bathroom; a bathroom; now think of that, Will – a whole room to wash in with a sky-light and a gas water heater. There's a proper kitchen, a proper dining room, and a proper sitting room. A real sitting room, Will, with places to sit and no smoke or drafts. And all lit by electricity. That makes us as good as Eric. Can you imagine it?" She went faster still. I suspected by now that she was adding rooms that were not there.

With father waving his arms like a drowning man, and the rest of us standing around gaping, mother described the garden. "Just think, Will, a proper garden. Not a pen on a cinder tip." She pummeled him with the garden. "Think what you could do with a garden like that, Will – front and back! Have you ever thought of the difference a hot-house would make to your plants?" she tempted him. "Have you ever thought what it would be like to go out of your front door and for the first time in your life step into a garden instead of into the street?"

Finally she talked about the view of the hills. "I want you to see the changing colours of the hills against the sky, Will. I want you to look up…" here she paused about to cry, "instead of looking at this sanded floor and these greasy cobbles."

She'd got it all worked out: my sister Jenny, who was about to marry Gordon Weall, would rent the front rooms overlooking the hills. Gordon, a painter, would paint and repaper the rooms. She rushed on. Then half-way through a sentence, tears rolling down her cheeks, she faltered. "Well?" she said, brushing the tears aside and looking at dad.

We all heid our breath. Surely, he couldn't say no. But he did.

"Tha off thi 'ead, woman," he shouted. "How can we live with toffs? We're 'and to mouth as 'tis."

"That's war ye're wrang," she sobbed, hiding her face in her hands. "That's war ye're wrang. Don't you understand? We've got to do summat or we're goin' te dee in this dirt."

Then Jenny and Brenda joined in. "We can do it dad, we can do it. Mother wants to move up, and you've got to help her. Your trouble is that you're not listening. You've got to listen to what she's saying. She's worn her feet off looking for a better place and all the thanks she gets from you is to say it's madness."

By now the three women were crying; the kitchen echoed to their sobs. I'd never heard the three of them at it before. Father stared at them with glazed eyes, slowly wiping the sweat off his brow.

My sisters needn't have cried so hard or stormed so much. Mother had no intention of being done out of the house. She knew only too well that father wouldn't want to change houses. He didn't want to change anything. He was happy to be where he was. Unlike mother, except for his Fall River years, he'd never known anything else. There was no ambition in him. But she was determined to change. It was her rainbow and her dream and she wasn't going to let anybody take it away. She was fighting for something better in life. Producing all kinds of papers from her blouse, she proceeded to deliver the final blow. "Look at these," she said. Dad looked at the papers and then covered his face with his hands.

"Oh Maggie," he muttered, "tha's really done it this time, lass."

Of course, he could have repudiated the contracts – mother could not read and what she'd signed, she'd signed with a cross[†] – but he didn't.

It took father some minutes, during which mother and my sisters continued to sob, to find his voice. "Hmm... hmm..." he coughed as if the shock had been too much for him. "Aw reet," he said with a nod. "Aw reet," provided tha'll promise no more shocks and no more fancy houses. A promise, mind?"

"Aw reet," Maggie answered, as she danced around the room, her eyes streaming.

"Aw reet" took us to Livingston Road.

After that we all became increasingly excited about the move. We kept going up to Livingston Road and sitting on the floor of our new house to see what it felt like. It was a most substantial two-story brick and stone house next to the last in a row. It was surrounded by duck and hen farms and open pastures. Its great bay windows looked out across the valley to Pendle Hill. It must have been several times the size of our Griffin Street cottage. The first night we went there, we were standing at the door of the tall, narrow bathroom wondering what it would be like to have a whole room in which to wash, when dad joined us.

"Too much washin' isn't good for you," was his only comment.

We loved the wrought iron gate and railings, the front garden, and the stone steps that led up to the front door. In Griffin Street we could stand at the front door and touch the horses and carts going by. We also loved the surrounding fields and farms. What a treat it was to breathe fresh air.

Everybody agreed that the house was "Champion! Aye, luvly!"

"Oh," said mother, striking further fear into father's heart, "wouldn't it be luvly if this was really ours." After which she gave a long sigh.

XVI   Livingston Road

We moved from Griffin Street to Livingston Road one Friday after midnight. We used a flat-topped hand cart with iron-shod wheels which father had hired overnight for one shilling. On to the cart we piled three beds and bedding, pisspots, four broken rocking chairs, four stools, a stand chair, a bench for sitting, a rough table, and several orange boxes, that served as bedside tables and cupboards combined. My sisters' orange box had a pretty curtain across the front. We also loaded several peg rugs, pots and pans, and cutlery. Personal belongings and clothing were packed in straw valises. All was tied down.

We took the rent-book with us. We also took the seven-and-sixpence. All we left in the little box behind the door was the key. Late as it was, Gordon Weall gave us fits pretending to be the rent collector taking down the empty box the next day. He took off the collector to a T: the cap and the turned-up collar, the shaking of the box, the sudden freezing, the dreadful frown, the terrier and the rat bit, the throwing down of the box and the book. His antics missed nothing. He glared at us and threatened us with the box, but then he broke down and laughed as much as everybody else.

Despite Gordon's clowning, it took little more than an hour in which to load the cart and make ready to leave. Other than turning off the gas, taking the penny asbestos gas mantle from the kitchen – we used open flames upstairs and the mantle in the front room had long since died – there were no utilities to bother about. Anyway, gas came at a penny a time and our penny's worth was almost done.

Father was the last out. He didn't look back. Having spat on his hands, he got between the shafts and began to push the cart along the cobbled street. Gordon took hold of one side of the cart, Harry Entwistle, a Derbyshire fellow who had recently started courting Brenda, took hold of the other. I ran behind father to ensure that nothing fell off the cart and was lost. My brother Dan was not there to help; for several months now he had been travelling northern Britain with his work crew cleaning and repairing mill boilers.

Despite the clatter, no neighbours' curtain moved. They knew perfectly well what was going on and deliberately kept out of the way. Without blinking, they could tell the rent collector the next day that they had no idea that the Woodruffs had gone. As for the police, they never interfered with a moonlight flit.

I was ten at the time and remember the cold starlit night well. This was the first move in my life. It gave me a glorious feeling. With our belongings piled high, and the chair legs pointing to the stars like masts, I saw the cart as a tall ship in which we were setting out on a voyage around the world.

It took less than an hour to get the cart up the hills to Livingston Road. At the worst points, Gordon, Harry, and I had to put our shoulders to the wheels to get the cart out of the ruts and to keep it moving. Father never left the shafts. The only sign of strain he showed was to wipe his forehead, adjust his cap, and spit on his hands. In time we drew up outside the house. It looked to me – accustomed as I was to a tiny cottage – like a glorious castle standing against the stars. We'd reached the shores of another land.

Mother and my sisters awaited us. They had lit the fires and were quick to give us a hand. Everybody worked with a will. To celebrate, we had hot tea on arrival. We hugged each other at our triumph, all talking at once. "We've done it!" we laughed. Our hearts were grateful. By four or five o'clock in the morning we were all in bed and fast asleep. By then the first pale streaks of light coming through the uncurtained windows were probing our unopened bundles lying about on the floor.

I woke the next morning for the first time in a room of my own. It smelled of fresh paint. I couldn't get used to the space and the amount of light. Going downstairs was like entering a ballroom. I was amazed at the distance between things – like how long it took to walk down a corridor from one room to another. I found mother making breakfast and singing. She was in high spirits. "You see," she said, "it can be done." She knew there was a better life because she had once lived it. She'd won. She wasn't going back to that squalor anymore.

With breakfast burning on the stove, she dragged everyone into Jenny's part of the house to look at the distant, sun-lit hills. "Look, look," she cried, pointing through the large bay windows: "Did you ever see anything so beautiful?" The sun was streaming in. With her hands under her breasts, her eyes soared across the valley, over the mills, the smoking chimneys, the mud and decay, until they came to rest on the coloured fells and the long straight line of Pendle's back standing stark against the sky. A dark tide of heather lapped the summit. The surge of emotion she felt when a rainbow lit the distant hills brought her to the edge of tears. "Well," she said to dad, who was standing by her, "do you still want to go back to Fall River?" Having drunk it all in, she gave a great sigh and went back to the kitchen. She couldn't have enough of it. For days she kept running through the house to see the hills, looking at them as if she were seeing them for the first time.

There was no stopping mother now. Unknown to us, and despite her promise to father, she was planning further shocks. We came home one night to find the house transformed into a palace. There were rugs on the floors. They were not new – later we noticed holes in them – but they were our very first rugs. We took off our clogs and stockings, and danced about in our bare feet. It tickled our toes. There were curtains instead of newspapers on the windows. There was furniture in every room. Dining room furniture, living room furniture, kitchen furniture, bedroom furniture. There were great upholstered couches and chairs such as none of us, except mother, had ever dreamt of possessing. I found it an extraordinary experience to lie on a couch. I felt I ought to be ill. None of the furniture was new, but it looked new. Forgetting money, mother had tastefully furnished the whole house. No more orange boxes for us. If ever she had a moment of glory, this was it.

Father nearly fell down when he limped in from work. He was tired out. For a moment he thought he was in the wrong house. He couldn't believe it. With a stunned look on his face, he went from room to room, his eyes getting larger and larger. This was Maggie on the grand scale. Father gingerly sat down on the edge of one of the new chairs in the sitting room, but not before he had covered it with a sheet of newspaper.

Mother just stood there silently, avoiding his gaze. With her hands across her apron, she looked a picture of abject guilt.

"Maggie, lass," father asked in a funny quaking voice, "where did you get all this stuff?"

Gradually the awful truth came out. She'd gone shopping for one or two little items of furniture, in the course of which she'd met such a nice man. He'd persuaded her that it was cheaper to hire furniture than to buy it. Buying furniture was out of date. For just a few shillings a week they could live as they ought to live. After all, they were living on Livingston Road. He had delivered the furniture the same day, and had worked hard putting it exactly where mother wanted it to give the family a great surprise. He had done that all right.

"But you promised..." father faltered.

"I didn't promise I wouldn't get a chair to sit on," mother shot back. "I promised I wouldn't get any more fancy houses. And I 'aven't."

Money aside, as mother would say, the next three years were the best years we would ever know together. We had never lived in such splendor. "Better than America," she'd say. She joked that we'd joined the middle class because she now stayed at home to look after the family instead of toiling in the mills. The pity was that grandmother Bridget could not have seen us – such a sight would have pleased her.

Helped by Jenny and Brenda, mother transformed the house into a comfortable home. This is where Jenny showed her talents. She sat in a corner, giving a little chirp now and again, while stitching the most marvellous curtains and cushion covers. Her needle flew as swiftly as the shuttle in the loom. As mother had the gift of making almost anything with scissors and paper, Jenny could do equal wonders with a needle and thread.

Outside, both around the house and in a pen at the back, father created an oasis of flowers. They grew so high and so thick that you had to hunt for him. I think there were moments when even he thought mother had done the right thing. He began to talk about building a hot-house. He came up with such wild ideas about growing red currents, gooseberries, and raspberries in the back garden – ideas that would have cost a mint of money – that even Maggie became alarmed. I think she felt he was appropriating her role as the squanderer of the family.

We knew that in joining the toffs we'd jumped the class barrier, but that didn't bother us. The rest of the working class would have jumped it too if they had had the chance. Father was mentally confined to a class; he was loyal to it. Mother wouldn't have known what to say about classes. She knew, as we all did, that there were classes within classes. "Loyalty to class", "Standing firm", or "Closing the ranks", meant nothing to her. She didn't use the terms "them" and "they" as other workers did. She knew that some people were rich and others were poor. If the working class meant dirt and poverty, then the sooner she was out of it the better.

It was our new neighbours, the Peeks, who did the worrying about class. As they were our next door neighbours on the row, they feared for their lives when we arrived. Later, one of the Peek boys told me so. His father, Terence Peek, had been a factory owner who had gone broke. As we'd gone up in the world, they had come down. We thought we'd reached paradise. They thought they'd fallen through the floor into a slum. Wakened by the din, Mr. Peek had seen us arrive in the moonlight with the flatcart. "Agnes, my dear," he had said to his wife, as he peeped through the bedroom curtains, "we are not only condemned to live in a slum, we are about to be overrun by savages." Clogs and shawls had not been seen on Livingston Road before. It took a year for Mrs. Peek to tell me this but eventually she did.

The Peeks had a rather affected way of talking to us, as if we were somehow inferior. There was a gulf between us; you could see it in the eyes. Brenda asked me if I'd noticed it. I said I had. It was a long time before we "savages" were accepted. Thanks to Roger Peek, who became my close friend, I led the way. Gradually, the barriers fell. I found the new neighbours quite different from those on Griffin Street – they dressed differently, they talked differently, and they were standoffish – but decent just the same.

The Peeks influenced me greatly in the three years that I knew them. There were five of them: Terence Peek, his wife Agnes, their sons Roger and John, and their daughter Millicent. Roger told me how well off they'd been before his father went bankrupt. One day they had lived in a large house set in spacious grounds, with servants, ponies, everything. The next day it had all gone.

Roger's only drawback was that every time he had a fall he broke a bone. I became quite expert at handling these emergencies. The brittleness of his bones, however, did not stop him from having the most dreadful fights with his younger brother John. Fortunately, when the fighting was over, it would all be love and sunshine again.

Millicent, sixteen, was the oldest child. She was just out of school. Like her mother, she was pretty in a doll-like way. She went in for flowery dresses and big frothy hats. She never took to us "savages." I think she found our presence jarring. It didn't help when my parents told her they'd been to America. We thought she was stuck-up. She was always putting on airs about their one-time superior wealth. Being "Lah-de-dah" we called it.

Our relations with Millicent were marred from the start. One bright moonlit night shortly after we had moved into Livingston Road there was the most frantic knocking on the Peek's front door. Something was dreadfully wrong for anyone to knock like that. There was a note of panic about it. Putting on the outside light, all the Woodruffs, including

Jenny and Gordon, rushed to the front door to see what was going on. Imagine our surprise to find Millicent pissing in the bushes, hiding underneath her latest frothy hat. The poor girl must have made a desperate dash up Livingston Road only to fail at the last moment. When Agnes Peek put on the light and opened the door, Millicent was still squatting among the shrubs.

"Milli!" Mrs. Peek shrieked in a shocked tone, before quickly switching off the light.

"I don't believe it," said mother, who was as stunned as Agnes, "not in Livingston Road;" after which she quietly switched off our own light, gently pushed us all back inside, and shut the door. We left Millicent out there, trying her best to merge into the shrubbery.

Once inside, we looked at each other for a moment. "Milli!" mimicked Gordon, and we all exploded. He made us rock with laughter. We laughed so hard that we could no longer speak. That night we laughed our way to bed.

We never met Millicent after that without her blushing like a peony.

Agnes Peek was my favourite. I always thought of her as plump, warm, and friendly. It may have been more as a result of sickness than of good health, but she had the loveliest round face. There was a haunting beauty about it. Like grandmother Bridget, she was always refined; never without her pearls and elegant shoes. Her fine fingers were covered with jewels. I used to look at them and think what Mr. Levy at the pop shop would give for them. Other than her wedding ring, mother had no jewelry. Grandmother Bridget's jewelry had long since been pawned. Strange, I thought, that the Peeks should call themselves poor.

Agnes had such a toff's way of talking that there were times when I couldn't tell what she was saying. But I knew her heart was good. Roger said she'd had tuberculosis, and had been treated in Switzerland. She gave me the impression of being lonely, of being cut off from former friends. She just couldn't adjust to her changed condition. It showed in her eyes and at the corners of her mouth. There were times when she looked non-plussed. She had a delightful way of fluttering her soft, white hands at any problem that became too much for her. Mr. Peek could escape from his troubles into books. There was no escape for Agnes. Little wonder that she had fits of moodiness.

If Agnes Peek was my favourite, Terence Peek was the man who changed the course of my life. He was as kind as any man I had met before; as kind as Willie Gill but in a different way; I never saw tears in Mr. Peek's eyes as I had seen them in Willie Gill's. To me he was all brain. He had a large forehead, yellowish skin, grey eyes, a little nose out of proportion to his face, and the largest ears. His hands fascinated me. They were nothing like father's hands. The palms were soft, the fingers long and delicate with broadish tips. I used to watch them as they drummed the table or the arms of his chair when he was talking to me. He wore an odd-looking pince-nez, and had his hair parted down the middle. He was forever shaking hands. We only shook hands after playing football or wrestling. He never worked – not as we understood the word. He spent most of his day either in his study or walking to and from the library in town.

I was astonished when, having won entrance to the house, I discovered that he had a whole library to himself. It was a darkish room with a long table, cluttered with books, papers, maps, and prints. It smelled of stale tobacco. He was forever smoking from an elegant cigarette holder. He had a framed picture on the wall of the factory he had owned. It appeared to be an enormous place, bigger than Hornby's. In a corner of the room stood a silent grandfather clock that he was always going to fix.

After several months, Mr. Peek began to take a deep interest in me; even though he continued to refer to me as "the young savage." I think he talked to me more than he did to his own children. I knew I'd won his confidence when he allowed me to borrow books. Sometimes I think he looked upon me as a young disciple.

One day Mr. Peek explained to me how it was possible for a man to be rich one day and poor the next. I had always thought that, outside America, where according to grandmother Bridget anything could happen, to be rich or poor was something you couldn't change; at least not as quickly as Mr. Peek had done. I thought you were born poor and you died poor, or you were born rich and you died rich. Uncle Eric was the only man I knew who had started poor and had become rich. No matter what reason Mr. Peek gave for his coming down in the world, most of which I failed to understand, his talk about being poor baffled me. By our standards, he was very well-off.

I learnt early on that Mr. Peek shared uncle Eric's belief in science. Like uncle Eric, he was a leading member of the local Mechanics' Institute. He was convinced that science was going to improve the workers' lot. He was writing it all down in a book upon which he worked every day. He never stopped talking about it; it would change the world. At least it was the only hope for Lancashire. I never understood half of what he said, but I had no difficulty following him when he argued that what the world needed was more money. Every cotton weaver knew that. Money was the one thing we lacked. Mr. Peek had worked out a scheme whereby we could all have the money we needed. He was so sure of this that even I thought him a little mad.

When I told him that I intended to follow my father as a weaver, he warned me to look elsewhere. He was the first to convince me that there was something irretrievably wrong with the Lancashire cotton industry. He knew that it had been dealt a fatal blow.

"Thank God," he said to me, "that I'm not younger. I couldn't stand to see a great industry die again."

"Rubbish," said father when I told him. "Cotton isn't dying. Peek is tapped, that's what he is. There will always be cotton."

204

Mr. Peek taught me much of what I came to know about the cotton industry. He told me that it was one of the greatest accidents in history that it was in Lancashire at all. Nobody had predicted its rise there. Not long ago, he said, Lancashire was a pastoral backwater; Blackburn was a village in the Ribble valley.

As the weeks and months passed, he told me how Lancashire had become the workshop of the world. With his help I began to learn how cotton had come to Lancashire in the 1600s, and how great textile inventors, such as John Kay, James Hargreaves, Richard Arkwright, and Samuel Crompton, had fostered its growth.

He listed other factors that had helped to bring Lancashire to the front: the older weaving tradition in linens and woolens; the damp climate which helped the cotton fibres cling together; the abundance of land, coal, stone, clay, slate, iron and other building materials; the cheap transport provided by canals and railways; the inexhaustible supply of English and Irish labour. In Liverpool Lancashire had an ideal port; in Manchester an ideal market place. Manchester was also the centre of Britain's best engineering skills. "There was a time," he said, his voice ringing with pride, "when Manchester challenged London for the commercial leadership of Britain. In 1913 Lancashire had exported seven billion yards of cloth. Imagine that, Billy, seven billion yards! We clothed England before breakfast, and the world after breakfast."

"But the people of the world must have worn something before we sold them cottons, Mr. Peek," I said.

"Of course they did. Most of the first fine cottons came from India and China. But the weavers of those countries, who used handlooms, were no match for the masters and men of Lancashire. Despite Asia's cheaper labour – sweated labour we call it – our steam-driven machines and our inventions beat them every time. We substituted machines and mass production for cheaper labour: brains for brawn. The air here was thick with inventions. We ploughed our profits back into the business; we took the long-term view. The factory owners of those days, and their sons, were known to every worker in the mill. They all took an active part. Absentee ownership was unheard of. The overriding loyalty of master and man, of capital and labour, was to the mill. This way we got bigger and bigger until we affected countries all over the world. Countries like America, India, and Egypt couldn't keep up with our demands for raw cotton. In the United States the growing of cotton with the aid of slave labour led to a terrible civil war.

"But then came the Great War of 1914–1918 which gave the other people of the world the chance to industrialize and take Lancashire's markets away. By the 1920s, India, China, and Japan had all made serious inroads into our foreign markets. They'd been doing it since the middle of the nineteenth century when Britain began to sell them textile machinery. The more machinery we sold them, the more cottons they produced for themselves and for export. The sun is setting on the British Empire, Billy, but it won't set for a long time on the machinery we've sold abroad. It's out there, Billy," he said, "working 24 hours a day to take our bread away. Many of those who are taking our bread were trained in Lancashire textile institutes; some of them right here at the Blackburn Technical College. We only have ourselves to blame."

On still another occasion he explained how, since 1921, the course of the Lancashire cotton industry had all been downhill. "Since then many parts of the world have shut out our goods, especially the low count products upon which Blackburn depends. When the Indians can't compete they find a political reason to boycott our goods, Billy. Gandhi was in Darwen yesterday. That fellow is costing England half a million jobs. For the low count cloth upon which we depend we simply can't match the Japanese, Indian, and Chinese prices. I know, because I've tried. The differences in prices gets worse. Somehow, we've got to match them. From the East and the West we're in trouble. America is taking the better trade. Technically, she's miles ahead of us now.[†] Foreigners are killing us, Billy."

At this point, tracing a line with his cigarette holder, he showed me on his maps and his globe where most of our raw cotton came from in America, 4,000 miles away, and where Blackburn sent most of its woven cloth, to India, 12,000 miles away. "Any industry that gets all its cotton from abroad and sells four-fifths of its cloth to foreigners, as we've been doing, is asking for trouble."

One day Mr. Peek was particularly down-hearted. "Nobody recognizes what is happening to cottons," he told me. "Nobody cares. Everybody tries to make a killing and get out. Those who plough their profits back into the industry and hang on get wiped out. There's no loyalty to the industry anymore. Those who run it are either daft or greedy. They still cling to the idea that Lancashire will go on leading the world. Yet they know as well as I do that our markets are disappearing and our factories are being shipped to Japan." I watched his fingers restlessly drumming the desk. "Something is missing," he went on, "we're not pioneers any more; we're hangers-on. Smugness and self-satisfaction rule. The money-spinners do the rest, they make a quick profit and get out. For us, Billy, the glory is over."

"Sounds serious, Mr. Peek."

"It is. There's only one thing the industry understands," he said as he went on tapping the surface of his desk, "Dog eat dog. Soon there will be no dogs to eat."

"What about the workers?" I said. "Where do they come in?"

"They're just as blind as the bosses," he answered. "They're sheep led by the nose."

"That's not fair, Mr. Peek, it was not the workers but the bosses that caused the General Strike."

"Nonsense," he replied puffing on a cigarette, "the General Strike was labour gone mad. There wasn't a chance of the strike succeeding. English workers aren't revolutionaries; they like to tinker, not to smash. They don't believe in tidal waves and big ideas like a General Strike; they believe in muddling through. They prefer to be haphazard. They're happier when they're arguing over price lists and pay lists. As a boss, I know. Anyway, there's no such thing as the working class; there's a dozen labour groups fighting each other. There will never be labour unity any more than there will be one church. In 1926 the workers squabbled among themselves and got what they deserved. They fought for a share of a cake that is fast disappearing. Without recognizing it, what they're squabbling over is the death of the Lancashire cotton industry."

My family's only comment whenever I told them what Mr. Peek had been saying was "Poor devil's barmy. If he goes on like that they'll lock him up."

In some things, I think, Mr. Peek probably was a little barmy. In other things he was practical and down to earth. I have to thank him for clearing up one great problem about which I had been complaining to my parents for years. To pass water had become agonizing for me; instead of flowing, it leaked out drop by painful drop. It was a crippling defect. Roger told his father of my plight.

Mr. Peek was appalled; even horrified at my parents' primitive view of medicine and their refusal to resort to surgery. He told them so. He came bouncing into our house one night determined to change their point of view. He became as committed to having them take me to a doctor as he was in providing the world with money. For him, it became another cause and he kept at my parents until they gave in. They took me to Dr. Grieves who decided upon immediate surgery.

Getting rid of the problem was as simple as Mr. Peek had predicted. Two mornings later Dr. Grieves arrived with an assistant. Fearful, I climbed on to the kitchen table, over which mother had spread a clean sheet. The table had been carried into my sister Jenny's room at the front of the house where there was more light. I could see the hills. A gauze cup was placed over my nose and mouth. "Give him a whiff," said Grieves to his aide. "All over in a tick," he said to me reassuringly. I can only remember a sickly smell. When I came to I was on the couch still facing the hills. I was still dazed from the chloroform. Dr. Grieves and his helper had gone. Mother was at my side hushing me. Mr. Peek came every day, sometimes with a book. Apart from what I recall as a week or two of agony, the cure was complete. It confirmed my confidence in Dr. Grieves; also that Mr. Peek was an ally worth having.

The reluctance to call in Dr. Grieves stemmed more from father than from mother. Although with the aid of doctors father had recovered from gassing in France during the war, he had no faith in either doctors or hospitals. Unless he was forced to, he never went near them. Once he had collapsed at work with what Dr. Grieves diagnosed as acute appendicitis requiring immediate surgery. Mother had been warning dad for years that the peanuts, which he ate by the pound, would land him in hospital with appendicitis. The ambulance was sent for. Against father's protests, he was bundled into it and despatched to the Royal Infirmary. But he never arrived. Somewhere en route he managed to persuade the driver, who was a mate of his, to take him home. His mate had great difficulty explaining the empty ambulance when he got to the Infirmary. Meanwhile father had put himself to bed. He cured himself with folk medicine: fistfuls of steam-heated bread placed between sheets of brown paper and applied to the inflamed area. Mother continued the treatment when she came home from the mill.

All that can be said is that father survived.

Dr. Grieves was never informed about his patient's escape. Meeting father later on, he asked him how he felt after the operation.

"Couldn't be better," father answered.

"You're a lucky man, you are," Grieves responded. "It was touch and go with you, you know. A few hours later and you would have been a goner."

"I can believe that," father replied.

Father always believed that if he entered a hospital he would die. It was a deep superstition he held. Many years later his fears were fulfilled precisely as he had foretold.

Dad may not have appreciated Dr. Grieves' skills, but there were many others who did. When I was a boy, Dr. Grieves was a legend in the community. Everybody knew him and his spaniel Joy. Everybody admired him. Not least because he sometimes forgot to send bills. House visits, when he remembered to charge, were two shillings and sixpence. His stock had soared after it got about that he had one day risked his life in a collapsed mine gallery tending injured miners.

While any kind of illness was considered shameful among my people, there were occasions when we were persuaded to take a bottle of his cure. Invariably, it was I who was sent to the surgery to pick up the medicine for sixpence a bottle. I always knew if I'd got the right bottle by the colour. Coughs and chest problems – goose grease and a home-made concoction of lemon, glycerin and cod-liver oil having failed to put things right – were treated with a blue liquid. Aches in the head, eyes, ears, and nose were dosed with yellow; joint troubles with red; troubles in the belly – there being no response to the usual doses of prune and fig juice – with a black, tar-like substance. I wondered what would happen if somebody confused the colours.

The only reservation I ever heard about dapper, bow-tied Dr. Grieves concerned his love of horses. He not only looked after humans, he dabbled in veterinary medicine as well. There was the catch. People swore that there had been occasions when Dr. Grieves got his medicines mixed up and that he had administered to humans what he meant to administer to the horses. Nobody in his right mind in the community ever followed Dr. Grieves instructions on the bottle to the letter and swallowed a tablespoon at one go. They first wet their tongue in it or took a smaller sip to make sure they were not going to be knocked flat.

It was while we were living at Livingston Road that Jenny was married to Gordon Weall. That was when I got my first long pants. Father took me to a shop called "Weaver to Wearer" where I was measured for a suit of a dark brown worsted wool. "Weaver to Wearer" was considered the cheapest tailor in town. Their cloth was thought to be much better than that sold by the workers' Cooperative Store, and Co-op prices were usually higher. Also, "Weaver to Wearer" offered two fittings, the Co-op only one. Not that it mattered. You shopped at the Co-op like you went to church. It was a matter of faith.

When I took the suit home in a big cardboard box, I felt like a millionaire. At last I had stopped being a boy and had become a man. I explored all the pockets and found the sixpence which a tailor always hid in a boy's first suit. One night I put the suit on and paraded before the family. There were many approving looks; many long "ooohs" and "aaahs". It was the first time in my life that I had ever worn anything over my knees. It made them itch.

The wedding itself was the most elaborate affair in the family's history. Mother was not prepared to settle for second best, not in Livingston Road. It was one of the high points of her life. That's how she thought life should always be.

At great expense to father we went the whole way. Everybody had new clothes. Mother was in her seventh heaven deciding what everyone should wear. Jenny wore white. Her dress had a low neck with a tight waist and sleeves all puffed up. She had a white veil and carried lilies of the valley. Beautiful she looked. She also had two little girls as train bearers. Gordon wore a hired frock coat, pin striped trousers, and a special grey waistcoat with a watch chain. He looked like the Lord Mayor. Nobody would have guessed he was a painter's apprentice. Like the rest of us, he got a new suit and new shoes for the wedding but kept them for going away on his honeymoon.

As it was a June wedding and the weather was kind, family and friends stood outside the church for a moment to say hello and wave greetings before going in. It's amazing what clothes will do to people when they are wearing their best. Everybody held themselves stiffly and spoke in funny voices. I never saw such a change; they weren't the same folk at all.

When we went in, the organ was playing quietly. We had a full service: organ, choir, and soloist. There were six little flower girls. Gordon and a fellow painter were waiting near the altar rail – white gardenias in their buttonholes. There were a lot of people there whom I'd never seen before. All the Wealls were present, Mrs. Weall constantly wiping her eyes. Mr. Weall, a little red-nosed man, who looked as if he had just stepped out of a hot bath, steadily supplied his wife with clean handkerchiefs. Mother put our neighbours, the Peeks, including Millicent, well up front. "Savages, are we!" I could hardly recognize mother and Brenda in their flowing pink dresses and enormous wide-brimmed hats.

Then father arrived with Jenny and the train-bearers in a shining limousine. What agony father must have suffered having to pay for that car with its chauffeur and its white ribbons and orange blossom! Jenny looked an angel; she glided down the aisle with her tiny toes peeping out of her white slippers. She had the same easy motions that made her such a good dancer. Mother had seen to it that Jenny wore "Something old, something new, something borrowed, something blue." Father walked at her side as if he had just fallen off a wall. It was one of the few times I ever saw him wearing a tie. If the organ hadn't been thundering, "Here comes the bride," we could have heard his new suit creaking.

Then Gordon and his best man stood up, and Jenny joined Gordon. We all stood and sang: "Rejoice and be glad." Then we sat down while a young woman sang, "Love divine, all love excelling." Then the preacher came forward and talked about matrimony, and what a serious business it was. He went on and on about loving and being faithful to each other, and bringing up children in the fear of God. "The fear of the Lord," he stressed, "is the beginning of all wisdom."

Then they got on with the marriage, with Bertha Weall crying so hard that she could be heard throughout the church. Then the preacher asked Gordon if he would marry Jenny, and Jenny if she would marry Gordon – which is what I thought we'd come for. You could hardly hear Jenny's reply, but Gordon's "I do" was strong. Then the preacher gave them his blessing. "What God hath joined together, let no man put asunder."

While Jenny and Gordon were in the vestry, the choir sang, "Blessed be the tie that binds." Then everybody together, including the married couple and the choir, sang, "God the creator, God the good."

Jenny and Gordon and the parents of both sides then went off in the limousine. The rest of us – relatives, friends, and those who hung on in the hope of a free meal – walked down town to Harper's where the reception was to be held. It wasn't far, the weather was good, and we made fun all the way.

Jenny told me later that both mothers cried their eyes out in the limousine. Mrs. Weall blubbered most. She kept saying, "I've lost my only son, Maggie, I've lost my only child."

In response to which mother sobbingly replied, "Aye, but tha's got a good daughter, Bertha."

"Hisht, women," father had scolded.

At Harper's we had family pictures taken and a proper sit-down ham and tongue wedding breakfast. Trifle followed, and there was lots to drink. Gordon made a speech in which he couldn't help being a clown.

While everyone was stuffing themselves and having a good time, Jenny and Gordon changed to go away. Then we all got up in our best clothes and trooped off behind the married couple, who went hand in hand, across town to the railway station. Gordon had already dropped off a suitcase there. We were a happy, laughing throng of about twenty or thirty people. Several excited children brought up the tail end of the procession.

"God bless you," passers-by called to the bride and groom.

"All the best."

"Never grow old."

"Here's to your health and wealth."

On reaching the platform we rained confetti and streamers upon the happy couple. The women hugged and kissed the bride. The men were more restrained. They patted the bridegroom on the shoulder as if he was going to war. Dad stood stiffly to one side, preoccupied with his thoughts. I'm sure he was still worrying about the cost of the ribbon-bedecked limousine that awaited him in the street outside.

It must have taken father a long time to pay for that wedding. He must have spent the family's savings on it, and gone into debt. It will always remain a mystery to me how a man who resented paying a penny on the tram, and who was not known for giving his children anything, could suddenly spend like a profligate. The money for all the clothes must have come out of his pocket, for none of us belonged to a clothing club in which garments were bought by payments made over time.

I can only think that marrying off a daughter was something special. Of course, mother was the driving force. She never let price interfere. Besides the Wealls were a cut above the Woodruffs and it was up to us not to let the side down. Pride demanded that we should impress them. Also, we lived in Livingston Road. A threadbare marriage from such an address would have been unthinkable.

In any event, money was never better spent. We had a wonderful time, we all got stuffed with food and drink; and everybody finished up with new clothes. Father's suit lasted him the rest of his life. We'd never spent like that before, and we never did again. "Everybody is entitled to go mad once," mother said. Mother saw to it that the wedding got into the paper. She kept asking father to read it to her over and over again. I think she often relived Jenny's wedding in her dreams.

It was also while we were in Livingston Road that Brenda became engaged to Harry Entwistle. They were both members of the Salvation Army. The Army thought the world of them. Harry was a Derbyshire man. Twice the size of Brenda, he had a ruddy, well-weathered face, a mass of blond hair combed back, hands like shovels, and a body like an ox.

He was one of the boilermen at Dougdale's mill. He'd been in Blackburn about a year. Not much was known about him. He didn't seem to have any family. When I first met him, he had two passions: Brenda and the Salvation Army. Brenda at this time was about twenty.

With all the tenderness of possession, Brenda brought him home one night to show him off to the family. Harry's big, bright eyes and his infectious, happy laugh exuded warmth. We took to him at once. He was so open, friendly and genuine that we were drawn to him instinctively. In an ox-like way he was also good-looking; handsome would be the right word. There were not many young men in town with as rich a blond beard as Harry's; his eyebrows were equally splendid.

Mother thought them a good match. At twenty-four Harry was four years older than Brenda. He had a job, and he obviously loved her. Brenda couldn't have enough of him. Without a dissenting word, the family came down on Harry's side.

Henceforth, Harry became a member of the Woodruff household. He was always coming up to Livingston Road; always eating with us, always engaging us in jolly laughter. Brenda and he often went off to Salvation Army meetings, their faces glowing.

One night they came back and announced to the family that they were going to get married. Harry didn't formally ask father for Brenda's hand, but then members of the working class rarely did. The couple just said they'd made up their mind.

Everybody was delighted. The date was set. According to Salvation Army tradition, they were to be married under the flag, which meant that the Army took responsibility for the service and the reception. The wedding breakfast had all been arranged; two bands had agreed to play. Brenda and Harry were to lead a short demonstration march, to be followed by prayers and massed singing. Nothing was going to be left out for the couple who had won everybody's heart.

None of us will ever forget the wedding day. There was such hustle and bustle in the house on Livingston Road. Other than Brenda, who wore her Salvation Army uniform, we all put on the new clothes we'd obtained for Jenny's wedding and hurried down to the Salvation Army headquarters where the marriage was to take place. We took umbrellas because the weather looked bad. Father and Brenda were to follow in a taxi. The Army captain received us and made us all real welcome. Scrubbed, glowing faces, black hats, and red bands were everywhere. Resting against the wall in the hall were the flags to be used in the march. Harry stood waiting with a Soldier of Christ as best man.

While one of the bands was playing, Brenda and dad arrived. They were just walking up to Harry when a young woman hurried toward them from one of the side doors and blocked their path. Her face was grey and drawn. Brenda stopped. She looked flummoxed. Everybody stared at the intruder.

"What can I do for you?" Brenda asked the stranger who appeared distraught.

"It's more what can I do for you," the intruder gasped.

"Who are you?" said Brenda, her face darkening.

"Mrs. Harry Entwistle," the woman sobbed. "Thank God I got here in time."

Brenda's face became distorted; her lips quivered and throbbed. She looked at the woman with stony eyes.

Mother pushed past me and threw her arms around Brenda. "Come home child," she pleaded. Everybody in the hall was so still, they might have been struck by lightning.

Brenda turned on Harry. "Harry Entwistle," she asked, "is this your wife?"

Harry shifted his feet uneasily; he was trembling; his face was flushed; he was staring at the floor. After a moment or two he looked up. "Yis," he stammered.

Snatching the umbrella from father's hand, Brenda struck Harry across the face. A red weal appeared. "You scum!" she screamed, as she delivered blow after blow. Harry didn't move. Didn't flinch. Nor did anybody else. The crowd just stared. "You rotten devil!" Brenda went on hitting him until the umbrella broke. So did her spirit. With a sob she collapsed on to a chair. With all the women weeping, the family somehow managed to get her home.

For days, Brenda didn't speak to anyone. When she did come downstairs her face was a frightful sight. She looked twenty years older. A vague sadness had replaced her distress.

She never wore the Salvation Army uniform again.

In time the wounds healed. She married a good man called Richard Paden. He was a clerk at a store in town with very little money and fewer prospects. I remember the wedding because – in contrast to Jenny's wedding – it was an in-and-out-of-church affair with no trimmings. Nobody said it, but I think everybody felt that the ghost of Harry Entwistle was there, mocking us with his hearty laughter. Somehow Brenda and Richard weathered the hard times. Like my sister Jenny and most other workers who had little to eat, they only had one child. Brenda remained with her spouse until death intervened.

It was shortly after Brenda's wedding that Agnes Peek was struck down with tetanus. She cut her finger on a piece of glass which was lying under the sink. I was standing next to her at the time. It was only a prick which she sucked clean. That night there was a giant commotion next door. The ambulance came and carried her off. Mrs. Peek lay at death's door in the infirmary for weeks. I often went with Roger to see her. She was never the same when she came home.

XVII   Earning my keep

It was while we were living at Livingston Road that I first began to really earn my keep. I had to: mother needed the money. I'd been doing odds and ends for Mr. Tinworth in Griffin Street for several years, but the work I took on when we moved to Livingston Road was almost full time. I started by delivering morning and evening newspapers for George and Madge Latham, a young, childless couple in their thirties, who ran a sweets, tobacco and newspaper business on Revidge Road. The Lathams were an honest, hard-working couple. They were Lancashire folk: active, tough, cheeky, resourceful. They were always cheerful. I was almost a year below the minimum age of eleven when I applied for the job, but they took me on just the same. No one enforced the law. They paid me the princely sum of two shillings and sixpence per week, of which I received a "dodger". My people took the rest. I was expected to earn my keep and I took pride in doing so.

Working as a newsboy was one of the happiest periods of my life. I came to love the Lathams and looked upon their home as my own. They treated me as their son, which meant not least, that Madge periodically put my head over their kitchen sink to scrub my neck. For the first time I started wearing woolen underclothing, which she provided. It made me feel so hot. She also insisted on my taking a weekly bath in their bathroom. I never left the shop to go to school without Madge tucking a bag of shortbread into my jacket pocket. I loved Madge because she was so kind to me, but when she asked me to part my hair on the other side, I pretended not to hear. Several times they tried to adopt me. My father was agreeable; my mother, conscious of her own childhood, always refused. I would have been happy to join them. In George Latham I found the companionship of a father I had never really had.

I came to spend so much time with the Lathams that home and school fell into the background. The wonder is I got to school at all, or that having got there, I fell asleep. Winter and summer, wet or fine, dressing silently by candlelight, I got myself up at five to meet George at the newspaper depot in the centre of town about a mile and a half away. To get there, I had to run through the dark, hushed streets for half an hour or so. I'd find George waiting for me with his bicycle. On cold mornings his teeth would be chattering. Together, we then fought our way in and out of an ill-lit warehouse which served as the newspaper depot. In a state of frantic excitement and confusion, we fought a daily hand-to-hand battle with other cloth-capped men to get our newspapers.

Once we'd got our warm, damp bundles, we loaded them and George's bike on to the first, usually empty tram to Revidge Road at six a.m. Kneeling on the ribbed floor, we sorted the papers as the tram lurched along. When there was frost on the tram windows and the wooden ribbed floor was wet with the melted snow off people's clogs, we used the seats. Before reaching the terminus at Revidge Road, George helped me off the tram. With a bag of newspapers on either shoulder, I'd begin my round. Minutes later, he got off at Revidge with his bike and the rest of the papers. Depending on the weather, I'd be running through the streets for the next hour, or hour and a half. I found it wonderful to have the world to myself. There was time to dream of impossible things.

I must have had a remarkable memory for I never had any difficulty finding the houses or knowing which paper went through which door. In time, I knew the politics of every house I visited. Labour people took the *Herald* or *News Chronicle*, conservatives the *Mail* or the *Telegraph*, liberals the *Manchester Guardian*, the toffs took the *Times*. A switch in newspaper usually meant a switch in political allegiance. I always knew how my customers would vote.

Delivering newspapers taught me a lot about human nature. I learnt to recognize the news addicts and the insomniacs. In summer these chaps would be pacing up and down their lawn awaiting my arrival. They almost snatched the paper out of my hand. It made me feel important. I knew by the way they rushed to the financial pages that, like most of the rich, they were fearful of losing their money. I'd nothing to lose so the financial crashes of the time left me cold. I decided it must be very worrying to be rich.

I met every type: the sweet and the miserable. In bad weather the kind-hearted would give me a cup of tea and a bun. The not so kind would stand there, wave the paper in my face as if I were responsible for the success of Labour at the polls, or the assassination of the head of a foreign state. I felt like saying: "Look, Mister, I don't write these papers, I just deliver them." Usually I kept my mouth shut. One thing I did learn was never to give a man the wrong paper. You've no idea how touchy some people can be. They used to bawl me out as if I'd permanently committed them to the wrong religion.

In time I came to have a large family of newspaper readers. I knew them more closely than they realized. I could assess them by the way their houses stared, sat, and slept; the lights, the curtains, the way they handled their garbage or their dogs – everything conveyed a message. It wasn't long before I knew everybody's business. I knew all about the births, weddings, divorces, and deaths in the district. I knew those who had gone broke, and those who, in business and politics, were doing very nicely, thank you. I knew when a move was underway. Nobody could tell me who was going to be mayor or who was going to jail. I followed the sicknesses in the different houses. I delivered Dr. Michael's paper. He was the great ear, nose and throat specialist of the time who found himself unable to save his own daughter from a fatal ear infection. "How is the Michael child?" my customers would ask me as if I were a consulting physician.

With a passion for the printed word, I not only delivered newspapers, I read them too. I opened every day's newspaper eager to see what the world was up to. I cannot explain why I had this appetite; I just did. The newspaper I remember best was the one announcing the successful nonstop solo flight of Lindbergh from the United States to France in 1927. Lindbergh's feat had a tremendous effect upon boys of my age. My friends and I never stopped talking about Lucky Lindy. The only airplanes we had seen till then were three single-engine aircraft flown by a group of American "rough riders" who came for three days to "barnstorm" from a field on the edge of town. They charged five shillings for a ten minute ordeal. My mates and I saw the whole show and were awestruck. The planes and presumably the passengers were thumped and banged about so much that we expected them to fall apart. When we saw people getting out of the planes and throwing up, we concluded that it was just as well that nobody was pressing a free ride on us.

The newspapers of those days were full of politics. That's how I first heard about world leaders such as Mussolini in Italy or Stalin in Russia. I used to cut their pictures out of the paper and line them up like a rogue's gallery on my bedroom wall. With the world depression in trade and industry at its height, the papers also had a lot to say about commercial crises, strikes and lockouts.

Sometimes the news of the day was so arresting that I stopped under a street light to read. I remember the banner headlines of 1929 announcing the formation of a second Labour Government; the first had held office for several months in 1924. We believed Labour would put things right. Ramsay MacDonald was to be Prime Minister.

With the further collapse of trade and industry in Britain, equally large headlines greeted the fall of the Labour Government in 1931. The man upon whom all our hopes were pinned – Ramsay MacDonald – then deserted the Labour Party to work with the Conservatives and the Liberals. My family couldn't believe that the workers' only hope had gone to pot.

One thing I did learn, was the way newspapers contradicted each other – that truth is not as straight-forward as I thought it was. A disaster in politics in one paper was a victory in another. I asked myself how could that be? How could people be so dissimilar in their opinions and beliefs? I also learnt to be suspicious of the writers who had a simple answer for everything. Every day I read the column by Hannan Swaffer in the *Daily Herald*. Why, if they'd have put Mr. Swaffer in charge, the country and the world would have been on its feet again in seven days. I found it all very confusing.

I asked George Latham what he made of it; after all, he had newsprint all over his hands as I did, and he was much older.

"I'd never deliver the news, Billy, if I tried to make head or tail of it," he answered. "We're businessmen, Billy. We have our work cut out delivering papers without worrying about what it all means."

216

Being a businessman did not deter me from reading the newspapers as I ran through the streets. By the time I reached the Lathams, where a wash and a hearty breakfast awaited me, I knew pretty well where the world was going. After school I read the evening paper as avidly as I had read the morning edition. At the end of the day, after George, Madge and I had eaten together, I was allowed to plunder the magazines and books from the Lathams small two-penny lending library. I must have read them all. I read Edgar Wallace's detective stories one after the other as they came off the press. In Latham's lending library I continued the education that grandmother Bridget had begun. When I got tired of reading, I'd play table tennis either with Madge or with George. Always before I went home I had tea and cake with them.

Each Christmas the Lathams raffled a box of chocolates – the largest and most extravagant box available. It contained several pounds of the finest confectionery. A ticket cost a "dodger". Everybody who visited the shop bought one. Sometimes people came from miles away to join in the raffle. As it was my first Christmas with the Lathams, I decided I would have a go.

Two days before Christmas, with hundreds of tickets sold, I stood in a packed shop waiting for George to draw the winning ticket. The crowd was so large that it spilled out of the shop on to the street. With a lot of shouting going on, "Cum on now, lad, don't keep us in suspense," George dipped his hand into the box of tickets held by Madge. In a loud voice he called out: "283!"

I couldn't believe my ears. "A've got it!" I shouted.

I was speechless with excitement; it was the first thing I had ever won. I hurriedly pushed my way through the crowd to claim my prize. After a struggle I reached the counter.

"Oh, not you, Billy," George said. He gave me a sickly smile. "Billy," he leant over and whispered, "would you like to sell your ticket? I'll make it right with you. We could raffle the chocolates again. It would look better." There was a desperate look in his eye.

"No!" I shouted; I was aghast at the thought of being robbed of my trophy.

An embarrassed George had to declare me the winner. Reluctantly he placed the box in my outstretched arms. After making one or two veiled comments about shops winning their own prizes – some of them good-humored, some not so good – the crowd dispersed. I expected the customers to slap me on the back and congratulate me; nobody did.

The box of chocolates caused a sensation in my family. They'd never seen anything like it. Nor had I. The colourful lid depicted a scene from St. Mark's Square, Venice. The wrapper said so. It was all ancient buildings and lots of gondolas and glistening water. There was gold ribbon round every corner of the box. It was an adventure to raise the lid.

There was a box within the box. There were several layers, drawers and hidden corners. There was even a secret drawer at the bottom, so that when you thought the feast was ended, you could start all over again. Neighbours came and admired and fingered the box. It was left to me to decide who could have a chocolate and who couldn't. And what chocolates they were! Great delicious, hand-made things wrapped in bright tinsel. Some of them actually contained liqueur; a fact which disturbed my sister Brenda who had become a rabid drink hater.

When the next Christmas came round, I had my three pennies ready. But I was not to be given the chance to repeat my victory. "Billy," George begged, "do me a favor and don't buy any more of my raffle tickets. It would ruin me if you won it again! You are, after all, part of the business." I put my three pennies away.

The other great event of my life some months after I had joined the Lathams was finding a collie dog. Well, really, she found me. She came from nowhere one day when I was delivering evening papers, and adopted me on the spot. In a transport of joy, she suddenly leapt all over me, licking and fussing me. She made real loving sounds at me. She was black and white; she had bright eyes and the most beautifully shaped head. She bestowed herself upon me there and then, as if she'd been looking for me all her life. We became inseparable companions. I called her Bess.

After Rosie Gill, Bess was the second great love affair of my life. Morning till night, we were never apart. Although she was allowed in the house, she was never permitted to go upstairs. Every morning she would greet me by the kitchen fire writhing and leaping around me as if I'd been absent for months. She ran through the streets delivering papers with me in the dark every morning. With George and me, she slunk on to the first tram. With her cold nose, she supervised the sorting of the papers on the ribbed floor. She knew where I had to get off, and where we had to deliver. She only got mixed up – as I did – when people stopped and started their papers. When I had to go to school or inside the mills, she waited for me outside. She was always there, lashing her tail with affection. Sometimes she would give me a little bump with the side of her head to tell me that she had missed me; other times she would rub her head against my knees. No one could have had a more good-natured or more loving companion. I paid no attention to my family's complaints that she smelled – she did, beautifully. Nor did I listen when they said that there was no room or food for her. Together, Bess and I overcame all opposition, solved all problems. We lived our own lives; the rest of the world did not exist.

The greatest crisis in our lives came one day when we reached home to find a big red-faced farmer with black leggings and a check cap waiting for us. He had a collar and a leash in his hand. His angry mottled brown eyes spelled trouble.

"Tha cumin' with me," the farmer said to the dog.

I was horrified. I got as far away from the man as I could and clung to Bess in a corner of the room.

"Doesn't ta know that stealin's a sin?" he asked me with an unblinking stare. "Tha'll finish up in jail, th' will. And then, by gum, tha'll go t' 'ell."

Bess and I trembled. Her head was down, her tail tucked in.

"'As t' told boy this?" he turned on father.

"Dust ta expect me t' look after all t' bloody stray dogs in town?" father grumped.

"Wot dus t' think a dog like this costs?" the man said, turning to me. "Well wot dust t' think? Ah'm waitin' fur an answer."

"I don't know." I said. I was shaking. Bess and I clung closer still. I could feel her heart thumping; she was as terrified as I was.

"Well, if ah'd got nothin' better to do, ah'd tell thee. As it is, ah'll just take me dog and go."

The farmer reached across and grabbed Bess by the neck. With Bess squirming to be free, he put the collar on her. He then attached the leash and began to drag the dog across the floor to the door. I didn't know what to do. Father just sat there as if nothing was happening. So I burst into tears. I sobbed as if my heart would break.

"You can't take Bess away from me," I spluttered. "She's the only thing ah've got." Over her shoulder Bess pleaded for my help. I cried harder. Much harder.

The man stopped at the door and looked back. Shifting his weight from one foot to the other, he seemed embarrassed and uncertain what to do. "Tha needn't bawl thi 'ead off," he threw at me. "Anybody'd think ah'd murdered thee."

Bess began to whine. In tears, I threw myself on the floor.

"Now, tha should stop that at once. It sounds as if tha being murdered. Ah've never seen sich. Tha could make thiself ill."

While father looked on in a disinterested sort of way, Bess and I kept it up.

"A fine pickle," the farmer said, "Ah've not only had me dog robbed, ah'm goin' t' lose me 'earin' as well." After that he stood there bewildered, opening and shutting his mouth. "Ah'll tell ye what ah'll do: rather than 'avin' thee caterwaulin' like that, ah'll give thee t' dog." He bent down to remove the collar.

Bess was with me in a flash. I put my arms around her and together we went on crying and shaking.

"'Tis been a bad day," the big man muttered aloud as he left the house. "A very bad day," he said, still shuffling his feet. "Yo two have just wasted my time."

The moment the door was closed, Bess ceased whining and licked my face and hands. She declared our victory by thumping her tail on the floor.

The man never returned, and Bess and I lived happily ever after. Well, almost. One winter's day an angry neighbour entered our house:

"Would ya remove yor dog from my kennel!" he demanded. "My own dog's in t' snow." In the night, Bess had left her own kennel, which stood outside the kitchen door, wandered down the street, found a better, warmer kennel, tossed out its occupant, and had taken possession.

When I left school in 1930 and began to look for a full-time job, half the workers of Blackburn were on the streets. The entire output of the Lancashire textile industry had been halved since 1914. Because it depended upon the export trade, our town was hardest hit. Exports fell steeply from 1929 onward. The number of workers in the mills in 1930 had shrunk to a tenth of what it had been in 1913. The poor were not only going hungry; they were pawning their bedding for a meal. Some of them finished up on straw and sacking, their "bed of sorrows." A diet of fish-head soup and haddock was all that kept many of them going. Well might England's leading medical journal *The Lancet* report that people in the depressed areas of Blackburn were literally dying of starvation. The birth rate declined; the infant mortality rate remained consistently higher in Lancashire than in most of the rest of the country. The maternal mortality rate rose. Things must have been desperate because the money lenders thrived. In those days, sickness wasn't feared for sickness' sake, but because of the threat of destitution.

Such were the conditions when I reached fourteen and prepared myself to go out into the world.

The idea of my leaving upset Madge Latham. She thought that I was going to stay with them forever, but did nothing to dissuade me. At fourteen I'd kind of come of age and felt I ought to make my own decisions. She knew I'd come back to the shop whenever I could. It was tacitly agreed that if I couldn't find a full-time job I'd come back and work for them. As indeed I did. Many's the time I returned to give George a hand, in return for which Madge fed me.

Had times been better I'd have had no difficulty finding a job. I'd have joined father in the mills. There was always a place in cotton textiles for cheap child labour. A child could easily be thrown out later on. But the depression was at its height and most of the mills were shut. Nor was there hope of becoming an apprentice to a plumber, carpenter, machinist, glazier, boilermaker or painter. They were all looking for work them-selves. People were fighting over pick-and-shovel jobs. The best I could find was a job as a shop assistant to Charles Grimshaw.

Mr. Grimshaw owned a large grocery store in the wealthier part of town. He lived above the shop. Everything about the building was pretentious: it had pseudo Tudor beams across the front; the entrance was flanked by hollow wooden pillars. Apart from himself, his wife and his daughter, there were two other assistants, Cyril and Arthur. The shop contained everything to eat, drink, or smoke. It had a bakery, and was licensed to sell wines, beer, and spirits. It also sold fresh fruit and vegetables. Its doors opened precisely at 8:00 a.m. and closed at 6:00 p.m. – later on Saturdays. It catered only for the needs of the rich.

I was interviewed by Mr. Grimshaw at 6 p.m. one evening as the store was closing. I don't think I'd ever seen anybody who looked more like an eagle. Tall, grey, with closely clipped hair and moustache, Mr. Grimshaw had the eagle's ever-watchful, baleful eyes, and its strongly carved, beak-like nose. I stood by the shop door for at least thirty minutes until he had finished struggling with a large ham. Having wiped his hands thoroughly on a towel, he recognized my existence and came over to question me.

"What's your name?"

"William Woodruff."

"Where do you live?"

"Livingston Road."

Mr. Grimshaw paused. "What does your father do?"

"He's a weaver, but he's out of work."

"How many of you in the family?"

The questions went on and on. They were sharp and precise. There was no end to what he asked. After I had finally assured him that I was "a God-fearing boy," he took me on at ten shillings a week. Of the sum, I received tenpence from my parents. The rest was needed at home. Mr. Grimshaw's last words before dismissing me were: "Watch thi P's and Q's and tha'll be aw reet. Don't sing in t' shop and don't whistle. Give me trouble, and tha're out on thi ear. Remember," he warned, "jobs these days are not two-a-penny."

The next day I stood with the other two assistants Cyril and Arthur awaiting Mr. Grimshaw's arrival. On the dot of eight, which he checked with his watch, Mr. Grimshaw emerged from the house and entered the store. He wore a stiff, stand-up collar, a well-pressed grey suit, a gold watch chain across his ample chest, and highly polished shoes. For a moment or two, watch still in hand, he looked around, taking everything in. Then he snapped the watch lid to with an air of finality. He looked as sharp as a razor. We assistants froze into place holding out our hands, palm up, for inspection. Nobody talked until the inspection was done.

The snapping of the watch lid was the signal for everyone to start work. Sometimes, before snapping the lid to, he'd repeat his Five Commandments, which I soon knew by heart: work hard; be humble; don't waste; be punctual; be clean. Henceforth, until the shop shut at six in the evening, Mr. Grimshaw never spared himself or others. I never saw him waste a moment. I never knew anyone as hard-working or as efficient as he.

It didn't take me long to realize that there was nothing anyone could teach Grimshaw about groceries; nothing anyone could do, as far as I could see, to improve the Grimshaw business. He had spent his working life getting everything right. He had built his business up from nothing.

He knew every nook and cranny of the store. Better still, he had a first-class mind for figures. He could trace every penny that came and went. No wholesaler dared to take advantage of him. He could smell a rotten basket of fruit at ten yards. No one embroidered accounts when he was about.

As a salesman, he had no match. Ticklish customers were his specialty. He'd have them eating out of his hand in no time. He was a marvel on the telephone. People had to be sharp or he'd sell them the shop. He never lost a sale. I think he felt an obligation to make money. I once heard him sell a number of chests of tea to a customer who came into the store looking for something for his poor relatives for Christmas. Grimshaw was poetic. "Why sir," he said, "in the circumstances, I can think of no better Christmas present than a chest of tea. Think of the cheer it will bring. Think with what gratitude they will remember you daily…" He was as good at selling tea as anything else. I learnt later that there was quite a high profit on tea.

It was taken for granted from the day I arrived at the store that the other assistants, including members of the family, would be free to take their frustrations out on me. "Billy, give a hand!" someone would yell. "Billy, why are you standing there?" "Billy, you're loafing." "Billy, look what a mess you've made!" "Billy, you'll never learn." "Billy, it's a wonder we pay you." Every crisis was solved, every problem explained, by somebody bawling at me.

Mildred, Grimshaw's daughter – a large, dark woman who lacked all the aggressive traits of her parents – was the exception. She never bullied me. Often she defended me from her parents. She taught me to be silent. In the early days when I was just about to get my blood up at Grimshaw and answer him back, I'd catch sight of her face. "No!" she'd warn me with her lips and eyes and a slight shake of the head. She it was who told me that I'd got the job because I came from Livingston Road.

Mildred was in love with the Reverend Black who lived a street away. For such a young man Mr. Black had unusually gaunt eyes. He used to carry a tin round with him in which he collected donations for foreign missions. "Don't forget the poor souls of the West Indies," he'd say, while shaking the can vigorously under someone's nose. I'm sure there was no connection between his name and his avidity to save black souls. The look he used to give me suggested that white souls were boring and beyond redemption anyway. Mildred put one of his collection cans on the shop counter, but her father removed it. "Nay, nay, mustn't mix religion and business."

I think Mildred's love affair made her brood. Sometimes I'd catch her, elbows on the till, lost in thought. On occasions, I had to cough to make my presence known. Every Friday night she slipped me a package of bacon ends and other scraps for my family. "Faith, hope, and charity," she said, emphasizing the charity. "Put it under your jacket, Billy," she cautioned. The only odd thing about Mildred was the way she paid us from the till on a Friday night. She always raised the money before our eyes before placing it in our eager hands.

Mildred was always kind to Bess, who followed our movements from across the road. Occasionally she would slip out with a bone. They were conspirators together. I cannot imagine how these things escaped her father's notice, especially as he was always going on about how businesses failed because people didn't watch the little things.

"Take care of the pence," he kept saying to anybody who would listen, "and the pounds will take care of themselves." He was always shooting off remarks such as "A stitch in time saves nine," or "Penny-wise and pound-foolish …"

"Oh father," Mildred would respond, "you are a one. You'll wear yourself out."

Mildred had a sister, Nancy, who was married to the Reverend Spick, a bright-eyed, vigorous young curate, with a scrubbed face, who seemed to be running a race. Nancy was not like Mildred, loving and warm. Despite her invariably shapeless dress and footwear, she was imperious. Whenever she visited the shop she threw me a very stiff, "And how do you do?" to which I always replied, "Quite nicely, thank you." Her husband never wasted time on me. He raced through the shop, as he raced everywhere. A half nod or an oblique glance was the best I ever got out of him. The shop assistants never called the Reverend Spick anything else but 'Spick and Span.'

It was while I was at Grimshaw's that the notorious Rector of Stiffkey in East Anglia, the Reverend H.F. Davidson, was defrocked. There had been a sexual scandal, following which the Rector, with an apparent disregard for doctrinal orthodoxy or the interests of the Church of England, proceeded to air his differences with the church in public. His case was heard before the Privy Council. The press wrote editorials about him under the heading "The Stiffkey Scandal." Questions were asked in the House of Commons, his picture was in all the papers, his church was inundated by a multitude of sightseers who came by special buses from neighbouring villages and towns. He never climbed into the pulpit without the church being packed to the nave and hundreds of men and women standing outside.

Once defrocked, the Rector fell on hard times. To make ends meet, he finished up sitting in a barrel on the fairground at Blackpool side by side with an exhibition of performing fleas where people peeped at him through a hole at twopence a go. It was all in the papers and it didn't do the Church of England any good. Mildred, her sister Nancy and the Reverends Spick and Black were appalled at the Rector's conduct. I remember Mildred shaking her head sadly when the unhappy details of the Rector's broken life were related to her – not without certain relish – by a customer in the shop. "Oh dear," Mildred said, "those who test the Lord's patience do so at their peril."[†]

I never liked Mrs. Grimshaw. She was as small as Mildred was large. She had a hard face, with deep grey eyes and a prominent nose. There was a crushed look about her. From start to finish, I never saw her wearing anything else but the same white lace collar, a string of coloured beads, a black blouse with large wooden buttons, and a thick black skirt. She had an unpleasant high-pitched voice. She used to croak and wheeze all the time. For reasons which were never clear, she carried a large pair of scissors on a chain around her waist. I never saw her use them. Except when customers entered the store – when she suddenly became all smiles and friendliness – Mrs. Grimshaw sat on a stool like a molting hen. She was as stiff with me and the other shop assistants as her daughter Nancy.

Of the two assistants in the store, Arthur and Cyril, I liked Arthur best. Several years my senior, Arthur was a handsome fellow with roguish grey eyes and thick, wavy black hair parted down the middle. He had the best teeth in the shop when he laughed. Like my brother-in-law, Gordon Weall, he was a born mimic. He loved to impersonate the Reverend Black shaking his collection can for the foreign missions.

Nobody got the better of Arthur. He was deft at his work – nobody could handle the butter paddles or cut bacon like him – and he had an answer for everything. I never knew anybody who could guard his flanks like he did. It amazed me the way he made excuses for jobs not done. Sometimes he'd get through a job in no time. "I gave it a lick and a promise," he'd say.

Other than Mr. Grimshaw, nobody could handle customers like him. We had three kinds of customers: ordinary, they took what you gave them; difficult, they were forever tasting the cheese, or saying that the bacon had been cut too thick; and sick, these were the customers who, no matter what you did, complained. Arthur could mold the lot like clay. No trouble at all. The sick customers actually smiled. Only Mrs. Grimshaw saw through him. She was always cool towards him. Yet women customers preferred Arthur to anybody else.

I always ate my lunch with Arthur in the dim-lit, dank cellar beneath the shop floor. It was the only room in the building where, as far as we knew, Mr. Grimshaw did not have a peep-hole. To avoid him over-hearing us we always spoke in low tones. We'd lots of fun sitting for our thirty minutes lunch break on soap boxes down there. We had to sit, the ceiling was too low to stand. Arthur was always laughing. He had a sly kind of humor. He took nothing and nobody seriously. Not even his boss. Grimshaw would have sacked him long ago had Arthur not been useful to him. In time I told him all about my family and the hard time they were having, but he never told me anything about his.

What astonished me was how well Arthur ate. Having finished cheese sandwiches, he would proceed to eat chocolate, fresh fruit, and cake, which he fished, one after another, out of a giant pocket at the front of his black apron. Not content with that, he'd then lie back and blow rings from a most expensive cigarette. He couldn't have been more generous with me. While he smoked, I ate what food was left.

One day I asked him how he could afford it all. For a moment or two he looked at me quizzically. Then he beckoned me over and placed his lips against my ear. "Y'elps yerself, that's 'ow," he whispered, while giving me a sly wink.

"But that's …" I began.

"Tommyrot," he broke in.

I was too shocked to know what to say, especially as for weeks now I'd been sharing the spoils. Good God, I'd been eating stolen goods! My mouth went dry.

"Cut your throat if you tell," Arthur warned in a low voice, while he held me with his eyes.

Not knowing what to do, I laughed nervously. I suddenly realized that I was in danger of losing my job. I was scared. Then we laughed together. He laughed uproariously at the effect his words had had upon me.

I later came to the conclusion that Arthur's philosophy in life was simple: it was for the poor to rob the rich. He must have been practising that philosophy at Grimshaw's for the past several years.

"Not 'alf," was his only comment when I asked him.

Mr. Grimshaw's chief assistant, Cyril, was a different kettle of fish. I couldn't stick him. He seemed to me to be full of malice and calculation. He had a funny little face which he hid behind large spectacles. He had black eyes and black hair. His handshake was soft and pulpy. At first I feared him as much as I feared Mr. Grimshaw. He was forever watching me and plotting against me. He made a habit of harassing me. He leered when I did anything wrong. He pushed and shoved me as if I were a piece of merchandise to be moved about the shop. He was my enemy without a cause. He also hated Bess. He would have stopped Mildred feeding her if he could. What put me off more than anything else, were Cyril's damp, fishy fingers.

The things he said about weavers and strikers made me mad. What he said about the striking textile workers he'd got from his boss, Mr. Grimshaw. "Shoot 'em," was Mr. Grimshaw's final word on strikers. Now and again Mr. Grimshaw would sound off to some prosperous customer on the subject of industrial unrest. "They're spoiled, that's what they are, these workers," he said. "Yes, sir, downright spoiled. It's not good for the likes of them to be mollycoddled. Only makes them lazy and ungrateful. They'll ruin any business. They'll ruin the country with their demands. You can't satisfy them. Having got a penny, they want a pound. If you don't keep them down, you won't get a thing done. They won't move. I know them – they have to be threatened: hunger in this world, hellfire in the next. Socialism can't take the place of hard work and the certainty of the Lord." Grimshaw would say these things with such heat that I expected flames to come out of his mouth. "Any man who strikes on me," he'd end, "goes through the window."

225

Cyril had no real skills, other than monumental servility. I think Grimshaw had bullied him for so long that there was nothing left. He must have been paid a pittance. One day I had occasion to go to his house in the woods on the outskirts of town. Cyril was at a relative's funeral. I was astonished how poorly he lived. I was badly off; Cyril was worse. I lived in a substantial house in Livingston Road, all he had was a leaking wooden hut and a bicycle.

His old father, whom I met on that occasion, was terrified that Cyril might lose what little income they had. A white-haired, bent old man, he clutched my hand on parting. "Look after my Cyril," he begged. "Tell Mr. Grimshaw that Cyril's a hard worker." He said much more about the merits of his Cyril, while moving bowls around to catch the rain coming through the roof.

Instead of fearing him, I came to pity Cyril. I knew from her eyes that Mildred felt the same. When he was not calling out: "Yes, Mr. Grimshaw. No, Mr. Grimshaw. Right away, Mr. Grimshaw," he was worrying himself to death what on earth he would do if Grimshaw fired him. I suppose he had conveyed his fears to his father, which is why the old man brought up the subject when I visited him. We were all frightened of being sacked – especially if it meant the loss of a character reference. There were simply no other jobs to be had. But Cyril was positively terrified at the thought. He clung to Grimshaw as a drowning man clings to a raft. His wildest dream, which he once confided to me, was to marry Mildred and inherit the business. There was a half-hopeful, half-gloating ring to his voice.

Arthur roared with laughter when I told him of Cyril's hallucination. He kept slapping his thighs as if it was the funniest thing he'd ever heard. "I suppose Cyril intends to get rid of the Reverend Black by sending him to the West Indies," he said, as he doubled over in stitches.

I happened to enter the shop one day at the moment that Grimshaw was sacking Arthur. He must have caught him helping himself. Or perhaps Cyril, who looked oilier than ever, had betrayed him. The only thing that surprised me was that Grimshaw had not got on to Arthur's pilfering sooner. "There's a week's wages," Grimshaw snapped. "Now get out!" Arthur was his usual cool self. He didn't seem rattled, not even when he was being fired. He knew from the shocked look on my face that I'd had nothing to do with it. "Ta, Ta! Woody," he said as he sauntered off, hands in pockets, trying to look casual. He whistled as he left. That takes some doing when you've just been sacked. I never saw or heard of him again.

Most of the time while I was working for Mr. Grimshaw I was too busy to worry about other people's troubles. My day began when Mildred let me into the store at 7:45 a.m. My first job was to carry out the trash and ashes from the house and the store from the day before. I then carried innumerable buckets of coal from the cellar up several flights of stairs to the rooms above. The main living room had a large glass cupboard containing fine china and silverware. It was richly carpeted. It had double curtains and a clock on the mantelpiece faced with black marble.

In winter my progress was speeded up by shouts from the rooms above. The grates cleaned and the fires lighted – the so-called house cleaning woman-cum-cook arrived later – I carried wood, coal, and flour to the bakery. I learnt not to stand about in the bakery talking to the cook. One morning when we were chattering away, a small wooden door slid back and Mr. Grimshaw's eagle head appeared. "I'm not paying you two to stand there gassing," he threw at us.

Having finished the house chores, I swept the shop, first sprinkling the splintery floor with used tea leaves. That done, I washed the shop windows and the pavement in front of the store. Whereupon I was ready to begin my day's work, which was to deliver groceries to customers. Cyril and Arthur had been round the district on bicycles earlier taking orders. I was never allowed to serve behind the counter.

I conveyed the supplies of food and drink in a two-wheeled hand-cart – a large tray on enormous iron-clad wheels – which I alternately pushed and pulled through the streets. On both sides of the cart were advertisements of Mr. Grimshaw's merchandise. The cart had a tarpaulin cover in case of rain. My only cover was a fustian cap pulled well down and a muffler wrapped round my neck. I could get wet, the groceries never. I also had an oil lamp which I used at night.

On the outward journeys, in order to keep my eye on the stacked boxes before me, I pushed the cart. Returning to the shop, I ran in front between the shafts like a donkey. Some passers-by asked me if I were a donkey. I doubt if a donkey could have handled some of the heavy loads I was expected to push. There were times when Cyril and Arthur had to help me make a wobbly start down the cobbled street. The pushing and pulling left me stiff and sore, but there was nothing like it for developing the back and shoulder muscles.

Wet or fine, I went out. Once started on the road, Bess appeared at my side. As rain was an almost permanent condition, I was accustomed to all kinds of it: dreary rain, slanting rain, driving rain; viciously cold rain that would beat against your face, blinding you until you yielded; rain that would soak you to the skin, and ooze in your clogs; rain that on occasions I found exhilarating and sang to.

Often the wind held me up, trying to drive me back. I became expert at waiting until the gust had finished and then pushing on. Sometimes sleet and snow would hit me. I averted the weather by holding my head to one side. Bess was smarter; she disappeared underneath the cart. Sometimes in winter a lighted tram would pull alongside us and the passengers would look lazily down at the strange apparition on the road. Bess and I were careful to yield to all other vehicles so that we would not be run over. We were the bottom of the heap; nobody gave way to us.

It didn't take me long to realize that Mr. Grimshaw's customers were living off the fat of the land. It was the same with their houses and their gardens. Everything they had was solid and prosperous. It puzzled me how it came about that while my family were fighting to make ends meet, others were eating sides of bacon, legs of lamb, whole hams, quantities of fish, eggs, milk, fruit including fresh grapes, vegetables, drink, fresh bread, pies, confectionery, and whole tins of Peak Frean biscuits. It didn't seem fair. The bad times meant self-denial for the workers, self-indulgence for the rich.

I was not alone in thinking thus. One day a gang of locked-out weavers stopped me and, despite my protests, began to rummage through the cart. Bess barked at them and ran between their legs, threatening to bite. I had trouble keeping her down.

"Just look at this," they shouted as they uncovered first one choice item of food or drink and then another. "Pigs at trough! Greedy buggers!" Then they turned on me. "What kind of a lackey are you?" they shouted. "Pandering to the gluttony of the rich. Tha working class and tha ought to be shamed."

Fortunately the demonstrators confined their anger to words. They didn't steal anything. After being pushed and shoved I was allowed to go my way. One of them shouted after me: "Tha'll get nowt but crumbs from t' rich man's table."

True, I thought as I went along. At ten shillings a week that's all I was getting: crumbs. But to anyone who was hungry, the crumbs from Mr. Grimshaw's table were worth having. For my family the crumbs were indispensable. It was the crumbs from the rich men's tables that kept Bess and me going. There was hardly a rich house where the servants didn't feed us. The servants were working-class people speaking my dialect. They knew that there were a lot of hungry people about. They also knew I wouldn't be pushing a cart through the streets in the pouring rain if I wasn't poor. Besides, I was only fourteen and I think they felt for me.

"Tha must sit thiself down, lad," they'd say, "and have a bite; tha looks clemmed." In those days servants and maids came cheap and were every-where. There were maids dressed in starched white, black, or brown; maids with fine aprons and pretty caps perched on their heads; maids with a rich Irish brogue.

And so, with a roaring fire in the grate and the pots spitting, Bess and I would sit in the kitchens and taste the food we'd just delivered before the rich could get to it. Many's the piece of hot pie or tart I had; many's the scrap that Bess got. There were so many of us eating the food in the kitchen that I sometimes wondered if there'd be any left to go upstairs.

During the year I worked at Grimshaw's the servants of the rich were my guardian angels. I couldn't have survived without them. I never met a sour one among the kitchen staff. They not only fed me and my dog, and dried my wet clothes before the great kitchen fires – sometimes they even provided me with cast-off clothing – they covered up for me if I accidentally damaged some of Grimshaw's goods. They were so kind to me that I sometimes stayed in the kitchens too long. Realizing that I was late, I'd race back to the shop like a mad horse, dragging the empty, bouncing, clattering cart over the cobble stones after me. Bess would lead, barking. Sure enough, as we approached the shop, I would catch sight of Grimshaw waiting for me on the sidewalk, red in the face, watch in hand. "Wher's ta bin?" he'd snap.

One of my special guardian angels was a sweet old lady called Mrs. Sand who lived in a large, gabled house surrounded by trees. She was a tiny, grey creature, with grey eyes, and a long grey dress. I sometimes thought of her as a ghost. In all the visits I made with groceries, I never saw anyone else entering or leaving the house, not even a gardener, or a maid, or a physician. The only other occupant of the large dwelling was her desperately sick husband who lay upstairs, making all kinds of choking noises. When he needed something he would ring a bell. The moment the bell rang, Mrs. Sand dropped what she was doing and rushed upstairs, calling out to her husband as she went. I never understood why she had to keep running upstairs when there were so many empty rooms downstairs.

Mrs. Sand's loneliness was so great that I could touch it. She always welcomed our arrival by feeding Bess. Then she'd sit and drink tea with me while telling me all the family business. The way the words came pouring out, I wondered if she had anyone else to talk to. She told me how her son's wild life – he was their only child – had caused her husband to have a stroke. Somehow the boy had got hold of their money and spent it on gambling and women and drink. They hadn't seen or heard of him since her husband's collapse. He had dropped out of their lives.

"Wouldn't it be awful," she said to me one day, talking more to herself than to me, "if he were to die in some God-forsaken place with no one to comfort him?"

"Yes," I said, "it would."

"He is our only child, you know."

In the time that I knew her, she must have said this a dozen times.

The trouble they had had with their only child did not seem to have undermined Mrs. Sand's faith in God's goodness.

"Never forget the glory there's to be," she would say. She had mother's faith in the future.

The tears rising freshly in her eyes, she vowed never to leave the bell-ringer as long as he lived. She said it as if I'd made the suggestion, or she was beating back a wrong thought. Staring through her window at the garden, she wistfully talked of the coming of spring.

In return, I told her all about the worlds I intended to conquer. I told her that I was thinking about getting a big job in Manchester or London. I also told her that grandmother Bridget had once urged me to go to America.

"Yes, yes, you must," Mrs. Sand encouraged me. "You must start at once. How exciting," she exclaimed, jumping up. "How I envy you."

And then, suddenly realizing that Grimshaw was waiting, I'd swallow my tea, eat my cake, and rush off.

When Christmas came she asked me in a faltering voice to drink a toast with her. There was a miniature fir tree on the table. I agreed at once. The two small glasses were ready. She insisted on pouring the drink, though I noticed how badly her hand shook.

"Merry Christmas," I said, raising my glass, and bowing slightly.

"Merry Christmas," she answered smiling, "and may all your dreams come true."

I stood in silence, not knowing what to say.

It was while I was working for Grimshaw that I fell in love with Betty Weatherby, the daughter of one of Grimshaw's customers. Of course, it was ridiculous. One can't have a fourteen year-old errand boy running off with a manufacturer's daughter. But nobody intended it that way. It was as much of a surprise to me as it was to everybody else, including Bess, who sat and stared at me as if I'd gone out of my mind.

It began one night at the town's indoor swimming pool where all the schools were competing. I'd learnt to swim in that pool. I've never forgotten the first time I let go of one side of the pool in the deep end and struggled to the other side. After that swimming became an obsession. The meeting was packed and noisy. The shouting in the confined space was deafening. I was swimming for St. Philip's. I'd taken up my job at Grimshaw's a couple of weeks earlier but I was still officially allowed to compete. I was pitted against the best in the town. Luck had brought me through several heats to the finals for my age group. Now I faced the ultimate test.

"Come on Woody," my supporters yelled. "You can do it."

As I stood poised, waiting for the starter's gun, I suddenly made up my mind to win. In all the other heats I'd never felt this sudden urge to come out on top. It was a funny feeling that came from inside me like a flash of anger. It said: "You've got to win."

At the crack of the gun, I and five others dived in. Dimly, I heard the thunder of voices. In the green, shimmering water I saw the black line on the bottom of the pool snaking away in front of me. To my left was another boy; at first I was level with his thighs, then he drew ahead and I caught glimpses of his feet. Gasping for breath, I chased after him. He was still leading when we turned for the eighth and last lap; the other swimmers had fallen behind. With my lungs bursting, I ordered my arms and legs to go faster. I strained until I was level with the other fellow's head. I heard the constant thump of his arms and legs. I wondered if I had strayed out of my lane. With one last frantic effort I hit the wall. When one of the judges touched me on the shoulder, I knew I'd won. I was more exhausted than elated.

The girl's final heat for my age group followed immediately. A short, small-waisted, dark-haired girl was the winner. I had no idea who she was. Together we stood in our dripping swimsuits before the judges to receive our silver medals. Real silver. On this occasion the town's poverty was forgotten. Amid all the shouting, she and I stole side-long glances. I noticed the full cheeks, the well-shaped mouth, and the rounded chin. She gave me the warmest smile. I smiled back. She smiled again. It was enough to make my face burn; enough to make me forget all about the judges and the medal around my neck.

While I wouldn't have dreamt of talking to her, I tried to follow her with my eyes after we left the dais. She was soon lost in the crowd. My friends pressed around me to see my medal; I dressed in a daze.

I slept badly that night. I didn't know what had come over me. I felt pierced from top to bottom. Rosie Gill, or Annie Morgan, or any of the other girls I'd met had never affected me like that. The next day I got up without any appetite.

Several days later, while delivering Grimshaw's groceries, I was amazed to see the same girl in a blue school uniform entering the Weatherby's driveway. Ahead of us lay the Weatherby mansion, a large brick building of several levels, standing among wide lawns and park-like shrubs. I was too flabbergasted to know what to do. I didn't want to bump into her; not pushing a handcart.

Instead of yielding to my immediate reaction, which was to flee, I slowed down and entered the driveway well behind her. As she went ahead of me, crunching the gravel beneath her feet, her doe-like body looked lovelier than ever. I hoped she wouldn't turn round. I think Bess knew what was going on, for, despite all my commands, she ran to the girl, wagging her tail, whining. The girl petted the dog but ignored me. Then she disappeared through the front door. Shamefaced, Bess and I went round the back.

In a round-about way I asked Mrs. Pegg, the head cook at Weatherby's, who the girl was.

She stopped what she was doing and looked at me curiously. "Tha not gettin' any fancy ideas in thi 'ead, ar' ta?" she asked jovially.

"Oh no, Mrs. Pegg," I answered, blushing.

"Tha'd better not, lad. That's Betty, the apple of Mr. Weatherby's eye. Mustn't throw thi cap at 'er."

"Oh no, Mrs. Pegg," I said. "Ah've got some gumption."

All the other kitchen hands laughed.

A week later, when Bess and I were leaving the Weatherby's drive, the same girl stepped out from behind the small, open pavilion which stood at the edge of the tennis court. She was wearing her school uniform, but was without hat. Her silky black hair was blowing in the wind. I reddened, she smiled. Bess ran to her, wagging her tail.

"I just wanted to congratulate you on your win at the swim meet," she said in a delightful voice. "I thought you were pretty good."

"Well, thanks," I stammered. I felt my face redden. "You were pretty good yourself."

She gave the gayest laugh and petted Bess. I saw the first blush on her face. How could anyone have such pretty, bright brown eyes, I wondered.

Every week after that, wet or fine, I met Betty Weatherby in the pavilion by the tennis court. For me, the whole week was simply the prelude to our meeting. I couldn't get her out of my head. My feelings went from utter joy, to utter sorrow, to utter joy again. It's a wonder my nerves stood up to it. I could not conceal my delight each time we met. Nor could she. She always ran toward me, arms outstretched, her face shining with delight and happiness.

With the handcart parked next to the pavilion out of sight of the house, Betty and I entered an imaginary world. It was a world without past or future, containing only the two of us. Holding each other's hands, we were deaf, blind, and dumb to everything except ourselves. Instead of talking about my job, or about Grimshaw, or about her family or mine, we teased each other light-heartedly. We lived only to be together.

The time came when I told Betty that I loved her. I followed this declaration by giving her an ill-contrived peck on the cheek. To my astonishment, she responded not by pecking me back again, but by nibbling my ear. For some odd reason, she became obsessed with my ears. The wonder is that I had any ears left; but then ears, surely, are a small price to pay for boundless delight. As the weeks passed, we began to love each other without reservation. We would have loved each other with even greater abandon had we known what was coming.

The Weatherby's housekeeper, Mrs. Shaw, was our undoing. I'd seen her in the kitchen once. She had cold, rebuking eyes, a beak-like nose, and a tight mouth. She had talked as if she was a cut above the rest. Her tall, thin body, with its funny little head sitting ill on her neck, suddenly appeared at the entrance of the pavilion where Betty and I were rolling about on the tennis nets. She was scowling. Bess had not warned us of her approach.

"Betty!" Mrs. Shaw yelled, as if Betty's delirious eating of my ears was the work of the devil. "Betty, I am surprised at you."

She was not half as surprised as we were. Suddenly, Bess came bounding up, growling.

"Young man," Mrs. Shaw pierced me, "you will take yourself and your dog off Mr. Weatherby's property." She looked grim enough to throw me, my cart, and my dog through the gate.

Betty and I squeezed hands. Then, head down, lips trembling, red-faced, she went with Mrs. Shaw up the drive. Dazed, I made my way back to Grimshaw's. Bess ran alongside, wearing a contrite look.

"Tha some use," I scolded Bess. "Tha's got us into real trouble, tha 'as." She knew she'd let us down, she ambled along, her tail tucked in.

Mrs. Shaw must have telephoned Grimshaw. He was waiting for me outside the shop. Even though there were customers about, he didn't hesitate to have it out with me.

"Tha 'ere to deliver groceries," he told me in a biting tone, "not to go courtin'. Tha deserves to be sacked." He really got himself worked up. The veins on his forehead protruded. I stood there between the shafts, with Bess cowering at my feet. He went on and on. "If tha must go courtin'," he ended, stamping his foot, "go in thi own time, not at my expense."

I was too dazed to make any response. For all the impact his ranting and raving had upon me, he might as well have blown smoke. I was more fascinated with the globule of sweat hanging from the tip of his nose. Had he run me through with a sword, I wouldn't have cared. My thoughts were still with Betty, romping on the tennis nets. All I cared about was seeing her again.

The next week, when I pushed my cart up the Weatherby's drive, Betty was not there. I thought I'd die. I tried to pump Mrs. Pegg in the kitchen, but she kept a tight tongue. She'd obviously had orders. A week or so later, while watching the other servants closely, she whispered that Betty had been sent to a boarding school outside London. No one seemed to know where the school was. The news made me sick for days. I became convinced that I was going to die. Bess seemed to sense my feeling of complete hopelessness. She would rub her nose against my hand, trying to gain attention.

Mrs. Pegg shared my sorrow. Every time I entered the kitchen she would look at me and sigh. "Tha just too young to 'ave anything in t' 'ead," she said to me one day. "Tha'll 'ave to learn that life can be very troublesome." She then relieved her frustration by pounding a lump of dough. Later, in great secrecy, she undertook to get a note from me to Betty. "They'd have me 'ead if they knew."

I returned the same day with my letter. I told Betty that I was dying without her; that I loved her; and that I'd wait for her forever. I also gave her my address. For weeks after that, Bess and I used to trail the postman through the streets to see if he had a letter for me. Nothing came. "Tha're out of luck, they've taken thi letter out of t' post at t' other end," Mrs. Pegg concluded after some reflection. "Tha'll have to wait," she counselled. "Others do. Tha not t' only one round 'ere with a broken 'eart."

It was about the time of Betty's departure that tragedy overtook the Grimshaws. I arrived one morning to find the shop in darkness. Grimshaw had had a stroke in the night, and was paralyzed down his left side. His speech and hearing had been affected. Although I continued to carry coal for the fires upstairs, he never spoke to me again. He lay on his bed, his face twisted beyond recognition, his ugly, shrunken body like half a sack of flour on the counterpane. To catch his saliva a towel lay under his chin. Once when I was sweeping the hearth, the sack-like figure flapped its hands at me and grunted. I dropped the hand brush and fled in horror.

For the business, hard times followed. The family did their best, but, without Grimshaw, the shop was a ship without a rudder. Wrong accounts were sent out. Some wholesalers took advantage of Mildred and her mother. The women were just not as sharp as Grimshaw had been in obtaining supplies. Cyril used the occasion to worm his way into the family business, but he didn't have the brains to help. Without Grimshaw on his back, he was at a loss what to do.

Grimshaw knew that his business was dying. He made heroic, if futile, efforts to get out of bed. One day he managed it. Mrs. Grimshaw, Mildred, and Cyril dressed him and dragged him downstairs as far as the shop floor. Held upright, he managed to get across the threshold. After each step he paused to gain strength for the next. For a few moments he stood in the shop shaking, his hands fluttering, his wild, bloodshot eyes taking everything in. What he saw must not have pleased him, for his already twisted face underwent further contortion. Gasping for breath, he began to make unfriendly, unintelligible noises. Then he wobbled around and turned his back on the store. With Cyril and Mildred lifting his stricken leg at every step, he was slowly dragged back up the stairs.

The final straw for Grimshaw was to fall into the hands of a charlatan couple from Manchester who pretended to be physicians. There had been some difference of opinion between Mrs. Grimshaw and the family doctor, as a result of which he was passed over. Alas, in the care of the Manchester couple, Grimshaw's condition became worse. Mrs. Grimshaw suspected nothing until the police came to the shop. By the time a warrant had been issued for the arrest of the fraudulent couple, the birds had flown. Everyone was dumbfounded when the story got around. Imagine Grimshaw being hoodwinked like that! It put Mrs. Grimshaw in a towering rage.

The shock of being diddled was too much for the old man. I heard Mrs. Grimshaw tell a customer how he'd sighed deep enough to break his heart. Mercifully, three days later, he had a second stroke and died. We put black ribbons on the shop door and on my cart. Two days later he was buried. Wearing black armbands, Cyril and I went to the funeral. It was a bitter day. The wholesalers and most of the customers had sent flowers. There was a mountain of them. I was too busy pushing cartloads of wreaths from the shop to the cemetery to attend the church service. I carried the flowers through a great crowd to the edge of the grave.

In deepest mourning, Mildred, Nancy, Mrs. Grimshaw, and the Reverend Black, stood by the graveside. The Reverend Spick read the funeral service for his father-in-law. It was the usual one about "the resurrection and the life." I was at the back of the crowd and heard only snatches. He spoke of my boss as a father, as a merchant, as a citizen, and as a God-fearing, church-going man. He said he was convinced that Mr. Grimshaw was already enjoying his heavenly reward. We were all the poorer for his passing.

I must confess that despite the Reverend Spick's moving oration, my thoughts were not so much concerned with the whereabouts of Mr. Grimshaw's soul as with the whereabouts of Betty Weatherby.

My stay at Grimshaw's did not long outlast the death of my employer. One day, on turning a corner with a heavily laden cart, Bess and I ran slap bang into another workers' demonstration. There were more of them this time. They were led by a man beating a drum. Boom! Boom! went the drum to help the men keep in step. It struck a sinister note. A sea of hungry faces approached me, some of which I remembered from my earlier encounter with them. Inwardly, I groaned. They marched straight at me with their banner emblazoned with the words: "WORKERS OF THE WORLD, UNITE!" No one else was about. The policeman who occasionally trudged along at the side of demonstrators was absent.

"Would you believe it," somebody bawled, "he's still serving the bloody rich."

"Bloody lackey," another yelled.

"Disgrace to his class, that's wot 'e is."

Barking loudly, Bess ran from me to the men.

In panic, I tried to turn the cart round, but someone grabbed one of the wheels. Several of my boxes fell over. As I reached down to secure them, a demonstrator wearing a long, black coat seized me by the collar in a violent manner. Bess attacked him; someone kicked her off. Another worker made a menace of striking me with the back of his hand.

The crowd shouted encouragement. "Why should he help them to eat while we go hungry?"

Shaking off the man who held me by the collar, I tried to stop the pillaging of the groceries.

"Leave bloody stuff alone," I bawled. I was hotted up by now and ready for a fight; so was Bess. Realizing that if I didn't escape there would not be a thing left, I clutched the shafts, put down my head and charged. "Fetch them, Bess!" I shouted.

The cart hit several bodies as I fought to break the encircling ring. My clogs stomping the cobbles, I hurled myself forward again and again. With Bess nipping their heels, the line began to give way. To my great relief, I broke through the crowd and began to run down a steep hill. Several of the men came after me. I heard their running footsteps behind me.

Panting and crying, with Bess at my side, I rattled away faster and faster. I ran so fast that I could neither guide nor stop the cart. I knew that if I didn't let go, it would drag me along the ground after it. With a cry of despair, I let go.

Transfixed, I watched the cart lurch away from me, stand on its end, and then flip over, wheels spinning in the air. Groceries flew in all directions. Trickles of vinegar, wine, milk, flour, eggs, and hot rhubarb pie began to make their way into the gutter. My heart sank into my clogs.

With several of the demonstrators, I ran to see what might be salvaged. Together, we got the cart back on to its wheels. Helpless, I looked at the pile of food lying on the ground. It was a terrible, chilling sight. There were pickles and jam, and broken glass everywhere. With Bess barking furiously, I stood there staring at the mess, not knowing what to say or do.

By the time I recovered my wits, the men were already helping themselves. They were like locusts. Hungrily, they rummaged through the packages. Whatever could be eaten was eaten on the spot; the rest was carried off. In no time all that was worth taking had gone. I was too bruised and shaken to intervene.

Distraught, I watched the crowd line up again in a quiet and orderly manner, raise their banner against the wind, beat their drum, and march off up the hill eating as they went. Boom! Boom! went the drum. With my heart thumping, I sat in the gutter wondering what to do next. Bess sat beside me, whining, and licking her wounds. Without really intending to, I broke into a passion of crying. I wished that the earth might open at my feet. "Oh Bess," I sobbed, throwing my arms around her neck, "what are we going to do?"

Eventually I got as much of the broken glass off the road as I could. Then I threw the empty boxes back into the cart and, with a silent, downcast Bess, slowly made my way back to the shop where, with Cyril listening to every word, I told Mrs. Grimshaw what had happened. Clutching at the beads around her neck, she nearly choked. Her mottled face became contorted. In her croaking voice, she sacked me on the spot. Not far from tears, I went home and announced to the family that my ten shillings had just been stopped. Ten shillings was a small sum, but it was the only earnings coming into our house. The rest of the family had been sitting about waiting for work for ages. My ten shillings and Mildred's bacon scraps had been an indispensable part of our welfare. The loss of that money, and those scraps, worsened an already desperate situation.

Later on I had a note from Mildred Grimshaw which made me feel better. She was sorry for what had happened. She asked me to go at once to Lady Fielden's estate on the edge of town where I might get a job as an assistant gardener. She had spoken for me. Lady Fielden, I knew, was one of the town's richest widows. I wasted no time in getting there. I arrived breathless. I simply had to get this job.

The house itself was a beautiful place surrounded with wrought-iron railings. Lilac trees and beds of peonies faced the street. I made my way through archways of roses, past an artificial rock garden and bright borders of flowers, to the back of the house. From there I was sent to the front.

To my surprise, it was not the head gardener but Lady Fielden herself who awaited me. Having been admitted to the house by a maid in starched white apron and pretty cap, I was ushered into a side room rich with tapestries and curious figurines. There I found a short, hard-faced woman in her seventies sitting perfectly upright on a high-backed chair.

She was dressed in lace from head to foot. A skein of pearls was around her neck. She smelled faintly of lavender. She had an unusual amount of hair on both sides of her face and almost a beard on her chin. I put on my best smile, "I'm William Woodruff," I said.

"I know, child," she said stiffly. She then smoothed her dress while looking over her wire spectacles; her searching look went right through me.

"Sit there," she commanded, pointing to a chair opposite her.

I did so quickly, but with a sinking feeling. I was intimidated by Lady Fielden and the large room with its high ceiling. I felt that if I moved I might break one of her treasures.

She proceeded to question me. The way she pursed her lips told me that I was giving all the wrong answers.

"Which church does your family attend?" she asked finally.

"My people don't go to church," I said, attempting to smile.

She shook her head deprecatingly, while fingering her pearls. I shifted uncomfortably inside my clothes. I began to revolve my worn cap in my hands. From the stern look she gave me I knew I'd said the wrong thing.

Curtly Lady Fielden made a dismissive gesture. "That will be all," she said. "I will write to you." I gave a stiff little nod. She never did write. Another gardener there told me later that I had failed the "religious test." I should have boasted membership of the Church of England, he said. Instead, I'd given her the impression that my family were heathens, which they were. She wasn't going to have any heathen touch her flowers.

The last thing I heard about Grimshaw's came from Mrs. Sand, whom I visited one day. She was delighted to see me again. I heard the bell still ringing upstairs. She told me that the errand boy who had replaced me had told her that Cyril had also left Grimshaw's. There'd been a storm between Mildred and Cyril and he'd been thrown out.

Weeks later, I saw a notice in the paper saying that Grimshaw's was up for sale.

XVII   To Nab Lane

While I'd been earning my living at Latham's and Grimshaw's, our neighbour, Mr. Peek, had been getting on with his book that would save the world. He never tired of talking to me about it. The more talk in the papers about a world depression, the more time Mr. Peek spent in his study. "The workers don't know what's coming," he muttered darkly one day when we were talking about the growing problems of the cotton industry. My family didn't thank Mr. Peek for his warnings. As long as they had some income, they seemed to have a vision which prevented Mr. Peek's fears from reaching them.

Alas, Mr. Peek's gloomy predictions gradually came true. In the summer of 1929 the cotton industry took another nose dive. In that year the spinners were locked out to enforce wage reductions. Jenny and Brenda lost their jobs, but it was only temporary. We were soon back on our feet. In 1930 the weavers were locked out to enforce the increase in the number of looms from two to six, or even eight. But that only affected father and the lockout was lifted. We breathed freely again for several weeks. One way or another, my family got along. We hung on for our dear lives to the house in Livingston Road.

In 1931, when stoppages and wage reductions became general, Mr. Peek's dire warnings could no longer be disavowed. Like a distemper, unemployment spread throughout the entire region. Since 1929 it had been spreading throughout Wales, Scotland, and the North of England. By 1931 there were three million people without a job, and perhaps a similar number under-employed. Most of my family were now out of work, working part time, or double shifts, or working for less. In late 1931 the industry had reached a state of collapse. By 1932 Britain had slipped into the depths of a world depression. At the workers' expense everything was done to keep the industry alive: wages were cut, the hours of work increased. For the same pay workers were forced to man six, even eight, instead of two or four looms. The fight against six and eight looms went on mill by mill, Todmorden and Burnley weavers leading the way. The workers could do nothing but surrender or fight back – and go hungry.

At the beginning of 1932 my family was surviving on little more than Gordon's dole and my ten shillings from Grimshaw's. When I got the sack that left us with Gordon's money only.

One week when Gordon went to pick up his dole, the lines outside the Labour Exchange – a dingy, moldy building – seemed longer than ever. There were so many people standing about, it was like after a football match. It took him ages to push his way through the shabby, hungry-looking crowd and join one of the queues shuffling toward the counter. When he got there he was faced by an unfamiliar clerk.

"How t' be?" the clerk said.

"Nicely," Gordon lied, expecting to sign his name, take his money and push his way out again.

"I've got a job for thee," the clerk went on, shuffling some papers.

"Tha 'as?"

"Yes."

"Wher' ist?"

"Cornwall."

"Where's Cornwall?" asked Gordon. "It sounds a long way."

"That it is. A very long way."

"What kind of painting is it?"

"It isn't painting."

"It isn't?"

"No."

"What is't then?"

"It's digging tin down a mine."

"I'm not a tin miner, I'm a painter."

"Does t' refuse to go to Cornwall?"

"I do."

"Then tha's just lost thee dole."

"Tha can't mean it." Gordon didn't just need the money; he needed it desperately.

"Ah, but I do. If tha not 'genuinely seeking work,'[†] and obviously tha not, benefits have to be stopped."

Gordon returned to Livingston Road dumbfounded. He couldn't understand how anyone could be so mean. The fellow didn't even say he was sorry; he just stopped Gordon's dole and that was that. Had Gordon harmed him, there might have been some justification for the man's gleeful savagery, but he had never met him before. We wanted Gordon to go and fight it out, but his pride wouldn't let him. For Gordon and Jenny it wasn't love on the dole, it was love without the dole. Once war came, Gordon volunteered as a trooper in the Tank Corps and fought for the country that had treated him so shabbily.

Somehow or other, by pinching and scraping, by using up our joint savings and by pawning whatever was left, we continued to pay for the furniture and hang on to the house in Livingston Road. Mother was prepared to fight to the death to stay in Livingston Road. We went on living day by day, watching our resources dwindle, knowing that disaster threatened. As winter gave way to the spring of 1932, and spring to summer, we sat around for hours trying to come up with schemes to make a few shillings, or discover ways to spend less.

Armed with a sledgehammer, father earned a few pounds smashing looms that earlier he had tuned with all the skill of a piano-tuner. I watched him destroy his idols – some of them a hundred years old, and thanks to people like him, still in first-class condition. I cannot imagine what went through his head as he tossed the broken pieces through the window. I think it took a lot of meaning out of his life. A hundred years earlier in Lancashire they'd hung people for smashing the first power looms. Now they paid them to do it. Mother and my sisters did odd jobs like washing up and peeling potatoes for club dinners in town, and sometimes for the hotels. Gordon – now that his dole was stopped – for the shame of it, put on a false nose and moustache and carried a sandwich board on his shoulders through the streets advertising Harper's lunches and dinners. Harper's was the restaurant where Gordon had had his wedding breakfast. He kept his eyes on the pavement as he walked along and he didn't try to make anybody laugh. I think they paid him twenty-five or thirty pennies a day, plus a bowl of soup. And that job didn't last long either. I added little to the kitty. I did some ditch-digging for the Town Council, but after several weeks that fell through.

So much for our income. As for our outgoings, after I'd been fired from Grimshaw's and my indispensable ten shillings had been lost, we fell behind on rent and furniture payments. We spent less and less on food. We got charity bread (public relief) where we could; for the rest we went hungry. Stealing was never considered. The local Public Assistance Committee refused help on the grounds that we were "living on a scale disproportionate to [our] position." It was their way of saying that poor people do not live on Livingston Road. Bess and I didn't do badly because the Lathams fed us, as they would continue to do as long as I had need. Also, many were the parcels of food they sent home with me at night. For the shame of it, we revealed none of these things to our neighbours, the Peeks, or for that matter, to anybody else. Certainly not to old friends such as the Watkins, the Gills, and the Morgans. They had troubles of their own.

With almost no money coming in, and everything going out, our resources continued to vanish before our eyes. Hanging on to Livingston Road was like trying to bale out a swamped boat with an egg cup. As each member of my family was thrown off the dole, and we struggled to hang on to a house and a way of life that was obviously beyond our means, we found ourselves with no resources at all. No amount of paring and scheming could help us. Whatever funds we still had were sacrificed in the struggle. Even father's war medals and Jenny's wedding dress were pawned for food. We would have given up earlier had we not been used to the roller-coaster kind of existence. We were hardened to it. But now our resources and wits were used up.

Meanwhile mother continued to postpone the inevitable. Time and again she'd find a way to get by. She was brilliant in fending off creditors. She had no trouble at all with the thin, insignificant men who came with fly-marked paper-files from the rental agency and the furniture store. She gave them a cup of tea and charmed them out through the door again. But they were the decent types who didn't want to hurt anybody. They were followed by the muscle men who knew exactly what was needed. They were impervious to mother's charms.

"Have you read your contract, Mrs. Woodruff?" the muscle men asked, knowing full well that she couldn't read. "It states clearly…"

"But we've nowhere to go," mother countered, fear in her eyes.

"That doesn't give you the right to occupy a large house rent free. The contract is quite clear and must be upheld."

"Even if it throws my family in the street?"

"The truth is harsh, Mrs. Woodruff, but it must be stated and upheld."

"We'd pay you tomorrow, if we had the money, you know that. We've always paid."

"Mrs. Woodruff, we've already lost six weeks' rent on this house. Others are prepared to pay a higher rent than the one you paid. They're waiting for you to get out. The papers have been signed. Do you want me to get the sack?"

"How long do we have?"

"Two weeks."

The muscle men from the furniture store didn't waste time talking. I came home to Livingston Road one day to find all the furniture gone. I found mother sitting on a stool, looking through the rain-washed windows. Streaks of snow marked the summit of Pendle Hill. The curtains (Jenny's curtains) had been drawn back. She didn't notice my coming. The muscle men must have caught her while she was washing her hair, for she wore a hand-towel wrapped round her head like a turban. Her head was lowered as if someone had struck her a blow. Tears streamed down her hollowed cheeks. I looked at her sad figure and thought how often she'd sung:

> I'm forever blowing bubbles, pretty bubbles in the air;
> Oh they fly so high, nearly reach the sky,
> Then, like my dreams, they fade and die.
> Fortune's always hiding. I've looked everywhere.
> I'm forever blowing bubbles, pretty bubbles in the air.

Poor Maggie, so many of her bubbles had burst. She had lost her father as a child; neglect had become her lot. The war had changed her man; the depression had ruined their livelihood. Tied to an industry of boom and bust, she'd lived on a precipice, always uncertain, always unable to relax, fearful that their living would disappear altogether. Now the Livingston Road bubble – the best bubble of all – was to die too. No wonder she sat there looking totally vanquished.

I wept with her.

Two weeks later we put our scant possessions on a flatcart and, in the middle of the night, pushed it to a lodging house in Nab Lane at the other side of town, close to the Leeds and Liverpool Canal. Out of shame we didn't want the neighbours on Livingston Road to see us go. I'd been avoiding Mr. Peek and Roger for days. I didn't want their sympathy. Now, when it came time to go, I couldn't face them. I never said good-bye. Yet I have never forgotten the man who shared his knowledge with me; I shall feel indebted to him forever.

The midnight flit from Griffin Street to Livingston Road had been a triumphal march. The journey through the streets to Nab Lane was like a funeral. There wasn't one of us who didn't feel sad and shamed. Father was his silent self. "Who cares what people think," mother had said when we were rising. I knew in my heart that she cared deeply what people thought now that we were falling. She walked arm in arm with Jenny and Brenda with a guilty look on her face. Even the family clown, Gordon, held his tongue.

We moved in the dark. I can't remember what we saw en route. We were all too miserable. We'd been robbed of the only really decent living conditions we'd ever known.

Although Gordon's parents took in Jenny and Gordon later on, no other relative offered help. Most of them didn't have anything to give.

Nab Lane was a come-down after Livingston Road; about as far as you could fall. It was worse than Griffin Street. At least we'd had our own cottage there. Nab Lane was chiefly lodging houses – all of them long past their prime and seedy looking – with vacant faces peering through dirty windows.

Six of us – mother and father, Jenny and Gordon, Brenda and I – occupied one room. Bess was kept outside. It was the cheapest thing we could get. Stacked with lodgers from cellar to roof, the place reeked. It wasn't the usual haddock and cabbage reek; it was a funny dead, musty smell. In Livingston Road, which out of shame I never visited again, I had had a room to myself and a garden to sit in. In Nab Lane there was foul, crowded shelter, nothing more. Without the Lathams to flee to, Bess and I would have been lost.

I was so offended by the move that I couldn't think straight. By then I was about fifteen and I had a lot of pride. It was a bad dream from which I felt I would waken. Thank goodness grandmother Bridget was not alive to see us in such squalor. I can remember the damp bricks, the dust-covered, broken windows, the sputtering gaslight, the peeling plaster and paint, the faded wallpaper, the crowded, greasy rooms, the dim landings where we washed, and the shaky banisters. Toilets were shared in the yard. After Livingston Road the noise of the place was deafening. Everybody spoke at a higher level – almost in a hoarse shout. There was an incessant clamor throughout the building. Doors were always being banged to. There was no such thing as privacy. Everybody's business came through the walls. Outside, the shouting of children went on all day. There was no end to it.

Even more vividly, I remember the enormous, one-eyed man, with tattooed arms and a bullock's neck, who ran the place – chiefly by bawling orders from the bottom of the stairs. Gross and unclean, he looked as if he never took his clothes off. Like the ceilings and the walls of the lodging house, his bald head was covered with sweat. He had a bad limp – "the war" everybody said – and was forever accompanied by a small, black Boston terrier. It had pricked ears and bulging eyes, which never lost their startled look. It was so silent and kept so close to the man that one could mistake it for one of his boots.

Periodically the landlord and his mouse-like wife had fights to the death; usually when we were about to go to sleep. As our room was directly above theirs, we could hardly avoid the din. The fights began with shouting and name-calling; there followed the throwing of dishes, which led to a free-for-all. There were such bangs and crashes that mother feared for the woman's life. It did sound as if the brute was throwing his wife against the wall. There would be a thud, followed by a deep groan, followed by silence; then another thud, followed by greater groans, followed by silence. Eventually, presumably when the combatants were lying on the floor unconscious, we were allowed to go to sleep.

As long as we were there, the woman and the dog survived. Sometimes the woman would appear with a black eye, a split lip, or a puffed-up face, but nothing bad enough to stop her going about her daily business. The wounds on her husband's face showed that she was giving as good as she got. I couldn't make head or tail of them. Having fought half the night, they'd spend the next day cooing, laughing, and chatting together like young lovers. Mother said it was ridiculous. "Rubbish," said father, "they're having the time of their lives."

The one redeeming feature about that dark hole was the sense of community among the poor wretches who lived there. They were like members of a great noisy family. They understood and sympathized with each other's hunger and desperation. They willingly shouldered each other's burdens. With nothing to lose, these people should have been revolutionaries and thieves. On the contrary, they were the most law-abiding people one could meet. Their luck was out; like ourselves, they'd gone on the dole; they'd then endured the Means Test[†] which – having assessed their non-existent resources – had either reduced or removed state aid[†] altogether. There was no work to be had. Their reserves had been used up. Their families and friends either couldn't afford to help them, or had deserted them. Beyond the workhouse, which they all feared, there was no one else to whom they could turn. "But don't worry," they said, "times will change. We maun bide His will till work coom again." With childlike innocence, they honestly believed that they would climb back to the level from which they'd fallen. Against all the misfortunes of their earthly lot they clung to the promise of Heavenly Salvation. God was their only balm.

Every night, the Catholics among them went down on their knees on the sanded floor to implore the Virgin to intervene on their behalf. We heard the drone of voices throughout the house:

"Remember, O most gracious Virgin Mary, that never was it known that anyone who fled to thy protection, implored thy help, or sought thy intercession, was left unaided. Inspired with this confidence we fly unto thee, O Virgin of Virgins, our mother. To thee we come, before thee we stand, sinful and sorrowful. O mother of the word incarnate, despise not our petition, but in thy mercy hear and answer. Amen."

They showed infinite patience. Nothing got better; nobody seemed to hear or answer them; the world remained pitiless. Yet they never stopped making their nightly appeal: "Remember, O most gracious Virgin Mary..." They answered the scepticism they detected in my eyes with: "Mary can't be expected to answer every supplicant at once."

A spindly, bright-faced Irishman with silver hair led them in prayer. He'd been the "boots" at the local railway hotel and, having spent his life working for a pittance, had fallen about as far down the ladder as he could go. I don't know how he got to Nab Lane. All I know is that it seemed wrong for a good man to end his life in such circumstances. I didn't know what a saint was supposed to look like, but every time I saw the Irishman in the house or on the street, he made me think of a saint. He radiated serenity and peace. When later in life, I learnt about "abiding grace and inner peace," I thought about him. Mother had a beautiful face, but it wasn't a saint's face. There was agony on it and the agony stayed there until father got a job and she escaped from Nab Lane to Polly Street by the railway line.

From there, my father went as a labourer to the Rolls Royce Company at Derby helping to make fighter planes. There was no end to the money dad earned from making weapons. As war approached, he was allowed to work as many hours as he wanted. Henceforth, there was no shortage of work or money. They had so much money that in 1939 they bought a new two-level house with garden, hot-house and all outside Derby. On the outbreak of war, on being drafted overseas, I visited them there for an hour. How well I remember Maggie, now grey-haired, stretching out her hands to greet me. The house was smaller than the one in Livingston Road, but for Maggie it was the ship which at last had come home. As long as the war continued my parents prospered.

I next saw Maggie when I held her hand as she lay dying. I'd rushed all the way from Jerusalem to Blackburn to reach her side. By then the war was over and my father's job at Derby, making fighter planes, had failed him. To join my sisters, my parents had returned to Blackburn once more. I arrived with only a few hours to spare. Maggie recognized me. She talked to herself a good deal that night. Toward dawn, she turned to me and said, "Do...you remember, Billy,...the first time...I took you to Blackpool?" By the time I'd stopped crying, she had gone.

It was while we were at Nab Lane that my brother Dan married Christine Bailey. It must have been a quiet affair because I cannot remember the ceremony at all.

Christine had met Dan while he was working away from Blackburn as a "devil." She didn't seem to object to soot, and fell deeply in love with him.

Mother was not happy about Christine at first. She was not prepared to have her Dan marry somebody just because the girl said she was pregnant.

"If he's put her in t' family way, then he's got to marry her," said father.

"How do you know she's in t' family way?" mother retorted.

"Grieves will tell you," dad answered.

He did.

Christine was about two months pregnant. Mother bowed to the inevitable. The wedding took place.

Against all odds, Dan and Christine lived happily ever after.

As with the other members of my family, the growing rearmament of the western world prior to the Second World War was Dan's saving. He ceased to be a "devil" and became a highly paid labourer in a defence factory. He gave the army a wide berth. He ignored the call-up papers that came through the mail. It took two years before the army caught up with him. In 1943 he found himself before the military police in Manchester. By then, the army had done some research into Dan's background and had discovered that he had been born in the United States. On that count, they treated him less severely than they might have done. Especially as he already had a black mark from the Argyle and Sutherland Highlanders.

Dan was given the choice to fight either for His Majesty, King George VI, or for President Roosevelt.

"Which do you prefer?" asked the officer.

"Neither," said Dan, whose Inverness experience still rankled.

"Gracious, what happened then?" I asked him.

"Chap got red in t' face. Reminded me of the Colonel of the Argyles."

"What then?"

"I was thrown out and told 'You'll hear from us, Mr. Woodruff.'"

"Did you?"

"No."

I can only think that the army concluded that Dan was more trouble than he was worth. He was a stubborn mule with whom they'd do well to avoid a legal tangle. Anyway, the Allies had to fight without him.

While we were living at Nab Lane, I was pulled in at the Darwen Brick Works by friends as a junior labourer. I was just sixteen. It was a temporary job which I was glad to get. With a gang of others, my job was to stack the bee-hive shaped kilns with unbaked bricks ("green bricks"), fire the kilns with gas, and days later take out the finished product. We used sacking to cover our hands; the alternative was suppurating blisters. The sallow-faced man in charge of the kilns was always rolling and relighting a cigarette. Having lit it, he would stare intently at the end to ensure that it was burning. It rarely was. Keeping his fag alight seemed to me to be his chief occupation.

Sometimes we gave a hand at the grinders, where the clay was crushed and forced through holes in the pan bottom, or at the pugmills, where a column of clay was forced through a die on to the cutting table. The bricks were cut automatically, loaded on to pallets, and then dried before we took them to the dome-shaped kilns to be fired. I learnt early on not to hustle at the Darwen Brick Works; slow and steady was the standard.

After several months there wasn't much I didn't know about bricks. Day after day, morning, afternoon, and night, I handled the same kind of bricks. Bricks that went into kilns, bricks that came out of kilns. I didn't think it was the sort of thing I'd like to do for the rest of my life. Yet, by the standards of those days, it was a good job. I could keep Bess with me. I had young, enjoyable workmates, who roared at each others' jokes and the accounts of their weekend escapades. The foreman, soft-voiced Arthur Dimbleby, was a pleasant change after Mr. Grimshaw. For a foreman he had unusually pleading eyes.

Best of all, I loved the moors where – because of clay – the works were sited. Most of the time I worked out of doors where I could hear the birds and see the fells. Every morning and every night, wet or fine, with Bess running alongside, I rode for the best part of an hour across the moors to and from Blackburn on a borrowed bike. Sometimes I'd stop to give Bess a chance to swim in a water-filled clay pit. In the spring and summer, the evening colours were so captivating that I often regretted it when the outskirts of Blackburn came into sight.

It's amazing what you'll do when you're poor. It was across those moors, at the end of a day's work, that I brought an unbelievably slippery kitchen sink all the way to Blackburn. I got a faulty one from the brick-works at a give-away price. The trouble began when I tried to take my give-away sink home. With Bess at my side, I trudged the whole six miles from Darwen to Blackburn, up and down hills, fighting to keep the forty-pound sink on the handle-bars of my bike. I never knew a sink so contrary. Anybody who thinks that such a balancing act is easy is welcome to try. I've never forgotten the ordeal. It was the greatest test of endurance I'd ever undertaken. On more than one occasion, I was tempted to abandon the wretched sink by the wayside. I was soaked through with sweat when I got home.

I came to know Arthur Dimbleby very well. He was a kind of quiet father figure whom we all respected. Well-built, tough, skilled, he had a benign face that was often crinkled in a huge grin. Sometimes he'd join us for a game of cards, or pitch and toss, at midday, or he'd sit with us on a plank supported by trestles, and yarn. He was always ready to join us in placing a small bet on the horse races at Aintree, Liverpool. One day he got talking about London where he'd worked when he was younger. His stories excited us. "It's the place for young uns like you," he said. "I'd be off to the South like a shot if I was your age."

Mr. Dimbleby's talk about London put all kinds of ideas into my head. It fired me up. I knew that my job at Darwen was insecure. I never knew when I got there in the morning whether I'd still be working for them at night. It kept me on edge. Later on I talked to Mr. Dimbleby about London again. I didn't mention Betty Weatherby.

"It'll do you no harm to try to get a job there," Mr. Dimbleby said. "You can always come home. I still know one or two people down there.

I might be able to give you a hand." Later on, he showed me a letter he was about to send to a Mr. Dent at the Bow Bridge Iron Foundry in Bow, East London. It said that I was a good labourer who needed a job, and could he help? Weeks passed without hearing anything from Mr. Dent.

"Give him a chance," was all Mr. Dimbleby said when I asked him if he'd had any news.

XIX   Politics

As I did not work Saturday mornings at the Darwen Brick Works, I kept in touch with the world by spending some time reading the newspapers and magazines in the Blackburn Public Library Reading Room. One had to get there early because it was always full.

I remember a particular Saturday morning very clearly. It was when my political education underwent a marked change. The room was crowded to the door with other workers wearing caps and mufflers, and long coats buttoned to the top. Some just sat there with vacant, watery eyes daydreaming, killing time, glad to be off the cold streets. Others stared blankly at the ceiling or leafed aimlessly through the magazines. Still others stood before the high reading stands to which the newspapers – minus the sporting pages to discourage betting – were fastened. Few readers studied the "Vacancies" column any more. A real job didn't have to be advertised; it was pursued and seized.

The only woman there was the mousy librarian with eye-glasses who invariably had a bad cold. She always wore a dark blue pullover, a light checked blouse with the collar showing at the neck, a pleated, blue skirt and a white belt. In really cold weather she wore a quilt-sized shawl which covered everything except her dark head. She was usually hidden behind a highly polished counter and a thick glass partition. Laden bookshelves stood in rows behind her. On the counter stood a large unneeded "No Smoking" sign. Even when cigarettes were selling at five for twopence, nobody had money to smoke. Equally large notices demanding "Silence" dotted the often damp, mud-coloured walls. One gained the librarian's attention by rapping hard on the glass. Earlier encounters and raised eyebrows had taught me that this was a foolish thing to do. The wise thing was to get a seat with your back to the hot pipes, keep your head down, talk to yourself quietly, and ask for nothing.

On that particular morning I was lost in my reading when I became aware of an unusually thin man standing behind me. He was in his thirties. He had a plain, pasty face with a small nose. His eyes protruded slightly; they had an intense look. He was dressed like the rest of us: cap, muffler, coat, clogs.

247

"After you with the *Herald*," he said.

I began to yield my place.

"No rush," said the stranger. "I can read something else while I'm waiting."

At that moment the sound of a band drifted in from the street as a procession made its way to the square. To satisfy our curiosity, we both hurried to the door to see what was afoot. It was cold out there and we wasted no time in getting back. We talked some more together in hushed tones. The man introduced himself as Peter Shad. Like most others in the room, he was an unemployed weaver.

I next saw Peter Shad one Sunday evening when I was wandering across the half-darkened town square. One could always pick up a copy of Left-wing newspapers there, such as the *Daily Worker*, the *Labour Leader*, and the *Daily Herald*. There were little knots of people standing about everywhere, talking politics. Many of them were at a loss for something to do. To my surprise, Mr. Shad was standing on a box haranguing a large crowd. His excited face was lit by an acetylene lamp hanging above his head. Behind him, flapping in the breeze, was the Red Flag bearing the hammer and sickle.† I simply couldn't believe it. As most of what he was saying was being drowned out by the drums and cornets of the Salvation Army band, which blared its way back and forth across the square, I pushed through the crowd until I stood directly in front of him.

For the next hour I lived under the spell of Mr. Shad. In place of the ordinary, passive, uninteresting man I'd met in the library, here was a dynamic, intense, passionate individual ready to die in the cause of social justice.

He spoke with his whole body as well as his voice. He threw his arms above his head to express despair, sprang forward, arms outstretched, to embrace us, threatened us with his fists, stabbed at us with his fingers, and, to emphasize his points, repeatedly slapped the palm of one hand against the other. He was never still.

He was expert at hurling thunderbolts into the crowd. "Theft! Theft!" he shouted. He really got you hotted up. Everything he said rang with conviction. There was so much fire in him that no one dared interrupt him. In contrast to the usual free-for-all, give-and-take discussions on the square to which I was accustomed, the crowd was hushed.

Mr. Shad opened my eyes to what was going on in Lancashire. "Those who say that things will buck up, those who tell us to wait and see are fools," he yelled. "Capitalism has taken whatever profits it can out of Lancashire, and has gone elsewhere. Fortunes have been made here, but they have never been enjoyed by the people who made them."

Mr. Shad took a long breath. "That's what free enterprise is all about," he went on, "the freedom to make a fortune out of the people and then clear off, leaving the dirt behind. Our looms are now being sold to Japanese capitalists so that whatever trade we still have will be taken away.

The Japanese will take all our looms for nought a piece. The problem is not cotton, it's capitalism. It will let Blackburn rot. It will let you rot. The capitalists are never sacrificed, you are. That's why fish and oranges are being thrown into the sea off Liverpool by the ship load. That's why vegetables are rotting in the fields, and milk – badly needed by our children – is being fed to pigs. All because of profit. Profit is all that matters. If more profit can be made in China, the capitalists will drop you and sweat the Chinese."

Here the speaker paused again. "Do you wonder why there are empty bellies, no clogs for the feet, no beds for some? Capitalism can never be changed. It can only be destroyed. To talk of loving our fellow-men in a capitalist society is just pie in the sky. To say that the rich have an obligation to the poor is tripe. Love does not make the world go round; money does. To the capitalist, making money is the only virtue. Everything is forbidden except making money and the exploitation of the working class. There are only two classes: the productive working class and the possessing master class. You exist to make the master class rich and for no other reason. That's why you are called "hands." Without money, you are helpless. That's why our mills are now owned by the bankers and financiers."

At this point he interrupted his tirade to throw still another thunderbolt into the crowd: "Drive the money changers from the temple!" he yelled. "The enemy is greed. You work for less and less while the usurers take more and more. Your condition cannot improve; there will be no peace on earth until the working class destroys the masters, and the money bags – the financiers. Private ownership of our mills and our lives must go."

After wiping the sweat off his forehead, the speaker was off again. The crowd stood entranced. "Not love, but hate is what matters – hatred of the capitalist class," he shouted. "It's madness to think, as many in the trade union and labour movement think, that you can make a deal with the bosses. It doesn't matter whether the bosses are Liberal or Tory. First and foremost they are capitalists. The bosses have to go."

Mr. Shad was now vigorously beating one hand against the other. "Only when the capitalist class has been overthrown" – here he struggled with an imaginary object and threw it to the ground – "only when we have robbed them of the ability to exploit others can there be true social justice. Only when the old order has been smashed to pieces can we hope to build on new foundations. All power to the people!" he ended.

The spell broken, the crowd stirred. Here and there, there was a gentle rumble of approval. Among us, any man who could hold a crowd was respected.

Later on I could not recall all that Mr. Shad had said in his speech. I know he had no difficulty in answering the questions that followed. He didn't strike me as scoring, or that he was trying to deceive us. He struck me as a man who really believed what he was saying. Except for the policeman, who stood to one side, a lamp on his belt, impassively watching and listening to all that was going on, and sometimes as impassively making a note, I'm sure most of the audience felt as I did. The meeting ended with Mr. Shad singing the "Internationale":

> Oh, comrades, come rally,
> For the last fight let us stand,
> The Internationale,
> Unites the human race ...

In a subdued tone, as if they weren't quite sure if they could get away with it – and with an eye on the policeman – two or three others sang with him. To one side, several youths, the worse for drink – "drink-sodden victims of capitalism" Shad had called them – were singing the well-known parody of "The Red Flag":

> The people's flag is palest pink.
> It's not as red as you might think.
> We've been to see, and now we know,
> They've gone and changed its colour so.
> While cowards flinch and traitors sneer
> We'll go on drinking bitter beer...

I had hoped to speak to Mr. Shad when he was through, but he deliberately ignored me. His eyes said "piss off!" He quickly furled his flag and was lost in the crowd.

The following Saturday morning I encountered Mr. Shad once more in the Reading Room. He was as I had seen him the first time: passive and soft-spoken. I could hardly believe that this was the same fellow who had held the crowd spellbound in the town square. He crossed the room to speak to me.

"Keep clear of me on the streets and on the square," he warned in a low voice. "Recognize me only in this room. It's the only place where we can find shelter and warmth, and where no one will bother us. Elsewhere it is dangerous for you to be seen with me. Capitalist repression is growing. Mosley's Black Shirts[†] will appear in the square any day. The Fascists are looking for victims. When you're older you can make up your own mind about Communism."

That Saturday morning, with Mr. Shad as my tutor, I began my education in political economy. Every Saturday thereafter, almost without fail, he would arrive and fish books out of his deep pockets. We sat at a table in a corner of the room with our backs to the other readers, talking in whispers. Chiefly he whispered and I listened. Nobody had to tell us that in bringing books into the Reading Room we were doing something expressly forbidden by one of the many notices on the walls. Mr. Shad first went over the *Communist Manifesto*, of Marx and Engels, line by line, word by word, explaining its inner meaning. I was over-whelmed by it. Why hadn't I heard of it before? It was almost a hundred years old. How right Marx had been to say that the working class had nothing to lose but its chains. Anybody who lived at the bottom of the heap in Blackburn knew that.

Mr. Shad was a born teacher. Whenever I got lost – as I often did – he would go right back to the beginning and start all over again. He had infinite patience, infinite generosity.

What I found difficult to swallow was his need to hate the bosses. He wanted me to hate the bosses with all my mind and with all my heart. He seemed to be possessed with the idea of killing and dying. Grand-mother Bridget had always taught me not to hate. "Hate will rot you," she'd said.

"Must we really hate the bosses?" I asked him.

"You can't fight evil without hating it," he answered, his eyes flashing. "You must hate evil until it is destroyed."

"Uh, huh."

"Tell me," he asked, "Do you hate sin and the devil?"

"Oh, yes."

"If you had the chance to kill the devil, would you?"

"Oh, yes." I had never forgotten the statue of St. Michael fighting the devil at St. Peter's School.

"Well," he concluded, "the devils are the bosses; they're the gangrene in the system; they won't go away peacefully; the rottenness has to be cut out. Rotten societies have to be toppled. That's what history is all about."

For several months I met Mr. Shad every Saturday morning in the library. Like grandmother Bridget, and Mr. Peek, he seemed honestly concerned with my education. Now and again he would give me a copy of the communist newspapers *The Daily Worker* or *The Young Worker*, but he never pushed them on to me. I looked upon him as my teacher. I have to thank him for arousing my interest in what was going on in politics and industry.

The only person to whom I said anything about Peter Shad was Harold Watkins. My Saturday morning meetings in the Public Library I decided to keep to myself. One Sunday night Harold went with me to hear Mr. Shad. The look in Harold's brown eyes told me that he was just as spellbound as I.

As in the library, so in the square, Mr. Shad would suddenly appear from nowhere. One moment we were waiting for him, the next moment there was the box, the lamp, the flag, and the speaker. He seemed to have dropped from the sky. People quickly gathered; you could almost feel the growing rustle of attention. By the time I'd finished wondering how he got there, he'd already begun to speak. He always started quietly, so that his listeners were forced to listen carefully. As he warmed to his subject, a new note entered his voice. The voice grew in pitch and volume until it echoed from the surrounding buildings. With the speech done, and the questions answered, Mr. Shad disappeared as mysteriously as he'd come. He simply melted into the crowd. He was the only human being I'd ever met who could disappear in a crowd like that.

Harold and I marvelled at him. There was magic in his words. He got our blood up. We believed him when he said that Russia was a worker's paradise: that it was the only country in the world where no one went hungry, where no one was out of a job, and where no one could exploit the workers for profit. There had never been such a revolution before. Like nothing else, his stories about the Russian Workers' Paradise turned our heads. Only in Russia had the workers come into their own.

We believed him when he said that the Russian Revolution would redeem all our sorrows and misfortunes; that it was a great light on the horizon, a moral ideal, beckoning the workers of the world. We believed him when he said that the revolution was coming in Britain. We believed him when he said that if we waited for the moneybags in Parliament to act, we'd wait forever. We believed him when he said that the world couldn't wait until capitalism died of its own weaknesses; it had earned the sentence of death and should be got rid of. We believed him when he said that religion was "the opium of the people." We believed him when he said that the two greatest "sins" crying out for vengeance were the oppression of the poor and the defrauding of labourers of their wages. We believed him when he said that you couldn't stop the revolution; that the world had been preparing for it and that it must come. He was so eloquent, so persuasive, that we couldn't do anything else but swallow what he said – hook, line, and sinker.

Unquestionably, we shared his dream and his vision. Not for a moment did we worry about how the revolution would be achieved. Not for a moment did we think it would be anything but plain sailing after the revolution. We didn't ask him and we wouldn't have thanked him for the details. It was the vision that mattered.

Why didn't more people take notice of Peter Shad, we wondered? Nobody uncovered the root of all evil – greed – as he did. Nobody could explain the source of all our troubles as he did. Nobody offered a better remedy. Increasingly, Harold and I became convinced that Communism was the only answer.

I knew Mr. Shad for quite a while, yet there was a side of him about which I knew nothing. I'd no idea where he lived. I suspect few others did. He always left the library before me. By the time I'd got to the door he'd vanished. I never tried to follow him, because he gave me nothing to follow. He never mentioned a wife or children. The only personal thing I knew about him was that he hadn't been sleeping well. His insomnia explains the shade of melancholy that marked him; I never saw him smile. It was only later on that I realized that not once had I ever seen him happy. Peter Shad never really lived; he was always preparing to live –

after the revolution and the bloodshed. Once he talked about becoming a weaver in Brazil. He could have gone to the United States, but he spurned that country. "Rotten with capitalism," he said. He didn't ask me to go with him to Brazil. In fact, outside the library, he had no time for me at all.

I don't know whether Mr. Shad ever reached Brazil. The last I saw of him was during a brawl on the square. He had predicted that Oswald Mosley's Blackshirts would turn up and they did. Having tried to deafen him with their shouts, the Fascists suddenly seized his flag. Shad fought back and was knocked to the ground. Most spectators backed away. The struggle for the Red Flag ended with Peter Shad in possession of a bare flag pole. Apart from the shouting, the affair was all over in minutes. The Communists around Peter were simply swept aside by the Fascists.

As Mr. Shad got to his feet, a policeman arrested him for "disturbing the peace." I had seen the same copper at many of Shad's meetings. There was a struggle in which Shad must have lost self-control, for he struck the officer across the face with the flagpole. With witnesses present, that condemned him. The policeman could strike Shad but it was a criminal offence to strike back. The moment the officer released his grasp on Mr. Shad's arm, Shad swung round and disappeared in the crowd. I didn't need to be told that Peter Shad had become "a fugitive from justice."

A warrant was issued for Shad's arrest. But his picture was in the paper under the name of Arthur Cray. It startled me out of my clogs. Why had he called himself Peter Shad when his name was Arthur Cray? Or was it? Harold and I puzzled over the matter so much that we didn't know what to think. He had been unbelievably kind to me; he had given hours of his time to educate me. Try as I might, I could not think badly of him. Nor could Harold; though Harold could never understand how a man like Shad could have committed an act which made him an outlaw. To strike a copper in front of a crowd, you had to be mad.

I was left in no doubt what the Reading Room librarian thought of him. "Born troublemaker, I'd say," she whispered primly. "Tell them anywhere. Good riddance. You needn't think I didn't notice you two plotting and planning in the corner there – breaking all the rules. I thought several times of having you thrown out. From now on you'll have to watch your step."

I went to the square the next night to see if I could learn anything from Shad's friends – from those who used to sing the "Internationale" with him at the end of the meetings. No one appeared. Peter Shad (or Arthur Cray) had left my life as mysteriously as he had entered it.

A man was found drowned in the canal about this time. It was in the paper. They said he had protruding eyes. No one claimed the corpse. Could it have been Peter Shad? I sat with the paper in my hands in the corner of the library where I had first met him and wondered. I became so curious that for several weeks I went on trying to find one or other of the faces that I'd seen alongside Shad on the square. None of them ever showed up. Where Peter Shad had stood with his Red Flag, the Fascist Black Shirts gathered.

Shad's disappearance left Harold Watkins and me in a quandary. We were lost without him. He had lifted us up so high with his talk of the Russian Revolution that we suddenly felt deflated. His weekly harangue on the square had kept us going. There was nothing for us in Blackburn. No work, no political future. The local Labour Party was splintered by warring factions; there were innumerable divisions. The Trade Unions were the same. No wonder Mr. Shad had called for a United Front. The failure of the General Strike in 1926, and the fall of the Labour Government in 1930, coupled with what we thought was MacDonald's betrayal of the Labour Movement in going over to the Tories and the Liberals to form a National Government, had undermined our earlier confidence in some of our leaders and in working-class politics. Too often the working-class leaders talked like the bosses. There'd never be a working-class government at this rate.

We decided to write to the Russians and offer to go to Russia as weavers. All the things that Mr. Shad had told us about, we'd go and see for ourselves. I couldn't weave as well as Harold – I was at that time working at the Darwen Brick Works – but provided we could work together as a team in Russia, we'd manage. I trusted Harold, we'd grown up together. I knew he wouldn't let me down.

But then came the problem: how does one write to the Russians? I sought the advice of the reference librarian. Her spectacles jumped off her nose when I whispered, "How can I get in touch with the Russians?"

"The Russians?" she whispered, frowning at me. "In heavens name, what would a good Blackburn boy be doing writing to the Russians? Don't you know they're godless atheists!"

"I'm just curious," I whispered, guardedly. "I want to learn what's going on."

"Curiosity killed the cat," she hissed back.

Had I gone on and told her that Harold and I intended to go to Russia, she would, I'm sure, have fainted dead away.

As there was no Soviet Embassy in Britain at the time – the British had accused the Soviets of spying – she gave me the address of the Russian Trade Legation in London.[†]

It was one thing to get an address, another thing to know what to say. Harold and I anguished over our letter for some time. Clumsily, my first effort began "Dear Sirs," which Harold thought ridiculous.

"Communists don't call each other 'dear' or 'sir'."

I substituted 'Comrades,' which pleased him. He also took out my reference to Peter Shad. Eventually we agreed to send the following note:

Comrades,

We are two unemployed Blackburn weavers. We are both skilled, fit, and in our teens. We believe in the Russian Revolution and want to share it with you. Can you find us a job so that we can come to Russia and see it for ourselves? If you will write to the above address, we are free to come any time.

<blockquote>
Fraternally,
Harold Watkins
William Woodruff
</blockquote>

Very deliberately, we stuck a stamp on the envelope and carried it to the main post office in the centre of town. I felt a great change come over my life as I slipped the envelope into the black mouth of the red letter box. All the way home we talked about what might happen. Would the Russians write or would somebody come in person? How would we get there? Well, that was up to the Russians. Anyway, we were determined not to turn back.

We never heard a word. Peter Shad's dream of a great and glorious new life in Russia was denied us. Perhaps the letter was removed from the mail by the police, or both the Russians and the police had more important things to do.

Not long after Peter Shad had disappeared, and our Russian venture had died, I decided to throw in my lot with the Labour Party. With a Red scare on in Britain at the time – there'd been one earlier in 1924–1926 when a number of Communists had been sent to jail[†] – it certainly wasn't the time to join the Communist Party. Indeed, to be called "an avowed Communist" in the courts at this time – even though the Communist Party was lawful – was to run the risk of being sent to jail. Anybody who put Russia before Britain was run down. Even in the trade unions anybody suspected of being a Bolshie was quickly rooted out.

It was a matter of following Harold, who already was a member of the Youth Labour League. By the time I joined the Labour League, when I was sixteen, we had become inseparable companions. Harold and I could go downtown, eat some potato pie or black puddings together, walk round the square, or go to the films, and that was a good evening. Occasionally, we'd take Rosie Gill and Annie Morgan to a dance.

With our Russian options closed we gave more thought to our political future in Britain. With unaffected simplicity, we built all kinds of dream worlds in Britain as previously we had built them in Russia. It didn't surprise me at all when Harold confided in me, over a cup of tea, that he would one day be Prime Minister of a British Labour Government.

"You know, Billy," he went on, throwing back his mop of dark brown hair, "I've been thinking about this for a long time. When I become Prime

Minister, I shall appoint you as my Foreign Secretary." Harold had a droll humor, but I knew he was serious. I was impressed, and thanked him.

Obsessed with politics, and eager to make my way in the Labour Movement, I began to make speeches for the Labour Party on the town square. At first the speeches only lasted a couple of minutes, and I was told what to say. With Blackburn streets full of unemployed, and things getting worse every day, there was no shortage of topics: the dole, the slump in the basic industries, the need to tax the rich. I wondered if the fellows who provided the speech outlines knew what they were talking about. I'd read too many different newspapers over too long a period to swallow their pat answers.

Blackburn square is where I heard all the best speakers of the land. MacDonald, Snowden, Henderson, Clynes, Thomas, Churchill: they all spoke there. Although some of them claimed to be socialist, they were all conservative or liberal minded – some, like MacDonald, Snowden and Clynes, were intensely religious. They were always saying God this and God that. I'm sure none of them had read Marx. Even though they admitted being socialist, most of them didn't like to be called a socialist in public. Politics for them, as for most Englishmen, started with a love of country. Singing the "Internationale" was a pretence. As Mr. Peek would have said, they were tinkerers not revolutionaries. Most of them, I suspect, were adept at muddling through. Violence was an anathema to them. None of the out-of-town speakers advocated the radical clean sweep of Peter Shad. They wouldn't have been seen dead with such a firebrand. They wanted to prune the tree; Shad wanted to uproot it.

My memory of Winston Spencer Churchill was of a bald-headed figure standing on a box wagging an admonitory finger at the crowd. I can remember him railing at "that little fakir, Gandhi,"[†] whose appearance he described as "nauseous." His idea that we should hang on to India at all costs was shouted down. By now I had come to realize the absurdity of England's sway over such a vast sub-continent in the East. Even those of us whose living depended on it had the common sense to realize that we could no longer go on ruling an alien people ten times greater than our own. Partly because we remembered Churchill's militant role in helping to break the General Strike in 1926, we listened to Gandhi, who visited England in 1931, rather than to Churchill. In those days Churchill was considered a "run of the mill" speaker. For the important statesman he became, he drew a small audience; a lesser-known labour leader like Clynes drew more.

I found public speaking unnerving – especially my maiden speech which was attended by an audience of two, one of them a wild, half-clothed figure who kept shouting that the Day of Judgment had arrived. The moment I got on to the box I became tense with excitement. Sometimes the Labour Party took me to speak at Accrington or Burnley where I was less nervous. But a five minute stint anywhere would have me running with sweat. Interruptions would grow louder and more frequent, the longer I spoke. Sunday night audiences on Blackburn square were particularly outspoken and aggressive. "For God's sake, shut up," they'd shout right in your face. "Don't listen to him, he's a silly bugger," a wild-eyed individual would go on. Hecklers would rough you up in no time. Their whole purpose was to get you rattled. After that they'd chop you up into little pieces. Some listeners seemed to have nothing better to do; they made a profession of heckling. They made no allowance for age. Anyone who got up on a box and began to shout his head off deserved all that was coming to him.

I would never have survived these ordeals had I not had the help of Elsie Briggs, a small woman dressed in black who wore a cap and smoked a pipe, and whose passion was politics. As grandmother Bridget had taught me how to read and write, as Terence Peek had taught me about the cotton industry, as Peter Shad had taught me about political economy, so Elsie Briggs set herself the goal of making me the best political speaker in Lancashire.

Elsie Briggs lived round the corner from us in Polly Street where – next to the railway line – my parents had taken refuge after the wrenching experience of the lodging house in Nab Lane. Polly Street wasn't much better than Nab Lane but at least we had a small weaver's cottage to ourselves. Elsie was a spinster in her thirties. She was one of the few spinners in town who seemed to be able to hang on to a job. Her bent, white-haired, widowed father ran a fruit and vegetable shop in one of their two downstairs rooms. The shop was minute and fly-blown; the fruit and vegetables invariably sad and tired. I cannot imagine what the old man made out of it. There was one other member of the family, Charlotte – also a spinner – who was a couple of years younger than Elsie. She was disfigured by smallpox.

Of the four people who had most affected my life – grandmother Bridget, Terence Peek, Peter Shad, and Elsie Briggs – Elsie was the most ruthless, more ruthless than Peter Shad. I never saw her dark face clearly because she always wore her black cap pulled down over her eyes; her face was usually puckered around the pipe which she smoked incessantly. Sometimes she shouted at me through a cloud of smoke. On the occasions when she removed her black cap and I could see her grey eyes, I saw only loneliness. She had decided that I was about the worst political speaker appearing on the square and that she was going to improve me or die.

Henceforth, life with Elsie was hell. On more nights than I care to remember, I stood before a stained, peeling, body-length mirror in her bedroom – in better days the mirror had been used to reflect the contents of the downstairs' shop window – throwing my arms about while addressing a circle which Elsie had drawn above the mirror on the bedroom wall. She used to write out short speeches which I memorized while cycling home from the brickworks at night.

In these speeches politics were incidental. All that she cared about was elocution. We never got halfway through any of them because she never let me. "It won't do! It won't do!" she'd interrupt while blowing clouds of smoke in my face. "I won't own you if you talk like that. You sound a gobbin. You'll be lucky if you're not lynched."

Elsie was pure Lancashire; blunt, rude, aggressive and sarcastic. She could also be grim and ironic. She was not the slightest bit interested in whether I liked her or not. She didn't consider my feelings. She treated me as if I were deaf, dumb, and daft.

"Start again! Start again! Start again!" she commanded in a deep mannish voice.

"Look at your hands! Look at your hands! Look at your hands!"

"Face the crowd! Face the crowd! Face the crowd! Take that silly grin off your face. You've nothing to grin about." The punching and kneading never stopped.

Sometimes I wondered if she wasn't trying to torture me. As there was a shade of melancholy in Peter Shad, so there was a touch of sadism in Elsie Briggs. Charlotte swore that her sister had a heart of gold. She might have had, but I didn't see any evidence of it. Not once did I see her smile. No wonder her white-haired father threw me a look of sympathy whenever I entered the shop. I hope Elsie didn't treat him as she treated me.

One night I complained to Charlotte about Elsie. "I'm thinking of chucking it," I said, "Elsie is inhuman."

"It's the war," Charlotte answered after a moment or two. "Elsie's never been the same since her bloke got killed on the Somme. That's why she always wears black. I wouldn't chuck it if I was you. She needs you as much as you need her. Why drop it now when you're improving? I know she says you're only middlin', but secretly she thinks you're coming on real gradely."

Charlotte was right. If I hadn't been improving, I wouldn't have put up with Elsie. But I was getting better. I wasn't as assertive or as sure of myself as Peter Shad had been – probably never would be – but I was getting that way. Whenever I spoke on the square Elsie would take up a position right in front of me, puffing on her pipe, umbrella in hand. She reveled in the heckling I got. The more I was ribbed, the more annoyance and hindrance caused by some crank in the crowd, the more she cheered. The involuntary movements of her head and shoulders told me that she was enjoying every minute. Yet there was a point beyond which criticism of me was not allowed to go. At that point Elsie would turn upon my tormentor, umbrella raised.

XX   The bitter years

In the fading light of a wintry afternoon at the beginning of October 1932, I watched a column of ragged hunger marchers form up to begin a long trek from Blackburn to London to make a direct appeal to Parliament and the King. The effort was nation-wide. It was the culmination of trouble between unemployed demonstrators and police that had been going on throughout the spring and the summer. There were pitched street battles in London, Manchester, Birkenhead, Glasgow and other towns. In Belfast demonstrators were shot and killed. Early in the year they had had to call out the army in Rochdale. Street fights were becoming common.

Harold and I had joined the crowd in the town square to give them a send-off.

"We're goin' to tell t' King that we need work and food," they said. "You'll see, he'll understand. Once he knows what's 'appening in Lancashire, matters will be put right, there's no doubt. After t' King, we'll tell Parliament. The government will sit up and notice when they've heard from us. It isn't going to be easy. But who cares if it puts matters straight again?"

In 1536 there had been a similar Pilgrimage of Grace to London, in which political, economic, and religious grievances had played their part. It was led by northern gentlemen rather than by northern workers and had been crushed savagely. In 1848 the Chartists had also tried to march on Parliament. That effort had fizzled out in torrential rain.

Just before their departure the Blackburn contingent was joined by a small group from Jarrow, which had missed the main Northumberland, Durham, and Teeside contingent then marching south through Yorkshire. The Jarrow men, each with a blanket over his shoulder, came marching into the square with a springy step. Most of them were young. Although they'd been on the road several days their faces were still bright. Some had regular walking sticks, others carried ash rods. Most of them wore cloth caps and mufflers. Their belongings hung from their back. The Blackburn people gave them great wedges of bread, steaming tea, and Tator-hash (stew). I helped to pour the tea. While they ate, a fellow with a banjo sang them a song:

> I'm a four loom weaver as many a one knows;
> I've nowt to eat and I've worn out me clothes.
> Me clogs are boath broken and stockings I've none.
> Tha'd scarce gie me tuppence for a' I've gotten on.
>
> Owd Billy o't Bent he kept telling me long,
> We might have better times if I'd nobbut howd me tongue.
> Well I've howden me tongue till I near lost me breath,
> And I feel in my heart that I'll soon clem to death...

Our Margaret declares if she'd clothes to put on,
She'd go up to London to see the great mon,
And if things didna alter when there she had been,
She swears she would fight wi' blood up t' th'een.[†]

I'm a four loom weaver as many a one knows;
I've nowt to eat and I've worn out me clothes.
Clogs we ha' none nor no looms to weave on,
And I've woven myself to t' far end.

Some of the Jarrow marchers had never been so far afield before. With our men the idea of going to London had fired them up. To see the King was better than sitting rotting. "Nothing between here and London can be worse than what we're already going through," they said. Three-quarters of Jarrow's entire labour force at this time were out of work, on the streets. Some had been out for years.

Despite all the talk of Communism and riff-raff which had appeared in the conservative press, the marchers were a good-natured lot: law-abiding, laughing, decent, patriotic. They looked a bit rough and ready, but I doubt there was a revolutionary among them. Some of them had just been to church to receive Communion before setting out. They'd fasted all day before receiving the Host.

Later on the Blackburn and Jarrow men formed up together. They seemed a bit clumsy and shy at getting into proper ranks. Someone ordered the column forward. With their heavy boots and laced up clogs ringing on the cobblestones the marchers moved off. They were going to march all night. We shouted "Good luck!" The fellow at the end of the column waved back his lighted lamp.

A little more than a month later they were back, thinner than ever, their blankets and their boots and clogs worn through. Somebody in London had either taken pity on them, or wanted to get rid of them, and they'd come home by train. The police had seen them off. This time their faces were tense and desperate. We greeted them at the station and heard their story. In London, although completely law-abiding, they'd been called Communists and Bolshies and had repeatedly been run down by mounted police. At times it had been like a battlefield. They hadn't seen the King, or Ramsay MacDonald the Labour Prime Minister, or anybody else of any consequence. They'd been blocked and fobbed off at every turn; promised all kinds of remedies. They told us that London was already full of unemployed workers from the north and from Wales. There were so many hunger marchers going south – eighteen separate contingents in October 1932 – that they had become a downright embarrassment to the London labour movement. It didn't have the resources to feed every fellow who took it into his head to talk to the King. "What are you thinking of," they'd been asked by the London workers. "Your heads must be stuffed with cotton wool. Food doesn't grow on trees."

Our men said that while marching to their billets in London, they'd stopped and listened to a group of Welsh miners singing hymns for pennies as they shuffled along in the gutter. Some of them were wearing their war medals. The singing, they said, had simply lifted them out of their clogs. It was as pure as a mountain stream. It was worth walking all the way to London to hear it. Enough to break your heart.

They told us that there'd been big meetings in Hyde Park and Trafalgar Square (20,000 strong said some, 100,000 said others) at which contingents from all over the north – including the women's contingent from Yorkshire – had participated. Labour members of Parliament had addressed them and poured oceans of praise upon them. They'd said that thanks to the hunger marchers the complacency of the government would now be broken. The marchers could return to their homes, knowing that something would be done to give them food and jobs. The speakers had promised to work night and day to ensure that something was done. They'd even deny themselves sleep. A manifesto had been approved calling upon the government to abolish poverty and provide work. A million-signature petition was to be presented to Parliament.

In the end, nothing was done. Bitterest pill of all, the police had seized the petition. Empty-handed, the deputation that had tried to reach Parliament Square had found its path blocked by an army of police – batons drawn – spoiling for a fight.

It didn't surprise me to see the marchers straggling back home again; though it pained me to watch their leaden footsteps. Peter Shad had long ago hammered it into my head that Pilgrimages of Grace get nowhere. It was bargaining from weakness rather than strength. The weak get nothing, he'd said.

Harold Watkins and I were in a teashop in Bank Top when some of the hunger marchers from Northumberland, having spent a night in Blackburn, went by on their way home. We were drinking the steaming brew which was sold as tea and sometimes tasted like it. For twopence you could have a cup of tea and two slices of bread and margarine. The shop windows were wet with condensation. Outside, row after row of muffled workers marched by, their clogs and boots pounding the melted snow into a dark slush. Fragments of paper-thin ice filled the gutters.

"Like the rest of 'em, they've been banging t' head against a brick wall," Harold said, jerking his cap in the direction of the marchers. "They look licked."

"What do you expect? They've been shoutin' so that somebody would hear 'em. Better than sufferin' in silence."

"Nobody gives a damn about the weak shouting to be heard. Didn't Shad teach you that? When will people learn?"

"These poor devils 'ave a real grievance, Harold."

"Of course. They wouldn't have marched all the way to London if they'd 'ad a job and their bellies were full. You'd have never heard from 'em if they'd been getting three meals a day. They felt helpless, with nothing to loose. Flotsam and jetsam. No one's going to listen to that tripe. They tried it in London and nobody listened. Some of them got a broken head for their troubles. For all the notice that was taken of 'em, they might as well have stayed home and marched round the park. The toffs don't give a damn for us. They don't know what we're putting up with and if they did they wouldn't care. You haven't forgotten the reception our hunger marchers got one night at Stratford-on-Avon, have you? Instead of being given a hot meal and somewhere to sleep, they were driven out into the night again; Lancashire's no longer part of England. So much for your 'This blessed plot, this realm, this earth, this England,' that we learnt at school."

"You've got a point, Harold. Paper says there are two Englands: one with an unemployment rate of six percent, the other with sixty."

I thought of my own family. I'd had years to think about them. The Watkins family was the same. They were all hard workers, all entirely law-abiding. None of them were feckless, or habitual drunkards, or gluttons, or gamblers, or profligates. Their needs were extremely simple. Yet, no matter how much they worked, and saved, and schemed, their lot got worse. Even if they got a job, it would be sure to die on them before they'd had a chance to pay off their debts.

"What do we do, Harold?" I asked.

"I don't know. I do know that hunger marchers aren't going to make any difference. It's not a genuine grievance they need; it's power. Anybody who goes on a hunger march, carrying a petition that "humbly prays" is asking for trouble. Somehow they've got to get power in their hands."

"How?"

"Turn the toffs out of parliament and put the workers in. We've got to send our own man. Bradford did it nearly thirty years ago."[†]

"But the workers vote for the toffs. They won't vote for their equals. Lancashire voted overwhelmingly for MacDonald when he deserted the workers for the bosses in 1931. You know what happened when we pushed Pat Murphy as our Labour candidate."

"As long as the workers go on doing that, they're going to go on marching like those poor, pinch-faced sods out there."

It says a lot for the Lancashire unemployed that they didn't revolt. They certainly had grounds for it. Some of them had been out of work for almost a decade. Many of them felt unwanted, of no use to anyone, living in vain.

Some of the things happening in the industrial areas of Britain in the 1920s and 1930s were not only wrong; for those who had to endure them, they passed all understanding. They seemed to be deliberately aimed at breaking the spirit of anyone who was proud, thrifty, honest, and upright. How could anyone "genuinely seek work" when there was no work to seek; or accept a Means Test which seemed designed not only to lower an already impossibly low standard of living, but also to deliberately break up family life – the only thing some of the poor had got left. Some of the regulations were not only hard to bear, they were mean and villainous, if not downright cruel. Hardship could be borne; meanness and cruelty had to be resisted.

There was no end to the madness. Blackburn was a town that at one time had clothed much of the world; yet in the worst years of the depression we didn't have enough clothing to cover our backs. We Blackburnians bought Japanese shirts and cottons at half British prices because we didn't have enough money to buy our own products.

Blackburn was close to some of the richest coal seams in the world, yet because we couldn't afford coal, we were reduced to burning cinders. We stuffed miserable little perforated cans with coal dust which we burned in our hearths during the coldest days and nights. The family sat over them like a lot of crows. Refusing to go cold, we stole the wooden railings of the rich. We wrenched the railings away from their supports, one after another as we went by, and stuffed them under our jackets. We must have been desperate. Whole fences disappeared. Anything that would burn was appropriated. Special guards had to be mounted on coal shipments. Any railway truck full of coal, left standing overnight in the railway sidings, was emptied. It was no surprise that the local cinemas should have advertised warmth not films. For threepence you could keep warm, be entertained, and forget the bleak world outside.

The system was inhuman. So inhuman that it could throw people out of work on Christmas Eve, casting them off like old clothing, or give them a cheap bottle of sherry as a reward for fifteen, thirty, forty or even fifty years' work in the mills. My father brought such a bottle home. He put it on the kitchen table and – with the rest of us – sat and stared at it. Then, without a word, he picked it up, opened the kitchen door, and flung it against the alley wall. There must have been factory owners – other than Terence Peek – who felt a social obligation to the workers and to the industry, but in all my sixteen years in Blackburn I never heard of them. My family was as close to the factory owners as we were to our landlords – we didn't know them. Pounds, shillings, and pence, not human relations, dominated our lives.

Meanwhile newspaper advertisements were persuading the rich to take Union Line cruises to Madeira, First Class £20, Second Class £15; and to buy bed-side 'phones with extension cords; "Why Get out of Bed to Answer the 'Phone?"

No wonder that the bottom dogs were brought up to sing:

> It's the same the whole world over,
> It's the poor wot gets the blame,
> It's the rich wot gets the pleasure,
> Ain't it all a blooming shame …

Cotton made unbelievable fortunes for some people in Britain, but not for the working class. At one time, the Lancashire spinning town of Shaw was said to be "the richest town in England." But they measured it by millionaires to the square mile. Fat lot of use that is to the working man.

Perhaps things were not quite bad enough for revolution; though they were bad enough to cause an unheard-of mutiny among the Home Fleet at Invorgordan, Scotland, in September 1931. Perhaps, as Mr. Peek believed, revolution wasn't in the workers' blood. He used to say if the British workers wanted a revolution, they'd have to import it. Muddlers and tinkerers have never made revolution; such people are too haphazard. Perhaps because poverty was so highly localized in Wales and the North of England it could be contained. So many were in the same boat together. Perhaps the dole helped to save the country from upheaval. Perhaps drink or religion helped to pull them through. Strong Non-Conformists and Roman Catholics don't sit well with Communism. No matter how bad things got, the British never became people of guns and armed risings. Except among the toffs and the toffs' newspapers there never was widespread talk of the workers seizing power by force. The workers were too level-headed and law-abiding for that. Above all else the leaders of the British working class were moderates. Most of them were kindly, religious people. Fiery extremists, such as Peter Shad, who really did believe in pulling the mighty down, were called Reds or Bolshies and were kept out.

One thing which did help to turn the country away from violence was the way in which the poor pulled each other through the hard times. No wonder we sang, "It's the Poor what Helps the Poor." In the absence of a mutual dependence between capital and labour, the workers had to help each other. There was a lot of pitching in, a lot of making do, and a lot of pluck. Too little has been made of working-class solidarity and community spirit. It wasn't the dole that saved Britain from revolution, it was the nature of the British working class. The British toffs will never know how lucky they were.

Moreover, the workers didn't revolt as Peter Shad had told them they must because they didn't live in Peter Shad's world of blood and fury. They wanted to get to the Promised Land all right, but they didn't want to kill people in order to get there. They weren't that kind of people. The poor are by nature meek. Most of them lived in the submissive world of the earlier peasantry and the newer industrial proletariat. It took a lot to get their blood up. It took even more to get them out on to the streets. Also, the beating they'd had since 1920 had undermined their confidence. They no longer believed in promised magic solutions, no matter from which corner of the political spectrum they came. Their world was a topsy-turvy one in which there were no iron-tight solutions. They didn't think in intellectual terms; they thought of life as a bit of a mess that would sort itself out in time. Not least, they didn't revolt because they never lost hope. Even the poor devils I'd known in the Nab Lane lodging house never lost hope. For a Lancashire man or woman to lose hope was to lose life.[†]

I refused to believe that the dire conditions in which we lived were, as Sister Loyola used to say, "an act of God calling for heroic fortitude and passive endurance." There was nothing heroic about having an empty belly and wondering where the next meal was coming from. Nor did I believe that material poverty was spiritually cleansing. Material poverty was no more a virtue to me than spiritual poverty. Peter Shad had taught me not to swallow the "act of God" business or to suffer in silence. Those ideas were put abroad by the toffs to keep the working class down.

I believed that Lancashire's plight was an act of man. One could either try to improve the system or overthrow it as Shad had urged, or escape from the system altogether. Harold and I had tried unsuccessfully to escape to Russia. We'd also talked about emigrating to Fall River in the United States where my father's brothers lived. But the fare was beyond our means. Failing Russia and America, we decided to escape to London. But where would we find a job in London? Mr. Dimbleby had talked about helping me. But he had produced nothing tangible. With no other option open, we waited and stagnated. Everything in Blackburn hung like wet washing on the line, dead. It was like waiting for a storm.

Meanwhile we Lancastrians neither revolted nor whined. Instead, those who could took to the fields and the hills. Things weren't so bad when it was getting warmer and summer was at hand. Some of my best days in Blackburn, before I got the job at the Darwen Brick Works, were those when I was unemployed. Provided I got something to eat I could wander about all day. I didn't have to get back for anybody. Nobody owned me. There was no work tomorrow; no clocking in. There were times when we even laughed at our plight. As our Lancashire comedienne Gracie Fields used to say, "It's so bad, luv, laughing is all that's left." It is hardly surprising that we sang and tap-danced the American song of the time:

> I can't give you anything but love, Baby,
> That's the only thing there's plenty of, Baby...

Little wonder that I should have decided to try my luck elsewhere.

Shortly before my departure for London, Mr. "Sharabang" Fisher married Mrs. Beatty. Mr. Fisher's ailing wife and "Up-and-at-em" Beatty had both died in 1932. There had always been a close connection between the two families. With a complete invalid on her hands, Mrs. Beatty had been relying on Mr. Fisher for years. He had done all the fetching and carrying. Old "Up-and-at-em," I was told, just faded away. He'd been in that basket dribbling for the best part of fifteen years. His body, that is. His mind had never left the trench in France where Mr. Fisher had picked up what was left of him so long ago. We thought it wonderful that Mrs. Beatty could at long last live a fuller life. They were married at St. Philip's and the reception was at St. Philip's Hall where my gang used to steal meat pies. It was a crowded wedding followed by a really good send-off.

The joy of the Beatty–Fisher wedding was marred by the death of Mr. Peek. I learnt of Mr. Peek's death by chance long after he had been buried. Chain-smoker that he was, he had accidentally set his bed alight and had died from burns. He never finished his book – the book that was to save the world. I was so appalled with the news that I felt I must sympathize with Roger, who by now had lost both parents. Agnes Peek had lingered on for a year or so after her attack of tetanus and had then died of other things.

I was on the point of returning to Livingston Road when I learnt that, following their father's death, the Peek children had left town. That was the last I heard of them.

I took my leave of Rosie Gill in a manner that neither of us had expected. One evening, shortly after the Beatty–Fisher wedding, Rosie Gill was rushed to the infirmary with acute appendicitis. While I was visiting the Gill house to inquire about Rosie, a nurse came in and told Gill that following surgery somebody had given Rosie fish and chips and that she was dangerously ill. Mr. Gill and I rushed to the hospital. He was beside himself. With me trying to keep up with him, he barged past everybody who got in his way. "Here, hang on! Where do you think you're going?" the nurses called after him.

When we got to the ward a commotion was going on. There were doctors and a priest around Rosie's bed which was crumpled and disarranged. Nurses were running in and out with slop basins and towels. There was a strong smell of methylated spirits. One of the doctors, with a stethoscope hanging down his front, was taking Rosie's pulse. The priest was administering the Last Sacrament. I'd stood by a number of Catholic deathbeds in my sixteen years. I knew that in the fifth chapter of James it is said: "Is anyone sick among you? Let him bring in the Priests of the Church; and let them pray over him, anointing him with oil in the name of the Lord ..." I knew what it meant. With tears pouring down his face, Mr. Gill made the sign of the Cross.

Rosie lay like a corpse, her eyes dead and staring. Her lips were blue; her body was drenched with sweat. Her long, curly hair lay tousled across the pillow. Her faded amulet of Mary and Christ crucified – the one she'd shown me years before – rested on the sheet. There had been times when I thought something might develop between Rosie and me, but it hadn't. We were always running in and out of each other's houses and meeting at dances, but we knew without saying it that we'd never be anything closer than good friends.

As I stood and stared at the scar on her left temple, it all came back, flooding my mind. I remembered how we'd been fooling around in the

Ribble one summer's day in our early teens; and how Rosie had finished up bashing her head on a rock at the bottom of a water hole. I got her out of the Ribble as she'd got me out of the Blakewater earlier – dripping with blood. Somehow I'd managed to get her over the bridge into Ribchester where Rosie's blood-stained towel, which I'd wrapped around her head, caught the attention of a policeman. He took us to a doctor who stitched up Rosie's wound. Then, without so much as by your leave, the policeman and his mate collected our bikes from the high bank of the river and, with Rosie, Bess, and me quaking in the back of the car, wondering what on earth was going to happen to us, drove us back to Blackburn. They were nice all the way. Poor old Gill almost swallowed his teeth when we drew up in a police car outside his front window – the one which still displayed a bowl of "Virginia fresh tobacco." I pushed my bike home afterwards, puzzled by what had gone on. I'd no idea that the police could be so kind. It changed my view of them.

Now Rosie was lying at death's door. The doctors and the priest, all of whom knew Willie Gill, moved aside as he bent over his child. Rosie made no response to his quiet pleadings. The older of the two doctors beckoned Mr. Gill away from the bedside. With a hand on Willie's shoulder, he began talking to him quietly. I caught snatches. "It's too late… You'll have to face it… It can happen at any moment." One of the nurses began to draw a curtain around Rosie's bed. All I could think of was Rosie helping me out of the Blakewater river when I'd been thrown in head first. I wished I could have rendered comfort unto her in her last moments, as years before she had rendered it unto me. Instead, I stood there helpless, holding on to the weeping Willie Gill.

Rosie died a few minutes later. She was just sixteen.

I knew she was gone when I saw the nurse cover Rosie's face, and the priest beckon us to begin the "De Profundis."

"Out of the depths I have cried to Thee O Lord," the priest began almost before we had time to take up our positions at the foot of the bed. I wasn't sure that Willie was going to respond until I heard his faltering, "O Lord, hear my voice." He spoke like a child, lips trembling, too afraid to be heard.

One of the nurses quickly followed: "And let Thine ears be attentive to the voice of my supplication."

And so in hushed tones, with the priest leading, we went on together until the end: "May she rest in peace, Amen."

Several times I'd stood with mother and her workmates while Patrick Murphy had said the same prayer for a dead mill-hand. Whether you make the appeal among silent looms or in a hospital ward makes no odds.

I took Willie Gill home. As he stumbled through his doorway, he turned and placed a hand on my shoulder.

"They've killed my child, Billy," he sobbed.

XXI   Good-bye Lancashire

At long last, having talked the subject to death with Harold Watkins, I made up my mind to leave Lancashire and go to London. I decided to risk my chance by going to Mr. Dimbleby's friend Mr. Dent at the Bow Bridge Iron Foundry with a letter of introduction and recommendation from Mr. Dimbleby. Better to make up my own mind than have the Brick Works make it up for me.

As the time for my departure for London approached I became more and more excited. I'd been promised a ride in a lorry from Manchester to London by another friend of Mr. Dimbleby, Mr. Tomkins. It would cost me five shillings instead of the twenty-five shillings charged by the railway. Failing the Bow Bridge Iron Foundry, I'd look for work somewhere else in London. Provided I could find a job to hang on to, Harold would join me in about a month's time. After that we'd fight it out together.

Going to London was not only a matter of finding a job, it was an adventure. Long before I went to London I used to stand at the railway level-crossing close to Polly Street and watch the trains chugging and huffing their way south. As I leant over the gate I wondered what the people of the south were really like. Were they like us? With Betty Weatherby in London I now had a compelling reason to go and find out. Meanwhile I was afraid that somebody would learn of my plans and stop me from going. Only Mr. Dimbleby at the brickworks, my sisters Jenny and Brenda, and Harold knew that I was leaving. I didn't tell the Lathams. I knew Madge would be against my going off on my own. I decided I'd write to them as soon as I'd landed a job in London.

At this time, unable to find a job as a weaver, Harold had become the Blackburn agent of the ACDO laundry soap company. It was a little job with big aspirations. He drove a motorcycle three-wheeler with a plywood box at the back shaped like a block of soap with the words "NEW, SCIENTIFIC, REVOLUTIONARY, MIRACULOUS, ACDO LAUNDRY SOAP," painted all over it. He was going to hang on to this job until he could join me in London.

Harold's parting gift to me was a day-long picnic through the Trough of Bowland in northern Lancashire. We took two girls with us with whom we'd clicked on the "chicken run" the week before. The "chicken run" was the way to meet girls. You walked backwards and forwards on a parade out Whalley way until you "clicked." Clicking meant that the girls, who always walked in twos, had responded to your greeting and that they were prepared to stop and talk. That's how many a man got a good wife. These two girls were game enough to come with us for the lark. They turned up with bobbed hair, cheery faces, and short skirts.

We rode in Harold's delivery van. Harold sat up front with goggles and gloves revving up the engine. With the moustache he'd begun to grow he looked very dashing. The girls and I sat on top of each other in the windowless ACDO soap trailer.

"Does your boss know we're taking his bike?" I asked Harold, as the two girls and I climbed into the trailer.

"He does and he doesn't."

"What do you mean, he does and he doesn't? You're not risking your job to give us a treat, are you?"

"Now there you go again, Billy, taking the blackest view. Who's to know? This van is too small to be seen."

"But Harold, it's the only brightly coloured block of soap on three wheels on the road."

My fears for Harold's future were not lessened when I learnt from a chance remark made by him later in the day that the "mighty" ACDO company was also paying for the petrol we were using.

Once we got under way Harold proceeded to shout and point at what we were meant to see. "Look at those trees!" he yelled. "Have you ever seen a cliff like that! What a wonderful view of the lake!" Although it was impossible for the girls and I to see anything, being thrown about in the trailer, we took everything in our stride, laughing all the way. We laughed when we had to get out and push the bike up the steep fells. We laughed when we noticed that our hands and clothing had begun to smell of ACDO. We didn't know which was worse: the fumes from Harold's bike or the smell of soap. We laughed harder still when we ate meat pies we'd bought at Clitheroe that had a decidedly ACDO flavour.

Sometimes, after much shouting from the girls and myself, Harold would stop and we'd unravel ourselves and get out of the soap bubble to see the sights. Not even the cramp in our legs stopped us from appreciating the beauty of the Trough of Bowland on a clear day. Sitting on the grass, with our backs against the trailer, we marvelled at the great vistas, at the seeming limitless expanse of the high moors and the windy fells – ridge after ridge with not a sign of human habitation. We watched the light, fair-weather clouds scudding in from the Irish Sea. We heard the curlew's lonely cry and the tumble of the streams. We smelled the lemon-scented flowering gorse. We were exhilarated by the heights and by the air. This was the Lancashire I would remember when choice and fate had carried me far away: a great expanse of wild hills and moorland brooding against the sky; a land of vivid green valleys and beckoning dales; the blue haze of distant fells with strands of water glinting in the sun. Even after the gas works, the railways, and the steam-driven factories had done their worst, the north of England would always remain for me a wild, lovely place.

And then, on full throttle, we were off again, bouncing and rattling up and down the dusty, winding lanes, through half-sleepy villages with pretty thatched cottages, grey-stone churches, and solitary spires pointing into the bright summer sky. Several times we had to stop for a shepherd and his flock. In no time the smell of sheep and dust lay upon us like a heavy mist. The bleating tide of bobbing black and white heads swept around us and held us in its grip. Only with the help of several sly, glistening dogs, which knowingly and effortlessly kept the flock on the move, did we gain our release.

I took leave of mother the next day without telling her what I was up to. I was afraid that there would be a scene and she would attempt to stop me from going. After all, I was the last of her brood to fly away. Mother had a way of knowing what was going on. Unlike father, who lived in another world, there was always a bond of understanding between us. We didn't have to declare our love. The hug I gave her told her all she wanted to know. Poor Maggie, she was always having to deal with people who ran away: her husband, her daughters, her sons. Running away seems to have been a recurring theme with the Woodruffs. But then, it was also true of the Kenyons; Bridget and Maggie had both run away. Questing seems to have been in the blood of both families.

I didn't think father would be interested in my departure, so I didn't say anything to him either. Not that there was enmity between us. His silence at times may have been hard to bear but it was something that we'd got used to. It wasn't that he just stopped talking or didn't want to talk to us. It was more gradual than that. He just drifted off into a world of his own: of work, flowers, and birds. It was a kind of happy disengagement from the more immediate matters going on around him. I respected him for what he was: an honest and a courageous man. I don't think he feared anything, not even hunger or death. He was quite content to plod along as a member of the "lower orders" as long as the "upper orders" left him alone. If he held a grudge against anyone, we never heard of it.

At least he set me the example of being a good worker. All he wanted was a fair day's pay for a good day's work. After returning from the war in 1918 he never sought money for money's sake; he never took an unearned pound; he never earned much beyond what he needed to survive. His sights were not high – he had become almost devoid of ambition; ambitious people worried him; he thought that in scrambling after their own self-interests they were likely to damage all those around them. To the end he remained a plain and a poor man.

I felt for him as I watched the cotton industry collapse under his feet. More than any of us, he had believed that it would never die. Mother said that it had been his secret wish that Dan and I should be weavers alongside him. It was not to be. Later, the war saved both my parents. Father got his hot-house and grew his flowers and his berries again but it was in Derby, not Blackburn. He went on working well into his seventies. He died at eighty-three from shock. One night on entering his house he was horrified to see a stranger hanging by the neck from a rope fastened to a skylight at the top of the stairs. By the time neighbours had arrived and were able to convince him that it was not a corpse he was looking at but paper scraped off the wall by a burglar who had forced the skylight and slid down a rope, the damage to his health had been done. Several days later, using the tram on this occasion, he entered the hospital for tests. As he had foretold, he died an hour later.

Despite the fact that I didn't have a job to go to and had neither friends nor a place to stay in London, Jenny and Brenda did nothing to dissuade me from leaving. I could tell from her eyes that Jenny was not as sure as Brenda about my going to London, but her doubts and fears remained unspoken. Both my sisters promised to explain to mother what I was up to when I had gone. I promised to write.

Elsie Briggs was the last person I said good-bye to. There was no emotion or sentiment about our parting; we just shook hands.

She turned aside when I tried to thank her. "You're a bit better speaker than you were," she said. I guardedly agreed.

She knew I was much better; but she didn't want to take credit for it.

"I'm sorry I won't be the best speaker in Lancashire," I said. "I know that was your goal."

She gave me the only smile I'd ever seen on her face. It warmed me through. "It's best that you should go," she said. "There's nothing here for you. Go and show London what you can do."

"Thanks, Elsie," I said, as I gently lifted her cap and, dodging her pipe, gave her a peck on the cheek.

Worst of all was the parting from Bess. It was the only thing that brought tears. Brenda was to care for her. Brenda and her husband Dick were fond of the dog, and I knew that Bess liked them. Harold promised to bring Bess to London when he joined me. It had been my original intention to take Bess with me. "You must be out of your mind," Harold had said, "taking a dog when you don't have a bed for yourself. What are you thinking about? First get your bed; I'll bring the dog."

I was persuaded. It was all arranged. When I said good-bye to her, Bess looked at me with unforgiving eyes and whined. (Months later Brenda wrote to me that the day after I left Lancashire Bess had run away and was never seen again.)

Harold saw me off at the station for Manchester. From that station, built in the 1840s, Blackburn cottons had been sent to the whole world. It was quiet and looked run down now. It was the station to which my family had come on their return from America in 1914. With thousands of other Blackburn men my father had gone to war from the same platform and had come home again gassed. From here I'd made my trips to Bamber Bridge, to Little Blackpool and Big Blackpool. From where I stood Jenny and Gordon had gone off on their honeymoon. A year ago, I'd met the ragged hunger marchers on this very platform on their return from London.

There was a drizzle about. The wet stood in beads upon us both. I wore a cap, a coat and rough trousers. I had toyed with the idea of buying my first hat, but considering my resources had decided against it. My worldly possessions, including my two pairs of overalls and my only suit – the suit I got for Jenny's wedding – I carried in a small, battered cardboard suitcase. The suit had been let out as far as it would go, and was still a bit short in the arms and legs, but it would have to do. Also in my bag was a pullover, a shirt, socks, a face cloth, soap, and a razor. Despite Madge Latham, who had introduced me to underclothing, I wore and took no underwear. With other odds and ends, my pockets contained my worldly wealth (five pounds), a watch, a comb, a handkerchief and a knife.

Neither Harold nor I said much on the platform. There were unusually awkward pauses in our conversation. I couldn't think of anything interesting to say and I was glad when the train came and we shook hands and said good-bye. I waved to him from the window. The engine gave a shrill whistle, there was a puff or two of steam, the carriages lurched forward and slowly slid out of the station. I was off. Tat-tattat, tat-tattat the wheels went. I looked down through the rain-streaked train window at streets and buildings and smoking chimneys that I knew so well. I should have been excited, instead I felt sad – as sad as the clouded, melancholy sky above me.

It was dusk by the time I found Mr. Dimbleby's friend in Manchester. I had been told to be at a garage by the central bus station not later than 6 p.m. and to ask for Mr. Tomkins. It was ten minutes from the hour when I hurried into the cavernous depot.

As I entered the building, a bundled figure of a man, wearing a box-like cap, a muffler, and a coat that reached down to his boots, left a little office in one corner and walked toward me. He had a blank, scrawny face.

"You the young 'un for London?" the bundled figure asked eyeing my valise.

Putting on a bold look, and trying to sound older than my sixteen years, I said I was.

"Well then," he went on – ignoring my "Are you – er – Mr. Tomkins?" – "don't muck abaht; jump in, we've got a long way to go."

As he didn't tell me whether he was Mr. Tomkins or not, I henceforth thought of him as Mr. Bundle.

Having put my suitcase in the back of the lorry among crates of machine parts, I clambered into the cab. It smelled of petrol and oil. It was unbearably warm inside. However, the great hole in the canvas above the door on my side told me that I'd better enjoy the heat while I'd got it. Mr. Bundle climbed into the cab from the other side. He took some time to adjust the controls on the engine, then he got out and swung the starting handle at the front, at which the engine sprang into life, and got back again.

Shortly after six, with a blaring of the horn, we rumbled from the garage in the direction of the London Road. At first, Mr. Bundle's constant crashing of gears and screeching of brakes unnerved me, but I got used to it. I also accustomed myself to the explosive sneezes my otherwise silent companion gave at seemingly fixed intervals. "Oh, oh, oh," he'd call out before shaking the cab with an "atchooo!" I feared that he would lose control of the wheel. But he didn't. Instead, we clattered, rocked, and sneezed our way into the open countryside.

Curled in my corner, trying to avoid the gale now blowing through my side of the cab, I continued to watch the lorry's headlights as they ran before us, piercing the gloom. Periodically other vehicles danced toward us out of the night, filling our dark cab with a blinding light. Now and again I saw the skeleton of trees in the background, the hazy lights of towns.

It was just as well that Mr. Bundle remained silent, for I had enough on my mind. As I watched the road, all kinds of thoughts raced through my head. I was overwhelmed at the idea of going all the way to London. For a sixteen year old who had hardly been out of his town, London seemed a long, long way. When I thought of Bess or mother, I was equally overcome with a great sadness. Only when I was on the London Road did I realize that I should have brought Bess with me. I shouldn't have listened to Harold. I'd allowed myself to be talked into the idea. I'd betrayed Bess. I felt like bursting into tears.

At that moment Mr. Bundle followed a sneeze by pointing through the windscreen. "See that?" he asked. I looked in the direction he was pointing. "For London," he said. It was the London train, a long string of lights slipping across the dark valley floor before us.

"More comfortable like that," he said.

"Oh, yes," I agreed, a catch in my voice.

"Tha mustn't take it badly," Mr. Bundle counseled, glancing at me. "If tha falls flat on thi face in London, tha can allus cum 'ome 'gin wi' me."

"Tha kind."

The truth was that now that I was running away I had lost the desire to do so. While I didn't feel like jumping out and running back, had there been a steady job or a steady girl to run back to, I might have done.

There must have been periods in Lancashire's history when it was possible to live a fairly contented life as a weaver without having to look elsewhere for a living. But that had not been my experience. The Lancashire I had known was a long story of broken work and broken pay; of being overworked or having no work at all; of being paid so badly that the whole family had to work or nobody ate; with only a narrow margin separating us from sinking altogether. I was sixteen when the hunger marchers returned to Blackburn. I had lived through the worst years Lancashire was to endure. By then I didn't need anybody to explain to me, as Mr. Peek had done earlier, that the Lancashire cotton industry had been dealt a fatal blow. I had no job to go back to. Best I could hope for was pick-and-shovel work. I either sought a better living elsewhere, or I lived from hand to mouth, forever paying "something off", forever "carrying over", forever worrying where the next meal was coming from – as the rest of my family did. London was the lure, but I might never have gone there had hard times and Betty Weatherby not made up my mind.

My great-grandfather Arne had come to Lancashire when the name of Blackburn was about to be known world-wide. Now the Lancashire cotton industry was dying – as was our pride and our loyalty to cotton. An industry that treats its workers, especially its defenseless women and children as inhumanely as cotton textiles had done, must die unsung. All my life I have been puzzled why we Lancastrians should have been so good at inventing machines, at starting an industrial revolution that had transformed the whole area and ultimately the entire world, yet so bad at human relations. In my whole sixteen years in Lancashire I had heard nothing but "us'n" and "they". The gulf dividing capital from labour was never bridged.

It never crossed my mind that in going to London I might be jumping from the frying pan into the fire. The obvious dangers accompanying my mad-cap scheme never penetrated my thick head. I never thought of discomfort or inconvenience. The fact that I had no idea where I would sleep the next night, or the one after that, added spice to the adventure. Somehow the solution to all my problems would be found at the end of the road that lay before me. I was blindly optimistic of the outcome.

I didn't hold it against anybody that I had to go. Because of what grandmother Bridget had taught me, I didn't hate anybody for it. I envied but I can't say I ever hated the rich. That is one conversion Peter Shad had not succeeded in making.

Least of all did I blame Lancashire, the county of my birth. Regardless of the fact that Lancashire had not offered me much of a living I was proud to be a Lancastrian, especially to be a Blackburnian. Blackburn was not just another Lancashire town; Blackburn had been the greatest weaving centre in the world. It had been the pioneer, the seed-bed of inventions in power weaving. It was unique. East Lancashire had developed the greatest concentration of manufacturing industry there had ever been. Without the textile industries of Lancashire and Yorkshire there would have been less "Rule Britannia" in the world.

Whatever else Lancashire had denied me, it had left me with a love of individual liberty and freedom. Lancashire had given me the liberty to run as wild as I wanted. I had always had the freedom to run from dark streets and alleyways into the open rolling countryside. Liberty and freedom were in the bones of my people. Lancashire folk might be rough and ready, but they were never servile. Servile people didn't take it upon themselves to walk out as I was doing. At least Lancashire had left me free to reject my birthplace.

My heritage was joyful as well as bleak. I knew not only the squalor of a factory town, I also knew the unforgettable beauty of the surrounding fields, moors, hills, and craggy fells. I shall never forget the long, joyful summer days playing on the banks of the Ribble; the hectic winter flights down icy hillsides on homemade sleds, or the happy hours spent flying a linen kite in the ever-present north wind. These things are rooted in my mind, they are part of my blood. More than anything else, it was the river, the rushing streams, the wind, the hills, and the moors that made me what I am. They are with me forever.

As a Lancashire boy and youth running wild, I'd never known boredom. There had always been something to do. I had never had the time or need to ask, "who am I?" I was a weaver's son, somebody close to the bottom of the social pile; somebody who could not evade reality; somebody who had been brought into daily contact with the conditions of labour; somebody who had been blessed by constant challenge: the challenge of poverty, the challenge of making do; even the challenge of a harsh climate and a cold north wind.

There was nothing dishonourable in all this. Hard times had bred resourcefulness and self-reliance. I knew by experience how to take setbacks. I also knew that nobody owed me a living. I took it for granted that in life I'd have to shift for myself. Lancashire schools hadn't taught me much. What schooling I had received was deplorable; so deplorable that I cannot remember one outstanding teacher or the subjects they taught. My schooling in Blackburn is a regrettable blank. But I had at least been taught common sense and how to survive; I wasn't quite the greenhorn I must have looked and sounded in those early days.

No, all things considered, I was lucky to have been born and reared in Lancashire; doubly lucky to have been born poor.

"Tha leaving Lancashire," my friend said, as he slammed in the gear. "Cheshire's at top of 'ill."

"Good-bye Lancashire," I said, a frog in my throat.

Notes

p.11   *Pakies*: Immigrants from Pakistan.

bloody at times: While the Children's Act of 1908 made it an offense to keep children in a verminous condition, I doubt that any worker had heard of the law. Despite our poor circumstances, I can never remember lice or fleas getting the better of us.

p.12   *clogs*: English working clogs had a stout leather upper; the wooden sole and heel were strengthened with iron cokers.

p.24   *gift of the gab*: He is a great talker.

p.29   *counts*: Counts refer to a number of hanks (a hank = 840 yards long) contained in a pound weight of cotton yarn; the higher the count the finer the yarn. While Blackburn counts were generally higher than those of the cotton textiles of India, China, and Japan, they were not as high as those of other Lancashire towns such as Bolton and Preston which produced high quality goods for the home market.

p.30   *picking sticks*: A piece of wood and metal, about the length of a man's arm, which struck the steel-tipped shuttle a powerful blow, propelling it across the loom through the warp threads to the other shuttle box. A pick was a throw of the shuttle. The speed of the loom was measured by the number of picks per minute.

p.34   *higher and higher*: The net profit in spinning a pound of yarn in 1912 was a halfpenny; in 1920 it was one shilling and six pence. The profit on a 38 yard piece of shirting in 1912 was five pence; in 1920 it was five shillings and three pence. Dividends paid in 1920 – as high as 40% – were six or eight times the more normal 5%–7% of earlier years. Figures drawn from B. Bowker, *Lancashire under the Hammer*, London, 1928, p.34

p.41   *Blackpool rock*: A stick of toffee (US candy).

p.44   *butties*: Sandwiches.

p.55   *Bridget Gorman*: I always knew my grandmother as Bridget Magory (Magory was her mother's maiden name). However, her marriage certificate bears the name Bridget Gorman – her father or stepfather's name. Bridget was long dead before I had cause to think about it.

p.58   *employer's liability*: The British Workmen's Compensation Act of 1897 established the liability of an employer to pay compensation to a workman or, in case of death, to his dependents.

p.73   *fatal*: The Contract Labour Law, passed by the United States Congress in 1885, was meant to discourage the recruiting by employers of lesser skilled workers in Europe, which in some respects had become akin to the Asian coolie trade.

p.80   *same skill*: In the mule, twisting and winding are separate operations. In the ring spinning process, the twisting and winding of a very much shorter length of yarn are done simultaneously. The ring is faster and more economical to operate than the mule.

home market: Between 1910 and 1913 the United States exported only 4 percent of its cotton goods. The figure for Lancashire at this time was 45 percent.

same hours: This was not to be compared with the $5 a day which the Ford Motor Company began to pay its workers in 1913.

p.83   *America*: The war certainly played a primary role in preventing my people, even if they had intended it, from returning to America. In August 1914 the sea lanes around Britain were mined. In the winter, Hartlepool and Scarborough on the North Sea coast were shelled by German warships. A German submarine attack on the *Carmania* – the ship in which they had sailed – must have come as a great shock to them. In February 1915 Germany declared that the waters around the British Isles were a war zone. To cap it all, in May 1915, the *Lusitania* was sunk off Ireland.

p.89   *twelve months*: In an attempt to share the industry's unusually high profits, in January 1918, the Labour Party Conference demanded a minimum wage of 30 shillings. They were rebuked. By December, 1918, there were 100,000 cotton workers on strike in Lancashire. Henceforth, especially after 1920, strikes in the industry were endemic.

age of thirteen: It was not until 1918 that children were required to attend school until they were fourteen. Moreover, the working class regarded such bureaucratic rules as something imposed from above. It was adapt at evading them.

p.111   *former students*: The Lancashire Fusiliers had won an unmatched seventeen Victoria Crosses in the First Great War, the highest military honour Britain could bestow.

p.164   *3 May 1926*: The coal miners struck on 1 May; a State of Emergency was proclaimed the same day; the strike became general from 3 May to 12 May.

p.198   *signed with a cross*: Mother had refused to use a cross on her wedding certificate. With father's help, she signed her own name.

p.206   *ahead of us now*: In 1930 almost all American looms were automatic compared with five percent in Britain. A survey in 1930 showed that almost half the looms and a third of the spindles in Lancashire had been built before 1900. Technical backwardness affected all the traditional British industries. For instance, in 1924 less than 19 percent of British coal was cut by machinery as compared to about 90 percent in the United States.

p.223   *at their peril*: The peril proved to be more serious than Mildred realized. In 1937 the ex-Rector made his appearance as a Modern Daniel in a lion's cage at Skegness Amusement Park. On 28 July he was mauled so badly that he died two days later. The headline at the fairground the next day was: "See the lion that mauled and injured the Rector."

p.239   *genuinely seeking work*: The phrase 'genuinely seeking work' was introduced in 1921. After 1927 it applied to all unemployment benefits. It caused hundreds of thousands to be denied assistance. Some relief came with the appointment of a Labour Government in 1930, but when Labour fell later that year, the old stringency and severity returned. It was a callous age that could reduce the number of unemployed by simply stopping people's dole.

p.243   *Means Test*: From 1931, anyone unemployed for more than six months underwent a means test, administered by the dreaded Poor Law Authority, in which every source of income (including that of family members) was counted and deducted.

        state aid: The maximum was fifteen shillings for a man, eight shillings for his wife.

p.248   *hammer and sickle*: Britain's Communist Party was founded in August 1920. It comprised existing Marxist groups such as the British Socialist Party, the Socialist Labour Party, and the Workers Socialist Federation.

p.250   *Black Shirts*: Their leader was Sir Oswald Mosley, Chancellor of the Duchy of Lancaster. Mosley, like Mussolini, had started out as a Conservative and had become converted to Socialism. The Fascist Movement was officially launched on 1 October 1932.

p.254   *Legation in London*: Diplomatic and trade relations between the United Kingdom and the Soviet Union had been on and off since their severance in 1927. Relations improved following the British Labour Party victory at the polls in May 1929.

p.255   *sent to jail*: Following the disclosure in the conservative *Daily Mail* of a letter purported to have been written by Zinoviev, chairman of the Communist International, instructing the British Communist Party how to infiltrate and control the British Labour Movement.

p.256   *Gandhi*: In 1931 Mahatma Gandhi was in London for the Round Table Conference on British-Indian affairs. He spent three days visiting the Lancashire textile industry. One day, with his coarsely spun white shawl and his homespun loincloth, his skinny legs, and his clumsy wooden sandals, he passed through Blackburn on his way to the idle Greenfield Weaving Mills at Darwen. A strange, little, bespectacled, ascetic figure, he was greeted by the poor of England as warmly as he was accustomed to being greeted by the poor of India. Despite the fact that the politically inspired boycott of British textiles was robbing the Lancashire workers of jobs, he proved to be immensely popular with them. A sharp observer, the antiquated condition of the British cotton textile industry did not escape him. "The machinery in the Bombay and Ahmadabad mills," he was quoted as saying, "is one hundred percent more efficient."

p.260   *'een*: Eyes.

p.262   *nearly thirty years ago*: In 1906 Bradford, Yorkshire, elected Independent Labour Party member Fred Jowett to the House of Commons.

p.265   *lose life*: On 2 January 1932, the following item appeared in the *Blackburn Times*: "Betty Jones, 39, took her life on Christmas Eve. A month earlier all her unemployment benefits had been stopped." Notices like that added to the already widespread fear of hunger and despair. No wonder that between 1921 and 1931 there was a two-thirds increase in the number of suicides among young men under age twenty-five. Sometimes they took their life only hours after being laid off. Gas ("'ead in't oven") was most commonly used.

Other books by
William Woodruff

The Rise of the British Rubber Industry during the Nineteenth Century
(Liverpool, 1958)

Impact of Western Man,
A Study of Europe's Role in the World Economy 1750–1960
(London and New York, 1966)

Vessel of Sadness
(London, 1970)

The Emergence of an International Economy 1700–1914
(London, 1971)

America's Impact on the World:
A Study of the Role of the United States in the World Economy, 1750–1970
(London and New York, 1976)

The Struggle for World Power, 1500–1980
(London and New York, 1982)

Paradise Galore
(London, 1985)

A Concise History of the Modern World: 1500 to the Present
(London, 1991)

Details of a selection of Ryburn
books appear on the following pages.
For a complete stocklist write to Ryburn Publishing Ltd
Tenterfields, Luddendenfoot, Halifax HX2 6EJ, England

Specialist publishers in architecture,
current affairs, literature, history
and the social sciences

BLACKBURN
The development of a Lancashire cotton town
Derek Beattie

By 1914, and in just over a hundred years, Blackburn rose from near obscurity to become the cotton weaving capital of the world. Derek Beattie, Senior Lecturer in History at Blackburn College, considers the progress and profound consequences of such rapid change in thematically defined chapters to build a general analytical history of the town. A central issue is the way in which a small middle-class elite influenced, moulded and guided Blackburn's physical, social and political outlook.

Dr Beattie also explores the way Blackburn has adapted to the present century. He looks at how it inherited 19th-century social and political traditions and has tried to come to terms with a declining economic base and new 20th-century pressures.

ISBN 1 85331 021 2   Illustrated paperback

BRADFORD
David James

A concise, accessible and authoritative history of Bradford to the present day, this was the first title in Ryburn's *Town and City Histories* series, edited by Stephen Constantine, Senior Lecturer in History at the University of Lancaster. Archivist Dr David James charts Bradford's growth from minor market town to worsted capital of the world, and the impact of the woollen industry on subsequent economic, social and political problems. He examines the changing economic foundations of the city and the ways they have affected its physical shape, built environment, employment, living conditions, urban character and politics. He also analyses how power was structured, who wielded it, and its effects on the social behaviour of ordinary people.

'Ryburn ... are to be congratulated on initiating what promises to be a valuable series with David James' coherently argued and clearly expressed account.'
– *Industrial Archaeology Review*

ISBN 1 85331 005 0   Illustrated paperback

MANCHESTER
Alan Kidd

According to Alan Kidd, Senior Lecturer in History at Manchester Metropolitan University and author of this first general history to appear for over 20 years, Manchester was arguably the first modern city and its history is more than the story of a town, rather a contribution to the history of the modern world.

Although Manchester has been inhabited for almost two thousand years, a process beginning just over two centuries ago was to put this hitherto remote Lancashire town on the international map. Changes wrought by the industrial revolution caused unprecedented growth, ushered in new ways of living and working and generated new ideas of economy and society. Dr Kidd divides the book into four sections: the period before industrialisation; the world's first industrial city 1780–1850; a commercial metropolis 1850–1914; and the city within living memory 1914–1990. He proposes many new interpretations in presenting his lively and closely-argued analysis.

ISBN 1 85331 016 6   Illustrated paperback

MARY BARTON;
A TALE OF MANCHESTER LIFE
Elizabeth Gaskell
Edited by Angus Easson

'The artistry, the emotion and the truth of Mary Barton are eloquent witness to the achievement of Elizabeth Gaskell', writes Angus Easson in his stimulating introduction. 'Gaskell participates in a new concept of history both as a form of imaginative writing and a record of people whom the big histories of kings and wars has ignored.'

A vivid and touching account of 'them and us', *Mary Barton* is also a gripping story of love, murder, death and forgiveness set against a chilling background of poverty and oppression in Manchester of the 1840s. Gaskell's descriptions of the suffering and successes, conflicts and plights, of classes and individuals, are brilliantly realized and full of timeless credibility. Her view of working-class life is vividly dramatised, and spurred by Gaskell's belief that only by social reconciliation between employers and workers could there be any cure to the appalling plight of the poor. The book is both a major literary feat and a fascinating insight into the class values and broader issues surrounding the social issues of the day.

Professor Easson has paid scrupulous attention to the text, employing the fifth edition as Gaskell's final and most careful overseeing of her work but incorporating 74 substantive variants. This edition also includes William Gaskell's 'Two Lectures on Lancashire Dialect', three appendices, and comprehensive explanatory notes.

ISBN 1 85331 020 4   Hardback   ISBN 1 85331 040 9   Bonded Leather

CALDERDALE: ARCHITECTURE AND HISTORY
Photographs by Ian Beesley and Andrew Caveney
Commentary by Alan Betteridge, Derek Bridge and Peter H. Thornborrow

'A photographic feast by a highly competent team from West Yorkshire.'
– Industrial Archaeology Review

'(This book) offers us another view of Calderdale – a place rich in wild scenery, dotted with marvellous medieval, Tudor and Georgian houses as well as the remains of early industry' *– Kenneth Powell, The Daily Telegraph*

From standing stones and medieval churches to modern developments which respect the existing fabric of conservation areas, this popular work includes over 100 remarkable black and white photographs and features examples of impressive stone-built yeoman clothiers' houses, magnificent Victorian public buildings, unique workers' cottages, mills, pubs, chapels – sufficient to indicate the great wealth and diversity of Calderdale architecture and also to enable the authors to give an outline history through the extended captions which accompany the photographs.

ISBN 1 85331 007 7   Illustrated paperback

VICTORIAN MANCHESTER AND SALFORD
Photographs by Ian Beesley
with an introduction and commentary by Peter de Figueiredo

'*Victorian Manchester and Salford* and *Calderdale: Architecture and History* set a new standard for books on local history and architecture; the restrained elegance of the presentation and the excellent photographs ... seem to me absolutely first class.' *– Mike Pegg, former Director,*
The John Rylands University Library of Manchester

A celebration of 'the most wonderful city of modern times' (Disraeli's *Coningsby*). As Manchester's role changed from being a manufacturing town to a centre of trade and distribution, modern warehouses, banks, offices, theatres, clubs, shops and hotels replaced the mills. 'There has been nothing to equal it,' commented *Building News* in 1861, 'since the building of Venice.'

'The atmosphere of Manchester in its heyday is still to be found,' writes Peter de Figueiredo. 'In spite of the terrible destruction of war and of brutal 1960s redevelopment, the achievements of Victorian and Edwardian architects still give the city a distinct identity ... reminding us that Manchester was a place not only of wealth and power, but a city with a clear vision of its cultural identity.'

ISBN 1 85331 006 9   Illustrated paperback

LANCASHIRE QUAKERS AND THE ESTABLISHMENT 1660–1730
Nicholas Morgan

The multi-faceted relationship between the Quakers and the civil, political and Quaker establishments of the late seventeenth and early eighteenth centuries is a complex and fascinating one.

In this detailed examination and explanation of the state and condition of Quakerism in the period, Nicholas Morgan, Archivist with United Distillers plc, traces the rise of Quakerism in the North West of England, its development, attitudes and principles, and considers such issues as the place of oaths, swearing and discipline in society. In contrast to the accepted view, this thorough and searching analysis of Quakerism shows how Friends in Lancashire sought to maintain the missionary dynamic of the earliest Quakers and that consequently the relationship which existed with the Establishment contrasted sharply between Friends in London and those in Lancashire.

ISBN 1 85331 015 8   Hardback

BRASS CASTLES
West Yorkshire New Rich and their Houses 1800–1914
George Sheeran

The West Yorkshire families who grew rich through commerce and industry during the Industrial Revolution used their newly acquired wealth to build houses and gardens that were markedly different from those of older landed and commercial families. *Brass Castles* is the first book to explore these 19th-century mansions as a group in their own right.

How did the industrial magnate view his position in society? What sort of house was appropriate to his station? In this fascinating sociological approach to architectural history, George Sheeran examines the urban as well as rural homes of 92 of the wealthiest families from the 'New Rich' section of the population. He analyses their wealth and where it came from, contrasts the architecture and functions of their houses, compares them with the general development of the 19th-century house and looks at how far they were modified by local or individual conditions. He also studies ten case histories in depth and includes a comprehensive gazetteer of surviving houses. The book is illustrated with more than 160 photographs, figures and specially drawn plans.

ISBN 1 85331 022 0   Illustrated paperback

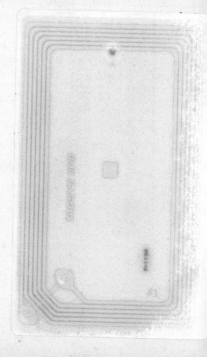